PSYCHOANALYSIS
AND BUDDHISM

PSYCHOANALYSIS AND BUDDHISM

An Unfolding Dialogue

EDITED BY JEREMY D. SAFRAN

WISDOM PUBLICATIONS • BOSTON

Wisdom Publications
199 Elm Street
Somerville, MA 02144 USA
www.wisdompubs.org

Library of Congress Cataloging-in-Publication Data

Safran, Jeremy D.
    Psychoanalysis & Buddhism : an unfolding dialogue / edited by Jeremy
D. Safran.— 1st Wisdom ed.
        p. cm.
Includes bibliographical references and index.
    ISBN 0-86171-342-7 (pbk. : alk. paper)
    1. Buddhism and psychoanalysis. 2. Buddhism—Psychology. I. Title:
Psychoanalysis and Buddhism. II. Title
    BF175.4.R44S24 2003
    294.3'375—DC21

                                                    2003000939

First edition
12 11 10 09 08
5   4

Chapter. 6: "Your Ordinary Mind" is adapted from material previously published in *Ordinary Mind: Exploring the Common Ground of Zen and Psychotherapy* (Boston: Wisdom Publications, 2002).

Wisdom Publications' books are printed on acid-free paper and meet the guidelines for permanence and durability of the Production Guidelines for Book Longevity set by the Council on Library Resources.

Printed in the United States of America.

This book was produced with environmental mindfulness. We have elected to print this title on 30% PCW recycled paper. As a result, we have saved the following resources: 19 trees, 13 million BTUs of energy, 1,635 lbs. of greenhouse gases, 6,786 gallons of water, and 871 lbs. of solid waste. For more information, please visit our website, www.wisdompubs.org. This paper is also FSC certified. For more information, please www.fscus.org.

To Karma Thinley Rinpoche
To Zen Master Richard Shrobe
And to the memory of Stephen A. Mitchell

***

My Tibetan teacher, Karma Thinley Rinpoche, the fourth incarnation of the sixteenth century lama, Karma Thinley, once asked me, in his broken, heavily accented English: " How does Western psychology treat nervousness?" "Why do you ask?" I responded. "Well," he replied, "I've always been a nervous person. Even when I was a little boy I was nervous, and I still am. Especially when I have to talk to large groups of people or to people I don't know, I get nervous." As was often the case with the questions that Karma Thinley asked me, I found myself drawing a complete blank. Part of it was the difficulty of trying to find the words to explain something to somebody whose grasp of English was limited, but there was another more important factor. On the face of it this was a simple question. But Karma Thinley was a highly respected lama, now in his sixties, who had spent years mastering the most sophisticated Tibetan Buddhist meditation techniques. Those who knew Karma Thinley considered him to be an enlightened being. In the West psychotherapists are increasingly turning to Buddhist meditation as a valuable treatment for a variety of problems including anxiety. Who was I to tell him how to be deal with anxiety? And how was it possible that Karma Thinley, with all of his experience meditating could still be troubled by such everyday concerns? How could an enlightened person be socially anxious? Was he really enlightened? What does it mean to be enlightened? My head swirled with all of these inchoate questions, and for a moment my mind stopped. I felt a sense of warmth coming from Karma Thinley and I felt warmly towards him. I felt young, soft, open and uncertain about everything I knew.

Jeremy Safran

Contents

ACKNOWLEDGMENTS

First I would like to thank Karma Thinley Rinpoche and Zen Master Richard Shrobe who were both there for me during difficult times in my life and who taught me the lessons of simplicity, ordinariness, constancy and compassion. I would also like to thank Philip Bromberg for his faith in me, for his guidance, and for his encouragement. I am particularly indebted to the late Stephen Mitchell for his intellectual stimulation, openness, and infectious enthusiasm. His support of this project in its early stages played a critical role in helping it to materialize. To Neil Altman, Joseph Bobrow, Jack Engler, Mark Finn, James Grotstein, Robert Langan, Barry Magid, Stephen Mitchell, Raul Moncayo, Stuart Pizer, Owen Renik, Philip Ringstrom, Jeffrey Rubin, Charles Spezzano, Neville Symington, Michael Thompson, Sara Weber, and Polly Young-Eisendrath: Thank you for your outstanding contributions to this volume and for your willingness to take part in this important—and at times difficult—dialogue; this project was a long time in the making and I am sure that there were times when some of you may have wondered if this book would ever be published. I know there were times when I did. My editor at Wisdom, Josh Bartok, has been delightful to work with: intelligent, knowledgeable, committed, passionate in his views, and open to dialogue. I would also like to thank John LeRoy for his exceptionally intelligent copyediting. To my wife, Jenny, my love and my companion in life: Thank you for your ongoing support of my work, your intelligent and constructive criticism (which I may not always react to well initially, but always end up appreciating), and your encouragement with this project in particular. To Marvin and Cathy Hunter: My gratitude for your warmth, generosity of spirit, and vitality. And finally to my daughters, Ayla and Eliana: Thank you for bringing such joy to my life. When I was young, my father used to say that my sister and I were his precious jewels. Now I know how he must have felt.

PREFACE

The roots of my involvement with Buddhism go back a long way, certainly as far back as my interests in Western psychotherapy and psychoanalysis. I first began meditating at a Zen center in Vancouver prior to beginning graduate training in clinical psychology in the early 1970s and long before undergoing psychoanalytic training. The teacher at the Zen center was an earnest young monk from England. He had a pious manner more reminiscent of my stereotype of a Presbyterian minister than of the iconoclastic Zen masters and Tibetan lamas who have had the greatest impact on me. But to his credit, he did manage to impress upon me the importance of actually sitting down and meditating in a disciplined fashion. Although I can't claim to have always been the most diligent of practitioners, my interest in Buddhism has remained consistent over the years. Nevertheless, while the influence of Buddhist thought and practice began to explicitly appear in my professional writing as early as 1990, it has taken considerably longer for me to undertake a project such as this one. As to what all the forces are that finally motivated me to attempt to bring my interests in Buddhism and psychoanalysis together as the central focus of a professional project, I can only speculate. No doubt, as Freud taught us, there are multiple determinants, both conscious and unconscious. And as Buddhism teaches us there are karmic determinants as well. What I do know is that the time for this project now feels ripe to me.

Although the dialogue between psychoanalysis and Buddhism has a long history, attempts to examine the interface of these two disciplines in a systematic fashion have been scattered and episodic in nature. Psychoanalysts who have been interested in this dialogue have tended to be on the margins of their field—functioning outside of the mainstream of analytic thinking. In recent years, however, there has been a deepening interest in Buddhism by psychoanalysts that parallels the growing interest in Buddhism both by Western psychotherapists in general and by the culture at large. This book is the first to initiate a formal dialogue between mainstream psychoanalysts and those who write about the interface of psychoanalysis and Buddhism.

It is structured in the form of: primary chapters followed by commentaries, followed by replies written by the authors of the primary chapters in response to the commentaries. The primary chapters are written by authors equally conversant with the worlds of psychoanalysis and Buddhism, and who in many cases have made seminal contributions to this interface in the past. The commentaries are all written by psychoanalytic theorists who in most cases have a rather limited familiarity with the topic of Buddhism, but sufficient interest to be willing to engage in the dialogue. I was fortunate to be able to enlist the participation of a highly prominent group of psychoanalytic thinkers, many of whom have had an important impact on the development of contemporary psychoanalytic theory. Their willingness to participate in this enterprise is a reflection of the changing cultural milieu, among psychoanalysts and the culture at large. Although there has always been an underground of "Buddhaphiles" within the psychoanalytic community, it is unlikely the type of dialogue represented in this book could have taken place as recently as a few years ago. My hope is that this dialogue will help to raise thinking about the interface between psychoanalysis and Buddhism to a new level of sophistication, and to stimulate an interest in the topic by both a wider audience of psychoanalysts and psychotherapists, and the general public.

I have written the introductory chapter, Psychoanalysis and Buddhism as Cultural Institutions, to provide a context for this dialogue. It does so by sketching out the cultural and historical factors that have influenced the development of both psychoanalysis and Buddhism, and that are currently influencing the accelerating interest in Buddhism. My secondary agenda is to review some of the major themes and developments within both psychoanalysis and Buddhism in order to provide some background for those who may be less familiar with either of these traditions.

A final objective of my introductory chapter, and of the book as a whole, is to provide those who are not familiar with contemporary psychoanalysis with a taste of some of the exciting and forward-looking developments that are taking place within it. Western psychotherapy began with the emergence of psychoanalysis at the beginning of the twentieth century and for many years psychoanalysis was the dominant form of psychological treatment. Although psychoanalysis has always provided a conceptually rich and sophis-

ticated framework for understanding human experience, the discipline provoked tendencies toward reductionistic thinking and pseudoscientific steril-
ity. As psychoanalysis became increasingly well established as a cultural
institution, it tended to lose some of its more revolutionary and progressive
potential, becoming somewhat arrogant, conservative, and insular. Then, in
the 1960s psychoanalysis began to fall upon hard times. Within the field of
psychiatry it was superseded by the biological revolution. And as a form of
psychotherapy, it was outflanked on one side by the cognitive-behavioral tradition, with its pragmatic emphasis and its claim to scientific legitimacy, and
on the other by humanistic psychotherapy emphasizing the fundamental
importance of human dignity and potential.

In recent years, however, there has been a revitalization in psychoanalytic
theory and practice that has broken the shackles of conservatism and that is
shaping it in a direction that is increasingly responsive to the yearnings of the
human heart and soul. I see this book as both a reflection of this revitalization process and a continuation of it.

Introduction:

Psychoanalysis and Buddhism as Cultural Institutions

Jeremy D. Safran

Freud and the Dalai Lama

Although there was a flurry of interest in Buddhism by psychoanalytic thinkers such as Erich Fromm and Karen Horney in the 1950s and 1960s, this interest to some extent went underground until recent years. Currently, however, there is a marked resurgence of interest in the topic, as reflected in the popularity of books by authors such as Mark Epstein (1995, 1998, 2001), Jeffrey Rubin (1996), John Suler (1993), Anthony Molino (1998), and Barry Magid (2002). Epstein's books in particular seem to have struck a chord with both a nonprofessional audience and the psychoanalytic community. This increased interest parallels the tremendous popularity of Buddhism in popular culture, where, to paraphrase John Lennon's quip about the Beatles being more popular than Jesus Christ, the Dalai Lama wins the contest with Sigmund Freud, hands down. While the devout analyst may regard this statement as sacrilegious, like it or not, Buddhism gives every sign of being here to stay within our culture. and its influence on psychoanalytic thinking is growing.

How can we understand the growing interest by psychoanalysts in Buddhism? Psychoanalysis emerged at the beginning of the twentieth century when the secular worldview was ascendant. During this period the modernist worldview and the remarkable achievements of scientific rationalism were making the belief in God increasingly difficult for many people. Freud (1927, 1930) recognized that one of the primary functions of religion is to provide people with comfort in the face of the inevitable cruelties and indignities of life. But he believed that religion is an immature and self-deluding attempt to find comfort in the belief in the existence of an all-powerful and divine father figure. Instead, like many secularly oriented people of his day, he placed his faith in science.

Today, at the beginning of the twenty-first century, people no longer have the faith in science they once had, and the existential vacuum created by the death of God has become more pronounced than ever. It has become clear that psychoanalysis is not a science in the same sense that physics or chemistry are, but rather a secular form of spirituality. In some ways it functions to fill the void that was once filled by religion. But psychoanalysis does not focus extensively on the deeper existential questions that religions ask: What is the meaning of life in the face of our mortality? How do we as individuals fit in with the larger cosmos? How do we find meaning in the midst of the pain, suffering, and loss that are inevitably part of life?

Although many people in our culture experience a spiritual hunger, it is difficult if not impossible for somebody with a secular worldview to return to the religious worldview of premodern times. As the sociologist Philip Reiff (1966) has pointed out, the *religious man* of premodern times has been replaced by *psychological man,* and psychoanalysis has played an important role in this transformation. One of the appeals of Buddhism to a secular, psychoanalytic culture is that it is not a religion in the Judeo-Christian model, with belief in God and a theological doctrine demanding a leap of faith. As Stephen Batchelor (1997) puts it, Buddhism is a "religion without beliefs," or in Alan Watts's (1996) words, "a religion of no-religion." This makes Buddhism an appealing religion for the post-religious, postmodern person with a hunger for religion but no stomach for religious belief.

While the assertion that Buddhism does not require any kind of religious faith is true up to a point, the reality is more complex. Buddhism, like psychoanalysis, is a heterogeneous tradition with different schools and conflicting and seemingly contradictory beliefs. Both Buddhism and psychoanalysis are cultural institutions that originally developed as expressions of the values and the complex tensions and contradictions within their cultures of origins. Both are systems of healing that have evolved over time as culture has evolved, as the configuration of the self has evolved, and as new cultures have assimilated them. And both have transformed the cultures in which they have evolved. Today's psychoanalysis is very different from Freud's, and American psychoanalysis is very different from French. The meaning of Buddhism is very different for a contemporary North American or European than for an Indian Buddhist in the Axial Age or for a medieval Chinese Buddhist, and the function that the assimilation of Buddhist ideas into psychoanalytic theory and practice plays can be understood only if we know something about how this process of assimilation expresses contemporary cultural values, tensions, and problems.

In this introduction I examine the cultural contexts in which both psychoanalysis and Buddhism emerged and the ways they have evolved. I also examine some of the internal tensions that both psychoanalysis and Buddhism have struggled with over time, as well as the various ways in which these two traditions have reflected these tensions. One source of this struggle in both traditions has been the tension between the poles of agnosticism (or atheism) and faith (or commitment). Another has been tension between the poles of individualistic and communal orientations. Through cross-cultural comparison I begin a dialogue between Buddhism and psychoanalysis, with the objective of exploring various ways in which the two traditions can complement one another.

The Cultural Origins of Psychoanalysis

As Reiff (1966) has argued, psychoanalysis developed during a period in which the traditional religious values and symbols that held the community together were breaking down. Religious systems play the dual roles of integrating the individual with the community and of providing a system of communally held symbols and rituals that heal individuals who experience emotional distress. These traditional systems of healing function by giving some sense of meaning to the individual's suffering and by reintegrating the alienated individual into the community. This process of healing involves an act of faith and commitment to the values of the community, and through that commitment, one experiences salvation. For this reason Reiff refers to these traditional systems of healing as commitment therapies. In order for therapies of this sort to work, there has to be an intact, coherent community to which one recommits oneself. When psychoanalysis originated, the religious world-view that had dominated Western culture was no longer functioning in a cohesive and fully viable fashion. The traditional value system was fragmenting. Neitzsche had already proclaimed the death of God, and the secular worldview was securing its hold on the modern mind. Reiff sees psychoanalysis as qualitatively different from traditional systems of healing. From his perspective, psychoanalysis is not a therapy of commitment but rather an approach that liberates people from the type of commitment required by traditional religion and other social institutions.

As he points out, the goal of psychoanalysis for Freud was not to help the individual to recommit himself or herself to the values of the community but rather to learn to manage the strains of living as an individual detached from community. Part of Freud's concern was that the existing cultural value system was repressive, or at least that people responded to the demands of society through harshly or rigidly repressing their instincts, thereby giving rise to psychological symptoms. He emphasized the importance of becoming aware of our underlying instinctual passions and then using our rational capacities to modulate or tame them in a reflective rather than a rigid fashion. In this way, Freud believed, people could develop the ability to choose how to act, rather than be ruled unconsciously by their instinctual passions or by their unconscious, rigid defenses against them. His emphasis was thus on rational renunciation rather than irrational or unconscious suppression.

Thus, as Reiff sees it, the analyst, unlike the priest who speaks for organized religion, "speaks for the individual buried alive, as it were, in the culture. To be thus freed from a tyrannical cultural super-ego is to be properly bedded in the present world. Analysis is not an initiation but a counter-initiation, to end the need for initiations" (1966, 77). Freud had no interest in providing people with any form of salvation. In important respects his value system was consistent with the values of science and the modern era. From this perspective, knowledge is power, and self-knowledge allows choice. To Freud's way of thinking, the mature individual is a realist, and the realist does not need the comforts of religion, which he regarded as illusion.

But as Reiff argues, there has always been an ongoing tension within psychoanalysis between Freud's insistence that psychoanalysis not be a therapy of commitment in the traditional religious sense, and the need to find the type of meaning and salvation afforded by more traditional cultural institutions of healing. In contrast to Freud's "hermeneutic of suspicion" (Ricoeur 1970), Alfred Adler offered a philosophy of social commitment. Jung attempted to breathe new life into religion by relocating the gods inside man as archetypes. Reich developed a psychology of sexual/energetic mysticism. More recently analysts such as Wilfred Bion (1970), Michael Eigen (1998), and James Grotstein (2000) have developed approaches that attempt to reincorporate the spiritual through what can by thought of as a type of psychoanalytic mysticism.

Moreover, what Reiff failed to realize is that in certain respects psychoanalysis itself is a therapy of faith or commitment. Increasingly, analysts are realizing that the analytic process is not free of suggestion and persuasion, and that a certain degree of indoctrination into the analyst's value system is both inevitable and desirable. Irwin Hoffman (1998) has been particularly articulate in his discussion of the role that "analytic authority" plays. He reminds us that Freud (1926) himself thought of the analyst as a "secular pastoral worker" and recognized that he or she plays the role of an intimate, loving authority who has continuity with the kind of authority that parents have. Freud believed that this authority should be used to persuade patients to come to terms with the truth about both their internal and external worlds.

Building on Freud's own conceptualization of psychoanalysis as an "after-education," Hoffman borrows the sociological concept of secondary socialization (Berger and Luckmann 1967) to account for the mechanism through which the analytic relationship influences the change process. He argues that just as the child's initial construction of reality is forged in the crucible of affectively intense human relationships characterized by dependency upon the parent, the change that takes place through psychoanalysis is inevitably dependent upon a new socialization process in which the analyst functions as an intimate and loving authority. Thus in contrast to Reiff, who makes considerable effort to distinguish psychoanalysis from the type of change process that takes place through what he termed therapies of commitment, many contemporary analysts argue that psychoanalysis inevitably involves some degree of socialization into the value system of the analyst and the analytic community (e.g., Hoffman 1998; Renik 1996).[1]

Another way in which psychoanalysis has elements of a therapy of commitment is in its tendency to develop doctrinal positions that the faithful must adhere to in order to be considered "true analysts." As Greenberg and

Mitchell (1983) pointed out, for many years Freud's drive theory was the litmus test of whether one was a real analyst, and rejection of drive theory could lead to excommunication from the profession. And even within postmodern and pluralistic circles, the belief in the importance of "throwing away the book" is becoming a new doctrine of sorts (Hoffman 1994; Greenberg 2001).

Psychoanalysis and the Culture of Individualism

Another important shift in psychoanalytic sensibility that has taken place over time has involved an increased emphasis on the importance of the development of an authentic, vital sense of self and on the construction of personal meaning. Freud emphasized the importance of learning to negotiate the tensions between our instincts and civilization in a constructive fashion. As Mitchell has argued, many contemporary analysts are more interested in helping patients construct personal meaning for themselves: "What the patient needs is not a rational reworking of unconscious infantile fantasies; what the patient needs is a revitalization and expansion of his own capacity to generate experience that feels real, meaningful, and valuable.... If the goal of psychoanalysis in Freud's day was rational understanding and control (secondary process) over fantasy-driven, conflictual impulses (primary process), the goal of psychoanalysis in our day is most often thought about in terms of the establishment of a richer, more authentic sense of identity" (1993, 24).

This shift in psychoanalytic sensibility corresponds to an important shift in cultural landscape from Freud's time to ours. Psychoanalysis was born during a period when individualism was in the process of becoming more pronounced. In the Victorian culture of Freud's time, the self was viewed as dangerous, and an emphasis was placed on self-mastery or self-control (Cushman 1995). Over the last century the culture of individualism has continued to evolve, and the individual has become increasingly isolated from the community. This is a double-edged sword. On the one hand, the more individuated person of contemporary culture is freer of the potentially suffocating influence of the community. On the other, he or she is cut off from the sense of meaning and well-being that potentially flows from being integrated with the wider community.

According to Philip Cushman (1995) the disintegration of the unifying web of belief and values that traditionally brought people together and gave life meaning has resulted in the development of what he refers to as the empty self. This empty self experiences the lack of tradition, community, and shared meaning as an internal hollowness, a lack of personal conviction and worth, and a chronic, undifferentiated emotional hunger.

Christopher Lasch (1979), in a similar vein, argues that the breakdown of traditional cultural values and the fragmentation of societal structures, which traditionally provided a unifying web of meaning, has resulted in the development of a culture of narcissism. The individual in contemporary culture tends to be narcissistic in the sense that he has a grandiose or inflated sense of his own uniqueness and abilities. This grandiose and hyper-individuated sense of self is a defensive attempt to cope with the underlying sense of fragility and isolation resulting from the breakdown of traditional social structures and unifying webs of meaning. As Lasch sees it, the institutions of psychoanalysis and psychotherapy have developed to fill the cultural void left by the breakdown of traditional cultural institutions. The danger, however, is that psychoanalysis and other forms of psychotherapy can perpetuate or exacerbate the pathology that they are attempting to remedy. By focusing on the enrichment of the self they can create pathological individualism. The popularity of theorists such as D. W. Winnicott, with his emphasis on the *true self,* and Heinz Kohut, with his normalization of narcissism, can be seen as a reflection of the deeply entrenched sense of individualism in contemporary culture.[2]

Whereas people once saw personal contentment as a byproduct of living a good or moral life, in contemporary culture the pursuit of happiness risks becoming a goal in and of itself. There is thus a perpetuation of the narcissistic goal of pursuing self-enhancement or of shoring up the self. Because of the sense of isolation produced by the breakdown of traditional social structures, people become increasingly desperate in their pursuit of intimacy. However, intimacy becomes unobtainable as a result of the same circumstances that lead to the intensified search for intimacy in the first place. True intimacy involves the letting go of rigid self-other boundaries that are necessary in order to maintain narcissistic defenses. Because people are so preoccupied with shoring up their narcissistic defenses, intimacy becomes increasingly elusive. In addition, because of the intense isolation resulting from the breakdown of traditional social structures, people have unrealistic expectations about their intimate relationships or place unrealistic demands upon them, thereby dooming them to failure. People look for the kind of spiritual transcendence in their intimate relationships that traditionally came from religion.

Relational Developments and the Postmodern Turn

One of the more important developments in contemporary psychoanalysis consists of the relational perspective (Aron 1996; Benjamin 1988; Ghent 1989; Mitchell 1988). This perspective involves a host of related theoretical developments, which share in common an emphasis on the relational field as the basic unit of study, rather than on the individual as a separate entity. Human beings are regarded as being fundamentally interpersonal in nature; mind is regarded as composed of relational configurations; and self is regarded as constructed in a relational context. Although relational theorists trace their roots as far back as Sandor Ferenczi, the growing impact of the relational perspective on the mainstream is, I believe, a reflection of the intensification of the crisis of individualism in contemporary culture. It can be regarded in part as an attempt to remedy the excesses of a more individualistic perspective. It is also interesting to note that although the relational perspective synthesizes theoretical perspectives from both sides of the Atlantic, American culture has played a particularly significant role in its origin and development. This, I believe, is a reflection of the particularly intense sense of individualism and isolation in the United States. While the relational perspective can be seen as a corrective to the excessive individualism of contemporary culture, at another level it represents a further embodiment of that individualism. By emphasizing the mutuality of the analytic relationship and the analyst's embeddedness in the relational field, it challenges the traditional sources of analytic authority. This is consistent with the Western democratic emphasis on the challenge of tradition and the location of authority within the individual rather than the social institution.

Another important trend in contemporary psychoanalytic thinking consists of the postmodern turn. Increasingly analysts are emphasizing the constructed nature of human knowledge and the inherent limits of our understanding as analysts (Hoffman 1988; Mitchell 1993; Stern 1997). Constructivist epistemology asserts that reality is intrinsically ambiguous and is given form only through our interpretation of it. This perspective has profound implications for the nature of analytic authority and goes hand in hand with the increasing democratization of the therapeutic relationship. As we shall see, the shift toward a constructivist epistemology and the recognition that all knowledge is positional is also consistent with developments in traditional Buddhist philosophy.

Associated with the postmodern turn has been a shift toward viewing the self as multiple rather than as unitary (Bromberg 1998; Mitchell 1993; Pizer 1998). This shift reflects a similar shift across a range of different disciplines including philosophy, literary criticism, anthropology, social psychology, cognitive sciences, and neuropsychology. Although it is beyond the scope of this chapter to speculate extensively about the factors underlying this widespread cultural shift, it is worth dwelling for a moment on its meaning within psychoanalytic thinking, given the parallels between the psychoanalytic conceptualization of self as multiple and the Buddhist conception of self.

In postmodern thought, one of the central impulses underlying the deconstruction of the self is to challenge potentially oppressive functions of tradition and authority. Jacques Derrida, for example, "kills" the author of a text, deprives him or her of ultimate authority, by arguing that the final meaning of a text cannot be settled with reference to the author's intentions. Constructing meaning is an endless hermeneutic enterprise, and the notion of truth is replaced by a ceaseless play of infinite meanings. Michel Foucault challenges what he considers the illusion of self as an autonomous free agent by analyzing the way in which intricate decentered networks of power relations within society lead to the construction of the subjective experience of selfhood.

The current psychoanalytic fascination with self-multiplicity has no doubt been influenced by the faddish nature of this type of thinking. But there are other influences. Susan Fairfield (2001) for example, argues that theories of selfhood do not accurately capture some underling reality but are shaped by various intrapsychic needs of the analyst. She draws our attention to the hidden smugness often associated with critiques of monists (believers in a unitary self) who cling to the comforting belief that there is a stable, cohesive, singular self. She also points out the aggressiveness potentially associated with the desire to challenge conventional boundaries. And she suggests that seeing the self as multiple may also be a counter-phobic attempt to master fears of self-fragmentation by arguing that the self really is fragmented. She further adds that North American analysts, consistent with the optimism of their culture, tend to think about self-multiplicity in positive terms. For them, a multiple, contradictory self has more potential than the unitary self. In contrast, European theorists who emphasize multiplicity tend to place more importance on the experience of alienation or loss associated with the lack of a unitary self.

Mitchell (2001), while applauding Fairfield's thoughts about why one might view the self as multiple, also highlights the clinical implications of this view. His central thesis is that the adoption of the perspective of self as multiple helps to liberate us from a view of mental health that emphasizes conformity. In an argument somewhat reminiscent of Jacques Lacan's, he claims that the American ego-analytic emphasis on ego integration tends to value rational analysis and synthesis and to pathologize emotional intensity. In contrast, openness to a range of different states of being is conducive to greater unpredictability and passion in life. It is interesting to note that in some respects Mitchell's understanding of the clinical implications of self-multiplicity is consistent with his earlier emphasis (Mitchell 1993) on the centrality of enriching and revitalizing the self. This sensibility is in keeping with Fairfield's argument that American analysts tend to view the multiple self as a "cornucopia" of possibilities.

Origins of Buddhism

Buddhism originated in what is now northeast India during the fifth century B.C.E. During this period Indian civilization was undergoing tremendous ferment. The rural society and agricultural economy were gradually being replaced by a market economy and urban centers. A new culturally diverse and sophisticated merchant class was on the rise; traditional cultural values and religious beliefs were being challenged, and a heightened sense of individualism was emerging. Just as present-day individualism is double-edged, the growing individualism in India seems to have been associated with both malaise and exhilaration.

The agricultural society in which Buddhism developed was static and conservative. It divided society into four rigidly hierarchical castes: priests, warriors, farmers, and servants. These castes were hereditary and were thought to mirror the archetypal order of the cosmos. Ethical conduct consisted of performing the duties and responsibilities appropriate to one's caste. This worldview, while providing structure and cohesiveness, left little room for social change or individual conscience. The Brahmans, or priests, were in exclusive possession of the sacred knowledge of the Vedas, which spelled out the responsibilities of the castes and the relationships between them. It was the Brahmans' duty and responsibility to enact various sacred rites including animal sacrifice in order to control the universe.

For some time preceding the emergence of Buddhism, a new religious trend had begun to develop, the Upanishadic tradition. It involved a reinterpretation of the Vedas that emphasized the importance of the internal meaning of things over the external, magical significance of sacred rites. At the same time it enshrined the caste system. Central to Upanishadic philosophy is the concept of *atman*, which is equivalent in some respects to our concept of soul. The atman is the essence of the person, which transcends phenomenal experience. It is thus the real self in contrast to the experienced self. This atman is conceptualized as identical with the single unified essence behind appearances. The individual experience of self, and all phenomena in the world, are thus illusions, behind which lies a transcendental reality in which all phenomena are one. The failure to see behind this veil of illusion keeps people trapped in the pain of individuation and the suffering of life and death. Those who fail to recognize their true nature as part of the universal essence experience the pain and sorrow of life, and at death are reborn once again into endless rounds of life and death. The goal is to recognize the illusory nature of the self and to unify the true self or atman with the underlying universal essence. As for the historical conditions that led to the perception of life as being so painful, this is a matter of speculation. It may in part have been related to the stress associated with increased urbanization and the breakdown of traditional values. The rapid buildup of urban centers may have led to an increased incidence of plagues (Gombrich 1988). Regardless of the conditions giving rise to this perspective, however, one of its consequences was a devaluing of sensual and worldly experience in favor of the transcendental.

Two primary practices used for gaining transcendence were meditation and mortification of the flesh. Meditation in this context involved sitting quietly and using a variety of concentrative techniques to focus the mind, thereby stilling discursive thought. Mortification of the flesh involved subjecting oneself to various physical extremes of cold, heat, hunger, and so on as a way of conquering the demands of the body, thereby experiencing transcendence.

Early Buddhism can be understood as a reaction to this worldview in a number of ways. To begin with, the Buddha denied the existence of an atman, or of any transcendental self or soul. At the same time, he never taught that the self does not exist (as he is often interpreted to have done), but rather argued that the self is nonsubstantial, in the sense that it is constructed on a moment-by-moment basis out of a variety of components: memories, physical sensations, emotions, concepts, dispositions (including both unconscious and inherited conditioning), and so on. Furthermore, he argued that the construction of self is always influenced by ever changing causes and conditions. There is some similarity between this teaching of the Buddha's and the Upanishadic formulation of atman. The underlying assumption in both cases is that the experience of the self as a substantial and isolated entity lies at the heart of the problem, and that the modification of that experience is the cure.

The Buddhist perspective is, however, more moderate in some respects. To begin with, it does not conceptualize the individual self as illusory. Again, what is illusory is the experience of self as substantial or unchanging. From a Buddhist perspective, the self, like everything in this world, is transient or impermanent. Death, illness, and loss are unavoidable aspects of life. Suffering arises as a result of attempting to cling to what we desire and to avoid what causes us pain. Liberation emerges as a result of recognizing the impermanent nature of reality and letting go of our self-centered craving. There is no transcendental self to be realized, as is the case in the Upanishadic worldview, and thus no self that is separate from the aggregates of form and psychological or mental experience. In this respect the Buddhist perspective is less dualistic than the Upanishadic worldview and less likely to give rise to extreme forms of asceticism. The Buddha emphatically rejected extreme asceticism as a spiritual practice and instead proposed what is referred to as the Middle Way, that is, a pathway between the extremes of asceticism and hedonism or sensualism. The goal in Buddhism thus becomes not one of transcending worldly experience but rather one of finding a wiser way of living within it.

This difference plays out in the form of the meditation techniques that are used in the two different traditions. In the Upanishadic tradition meditation tends to involve the concentration of attention upon a particular object of focus for purposes of experiencing an absorption. This results in a withdrawal of the senses from worldly experience, a reduction of internal stimulation, and a resulting experience of peace or tranquillity, which is believed to be associated with the transcendental reality that one wishes to realize.

This form of meditation, which is sometimes referred to as concentration meditation constitutes one form of Buddhist meditation, but in and of itself it is not considered to be sufficient for liberation. The second form of meditation, which plays a role in most Buddhist traditions, consists of detached observation of one's own mind. Concentration meditation plays an important role in helping the individual develop the attentional skill necessary to observe his or her experience in a mindful fashion, but the experience of meditative absorption is not the goal. The objective of this second form of meditation, which is referred to as *insight* or *mindfulness* meditation, is to help the meditator develop a greater awareness of the manifold contents of awareness as they unfold, and an ability over time to develop an attitude of nonjudgmental acceptance of the full range of experience. This objective is in keeping with the Buddhist emphasis on learning to live fully in this world rather than on pursuing otherworldly experiences. Mindfulness meditation leads to a greater appreciation of the impermanent or ever changing nature of all phenomena, including the self. It also leads to an appreciation of the role the mind plays in constructing reality.

Another important characteristic of early Buddhist thinking is the rejection of all metaphysical speculation. In this respect Buddhist thinking, at least in its early form and in some contemporary variants, is essentially pragmatic and agnostic in nature. It is pragmatic in the philosophical sense (e.g., Rorty 1982) insofar as truth is defined as that which is effective in relieving human suffering. And it is agnostic in the sense that it refuses to engage in metaphysical speculation. There is a story in which the Buddha used the analogy of a man who is shot by an arrow. In a situation of such urgency, questions such as who made the arrow and what type of bow was used are irrelevant. What is critical is the practical affair of removing the arrow. Similarly, argued the Buddha, metaphysical and cosmological speculation are irrelevant to the task of relieving human suffering. Moreover, committing oneself to a metaphysical view or a theological doctrine is a form of enslavement. It interferes with the openness essential to enlightenment or true existential awakening.

One of the implications of this feature of early Buddhist thinking was that it undermined the theological structure supporting the caste system. At a social level, then, early Buddhist thinking was a profoundly democratizing force. It subverted the authority of the priestly class and denied the value of ritual observances of a magical nature. Ethical behavior was no longer defined as performing one's duty as a member of one's caste, and no merit was accrued from observing rituals or depending upon the priestly class. Instead ethical action was defined in terms of acting selflessly, according to the precepts of right action.

In some respects the thrust of the early Buddhist tradition was analogous to the thrust of the Protestant Reformation in Europe. Early Buddhists were interested in purifying the Upanishadic tradition of features that they saw as problematic, just as Luther and Calvin wanted to purify Christianity. They wanted to eradicate the magical or superstitious elements, eliminate empty ritual, and establish a more direct relationship between the individual and the experience of salvation (or what the Buddhists refer to as enlightenment). Just as the Protestant Reformation contained a democratizing element, challenging the role of the clergy as divinely empowered intermediaries between the individual and God, Buddhism eliminated the divinely sanctioned role of the priestly class and emphasized the responsibility of the individual for his or her own spiritual destiny. And just as the attempt to purify Christianity of its magical elements had both desirable and undesirable consequences, so did Buddhism's attempt to purify Indian religion of its magical elements have such consequences. Both developments placed greater emphasis on the inner meaning of spirituality, but both sacrificed some of the magic and mystery that the human heart hungers for.

Tension and Evolution within Buddhist Thinking

Since its inception, Buddhism has struggled with the tension between the pragmatic/agnostic perspective at its core and the need for faith and epistemological certainty and metaphysical absolutism. In many ways this parallels the tension in psychoanalysis between Freud's vision of psychoanalysis as a purely rational, scientific, analytic approach and the tendency to develop a new therapy of faith and commitment. One reflection of this tension can be seen in the evolution of Buddhist philosophy. Early Buddhist philosophy and psychology were codified in a body of literature referred to as Abhidharma. This literature emphasizes that the self can be deconstructed into a number of constituent elements. These elements are viewed as arising in dependence upon one another and upon fluctuating causes and conditions. It is on this basis that the self is seen to be lacking in substantiality. In practice, it is held that the meditative process allows one to experience the arising and departing of various constituent elements of the self, and this insight leads to the experience of enlightenment.

Over time, this perspective became reified, and there was a tendency to view the various constituent components of the self as having a fundamental or substantial nature. Various alternative perspectives were offered as to what these fundamental constituents of the self were. Partially in reaction to this trend, the Madhyamika school of philosophy developed. This perspective employed sophisticated linguistic and logical analysis to deconstruct the Abhidharmic analysis of the self into constituent elements and to demonstrate that none of these elements have intrinsic reality. The argument is not that such phenomena are nonexistent, but rather that they are empty of inherent existence. In other words, all phenomena exist in dependence on our construction of them. This perspective anticipated contemporary hermeneutic and constructivist thinking by hundreds of years. The Madhyamika perspective is not a radical constructivism, but rather closer to what Hoffman (1998) refers to as dialectical constructivism. It extends the Buddhist principle of the Middle Way to the epistemological level, by arguing for a position between the extremes of naive realism and radical constructivism. It emphasizes that emptiness itself is only a concept and does not have any intrinsic reality. As Madhyamika philosophers put it, the concept of emptiness is like a medicine—a medicine for the illness of naive realism. But like any medicine, too much of it can make you sick.

Nevertheless, critics of the Madhyamika position interpreted it as a form of radical constructivism, leading to nihilism. The Yogachara school of philosophy attempted to correct what it saw as a tendency toward nihilism in Madhyamika thinking, adopting a position that, in turn, tended toward the metaphysical and transcendental. The Yogachara school holds that both perception and the object of perception spring forth from a single seed, which is contained in a type of substratum consciousness. This substratum consciousness is likened to a river, which is constantly changing and yet remains the same. It has both personal and universal aspects to it.

Then there is what is referred to as Tathagatagarbha tradition in Buddhism, which holds that all sentient beings are endowed with Buddha nature, and thus have the potential for "awakening" and realizing their intrinsic identity as enlightened beings. This Buddha essence, also referred to as *suchness*, or in Sanskrit as *tathata*, is often spoken of as equivalent to *emptiness*, but it has a more positive quality. It is described as beginningless and endless and as pervading everything. In some traditions this concept of Buddha essence or suchness appears to be taken more literally, thus bordering on the type of substantialism that early Buddhism was reacting against. In other traditions, however, the concept is subjected to the type of deconstructive logic characteristic of the Madhyamika approach.

At a more practical level, the tension between the poles of pragmatism/agnosticism and faith/absolutism is reflected in the way in which the Buddha is conceptualized in different Buddhist traditions. In early Buddhism, and in some forms of contemporary Buddhism, the Buddha is emphatically not seen as a divine figure. He is a human being who became enlightened through his own efforts, and who serves as a model for other spiritual seekers. After his death he was seen as no longer directly active in the world. The Buddha is thus not somebody to be prayed to. Over time various doctrines and traditions developed that viewed the historical Buddha as only one embodiment of the principle of enlightenment. In this view, the cosmos is inhabited by an infinite number of Buddhas—past, present, and future, all of whom have an active presence in the world and help sentient beings attain enlightenment. In various Buddhist traditions, practitioners pray to or petition one or another of the Buddhas, just as Catholics pray to the saints. At the level of philosophical doctrine, there is recognition that these Buddhas do not exist in any absolute sense, that like all phenomena they are empty of intrinsic existence. Nevertheless, at a psychological level they function for people in the same way that saints function in the Catholic tradition, or that gods and goddesses function in premodern cultures.

Another example of this tension can be seen in the role that the belief in rebirth plays in various Buddhist traditions. Despite the fact that early Buddhism rejected the notion of an eternal self or atman, it accepted a notion of rebirth. As in the Upanishadic tradition, a formulation of the goal in early Buddhism was (and in some forms of contemporary Buddhism continues to be) obtaining release from samsara, or the cycle of death and rebirth. This state of release, referred to as nirvana, is conceptualized as one in which all self-centered craving ceases. And yet at the level of practice the goal is often regarded as one of achieving a better life at the next cycle of rebirth. My impression is that there has always been a tension between the official Buddhist doctrine of anatman, or no-self, and the belief in rebirth. Buddhist philosophy attempts to reconcile this tension in various ways. For example, it is argued that what continues from life to life is not a substantial self or soul but rather a subtle causal connection. The analogy that is used is that of flame passed from candle to candle. The flame that passes from one candle to a next is not exactly the same, but not exactly different either. But to my mind, this resolution is less than completely satisfying. Some Buddhist traditions downplay the importance of the doctrine of rebirth. The Zen tradition, for example, tends to emphasize that good rebirths and bad rebirths are both states of mind.

On the other hand, Tibetan Buddhism places considerable emphasis on the principle of rebirth. In fact there is a tradition of picking important spiritual leaders at an early age because they are believed to be reincarnations of deceased spiritual leaders. For example, the Dalai Lama, who is the supreme spiritual and temporal leader of Tibet, is viewed as the fourteenth incarnation of the first Dalai Lama.

When Buddhism spread to China, it was transformed by the existing culture and by the Taoist and Confucian philosophies that were dominant at the time. Although a variety of different forms of Buddhism developed in China, Chan Buddhism (more commonly known by its Japanese name, Zen) is perhaps the most distinctively Chinese. Zen is often characterized by its direct and down-to-earth quality. Ancient Indian culture tended to prize abstract philosophical thought and metaphysical speculation. It tended to have a world-weary quality. As we have seen, in Upanishadic thinking, life is suffering, and the goal is to seek liberation from the endless round of rebirth by seeing through the illusion of one's individuality. Ancient Chinese thinking had a more optimistic, humanistic, and earthy flavor to it. In Taoist thinking, liberation is obtained by attuning oneself to the natural, spontaneous harmony of the universe—the Tao. This Tao is not something that can be defined in words or grasped conceptually, and in fact any attempt to do so only interferes with one's ability to function in harmony with it. One can act in accordance with the Tao only when one is able to let go of attempting to grasp it, thereby acting in a spontaneous and unselfconscious fashion. This allows one to be attuned and receptive to the configuration of the moment.

Although the Buddha originally served as a model for the way in which all human beings could become enlightened through their own efforts, subsequent developments in Indian Buddhism tended to present enlightenment as a more and more extraordinary, rarefied, and otherworldly state, available to only the few. Zen tends to bring enlightenment down to earth, as it were, and to demystify and demythologize it.

There is an iconoclastic element to Zen, which was probably influenced by the ancient Taoist image of a sage as somebody who was liberated from convention and from stereotypical thinking. Enlightenment in the Zen tradition tends to be associated with spontaneity and freedom from inhibiting self-consciousness and conformity. Enlightenment is conceptualized as a state in which events are experienced immediately, without the intrusion of reflective self-consciousness. There is a selfless openness to experience.

Buddhism in Tibet took a very different turn from Chinese Buddhism. In Tibet certain developments in Indian Buddhism (referred to as Tantric Buddhism) blended with the indigenous Tibetan tradition of Bon, which had strong magical and shamanistic elements. This resulted in the development of an interesting synthesis of magical and shamanistic practices with Buddhist worldview and epistemology. The Tibetan tradition places great emphasis on the importance of the teacher (referred to as the guru or lama), who is seen as an embodiment of the Buddha and as the gateway to enlightenment. Tibetan Buddhist cosmology is populated by a pantheon of male and female deities, who are invoked during meditation sessions that involve elaborate visualizations. Yet at the same time, these deities are seen as empty of inherent existence and as creations of the meditator's own mind.

In Tibetan Buddhism, one of the foundational meditation practices is what is referred to as guru yoga. The purpose of guru yoga is to facilitate the development of faith and devotion to one's lama. In psychoanalytic terms the Tibetan tradition attempts to cultivate an idealizing transference toward the teacher, and to use that as a vehicle for change. This transference provides an ongoing inspiration for the student to continue on the arduous pathway of spiritual development despite its many difficulties, by helping to generate and maintain faith that change (or relief from suffering) is possible. The lama or guru serves as a living reminder that such change is possible, since he functions as an embodiment of the principles that the student aspires to realize. In addition, being in relationship with a lama who embodies special qualities helps the student feel empowered.

In the Tibetan tradition, the relationship with the lama is never interpreted as it is in psychoanalysis. From the beginning, however, the student is taught to cultivate a paradoxical attitude toward the lama, who is seen, on the one hand, as an embodiment of the highest ideals and values in the Buddhist traditions and, on the other, as a human being with human flaws and failings.

As with so much of the Tibetan tradition, guru yoga is reminiscent of the old Indian rope trick, in which the yogi climbs up a rope suspended in midair, pulls the rope up after him, and disappears. The student is taught to conjure up a world of meditation deities in his imagination, or to imbue the lama with special powers, and then to use the constructed images of his imagination in order to help him to cultivate certain attitudes toward reality. At the end of every meditation session, the meditator dissolves the image back into the nothingness from which it arose. He pulls up the rope.

Although there are many variations of guru yoga, they all involve some combination of visualization practice and prayer or incantation designed to help the student see the lama as an embodiment of the Buddha (and of the qualities a Buddha embodies) and establish a deep connection with him, thereby ultimately internalizing his qualities. For example, the meditator visualizes the lama as manifesting in the form of a Buddha or other deity surrounded by a retinue of important figures in the lineage and by various dakinis (female deities visualized in order to focus the mind). Various colors of light are then visualized as emanating from the dakinis and from the lama, bathing and purifying the meditator of self-centered craving and helping him or her to recognize all phenomena as empty of inherent existence.

This particular practice illustrates two characteristics of Tibetan Buddhist visualization practices. First, the visualization is permeated by a kind of transitional logic or reality, to use Winnicott's term. Although the visualization is intentionally constructed by the meditator, it is also treated as if it had a life of its own (you pray to the visualized lama). At the same time you explicitly remind yourself by means of prescribed incantations that neither the visualization nor even the lama himself has any inherent existence. The meditator thus attempts to enter into a type of transitional space in the sense that the boundaries between subjective and objective reality are intentionally blurred. He or she strives to maintain a type of double vision, on the one hand knowing that the experience is subjective and, on the other, treating it as if it were objective or real.

Second, it involves the imaginary construction of a world in which the normal boundaries of personal identity become permeable. In the visualization the lama becomes identical with the Buddha, and the lama's mind becomes inseparable from that of the meditator. This identification helps to loosen the constraints of ordinary dualistic logic and challenges the conventional self-other distinction. When the meditator conjures up an entire pantheon of lesser and greater deities and, while doing so, recognizes that they both are and are not creations of the mind, the meditator taps into a rich and vast experience that dwarfs conventional reality.

Buddhism and the Culture of Psychoanalysis

SECULARIZATION AND THE RETURN OF THE REPRESSED

The trend toward secularization in the modern world, while profoundly liberating in some respects, has also contributed to the experience of the self as empty, and in some more traditional cultures has been seen as a form of oppression and an assault on traditional ways of life. In some cases this has caused a resurgence of religious interest in a variety of different forms, a type of return of the repressed. In the middle of the twentieth century, few would have predicted that religion would once again become an important societal force. And yet, from the dramatic influence of Islamic fundamentalism in the Middle East and internationally, to the growing influence of the Christian Right in North American politics, it is becoming increasingly clear that the trend toward secularism has dramatically reversed. As Karen Armstrong (2000) has pointed out, the rise of religious fundamentalism must be understood, not as a return to an earlier form of religious belief, but as a reaction to the spiritual and cultural crises of modernity. In its extremity and rigidity it involves a brittle and defensive attempt to revitalize a fragmented culture and to shore up a sense of self under assault.

Another response has been the emergence of New Age spirituality, which involves a syncretic blend of various traditional Eastern and Western spiritualities with pop psychology. This form of religious expression stems from a thirst for meaning and a genuine spiritual yearning. But in contrast to more mature forms of spirituality, which emphasize balancing the needs of the self with the good of the larger whole, it tends toward strong elements of narcissistic self-absorption and personal omnipotence.

We have seen how both Buddhism and psychoanalysis have struggled over time with the tension between the poles of agnosticism or atheism versus faith and commitment. Within psychoanalysis the tendency to deify Freud and to treat his words as gospel can be seen as another form of the return of the repressed.

From a contemporary psychoanalytic perspective, one of the appeals of Buddhism is the way its agnostic sensibility and its grounding in a constructivist epistemology resonate with the postmodern turn. Certainly Buddhism, like all religions, has gone through various forms of institutionalization and has often lost this agnostic sensibility. It is thus important not to idealize Buddhism, a particular danger for Westerners who have become alienated from their own spiritual traditions and seek spiritual meaning in a foreign tradition uncontaminated by negative associations. The postmodern emphasis on critiquing authority, which plays an important role in contemporary psychoanalytic dialogue, can, however, help challenge the institutionalized aspects of Buddhism that obscure its more emancipatory dimensions. Postmodern critique can help shed light on the various insidious ways in which Buddhism, like all religious traditions can be used to serve the interests of the privileged.

CONSTRUCTIVISM IN BUDDHISM AND PSYCHOANALYSIS

One of the attractions of Buddhist thinking from a psychoanalytic perspective is that the constructivist epistemology that is so prominent in Buddhist philosophy is compatible with the trend toward constructivism in contemporary psychoanalytic thinking. In light of this compatibility it is interesting to think about the impulses behind this trend in the two different traditions. In psychoanalysis an important influence has been the general shift toward constructivism in philosophy and other disciplines. In addition, however, a central impulse has been the desire to democratize the therapeutic relationship, by emphasizing the limits of the analyst's knowledge. Related to this is the emphasis on the mutuality of the analytic relationship and the coconstruction of reality by patient and analyst. These emphases are consistent with the Western tradition of democratic individualism and wariness of various forms of authority. The trend toward constructivism in psychoanalysis is also consistent with the growing emphasis on the importance of constructing healing narratives in the context of the postmodern crisis of meaninglessness.

In Buddhist constructivism, the primary thrust is to cultivate a radical sense of openness. The belief is that concepts enslave us and that the tendency toward reification creates suffering. The emphasis is not on constructing adaptive narratives but rather on the radical deconstruction of all narratives. It is interesting to note that this emphasis on radical openness is similar in some respects to the growing awareness in analytic thinking of the importance of the analyst's openness and tolerance of ambiguity (e.g., Bion 1970; Stern 1997; Eigen 1998).

There can be a valuable complementarity between the two traditions here. Analysts, for all of their fascination with constructivist thinking, still tend to have a bias toward wanting to understand and help their patients to understand. There are times when the experience of understanding can be helpful; especially in a more individualistic culture such as ours, the construction of personal meaning (which Buddhism tends to neglect) can be very important. Yet, letting go of the need to understand can lead to the experience of awe, acceptance, and reverence in the face of the mystery of life.

Multiple Selves and No-Self

The Buddhist emphasis on recognizing the insubstantiality of self offers a possible antidote for the narcissistic or "empty" self-configuration characteristic of our culture. First, however, it is important to bear in mind that, just as the adoption of the view of self as multiple can reflect a counter-phobic attempt to master fears of self-fragmentation (Fairfield 2001), the adoption of the Buddhist perspective of self as empty can be an attempt to deal with one's subjective sense of self as empty, by normalizing this state.

On the face of it, there are similarities between the Buddhist notion of noself and contemporary psychoanalytic conceptions of self as multiple. And in

fact the growing interest of analysts in self-multiplicity may help create a climate of receptivity to the Buddhist conceptualization of the self. It is important, however, to be aware of the different functions that challenge the
conventional conception of self serves in the two traditions. As we have seen,
the contemporary psychoanalytic fascination with self-multiplicity appears
to stem at least in part from a desire to challenge monolithic views of mental health that are implicitly conformist in nature. The emphasis in the Buddhist conception of no-self is on decreasing the sense of existential isolation,
by emphasizing the constructed nature of the boundary between self and others and the interdependence of all living beings. As Francis Cook puts it, in
Buddhist thinking: "There is no absolute reality beyond or distinct from this
world of interdependent being. It is a place where the individual arises out of
an extremely extensive environment of other individuals—parents, grand-
parents, culture, soil, water, stone, mist, and many, many more—and takes
its place as one other individual. Once in the world, the individual is constantly and massively conditioned by the extensive environment of other individuals" (Cook 1989, 24).

It is interesting to note that in some respects this perspective parallels the
object relations perspective, in which the self is constructed through the internalization of others. From an object relations perspective, however, the goal
is to liberate the self by freeing oneself from one's ties to old internal objects.
From a Buddhist perspective, freedom comes from recognizing that there is
no self independent of others.[3]

There is a famous passage from Dogen, an influential thirteenth-century
Japanese Buddhist teacher that goes as follows:

> To study the Buddha way is to study the self
> To study the self is to forget the self
> To forget the self is to be authenticated by the myriad things

Thus, when we are able to truly see the way in which we construct our
experience of self, the barrier between self and other dissolves. An experience
of authenticity then emerges, not out of an experience of true self as an individual, but out of an experience of being related to others as one finger of
the hand is related to the others. Somewhat parallel to this perspective is
Buber's notion of the I-Thou relationship, which emphasizes that relating

to the other as a subject (rather than as an object) is associated with an experience of interconnectedness. Further dialogue between the Buddhist and psychoanalytic perspectives on the self can help to recover a mystical dimension to psychoanalysis—mystical in the sense of experiencing a sense of oneness with the cosmos. The danger with any type of spiritual solution, of course, is that it can be used defensively, as a way of avoiding dealing with emotional conflicts, or in an attempt to fill up the empty self or support a narcissistic sense of omnipotence. The Buddhist tradition, while certainly not immune to these temptations, at least attempts to counteract them in various ways. The Zen tradition in particular emphasizes the "this-worldly" or ordinary aspects of Buddhist practice and consistently focuses on undercutting spiritual escapism and poking holes in students' spiritual narcissism.

In a well-known Zen story, for example, a student asks his master, "How do I attain enlightenment?" The master asks, "Have you finished your rice?" "Yes," replies the student. "Then," responds the teacher, "wash your bowl." As this story illustrates, the emphasis is on the "ordinary magic" of immersing oneself fully in one's everyday life rather than looking for idealized or escapist solutions. In the words of the Zen poet P'ang-yun: "Miraculous power and marvelous activity—Drawing water and hewing wood" (Watts 1957, 133).

There is also an iconoclasm intrinsic to Buddhism that is consistent with some of the more recent developments in psychoanalysis that emphasize the importance of the therapist's spontaneity and personal responsiveness (e.g., Hoffman 1998; Ringstrom 2001). The Zen teachers of legend are often distinguished by their spontaneity and unconventionality and their tendency to use unexpected tactics to shock students out of their conventional ways of looking at things, in order to allow them a glimpse of enlightened or unconditioned experience. In Tibetan Buddhism there is a tradition of "crazy wisdom": certain unusual and highly respected teachers act in a way that may look odd or crazy from the perspective of conventional standards, and yet it is believed that their unconventionality, their willingness and ability to transgress conventional standards, is a mark of their enlightenment rather than a sign of psychopathology. So, for example, one of the most beloved folk heroes in Tibet was a character named Drunkpa Kunley, who was notorious for outrageous behaviors such as getting drunk and consorting with prostitutes. At the same time he was seen as an enlightened teacher who guided (or perhaps more accurately provoked) many people to the experience of enlightenment.

Like any religion or established social institution, Buddhism has deeply conservative elements, and there has always been a tension between the more conservative and the more radical elements of Buddhism. But for all of its conservatism, there was something subversive about Buddhism from the beginning. The Buddha himself, very much aware of the limits of words and concepts, reputedly compared his teachings to a raft with which one crosses a river. Just as one leaves the raft behind after one has crossed, one recognizes that the various Buddhist teachings are only a vehicle to transport one along the path to awakening or enlightenment. To cling to these teachings as if they had some intrinsic reality would be counter to the basic thrust of Buddhism. In the Zen tradition they say, "Do not confuse the finger pointing at the moon with the moon," once again emphasizing the pragmatic nature of concepts.

The Reenchantment of the World

Premodern cultures regarded the world as an enchanted place. In these cultures the distinctions between internal and external reality and between subject and object were less clear-cut than in modern culture. The sociologist Morris Berman refers to this as "participating consciousness." As he puts it: "The view of nature which predominated in the West down to the eve of the Scientific Revolution was that of an enchanted world. Rocks, trees, rivers, and clouds were all seen as wondrous, alive, and human beings felt at home in this environment. The cosmos, in short, was a place of belonging. A member of this cosmos was not an alienated observer in it but a direct participant in its drama. His personal destiny was bound up with its destiny, and this relationship gave meaning to his life" (Berman 1981, 16).

In contrast, for modern consciousness the universe is a mechanistic one, operating on the basis of impersonal principles and matter that is inert and devoid of life. Human beings live outside of nature. Modern consciousness is thus fundamentally alienated. There is no ecstatic merger with nature and no sense of belonging to the cosmos.

Ernest Becker makes a similar point: "The characteristic of the modern mind is the banishment of mystery, of naïve belief, of simple-minded hope.

We put the accent on the visible, the clear, the cause-and-effect relation, the logical—always the logical. We know the difference between dreams and reality, between facts and fictions, between symbols and bodies. But right away we can see that these characteristics of the modern mind are exactly those of neurosis. What typifies the neurotic is that he 'knows' his situation vis-à-vis reality. He has no doubts; there is nothing you can say to sway him, to give him hope of trust" (Becker 1973, 201).

As Hans Loewald (1980) and more recently Mitchell (2000) have pointed out, psychoanalysis has tended unwittingly to reproduce the values of a culture that experiences the world as disenchanted. By privileging secondary process over primary process, and regarding the triumph of the reality principle over the pleasure principle as the essence of mental health, it has contributed to a loss of meaningfulness.

The move toward a constructivist epistemology within psychoanalysis, however, has opened the doors for a reconsideration of the relationship between reality and fantasy. Traditionally fantasy was viewed as distorting reality, and the analytic task consisted of gaining insight into the nature of this distortion. But as Mitchell puts it in his exegesis of Loewald's perspective: "Separating fantasy and reality is only one way to organize experience. For life to be meaningful, vital, and robust, fantasy and reality cannot be too divorced from each other. Fantasy cut adrift from reality becomes irrelevant and threatening. Reality cut adrift from fantasy becomes vapid and empty. Meaning in human experience is generated in the mutual, dialectically enriching tension between fantasy and reality; each requires the other to come alive" (Mitchell 2000, 29).

It is impossible for us to return to the worldview of our ancestors in a genuine or authentic fashion. We can reject the modern worldview, but we can never completely escape it. It inevitably colors the way we experience reality. Is it possible to achieve some degree of reenchantment of the world in which we experience a sense of participating consciousness, without an act of denial or self-deception? The Tibetan Buddhist approach to integrating practices and rituals of a more magical nature with a constructivist epistemology may provide some leads. The Tibetan culture in which such practices were originally developed was a prescientific, traditional culture in which magic and supernatural reality existed as a part of everyday experience, just as they did in Western culture prior to the Enlightenment and the dawn of the scientific era.

In this culture what was distinctive about Tibetan Buddhism was not the use of practices of a magical nature, but rather the co-option of the rituals and symbols of magic in order to pursue the Buddhist goal of realizing that all phenomena are empty of intrinsic existence. In contrast, in a contemporary Western context, the use of Tibetan Buddhist meditation techniques, or of practices informed by them, can have a different function. It can become a way of participating in the experience of an enchanted reality that is not normative in contemporary culture, while at the same time reminding ourselves of our own role in constructing that reality. A careful scrutiny of the processes through which such practices operate can thus play a role in refining current psychoanalytic thinking of how change can take place.

Reductionism versus Nondualism

As Becker (1973) has emphasized, one of Freud's fundamental insights had to do with the recognition of the irrevocable *creatureliness* of human beings. Always the iconoclast, realist, and destroyer of illusions, Freud insisted on reminding us that in the end, for all of our noble aspirations and pretensions, we are ultimately animals motivated by sexual and aggressive instincts. Many contemporary analysts are critical of this perspective and view it as reductionistic. And yet it is important to recognize the brilliance of Freud's vision in this respect and his passionate commitment to puncturing our pretensions and revealing our self-deceptions. A problem emerges when the spiritual is seen as something separate from our baser instincts. We imagine that somehow we can be free of our creatureliness, and that there is a clear distinction between the sacred and the profane. The ever present danger is that spirituality can lead to moralism rather than morality, and to dissociation and projection rather than acceptance.

From a Buddhist perspective this attempt to separate the sacred from the profane lies at the heart of the human dilemma. Rather than seeing spirituality as a derivative of baser instincts, however, the emphasis is on helping people recognize that the sacred and profane are one. In the Mahayana Buddhist tradition, for example, it is emphasized that samsara (i.e., conditioned, unenlightened existence, or the wheel of life and death) is no different from nirvana (i.e., the state of enlightenment in which all self-centered craving ceases to exist). In other words, there is no paradise or ideal state to be attained. There is only this world and this present moment, and enlightenment consists of the experiential realization of this. The Zen tradition is notorious for its earthiness. For example, the Zen master Lin-chi said: "There is no place in Buddhism for using effort. Just be ordinary and nothing special. Relieve your bowels, pass water, put on our clothes, and eat your food. When you're tired, go and lie down" (Watts 1957, 101).

In Tibetan Buddhism, some meditation techniques use sexual imagery as a way of expressing the non-dual nature of the relationship between the sacred and the profane. While there is something right about Freud's insistence on seeing our highest sensibilities and accomplishments as derivatives of sexuality and aggression, there is also something off base about it. His reductionism ends up devaluing the worth of our highest achievements and aspirations rather than celebrating the beauty of human nature with all our flaws, imperfections, and self-deceptions. The Buddhist emphasis on nonduality provides a perspective that resonates with Freud's important insights about our baser motivations, yet at the same time provides a corrective to his reductionism.

Locating Psychoanalysis within Life

In a laudatory review of Irwin Hoffman's *Ritual and Spontaneity in the Psychoanalytic Process,* Donnell Stern states that Hoffman's book is distinguished by the fact that it "locates psychoanalysis within life rather than the other way around" (2001, 464). What he is referring to here is Hoffman's commitment to an existential perspective, which emphasizes that the ongoing struggle to create meaning in the face of mortality lies at the heart of the human dilemma. One of the reasons Hoffman's book stands out is that with rare exceptions (most notably Otto Rank) mainstream psychoanalysts have tended to not focus on this dialectic or at least to not place it at center stage.

Traditionally, of course, these existential concerns have been at the heart of all religious systems, and it is understandable that psychoanalysts in their eagerness to distance themselves from their religious predecessors would be reluctant to tread on this territory. And yet we all know at some level that our hearts and souls are left untouched unless we are able to address our fundamental existential concerns about the meaning (or potential meaninglessness) of life in the ever-present shadow of death.

During periods of our lives when things are going well, when both we and our loved ones are healthy, we are able to quickly retreat behind a shield of denial, and death becomes an abstraction rather than something of immediate concern. Like the protagonist in Tolstoy's *Death of Ivan Ilyich* before his illness, we all relate to death as something that happens to others but not to ourselves—or as something that will happen to us someday in the remote future.

Buddhism places the confrontation with death, loss, and suffering at the heart of things. And ultimately it offers refuge, not in the promise of a better afterlife or protection by a divine figure, but in the form of a pathway toward greater acceptance of life as it is, with all its pain and suffering. There are two key features of this pathway. The first is the belief that, paradoxically, the full recognition and acceptance of the impermanence of everything leads to an experience of peace and the ability to truly cherish life. Interestingly, Freud himself expressed a similar sensibility in a short paper written in the shadow of the First World War. In this article (Freud 1915), he recounts a conversation with a young poet who had expressed despondency in contemplating the transient nature of existence. Freud responds that the recognition that all we value and cherish is intrinsically transient can give rise either to despondency or to a greater appreciation of that which we cherish. The determining factor is whether we are able to fully accept this intrinsic transience and not recoil against the mourning that is linked to this acceptance.

The second principle is the recognition that we are all members of the human community, who are linked together by the bond of sharing in the pain and suffering of life. There is an old Buddhist story that captures the importance of this sense of community. A mother whose son had recently died went to the Buddha to ask him to bring him back to life. The Buddha told her that if she would bring him a mustard seed from the home of somebody who had not known loss, he would help her. As the mother went from house to house she came to realize that no such home could be found. She gradually came to feel less separated from others in her grief, and able to find peace in the midst of her pain.

Freud (1927) believed that religion coerces people into renouncing their instincts through promises of illusory salvation and threats of everlasting punishment. He believed it was important for people to have the courage to genuinely acknowledge and accept the hardships, cruelties, and indignities of life, and to relinquish the illusory comforts of religion in order for them to be able to devote their energies to creating a better life here on earth. Given

Freud's antipathy to religions of any type, there is an ironic affinity between his worldview and the Buddhist perspective on this issue. Both visions have a stoic, courageous, and uncompromising quality to them. While Freud's vision at times lapses into pessimism and cynicism, however, the Buddhist worldview is a more optimistic one. This optimism is by no means naive or straightforward. As I have elaborated at various points throughout this chapter, the Buddhist vision of what type of change is possible has a subtle and paradoxical flavor. As Ch'ing-yuan famously expressed it: "Before I had studied Zen for thirty years, I saw mountains as mountains, and waters as waters. When I arrived at a more intimate knowledge, I came to the point where I saw that mountains are not mountains, and waters are not waters. But now that I have got its very substance I am at rest. For it's just that I see mountains once again as mountains, and waters once again as waters" (Watts 1957, 126).

If we are going to locate psychoanalysis within life rather than the other way around, it will be necessary to take up the challenge of confronting what Hoffman (1989) refers to as the dialectic of meaning and mortality in a more sustained and systematic fashion. The dialogue between Buddhism and psychoanalysis can play a valuable role in facilitating this process.

A Dialogue

Postmodern thinking has challenged the scientific worldview that was dominant in Freud's day. It has relativized the values of rationality and science and demonstrated the dangers of any type of master narrative—religious or scientific—that marginalizes or excludes the values of the other. Freud saw religion as an illusion. But from a postmodern perspective, Freud's faith in the scientific worldview is itself a form of religion. The dialogue between Buddhism and psychoanalysis provides a confrontation between two divergent pathways to liberation. Contemporary psychoanalytic practice in many respects embodies the Western values of democratic individualism. On one hand, the growing emphasis on the relational nature of all human experience can be seen as a corrective to Western culture's excessive individualism. On the other hand, the growing emphasis on the mutuality of the analytic relationship and the positional nature of all knowledge is consistent with this emphasis on the value of the individual and the challenge of traditional sources of authority. The contemporary emphases on the construction of personal meaning and the enrichment and vitalization of the self are also consistent with those values. Liberation in this model tends to be associated with personal freedom.

The Buddhist model of liberation emphasizes freedom from self-centered craving. In this perspective the experience of the self as masterful and bounded lies at the heart of the human dilemma. In certain respects the Buddhist perspective can serve as a corrective to the excesses of Western individualism that are reflected in the psychoanalytic perspective. It can also help to recapture the missing spiritual dimension in a fashion that is in tune with a contemporary postmodern sensibility. In other respects psychoanalysis can provide an important counterpoint to certain Buddhist perspectives. The value of democratic individualism can provide a corrective to the tendency that Buddhism shares with all religions to crystallize into religious orthodoxy. Moreover, the psychoanalytic emphasis on unconscious motivation can reduce the risk of using spirituality in a defensive fashion. The dialogue between Buddhism and psychoanalysis thus holds a potential for enriching both traditions. Through this encounter, Buddhism will inevitably be transformed, just as it was when it spread beyond India to other Asian cultures. And psychoanalysis will inevitably be transformed, just as it was when it spread beyond its culture of origin in fin-de-siècle Vienna. While it is impossible to predict what new therapeutic and spiritual forms will ultimately emerge out of the encounter, the contributions to this book provide an important glimpse of an ongoing evolutionary process.

Notes

1. Of course this is an oversimplification. It is probably more accurate to conceptualize psychoanalysis as a process through which values are negotiated by patient and analyst (e.g., Mitchell 1993; Pizer 1998). Moreover, as Lewis Aron (1999) points out, it is important to distinguish between the values of the analytic community and the values of a specific analyst. As Aron suggests, the analytic community can be conceptualized as a "third" that mediates the dyadic relationship between the patient and the analyst. It is critical for the analyst

to recognize the way in which personal and community values interpenetrate and influence one another, and to negotiate tensions between them in a reflective fashion when they emerge. Even given these qualifying factors, however, it is still important to recognize that the analytic process inevitably involves social influence.

2.   I recognize that Winnicott's conceptualization of the "true self" includes a recognition that it consists of an ongoing evolving process—a "going on being"—rather than a static entity. Nevertheless, I would still argue that the popularity of this aspect of his thinking reflects a culturally entrenched sense of the importance of the individual.

3.   Of course, one can argue that the goal of being liberated from one's ties to old objects is not necessarily incompatible with the goal of recognizing that that there is no self independent of others. For example, W. R. D. Fairbairn would argue that freeing oneself from one's attachment to bad internal objects allows one to be open to new relationships. This is still different, however, from the experience of interdependency valued in Buddhist thinking.

References

Armstrong, K. 2000. *The Battle for God.* New York: Ballantine Books.

Aron, L. 1996. *A Meeting of Minds: Mutuality in Psychoanalysis.* Hillsdale, N.J.: Analytic Press.

——1999. *Clinical Choices and the Relational Matrix.* Psychoanalytic Dialogues 9:1–29.

Batchelor, S. 1997. *Buddhism without Beliefs.* New York: Riverhead Books.

Becker, E. 1973. *The Denial of Death.* New York: Free Press.

Benjamin, J. 1988. *The Bonds of Love: Psychoanalysis, Feminism, and the Problem of Domination.* New York: Pantheon Books.

Berger, P., and Luckmann, T. 1967. *The Social Construction of Reality.* Garden City, N.Y.: Anchor Books.

Berman, M. 1981. *The Reenchantment of the World.* Ithaca, N.Y.: Cornell University Press.

Bion, W. R. 1970. *Attention and Interpretation.* London: Heinemann.

Bromberg, P. M. 1998. *Standing in the Spaces: Essays on Clinical Process,*

Trauma, and Dissociation. Hillsdale, N.J.: Analytic Press.

Cook, F. H. 1989. *Sounds of Valley Streams.* Albany: State University of New York Press.

Cushman, P. 1995. *Constructing the Self, Constructing America: A Cultural History of Psychotherapy.* Reading, Mass.: Addison-Wesley.

Eigen, M. 1998. *The Psychoanalytic Mystic.* London: Free Association Books.

Epstein, M. 1995. *Thoughts without a Thinker: Psychotherapy from a Buddhist Perspective.* New York: Basic Books.

———. 1998. *Going to Pieces without Falling Apart: A Buddhist Perspective on Wholeness.* New York: Broadway Books.

———. 2001. *Going On Being: Buddhism and the Way of Change.* New York: Broadway Books.

Fairfield, S. 2001. *Analyzing Multiplicity: A Postmodern Perspective on Some Current Psychoanalytic Theories of Subjectivity.* Psychoanalytic Dialogues 11: 221–51.

Freud, S. 1915. *On Transience.* In Standard Edition, 14:303–7. London: Hogarth Press, 1957.

———. 1926. *The Question of Lay Analysis.* In Standard Edition, 20:179–258. London: Hogarth Press, 1959.

———. 1927. *The Future of an Illusion.* In Standard Edition, 21:3–56. London: Hogarth Press, 1961.

———. 1930. *Civilization and Its Discontents.* In Standard Edition, 21:64–145. London: Hogarth Press, 1961.

Ghent, E. 1989. *Credo: The Dialectics of One-Person and Two-Person Psychologies.* Contemporary Psychoanalysis 25:169–211.

Gombrich, R. F. 1988. *Theravada Buddhism: A Social History from Ancient Benares to Modern Colombo.* London: Routledge.

Greenberg, J. 2001. *The Analyst's Participation: A New Look.* Journal of the American Psychoanalytic Association 49:359–81.

Greenberg, J., and Mitchell, S. 1983. *Object Relations in Psychoanalytic Theory.* Cambridge, Mass.: Harvard University Press.

Grotstein, J. S. 2000. *Who Is the Dreamer Who Dreams the Dream? A Study of Psychic Processes.* Hillsdale, N.J.: Analytic Press.

Hoffman, I. Z. 1994. *Dialectical Thinking and Therapeutic Action in the Psychoanalytic Process.* Psychoanalytic Quarterly 63:187–218.

———. 1998. *Ritual and Spontaneity in the Psychoanalytic Process: A Dialectical-Constructivist View.* Hillsdale, N.J.: Analytic Press.

Lasch, C. 1979. *The Culture of Narcissism: American Life in an Age of Diminishing Expectations.* New York: W. W. Norton.

Loewald, H. 1980. *Papers on Psychoanalysis.* New Haven, Conn.: Yale University Press.

Magid, B. 2002. *Ordinary Mind: Exploring the Common Ground of Zen and Psychotherapy.* Boston: Wisdom Publications.

Mitchell, S. A. 1988. *Relational Concepts in Psychoanalysis: An Integration.* Cambridge, Mass.: Harvard University Press.

———. 1993. *Hope and Dread in Psychoanalysis.* New York: Basic Books.

———. 2000. *Relationality: From Attachment to Intersubjectivity.* Hillsdale, N.J.: Analytic Press.

———. 2001. *The Treatment of Choice: Commentary on Paper by Susan Fairfield.* Psychoanalytic Dialogues 11:283–91.

Molino, A. 1998. *The Couch and the Tree.* New York: North Point Press.

Pizer, S. 1998. *Building Bridges: The Negotiation of Paradox in Psychoanalysis.* Hillsdale, N.J.: Analytic Press.

Reiff, P. 1966. *The Triumph of the Therapeutic: Uses of Faith after Freud.* Chicago: University of Chicago Press.

Renik, O. 1996. *The Perils of Neutrality.* Psychoanalytic Quarterly 65:495–517.

Ricoeur, P. 1970. *Freud and Philosophy.* New Haven, Conn.: Yale University Press.

Ringstrom, P. A. 2001. *Cultivating the Improvisational in Psychoanalytic Treatment.* Psychoanalytic Dialogues 11:727–54.

Rorty, R. 1982. *Consequences of Pragmatism.* Minneapolis: University of Minnesota Press.

Rubin, J. B. 1996. *Psychotherapy and Buddhism: Toward an Integration.* New York: Plenum Press.

Stern, D. B. 1997. *Unformulated Experience: From Dissociation to Imagination in Psychoanalysis.* Hillsdale, N.J.: Analytic Press.

———. 2001. *Constructivism, Dialectic, and Mortality.* Psychoanalytic Dialogues 11:451–68.

Suler, J. R. 1993. *Contemporary Psychoanalysis and Eastern Thought.* Albany: N.Y. State University of New York Press.

Watts, A. 1957. *The Way of Zen.* New York: Vintage Books.

———. 1996. *Buddhism: The Religion of No-Religion.* Boston, Mass.: Charles E. Tuttle.

Chapter 1

Being Somebody and Being Nobody: A Reexamination of the Understanding of Self in Psychoanalysis and Buddhism

Jack Engler

"You have to be somebody before you can be nobody." I wrote this nearly twenty years ago in an attempt to summarize my first effort at integrating two perspectives that appeared irreconcilable at the time: Buddhist teaching about no-self and newer psychodynamic thinking about the importance of self-development in object relations theory and self psychology. Originally this notion of needing to be somebody before trying to be nobody seemed to strike a chord with Western practitioners who were struggling to integrate newly discovered disciplines of liberation like Buddhism into their personal and professional lives, and were finding, sadly, with a lot of heartache and confusion, that progress was slow and that spiritual practice alone was not enough to manage problems in day-to-day living or provide direction in love and work. More recently, however, the epigram has attracted a fair amount of notoriety and criticism from friends and colleagues for its developmentalist position (Kornfield 1993; Suler 1993; Epstein 1995; Rubin 1997). I am invariably confronted at conferences and workshops, even at meditation retreats, and asked whether I still hold "that position." "That position" has become a bit of a straw man, a convenient foil/fossil against which to mount an argument. So when I was invited to write a chapter for this volume, I saw it as an opportunity, probably long overdue, to revisit the issue and the controversy it generated. The first part of my essay accepts the main point of the criticism, but still argues the importance of being "somebody"—that is, facing crucial developmental or life tasks head on instead of attempting to avoid them in the name of spirituality or enlightenment. The second part makes the case for the importance of being "nobody"—recognizing that the integration or enhancement of the self is at best a resting place, not the goal, that the experience of being or having a self is a case of mistaken identity, a misrepresentation born of anxiety and conflict about who I am.

On Being Somebody

The first point I wanted to make in that epigram was that it takes certain ego capacities just to practice meditation or any spiritual practice. This is especially true of *vipassana* (insight) meditation and other forms of mindfulness meditation that, like most therapies, are based on observing moment-to-moment experience—the desires, excitements, pleasures, satisfactions, anxieties, fears, humiliations, frustrations, rages, disappointments, self-doubt, and even ecstasies that self-discovery entails. Psychologically, this kind of practice strengthens fundamental ego capacities, particularly the capacities for self-observation and affect tolerance. It also increases the synthetic capacity of the ego by allowing for potentially destabilizing insights and experiences that conflict with normative representations of self and others. "Transcending the ego," which is often proposed to students as a goal in spiritual practice, has no meaning to a psychodynamically oriented therapist for whom "ego" is a collective term designating the regulatory and integrative functions. To "transcend the ego" in this frame of reference would mean to surrender the very faculties that make us human—the capacity to think, plan, remember, anticipate, organize, self-reflect, distinguish reality from fantasy, exercise voluntary control over impulses and behavior, and love.

The other point I wanted to make was that spiritual practice doesn't exempt us from normal developmental tasks. This would not be an issue in traditional Buddhist cultures. But part of Buddhism's attraction to Westerners is that it can seem to offer a way to circumvent the developmental tasks and challenges of identity formation that are inherent in certain stages of the life cycle, especially young adulthood and the mid-life transition (Levinson 1978). The Buddhist teaching that one has no enduring self ("emptiness," "no-self") is open to a fateful misinterpretation in our

Western context, namely, that I do not need to struggle to find out who I am, what my desires and aspirations are, what my needs are, what my capabilities and responsibilities are, how I am relating to others, and what I could or should do with my life. The no-self doctrine seems to relieve me of the burden of these tasks and to justify their premature abandonment: if I am (spiritually) nobody, then I don't need to become (psychologically) somebody.

At times, these vulnerabilities and disturbances in personal identity may reflect disturbances in the subjective sense of self. Here the Buddhist anatta teaching can unwittingly serve a different purpose: it can explain and rationalize, if not actually legitimate, a felt lack of integration, feelings of inner emptiness, feelings of not being real, of not having a cohesive self. "No-self" in this (non-Buddhist) sense seems an apt term for what a number of practitioners actually feel. Ontological "emptiness" becomes confused with psychological emptiness. Subjective feelings of inner emptiness are mistaken for the experience of *shunyata,* or the absence of inherent existence; and the experience of not feeling inwardly integrated for anatta, or selflessness. Epstein (1989), for instance, describes seven states of subjectively felt "emptiness" that are actually pathological. Intrapsychically, each reflects a debilitating *loss of self,* either through grandiose autonomy or symbiotic merger. The teaching of nonattachment can also be heard as rationalizing an inability to form stable, lasting, satisfying relationships.

The enlightenment ideal itself can be cathected narcissistically as a version—the mother of all versions!—of the grandiose self: as the acme of personal perfection, with all mental defilements *(kilesas)* and fetters *(samyojanas)* eradicated—the achievement of a purified state of complete self-sufficiency and personal purity from which all badness has been removed, which will be admired by others, and which will be invulnerable to further injury or disappointment. "Perfection" unconsciously comes to mean freedom from symptoms so one's self will be superior to everyone else's, the object of their admiration if not envy.

Spiritual practice also offers the possibility of establishing a mirroring or idealizing type of selfobject transference with teachers that remains impermeable to reality-testing for far too long, especially in the case of Asian teachers who are often perceived as powerful beings of special aura, status, and worth. In their unique presence one can feel special oneself, thereby masking actual self-feelings of inferiority, unworthiness, and shame or, even worse, feelings of being defective or flawed at the core.

It is more clear now than when I first made these observations that narcissistic vulnerabilities aren't unique to a specific character disorder or to the character-disordered range generally. They exist across the developmental and diagnostic spectrum. They can coexist with reasonably normal functioning in otherwise relatively integrated ego structures. If anything, narcissistic dynamics are probably far more intertwined with everyone's spiritual practice than I originally thought.

The fact is that there is no way to practice meditation that is immune from the anxieties, needs, cognitive-emotional styles, and dynamics of our own character structure. Spiritual practice, like psychotherapy itself, can serve defensive aims. This makes it even more imperative to understand that the no-self teaching does not mean we do not need to work with our own psychological self, our own character, or our relationships with others, either as a next step in our own development or as unfinished business from the past that continues to get in the way.

CHANGE IN SPIRITUAL PRACTICE: GRADUAL OR SUDDEN? PARTIAL OR COMPLETE?

Philip Kapleau Roshi relates a telling exchange with a student during a question-and-answer session in a Zen workshop that directly addresses this issue (Kapleau 1979: 31):

> QUESTIONER: But doesn't enlightenment clear away imperfections and personality flaws?
>
> ROSHI: No, it shows them up! Before awakening, one can easily ignore or rationalize his shortcomings, but after enlightenment this is no longer possible. One's failings are painfully evident. Yet at the same time a strong determination develops to rid oneself of them. Even opening the Mind's eye fully does not at one fell swoop purify the emotions. Continuous training after enlightenment is required to purify the emotions so that our behavior accords with our understanding. This vital point must be understood.

This is not what the student wanted to hear. You can palpably sense his desperate hope that becoming enlightened, experiencing *kensho*, will solve all his personal problems and doubts.

The enlightenment traditions often seem to promise this. In an interview for an issue of his journal devoted to the question "What is Ego?" Andrew Cohen (2000) asked me whether I didn't agree that if one's enlightenment is deep enough, the fixation on the personal self and all the suffering associated with it will disappear because one's perspective will shift completely, from seeing oneself as the one who was wounded to recognizing oneself as that which was never wounded by anything. Won't realization of the emptiness and ultimate insubstantiality of the personal self and its suffering completely change one's relationship to personal experience? My reply was that this is an idealized view. In practice, it just doesn't seem to work that way.

First of all, this happens *only* if one has truly gone to the end of the path. It is true that each moment of mindfulness shifts our normal relationship to experience in that moment. If a painful experience can be held without reactivity—without judgment, censorship, condemnation, or the wish to extrude—with clarity, openness, and compassion—the pain will not produce avoidance or aversion. Pleasurable experience will not produce attraction and clinging. Pain will simply remain pain, pleasure simply remain pleasure, without the reactive approach-avoidance response that much of psychoanalytic affect theory, by contrast, tends to consider innate and views as leading to the constellation of enduring drive or motivational states (Kernberg 1976; cf. also Engler 1986; Brown 1993). "Leave the arising (what arises) in the arising," a Tibetan teaching says, and the mind's natural clarity and ease will remain undisturbed. But the question is what it takes to shift one's relationship to experience so completely that *every* moment is held in this fashion. All enlightenment traditions agree that at the end of the spiritual path all forms of self-generated suffering end. But this is a huge "if." I know no one who claims it. Short of that, the reality is much more complex.

In the Theravada tradition, for instance, and in Buddhist traditions generally, freedom from self-generated suffering doesn't happen all at once—a position I've always found more credible. Both the classical and the contemporary commentarial traditions (Buddhaghosa 1975; Mahasi Sayadaw 1965) describe it as a process occurring by stages or increments, much as change occurs in psychotherapy. This was supported by the self-reports of the Buddhist practitioners I studied in India (Engler 1983a), all of whom had experienced at least the first of the four enlightenment experiences that are said to occur in Theravada practice.

Self-generated suffering is said to end in this tradition through a *progressive* and *irreversible* "extinction" *(niroda)* of the unwholesome mental factors *(samyojanas)* that cause it. These pathogenic mental factors are said to be *extinguished in a specific and invariant sequence* of four enlightenment experiences or "path-moments" *(magga)*. On each occasion, a specific group of pathogenic mental factors are eliminated from the mind once and for all and the practitioner will never again act in these conflictual ways. In Theravada teaching, this is the *real significance of the moment of "enlightenment"*: not the subjective experience, which Western psychology tends to emphasize in its preoccupation with individual subjectivity, but the extinction of these unwholesome mental factors leading to the progressive end of suffering and freeing the mind's natural joy, ease, equanimity, and unbounded compassion and care for others.

The group of factors said to be extinguished at first enlightenment *(sotapatti)* comprises core beliefs about the self—"maladaptive cognitions" or "core assumptions" in the language of cognitive psychology—pathogenic beliefs about who we are and how we become free. The most important of these is the representation of self as singular, separate, independent, and self-identical. This is now recognized as illusory, a construct or representation only. But insight in meditation doesn't immediately change behavior any more than insight does in psychotherapy. Modification or abandonment of this basic self-belief doesn't automatically shift the underlying reactive states—conditioned motivations, affects, and impulses—that can still influence the practitioner to act in unwholesome, selfish, and uncompassionate ways.

These core motivational states comprise the second set of "fetters," in particular the two basic motivational states of classic psychoanalytic theory, libido and aggression—in Buddhist terms, *kama-tanha*, literally "desire for sense pleasure" or behavior governed by the Pleasure Principle, and *vyapada*, literally "ill-will" or aggression toward others in its various forms. These motivational states are experienced as much more deeply conditioned and much more difficult to modify or extinguish than core cognitions. Accordingly they are said to be only "weakened"—"modified" in the language of behavior therapy—at the second stage of enlightenment *(sakadagami)* and not extinguished until the third *(anagami)*. But unlike psychoanalytic theory, they are viewed as conditioned behaviors, not instinctually based drives and not inherent in personality.

The final group of fetters clusters around the mental factor of *mana*, the "conceit" that "I am" and the remaining residual tendency to compare self with others. This is the root of all narcissistic striving and is said not to be extinguished until the fourth and final stage of enlightenment *(arahatta)*.

Note how similar this progression is to change processes in therapy: cognitions, beliefs, perspectives are more amenable to modification. Core motivational and drive states and their bases in affective reactivity are much more resistant to intervention. Hardest of all to change are narcissistic investments in the core sense of being a separate self. This is exactly what we would expect: cognitive change first; affective change next; change in core sense of selfhood last.

Zen tradition makes a similar point in distinguishing between little kensho and great kensho. The realization of emptiness can be small or large, but it's still just a first glimpse of enlightenment. My teacher, Anagarika Munindra, used to call it "a little bit of enlightenment," holding his thumb and forefinger an inch apart. That first glimpse by its nature is not complete and does not shift everything—as we know all too well from the misconduct of so many spiritual teachers in all traditions, East and West.

Teacher misconduct actually contains an important teaching. Misconduct certainly occurs in Buddhist Asia, but my experience in India and Burma was that cultural norms and expectations as well as centuries-old social role requirements impose constraints on behavior that is often mistaken—by teachers themselves—for spiritual attainment, even the "extinction" of samyojanas. In Western settings, when these constraints are removed and Asian teachers by necessity are thrown more onto their own resources and have to be much more self-determining, particularly around issues involving money, sex, power, and the idealized projections of admiring students, none of which they have been trained to handle except in the most cursory way, my impression is that they themselves—not to mention their students—are surprised by what they find themselves doing. It is important to understand that certain misconduct, by itself, does not mean they do not have deep understanding about the nature of reality. It doesn't mean they haven't experienced enlightenment. It means that freedom from the maladaptive beliefs, the identifications, the inner conflicts, and the narcissistic investments that create suffering for ourselves and others aren't extinguished—even granting you accept that notion—all at once. First enlightenment is still first enlightenment. Much work remains.

The Need for Personal Work

It seems to me that some of that work is and must be personal work. I also don't think this is simply a matter of applying spiritual insight to the rest of one's life or character as Kapleau Roshi's reply suggests. The "continuous training" after initial enlightenment that he says is necessary can—if it just means more practice—still leave character flaws, personal conflicts, and difficulties in love and work untouched. This is because awareness in one area of life doesn't automatically transfer into other areas of life (Kornfield 1993). Spiritual awareness, as Buddhism and other traditions define it, does not automatically yield psychological and emotional awareness in a Western sense. The profound need to defend against trauma and threats to bodily and psychic integrity, as well as our capacity for horizontal and vertical "splits" in personality (Kohut 1977), leave sequestered compartments where the memories of past injury and the anticipation of future hurt are deepest. Entrenched characterological defenses and flaws can remain untouched. So we can encounter teachers who have deep realization into the nature of self and reality, but who sleep with their students, encourage dependent relationships, need uncritical admiration, are intolerant of criticism or dissent, and insist on an authoritarian structure in their community. Or more simply, teachers who are powerful in front of a meditation hall, but who can be anxious, confused, immature, or withdrawn in their personal interactions with others.

In a conference I moderated at the Barre Center for Buddhist Studies between teachers from different Buddhist traditions, the topic was compassion. One of the Tibetan lamas, a lifelong monk who had recently disrobed, admitted, quite courageously I thought, that he had no difficulty generating compassion toward the "thousand beings of light" in traditional Tibetan visualization practice. Now that he was no longer a monk, what he found much more difficult was dealing with the real person in front of him. Jack Kornfield (1993, 249–50) writes: "Only a deep attention to the whole of our life can bring us the capacity to love well and live freely.... If our spiritual practice does not enable us to function wisely, to love and work and connect with the whole of our life, then we must include forms of practice [he specifically refers to psychotherapy] that heal our problems in other ways." And in fact, in Buddhist societies this has always been the case. One never took every problem in love and work to the spiritual teacher.

Because the psychological self seems to be much more a personal construct in the West than in Asia and much less embedded in a preexisting social and cultural matrix that defines it, practice also seems to unfold differently in the West in a way that makes the issue of being "somebody" unavoidable. Several features of Western practice stand out in this regard:

First, even in spiritual practice, the need to deal with emotional and relational problems seems to be more the rule than the exception. This is because practice itself uncovers personal issues by holding up a mirror to the mind. A worry or preoccupation of the moment can emerge with greater force or in a new light. Some issues close to awareness can suddenly emerge: a conflict we've been feeling all of a sudden becomes clear. Or repression may be lifted and we confront recovered memories long dissociated or repressed, buried affects, unconscious grief or longing, or intense fantasy and imagery encoding wishes and fears in the primary process. No doubt this occurs in part because, like psychodynamic therapies, mindfulness meditation is an "uncovering" technique based on the same procedures that guide psychodynamic inquiry: removal of censorship on mental content and affect, suspension of judgment, abstinence, and the injunction to observe experience while experiencing it—Sterba's "therapeutic split" in the ego (Sterba 1934; Engler 1986). Especially when practiced intensively in retreat settings, it cannot help but access suppressed, repressed, or dissociated material. It cannot help but eventually force the practitioner to confront areas of deep pain, confusion, and constriction in his or her personal life.

But uncovering in meditation doesn't automatically facilitate insight in a psychodynamic sense. It may for some meditators some of the time, but this depends on the individual's psychological astuteness and past experience in working with this kind of material, on the response of the teacher, and, most important, on whether the practitioner chooses to work with it. The meditation traditions themselves discourage working with any mental content, at least when doing formal practice. Zen, for instance, dismisses most of these phenomena, particularly altered-state phenomena, as *makyo,* or manifestations of delusion. The student is encouraged to dismiss them as a distraction and to avoid getting caught up in them at all costs. But whether explicitly worked with or not, practice will often access some of this material.

In a Rorschach study of vipassana meditators before and after one of the early intensive three-month retreats at the Insight Meditation Society in Barre, Massachusetts, Dan Brown and I found that the practice of at least half the practitioners continued to be dominated by primary process thinking, as well as by significant fantasy, daydreaming, reverie, imagery, spontaneous recall of past memories, depression of conflictual material, incessant thinking, and emotional lability, including dramatic swings in mood (Brown and Engler 1986). Kornfield's (1993) observation a decade later was still much the same: about half of the practitioners during the same intensive three-month retreats found themselves unable to sustain mindfulness practice in its traditional form because they encountered so much unresolved grief, fear, wounding, and unfinished developmental business with parents, siblings, friends, spouses, children, and others. This then became the focus of their practice. As it needed to. Attempts to get them to redirect their attention to note the simple arising and passing away of objects in the field of awareness are usually unsuccessful. The press of personal issues and confusion is just too great.

Kornfield has further observed that even advanced Western students find that periods of powerful practice and deep insight will often be succeeded by periods in which they re-encounter painful patterns, fears, and conflicts in other parts of their lives. Or they may come to some important understanding and balance in formal practice, but find that when they return home to the problems of day-to-day living, visit parents, fall in love, or change jobs, suddenly old neurotic and dysfunctional patterns of behavior are as strong as ever and have to be faced. If not, there is a strong likelihood that practice will be unconsciously used in part to avoid dealing with them. If that becomes too salient a motive, meditation itself will eventually become dry or sterile and feel increasingly unrewarding, like a therapy in which therapist and patient unconsciously collude to avoid the real issues or unwittingly collaborate only through the patient's false self system (Winnicott 1960).

Second, it appears that many of these personal issues uncovered or confronted in Western mindfulness practice aren't being healed simply by more meditation or other forms of spiritual practice alone. That's hard to accept and not what those of us who were drawn to these traditions and their promise of total liberation may want to hear. But specific problems such as early abuse, addiction, conflicts in love and sexuality, depression, problematic personality traits, and certainly mental illness require specific attention, and probably ongoing personal, professional, and communal support to resolve. Problems in love and work, and issues around trust and intimacy in relationships in particular, can't be resolved simply by watching the moment-to-moment flow of thoughts, feelings, and sensations in the mind. Thirty years of watching students try this approach bear that out. Kornfield notes that many students leave ashrams or monasteries or meditation centers after years of devoted practice and find, with a great deal of confusion and discouragement, even disillusionment, that they still have not faced the core anxieties and conflicts that constrict them.

Traditional Buddhist meditation manuals don't mention these issues. Systematic Buddhist psychology (Abhidhamma) lists fifty-two mental factors defining discrete states of consciousness and their karmic value, including a range of afflictive emotions—greed, envy, hatred, doubt, worry, and so on. But there is no mention of sadness, except as a kind of unpleasant feeling that can tinge other mental states. There is no mention of depression, no mention of mental illness as we understand it or of psychiatric disorders. No mention of personality, family, or relationship issues as such.

When Burma's most renowned scholar and meditation master, Ven. Mahasi Sayadaw, visited America in 1980, he held a meeting with Western vipassana teachers about teaching. I remember Jack Kornfield asking in his intrepid way, "What do you do when students bring psychological problems to you?" There was a hurried consultation with the other sayadaws (teachers) and some evident confusion. He turned back to Jack and asked, "What psychological problems?" At the end of his U.S. visit, the sayadaw remarked on how many Western students seemed to be suffering from a range of problems he wasn't familiar with in Asia. A "new type of suffering," he said—"psychological suffering"! As is now well known, the Dalai Lama, too, on his first visits to the West, expressed shock at the degree of low self-esteem and self-hatred he encountered in Western practitioners.

In the Theravada Buddhist meditation centers where I practiced in Asia, students typically do not present "psychological' problems to teachers. Why they don't is a complex issue. If you observe teachers working with their students, it is clear that they don't cue for personal issues or become involved in the content of students' experience. Their emphasis is exclusively on noting objects of awareness simply in their arising and passing away. By the end of the third day of practice at Venerable Mahasi Sayadaw's center in Rangoon, the senior sayadaw guiding me asked if I had "seen the great light yet"—a very advanced stage of practice. Evidently he expected it should only take me a few days!

But this phenomenon seems to be more than simply a difference in technique. Mindfulness as a rule does not seem to facilitate uncovering in a psychological or psychodynamic sense in Asian students as it does in Western students. This struck me in the accounts that very advanced Indian Buddhists gave of their practice (Engler 1983a). With one minor exception, their self-reports were notable for the absence of just the kind of material that emerges for Western practitioners when censorship is lifted. This may have more to do with a different self-structure or experience of self in those cultures than with how mindfulness is practiced and guided (see below and Klein 1995).

The wish that spiritual practice could, by itself, prove a panacea for all mental suffering is widespread and certainly understandable. But it unfortunately prevents teachers and students from making use of other resources. And worse, students are sometimes led to believe by their teachers or their own superego that if they encounter difficulties, it's because they haven't practiced long enough or haven't been practicing correctly or wholeheartedly. The message too often is that the problem is in the quality of the student's practice rather than in the mistaken assumption that practice should cure all. This leads to needless self-accusation and guilt, compounding how bad they already feel.

There is a second serious problem with this approach. Not everyone is capable or ready to devote themselves exclusively to spiritual practice, or to pursue it single-mindedly to its depth. If they try to force themselves, or are encouraged to by their teachers or fellow students, there is risk of serious disorganization, decompensation, regression, and loss of function. Most will simply give up, but may then carry the burden of shame and guilt for "failing." Others will get discouraged, quit, and give up a practice and a community that could have been immensely helpful to them.

Third, when basic developmental tasks are neglected or remain largely unfinished, Western students often find it difficult to deepen meditation practice beyond a certain point. One sign of this is problems focusing and concentrating. Another is a low-level nagging irritability and discontent with practice, teachers, and the community. Another is trouble bringing practice into daily life. Toynbee's dictum applies in spiritual life as well: those who don't remember history are compelled to repeat it. Whatever the origins of personal conflictual patterns, if they aren't consciously faced and healed, they will continue to repeat in practitioners and their communities. After the teacher of a well-established spiritual community not long ago was forced to acknowledge his sexual misconduct with students, community members were surprised to discover how many students had histories of incest or came from families of incest. Time alone doesn't heal these wounds. If they aren't faced, time only entrenches them further.

In summary, then, I completely agree with Kornfield that the need to reclaim and develop a healthy sense of self and self-esteem, a capacity for intimacy, and a creative way to live in the world with full commitment cannot and should not be separated from Western spiritual practice.

LIMITATIONS OF A DEVELOPMENTAL MODEL

The real problem with my statement was the notion of being somebody *before* becoming nobody. I agree with those who have taken issue with this. For a long time I've thought that a developmental model is not the appropriate framework for integrating Buddhist and clinical perspectives.

Thinking in terms of linear progression and stages leads to placing the attainment of self and no-self at different levels along a developmental path and, as John Suler (1993) points out, implies a hierarchy between psychological and spiritual development: first psychological health, then spiritual insight and transformation. This tends to devalue meditative experience prior to the classical "stages of insight" *(ñanas)* that precede awakening. It overlooks meditation's potential to promote many changes that are consonant with expressed goals of psychotherapy, such as developing a sense of self that is more cohesive and yet more flexible and malleable at the same time, as well as a greater acceptance of disavowed aspects of self and others. It also overlooks the ability of mindfulness to effect deep insight into impermanence, suffering, and selflessness prior to the formal "stages of insight." As I hope I've already shown, I didn't intend such a dichotomous view. My original focus was on intensive practice and the transformations that occur in moments of enlightenment or "path." I was trying to understand what inner psychological self-structure was required.

Some minimum degree of structuralization is certainly required: the capacity for moment-to-moment observation of thoughts, feelings, and body sensations; the ability to gradually attend to experience without censorship or selection; the capacity to tolerate aversive affect; some capacity to tolerate primary process material; the ability to suspend or mitigate self-judgment and maintain a benign attitude toward one's experience; the capacity for moral discrimination and evaluation of one's own behavior; and the capacity to mourn. I once asked Munindraji how old a person needed to be before they could experience enlightenment. He said around seven or eight—you need to be able to distinguish wholesome from unwholesome actions. In other words, superego integration needs to be somewhat complete.

All of these psychological capacities obviously fall along a continuum of development. The more intensively mindfulness is practiced, the more important these capacities become and the more capacity is required. But this is a different issue from locating self and no-self in a developmental hierarchy.

A linear and progressive model also doesn't allow for the fact that we do not function exclusively on one level or another. What we see as a rule in clinical practice, for example, are different blends of oedipal and pre-oedipal issues. Even in severe narcissistic disorders, oedipal themes can still be a predominant thread. Within individuals whose overall level of organization is neurotic or even normal, there are often residues of narcissistic problems. Margaret Mahler's (1975) earlier notion that psychological development pushes progressively toward higher and higher stages of separation and individuation—the premise I also accepted at the time—has largely been replaced by Heinz Kohut's (1971, 1977) more accurate perception that the need for selfobject ties is normal and remains necessary throughout life.

We are also much more aware today that the developmental lines for different psychological functions do not progress in tandem. There can be developmental lags in one line, precocious development in another (Blanck and Blanck 1974, 1979). The interactions and interweavings between all these different developmental lines at any one time is extraordinarily complex. Experience over the years has shown me that different levels and types of functioning can also coexist and interact in Buddhist practice. Deep spiritual insight and realization can (fortunately!) coexist with a certain degree of clinical psychopathology. The series of case studies of practitioners who experienced a traditional enlightenment, which I am preparing, will show this.

The most telling critique, however, is seldom mentioned: a developmental model implies that spirituality has its own developmental line, or is part of a developmental line—that the experience of no-self, for instance, is the culmination of the line of self-development. There is no basis for assuming this. Buddhist teaching views the state of no-self as altogether outside the realm of coming-to-be and passing-away. What is not born and never dies can have no "developmental line" in a psychological sense.

There is a certain complementarity to Buddhist and psychodynamic psychologies, each investigating a range of functioning the other does not. Buddhism assumes a relatively intact ego and structured sense of self and does not investigate the type and range of functioning, particularly the self-disorders and narcissistic deficiencies, that we address in Western clinical practice. Psychodynamic psychology equates optimal functioning with the attainment of psychological selfhood and has no concept of the type and range of functioning and well-being that accompany the realization of the self's constructed nature. Hence my originally calling the integration of these perspectives a "full-spectrum" model. This "full-spectrum" view also makes it clear that enlightenment and the associated experience of no-self is neither a return to the child's pre-intellectual, pre-rational experience of immediacy and oneness, nor a regression to some oceanic state of primary narcissism as Freud (1930) and the early analysts (Alexander 1931) thought. But the notion of a "spectrum" still carries developmental connotations that do not apply.

Instead of taking a developmental perspective, I think it is more useful to view the pursuit of a spiritual practice, like any other behavior, as multiply determined. Individuals inevitably begin practice, as they do therapy, with a mix of motives, some conscious, some unconscious, some adaptive, some maladaptive. Suler (1993) identifies ten psychodynamic issues in particular that revolve around meanings related to having or not having an autonomous self. These partially underlie the attraction to eastern forms of spiritual practice. They also predispose to employing practices like meditation in the service of defense rather than self-awareness. Each is more a cluster of related issues than an isolated motivation. These include using practice to (1) pursue narcissistic perfection and invulnerability, (2) calm fears of individuation,

(3) avoid responsibility and accountability, (4) rationalize fears of intimacy and closeness, (5) suppress unwanted or conflictual feelings, (6) avoid anger, self-assertion, and competitiveness by adopting a passive-dependent style, (7) satisfy superego needs for self-punishment for feelings of unworthiness, shame, or guilt, (8) escape from internal experience, (9) devalue reason, intellect, and reflection on one's motives and behavior, and (10) substitute for grief and the need for mourning in the face of loss.

One or more of these motives often continue to influence practice for a long time. It takes effort and courage and a willingness to look at one's motives before this gradually becomes apparent. Often it requires the guidance of a teacher or therapist. Or it may take some disillusionment or disappointment in one's progress, or feeling stuck for a long time, or some painful event like a teacher's betrayal of trust, to wake one up and force one to look and see.

On Being Nobody

I now want to readdress the entire issue of self-experience, from both psychodynamic and Buddhist perspectives, and offer a different way of conceiving the origins, role, and function of the psychological structure we call the self. Hard as it may be to believe, my thinking has actually moved on in the past twenty years!

PSYCHOLOGICAL SELF VERSUS ONTOLOGICAL SELF

It is crucial at the outset to understand just what kind of "self" Buddhist analysis is aimed at. Confusion over this has led to a basic category error and hence a misplaced argument with Buddhist teaching among a number of contemporary commentators, particularly those writing from a psychodynamic perspective.

The Buddhist critique is *not* aimed at the psychologically differentiated "self" of contemporary psychoanalytic theory and practice. As Anne Klein (1995) has pointed out in her study of contemporary feminist reflection and traditional Buddhist thought, the psychological self is a product of the last three or four hundred years of Western civilization: an autonomous individual with a sense of differentiated selfhood having its own nuclear ambitions, goals, design, and destiny. According to the anthropologist Clifford Geertz (1979, 59), the Western conception of the person as a bounded, unique, more or less integrated motivational and cognitive universe, a dynamic center of awareness, emotion, judgment, and action organized into a distinctive whole and set contrastively both against a social and natural background is, however incorrigible it may seem to us, a rather peculiar idea within the context of the world's cultures.

This "rather peculiar" sense of independent and autonomous selfhood was unknown in the Buddha's day. Even in our own day, this is not the ordinary, everyday experience of "self" in most non-Western cultures, or in Native American cultures for that matter. In the cultures from which Buddhism has emigrated west, preeminently India and Japan, the sense of self is much more merged with others in a "we-sense" that is profoundly different from the separate, autonomous "I-self" of Western experience (Kakar 1970; Suler 1993). The self is experienced as embedded in a matrix of relations and as defined by those relations, not just the matrix of human and social relationships but the more encompassing matrix of relationships within the world of nature, and ultimately the cosmos as a whole (Roland 1988).

But the absence of the psychological self in a Western sense certainly does not mean that Buddhist teaching and practice lacks an appreciation of the importance of basic ego strengths or the nuances of normal psychological functioning. As Harvey Aaronson (1998, 66) points out, for example, "the entire thrust of Buddhist philosophy is to emphasize the workings of personal agency through exploration of cause and effect," particularly the psychological consequences of wholesome and unwholesome behavior toward self and others. Even using criteria of contemporary psychoanalytic self psychology—the capacity for self-reflection and evaluation, vision, ambitions and goals, an ability to follow through effectively, empathy for others—"the extant Buddhist material illustrates that the Buddha and his disciples had fairly rich and effective psychological selves" (Aaronson 1998, 67), if not the Western sense of self. In fact, "looking at the model of various Buddhist sages, with their capacity to work in the world and be effective, signs of a healthy psychological self seem actually enhanced" (72).

The Buddhist critique is aimed instead at what Aaronson calls the *onto-logical* self: the feeling or belief that there is an inherent, ontological core at the center of our experience that is separate, substantial, enduring, self-iden-tical. The Pali Buddhist term for "self," *atta*, is used in this ontological or metaphysical rather than psychological sense. Whether through philosophical investigation or through meditative observation of moment-to-moment mind states, the aim of Buddhist analysis is to show that this kind of self cannot be found in any of the constituents of experience as an autonomous, ontologi-cal core. The commentaries use the example of a chariot: a "chariot" does not exist as a findable entity or essence; it is a designation given to an assemblage of parts, not an "essence" that exists independently of that essemblage. This doesn't mean that the assemblage we call a "chariot" doesn't function. Sim-ilarly, "self as a findable entity or essence is denied, but not psychological functioning" (Aaronson 1998, 66). "Self" no less than "chariot" is a name or designation only, not a "thing" which exists and can be found. Translating Buddhist analyses of "self" into the more familiar psychological language of narcissism, as a number of psychoanalytic commentators tend to do, mixes categories. The analysis is ontological, not psychological.

However, I don't agree with Aaronson (1998, 66) that this analysis has "no direct correlation to the discussion of self in psychoanalysis or therapy." On one level the issue is about reality: is there an ontological core to the per-son we may call a "self"? The answer is no. But on another level the issue is about representations: how we represent ourselves to ourselves. And self-rep-resentations matter—they have profound effect on functioning and well-being. Buddhist analysis says, in effect, you cannot appropriately represent yourself to yourself as independently existing. If you do, there are serious consequences for your own mental health, and if you act out of this belief you will cause harm to others. In this sense, the argument *is* psychological in a contemporary sense, though not about the psychological self: it is about a particular self-representation and its implications for self-generated suffering.

Self as Adaptation?

I agree with this Buddhist analysis of the concept of self. But I have never been satisfied with it. To my mind it still leaves the crucial question unanswered:

Why would we represent ourselves to ourselves in just this way if it only produces suffering, as Buddhism maintains? This doesn't make sense. We have to assume that every mental structure, every pattern of behavior, emerges only because it is an attempt at adaptation, either to meet a specific developmental task or to deal with some internal or external need. The way we organize ourselves, the way we present and represent ourselves, always constitutes a best effort to solve or negotiate some task or problem. Psychodynamically, our intent is never simply to create more pain for ourselves, even if this is often an unintended outcome. The most maladaptive beliefs and behaviors have some adaptive intent, misguided and pathogenic though they may be.

Buddhist psychology doesn't address this issue. While it describes in great detail the processes of identification by which the experience of being a separate self can arise, Buddhist thinking doesn't explain *why* we construct our experience in this way. It is only interested in how this mistaken self-construct contributes to suffering and how its hold on the mind can be released. But if it isn't necessary for healthy functioning, as Buddhism maintains, and if fully free and liberated action is not dependent on a sense of separate selfhood at all (as I will argue below), then why is this sense of self so real and pervasive in our psychic life and our day-to-day experience?

We can accept the Buddhist analysis of the concept of self but still ask the kind of question we would ask about any other kind of behavioral psychological structure: What purpose does it serve? What situation is it attempting to address? To what problem is it an attempted solution? In other words, can we view the self as an adaptation in a way that would explain its emergence, its pervasiveness, and its function as something other than simply a delusional belief? This might cast light on its stubborn entrenchment in the psyche, the great difficulty and resistance we encounter in seeing through its illusory nature, and why attachment to this self, as Buddhism maintains, is the root source of self-generated suffering.

Four Experiences of Self

In trying to answer this question, I want to look at four fundamentally different types of self-experience. Each seems to embody a different core experience of selfhood. All, I would argue, are normal ways of experiencing self, though not all are equally common. In discussing the first two types, I am following Stephen Mitchell's (1993) analysis of the two accounts of self he sees in contemporary psychoanalytic thought: self as multiple and discontinuous; and self as layered, singular, and continuous. The first type of self-experience is the focus of object relations theory; the second, the central concern of self psychology.

Self as Multiple and Discontinuous

We all have the experience, sometimes disconcerting, sometimes quite natural, of thinking, feeling, and acting differently at different times. We can be quite different with different people, or conduct and experience a relationship in very different ways with the same person in different contexts. The reason for this is that "we learn to become a person through different kinds of interactions with different others and through different kinds of interactions with the same other" (Mitchell 1993, 104). This yields an experience of self that is "discontinuous, composed of different configurations, different selves with different others." Mitchell cites Harry Stack Sullivan's (1964) description of these as "me-you" patterns: very different, discrete "me-you" patterns arise in different circumstances. Each configuration embodies not only a representation of self but a representation of the other(s) with whom I am engaged. And each relational configuration can be experienced in two ways: there are times when I experience myself as myself in relation to the other—Mitchell gives the example of a dependent child being cared for by a solicitous mother; and other times when I organize my experience and sense of meaning around an image of that other in relation to me—a solicitous mother taking care of a dependent child. Each actual relationship may contain multiple self-organizations. And of course we have many such relationships. Different configurations of self-experience can be encoded in different uses of language, or accompanied by and experienced in different physiological states. The most extreme case is the different physiology that accompanies different alter egos in multiple personalities. But even in our ordinary experience, we know that different bodily states accompany different states of mind: "Happy versions of self are often distinctly different, both emotionally and physically, from depressed versions of self" (Mitchell 1993, 105). Conflict within this framework is experienced not as a clash between impulses, regulatory functions, moral prohibitions, and the constraints of reality, but as "a clash between contrasting and often incompatible self-organizations and self-other relationships" (104).

"I am not myself today." A common and simple complaint. But as Mitchell points out, a profoundly complex one in terms of self-experience. There can be more than one "I," more than one version of "myself."

Self as Integral and Continuous

And yet despite this variable "I" that feels different today from other days, despite the discontinuities, we usually still recognize all these differences as "versions of a more or less invariant 'myself' (Mitchell 1993, 107). This sense of self feels independent of changes in circumstance, mood, time, and mental state. And it is this sense of self that provides a feeling of continuity from one subjective state, one experience, to the next. To cite Mitchell again: "I can represent that enduring sense of self as 'myself' and assign it specific content, which my current experience can either match or not match, and which enables me to feel either very much 'myself' or 'not myself.' But even when I am not myself, I experience a continuity with previous subjective states." The subjective meaning each experience has for me will depend on which internalized object relation or "me-you" pattern I am operating out of at the time. But the "I" that organizes each experience and finds/assigns a particular subjective meaning in it feels like the same "I" that did this yesterday and will do it again tomorrow. This is because I experience a distinctive subjectivity that feels like my own, that feels like "me."

Three aspects of experience are closely connected with this feeling of self as singular and integral. The first is cohesiveness. Self-cohesion is comprised of three elements: the sense that my experience "coheres" or hangs together and constitutes a meaningful whole; the sense that "I" am the same "me" across time, place, and state of consciousness; and the sense that "I" am a stable, ongoing point of reference to which all my discrete experiences refer back—they all feel like "mine." A second aspect of this self-sense is the sense of personal agency, or in Kohut's (1977) term, the sense of being a "center of initiative." A third aspect is the sense of personal worth or self-esteem: that "I" am valued in my own eyes and in the eyes of others.

Mitchell points to yet a further aspect of this mode of self-experience that is particularly crucial from the Buddhist perspective: the experience of our most personal self as "*an entity residing deep inside us*" that we can reveal or conceal from others as we choose: "It feels as if our personal self is ours in some uniquely privileged way; we control access to its protective layers and its 'core'; only we know and understand its secrets. It feels as if the self is *not* inevitably contextual and relational, but has an existence and a life that is separate and autonomous from others" (1993, 111). The core of "my" experience, my innermost identity, feels "immutably and profoundly private" (114), unknowable by others. Winnicott's notion of the "true self" refers to this mode of self-experience.

Mitchell goes on to argue that these apparently dichotomous experiences of self are actually not mutually exclusive: we act both continuously and discontinuously; we organize our experience into both multiple and integral configurations. And healthy functioning requires an ability to move flexibly back and forth between both.

It is not so difficult to establish a theoretical basis for this dialogical and interpersonal view of self, and Mitchell argues this convincingly. We define and experience who we are largely by contrasting ourselves to others and in relation to them. In the process of deciding "This is me," I am deciding "This is who or what I am not." Self and not-self are created in the same process. Winnicott (1958) earlier pointed out the paradox that the capacity to be alone, to be most private and interior, is developed in the experience of being alone in the presence of another with whom we feel connected and through whom we first learned to be a self. This mutual definition of self and other, both as singular selves and as different selves in different contexts at different times, continues throughout life. As therapist and client learn, even that which is most personal is usually arrived at, discovered, known, through interaction and dialogue with another. It is not preformed, accessible to direct introspection. It is discovered, actually created, in conversation and interaction with another. This is true for both participants. In an intersubjective view of therapy (Stolorow, Brandchaft, and Atwood 1987), the client brings the therapist into being as much as the therapist brings the client: both find meaning together, discover aspects of self and other through their interaction, co-create each other.

But this intersubjective, relational, dialogical perspective still doesn't address the root problem from the Buddhist perspective: namely, that this experience of self as singular and integral has a privileged position in the psyche. No matter how differently we may experience ourselves in different contexts, and no matter how compelling the theoretical—and clinical—support for a more dialogical understanding of self and other, this sense of our most personal self "as an entity residing deep inside us," as independent and separate from others (never mind the rest of life and the cosmos), is undeniably cathected in a way no other sense of self is. This brings us back by another route to the issue I want to address: Why is this particular way of representing ourselves to ourselves so compelling, so intractable to inquiry and insight?

Psychoanalytic writing about the self often confuses psychological and ontological categories here. It is incorrect to say the self *is* multiple or singular. We have a "sense" or an "experience" of self *as* multiple or singular. In other words, we are talking about representations: how we construct and represent our self-experience. Reframed in those terms, why do we represent ourselves to ourselves as singular, integral, and continuous, "an entity residing deep within us"? It is interesting that Mitchell himself acknowledges the illusory nature of this representation—"one might argue that the feeling of continuity in self experience is thoroughly illusory" (1993, 110). He even embraces Sullivan's (1964) view that the idea of possessing a unique personal identity is a narcissistic illusion—"the very mother of illusions," according to Sullivan. Buddhist analysis reaches exactly the same conclusion. But Mitchell then goes on to argue that this illusion has an adaptive, psychological advantage, at least in Western cultures where the sense of continuity and invariance is no longer carried and maintained by the supra-individual, invariant group:

> Without a sense of self as constant and unaffected by time, as continuous and unvarying (even though from a temporal perspective it is discontinuous and continually changing), we would have no way to prioritize our goals, motives and impulses—we would be all over the place.... So we need to feel we have an innermost identity and act accordingly, even though the content of that identity may change considerably over time.... What may have begun as an illusion often becomes an actual guide to living by virtue of our necessary belief in it. (1993, 111)

Buddhism completely agrees that this illusion becomes "an actual guide to living." But it sees this as precisely the problem! And it questions whether it is a "necessary belief" or illusion, as I hope to show. Still, Mitchell is asking the same question I am: how to account for the emergence of this particular self-sense if it is illusory (in the psychoanalytic sense) or "empty" (in the Buddhist sense)?

First it is necessary to describe two further types of self-experience and subjectivity.

Unselfconscious Experience

There are other moments, other times, when the sense of self drops away altogether, when we are not aware of ourselves as an independent self separate and distinct from our experience. We feel completely one with what we are doing. Even that is inaccurate, because there is no sense of "I" who feels "one." Experience at these times is not structured/constructed in a subject/object mode. Awareness is "non-dual": there is just the activity and the awareness of it; not even activity *and* awareness—the knower, the knowing, and the known are experienced as one—not distinguishable or "not different" in the terminology of later Buddhist traditions. In the previous two types of self-experience, experience is organized around self-representations by the ego; in the states here, the ego functions as a synthetic principle without organizing experience around a self.

This is the type of self-experience that has traditionally been associated with meditative and mystical experience, though it actually comprises a range of experience from the ordinary to the non-ordinary. It is a blind spot in psychoanalytic theory. When an autonomous, differentiated identity and sense of selfhood is viewed as the fulcrum of development, this mode of experience inevitably tends to be interpreted as a regressive de-differentiation of hard-won ego boundaries and a symptom of psychopathology—another example of how paradigmatic commitments determine which data are deemed relevant to theory.

Psychoanalytic theorists have viewed this mode of subjectivity more positively in the realm of cultural experience—play, creativity, art. Earlier theorists (Kris 1952) conceptualized this type of self-experience as a healthy "regression in the service of the ego" as opposed to pathological ego regression. Recent theorists have tended to view these experiences as "transitional" phenomena in Winnicott's sense. But these seem like default positions, attempts to incorporate a different mode of functioning within existing theory without recognizing its uniqueness. There is no natural place for this mode of self-organization in the standard model of psychological functioning. It does not inform the core of psychoanalytic thinking about the person.

In fact, we have experiences of non-dual awareness all the time, though we are usually unaware of it, or we tend to dismiss them as unimportant—an interesting reaction in itself. These are moments in which there is *full awareness without any reflexive consciousness of self.* Some common instances: we hear our name called and we respond spontaneously, without thinking about it; we are doing something that normally makes us feel uncomfortable, anxious, or self-conscious, and suddenly, this time, we just do it, without anxiety or self-consciousness—taking out the garbage, allowing someone to cut in front of us while driving, responding to our child's request for help with their homework; working through and resolving a misunderstanding or distortion with a client and both of us sitting in silence together, aware of each other as if for the first time.

In addition to these "everyday" moments of non-dual awareness, there are "peak experiences" when we feel totally alert, alive, one with our action: an athlete "in the zone" when action is completely clear and effortless; a Zen archer who lets the arrow loose without deciding or intending to let it go (Herrigel 1971); a child who finally balances on her bike and experiences herself riding for the first time.

Hans Loewald (1978, 67) describes the kind of "losing oneself" that restores and rejuvenates and is a source of sanity and health—in creating a work of art, in aesthetic contemplation, in love or intimacy:

> We get lost in the contemplation of a beautiful scene, or face, or painting, in listening to music or poetry, or the music of a human voice. We are carried away in the vortex of sexual passion. We become absorbed in …a deeply stirring play or film, in the beauty of a scientific theory or experiment or an animal, in the intimate closeness of a personal encounter.

The therapist's empathic listening, in those moments when there is complete attunement without thinking or distraction—the pianist who plays without thinking about his or her fingers or the notes he or she is playing (Kohut's example)—fall into the same category of non-dual awareness. It isn't hard to think of many other instances. In fact it is surprising to realize how common such experiences are and how completely they permeate our life. And yet this mode of subjectivity has remained peripheral to psychoanalytic theorizing, just as we tend to downplay, dismiss, or ignore it in daily life.

Earlier theorists recognized that these states are quite different from archaic states of nondifferentiation. But such notions as "regression in the service of the ego" miss the point. It is not that the self de-differentiates. There is no "transient loss of self-differentiation," as Jeffrey Rubin (1997) and other theorists maintain. This conceptualization assumes that a differentiated self—a self experienced as singular and continuous—is the ideal or preferred form of self-experience. This self is not "lost" here. Experience is simply organized differently—not around a sense of self as separate from its experience. Some writers describe this mode of subjectivity as an "expanded sense of self," which is paradoxical since awareness of self, or self-consciousness, is absent. But the term does capture the experiential feeling in these moments of "going beyond" the limited, differentiated, bounded "me" that feels separate from "my" experience.

This mode of subjectivity is characterized by *non-dual* awareness in which we are unselfconscious but acutely aware, attuned to the realities of the moment. Discrimination is enhanced; faculties of perception are heightened. We are focused and engaged, but relaxed and confident at the same time, without self-preoccupation or anxiety about our performance or results—success or failure, praise or blame, gain or loss, happiness or unhappiness—the eight "worldly conditions" *(lokadhamma)* identified in Buddhist psychology. We feel complete in the moment, and completely present: alive, rejuvenated, transformed. There is a sense of timelessness, efficacy and peace. We feel and are more creative, playful, joyful, effective.

What makes this possible is that internal tension and conflict are absent or in abeyance. Suler (1993, 54) describes what happens intrapsychically:

> This unified [mode of subjectivity] contains no rigid or abrasive boundaries between its intrapsychic components. Any conflict involves a tension between two or more opposing affects. Pathological self or object repre-

sentations are pathological because they grate against
other self or object representations. Repressive barriers
between them prevent their being integrated or harmo-
nized. In the spontaneity of [this mode of subjectivity],
all intrapsychic spheres are [at least temporarily] united
seamlessly, effortlessly... . this does not mean that
intrapsychic distinctions are lost, dissolved into a condition of chaotic undifferentiation.

The result is spontaneity in thought, will, and action. There are two aspects
to this spontaneity. First, there is little or no sense that "I" am "doing" anything.
Thoughts, feelings, actions occur, but they are not experienced as originating
in or by "me." They simply occur as a response to the exigencies of the moment,
fluidly, easily, spontaneously, unhampered by extraneous thought—without, as
Alan Watts (1957) said, the sensation of a second self, mind, or awareness separate from the thought, feeling, or behavior that is "doing" it. I do not experience myself as "thinking" my thoughts, "feeling" my feelings, "doing" my
actions. They simply happen of their own accord, without force or conscious
intention. And yet even though one acts without thinking or reflecting, "the
plan and precision of "thoughtfulness" remains" (Suler 1993, 54).

I was told the following story. I cannot vouch for its authenticity, but perhaps a reader who was there will write me and confirm or disconfirm it. The
members of the San Francisco Zen Center drove out to the country one day
for a community picnic. The idea was to climb a small hill and dig a fire pit
on the top. Suzuki Roshi was at that time suffering from terminal cancer and
was quite ill, and so was lagging behind. When the community reached the
top of the hill, they realized no one had remembered to bring the shovel to
dig the fire pit. While they were complaining and remonstrating about who
forgot to bring the shovel and why, Suzuki Roshi reached the top, took in the
situation at a glance, and without breaking stride or saying anything, turned
around, walked back down the hill, got the shovel, and brought it back up
the hill.

In unselfconscious experience, action and behavior in everyday living
tend to be commensurate with the situation and need of the moment—neither more nor less than what is called for or what one is capable of, as long
as no special competence is required. There tends to be a "rightness" and

sense of "fit" between one's behavior and what the situation requires. We are not on automatic pilot in these moments. Spontaneous action isn't automatic or habituated behavior. When we act without anxiety, we find ourselves acting spontaneously, purposefully, appropriately, fully aware of our actions, without the weight of self-conscious thought. It becomes possible when walking, as Zen says, to just walk; when running, to just run. Conflict or anxiety doesn't rush the walk into a run, or constrict the run to a walk. When hungry, it becomes possible to just eat. There is no painful self-conscious attempt to direct or control what we are doing, and no need. Contrary to T. S. Eliot's modern sensibility in *The Hollow Men*, "Between the idea / And the reality / Between the motion / And the act" does *not* "fall the Shadow."

In his last writing, Kohut (1984) came to see this kind of experience not only as the self's intrinsic potential, not only as a transient mode of subjectivity that we sometimes experience and sometimes don't, but as a more stable way of being that represented the outcome of successful therapy. Paradoxically, he still attributed this kind of functioning to "the self," an unnecessary and confusing reification, especially when the chief characteristic of this mode of subjectivity is awareness and action that is unselfconscious. Nevertheless, he describes the ideal outcome of psychoanalytic treatment as a self functioning spontaneously, in accord with its own internal design, without the burden of superfluous thought and reflection, the details of the process—interpretations, insights, empathic failures and disappointments, rages and reparations—sinking into the background, not through repression but because the patient no longer needs them. Ideally, the result is a self that is aware of its actions without having to be aware of its own workings because these proceed seamlessly, silently, smoothly.

In a neglected but profound study of the stages in self-transformation, Herbert Fingarette (1963) came to a similar conclusion about the ideal outcome of analysis, but went a step further to apply this notion to descriptions of "mystical" states as well. He noted the similarly contradictory way in which both mystics and successful analysands talked about acting, deciding, or feeling unselfconsciously: fully aware of their actions, but without self-consciousness. He saw self-consciousness as consciousness tinged by conflict or anxiety. It is conflict or anxiety that turns us back to check up on and reassure ourselves, and in so doing literally brings a "self" into being as a structure separate from its experience. When conflict is resolved or anxiety is absent, there is awareness, purpose, intentionality, but no consciousness of self. The confident person does not have a conscious feeling of confidence—does not "know" himself to be confident, as Lao Tzu might say. The person who is genuinely compassionate does not have a conscious feeling of compassion—he or she simply is and acts compassionately.

In addition to "ordinary" unselfconscious subjectivity and non-dual awareness, there are "non-ordinary" states. Most psychoanalytic commentators are not familiar with them. These are the states of consciousness associated with meditation and spirituality in the Great Traditions from time immemorial. In Theravada Buddhism they are called *jhanas* or "absorptions" (Buddhaghosa 1975; Vajirañana 1975). They are accessed through concentration meditation rather than through mindfulness, and are based on the mind's becoming "one" with the object of concentration through sustained one-pointed attention. This is the opposite of mindfulness in which one attends to the flow of any and all objects as they arise in awareness without preference or judgment. The tradition identifies eight discrete levels of absorption, none of which have been recognized let alone incorporated into psychoanalytic thinking.

At each progressive level of absorption, mind and body become more silent, more unified in their functioning, more expansive and peaceful, so much so that even the qualities of mind that distinguish the earlier jhanas—feelings of rapture and happiness—are systematically and consciously surrendered for still more refined states of absorption. The first four levels are reached through single-pointed concentration on specific meditation objects. From the degree of refined concentration developed at the fourth jhana, one can go on to develop the traditional psychic powers described in all yogic and shamanic traditions, though most Buddhist lineages do not teach these because they are enormously seductive, open to misuse, have nothing to do with liberation, and can actually impede it by inflating both the ideal ego and the ego ideal. The next four levels are described as "beyond form": consciousness lets go of any specific meditation object altogether and expands to experience boundless dimensions of silent and pure awareness that are completely unknown and unenvisaged in Western psychology.

From a Buddhist perspective, there are three problems with all these forms of unselfconscious subjectivity, "non-ordinary" as well as "ordinary." First, however long they last, they are temporary and transient. Like all states of consciousness, they arise and pass away. They are time limited and not sustainable. Second, they are essentially states of concentrative absorption in which we become "one" with our perceptions and actions only temporarily; they do not represent an enduring condition of liberation. Concentration is viewed as reciprocally inhibiting the operation of mental factors that cause anxiety and conflict, not as extinguishing them. Buddhist psychology uses a technical term *vikhambhana* to distinguish "suppression" from "extinction" (Buddhaghosa 1975). The underlying factors that cause self-generated suffering remain latent potentials and reassert themselves when concentration wavers or the state of absorption ends. Third, concentrative states of "oneness" are amoral by nature when they are based primarily on absorption. Concentration can be used for good or ill: one can use it to become an enlightened Zen master or a samurai. A thief thoroughly absorbed in breaking into a house is "one" with his action. Genuine, enduring liberation from suffering has to involve a moral component, since "unwholesome" (immoral) states of mind *(akusala citta)* and unethical actions inevitably result in intrapsychic and interpersonal conflict. From the Buddhist point of view however, unselfconscious subjectivity and action does have a value. It shows us that there is a mode of being, thinking, feeling, and acting that is not organized around a separate sense of self. "Thinking" can happen quite nicely, and does, without a "self" or "I" to think it. In fact, it happens much more efficiently and without anxiety or conflict. The same for feeling, intention, and action. Moreover, what is experienced in the absence of this particular self-representation is natural and spontaneous compassion and joy. In the Tibetan tradition, these experiences are sometimes called "glimpses" of liberation, "glimpses" of what it is like to be freed of the burden of this particular way of representing self and constructing experience.

But a glimpse is only a glimpse. We do function in this conflict-free mode of unselfconscious subjectivity—but only at times. The next time another driver cuts me off or my daughter asks for help with her homework while I'm working on this essay, the next time my therapist does something unempathic, lo and behold! I don't seem to feel very at one with the action that pops out of me—or maybe all too "one" with it in a different sort of way! Non-dual awareness, I hope to show, is absolutely, always, available—in fact is always the case—but under ordinary circumstances acting out of non-dual awareness remains short-lived, a transient state of consciousness. The propensity to again construct my experience in terms of a singular, separate, enduring self remains.

No-Self

The goal of meditation practice in all enlightenment traditions is to extinguish this latent potential and, with it, the roots of self-generated suffering.

It is one thing to realize that none of the core attributes or functions of the "self" require that they be attributed to a separate self—that there can be very good cohesion, continuity, and agency without this representation. In fact all the functions formerly attributed to my "self" operate even more efficiently and effectively than before. Thoughts do not need a "thinker." Actions do not need a "doer." But it is another and even more extraordinary thing to discover this not as a transient altered state but as a way of being.

Both historically and cross-culturally, there seem to be two routes to this discovery. In both the goal is a permanent and irreversible reorganization of self-structure, changing the very experience of self—not just induction of a special or altered state of consciousness.

One approach is *to shift the locus of subjectivity from representations of self to awareness itself:* to *who* it is that is thinking this, feeling this, experiencing this, having this sensation, behaving in this way.

To catch a "glimpse" of this in everyday experience: suppose I introspect for a moment and ask, What am I aware of (actually, what am I aware of being aware of)? Probably a thought or a feeling. Let's say it's the thought, "I'm writing this paragraph." There's an implicit metaphysics in this way of representing things: it posits a self, an "I," that exists apart from the flow of experience—who is thinking—"me"—and a more or less "objective" world out there—a word processor, an editor, a contract, a publication date—to which this "I," this self, must respond.

Suppose now I redirect attention away from the object of my awareness to the subject: *who* is it that is thinking? If I say, "I am," who is this "I"? When I turn around to find this "I," I can't find it. It's nowhere to be found. Because of my deeply held sense of myself as a personal center of subjectivity, this is a little unnerving. If I pursue the inquiry in earnest, it rapidly becomes very unnerving! Why is this sense of "I" that I normally take for granted so elusive?

It's important to understand that this isn't a trick. It exposes the episte-mological dilemma at the base of awareness and self-observation when we organize experience around a separate self.

Freud noted the extraordinary ability of the ego to take itself as an object: "It can treat itself like any other object, observe itself, criticize itself, do heaven knows what besides with itself" (quoted in Sterba 1934, 120). But there is one thing that it cannot do which Freud did not call attention to or incorporate into psychoanalytic therapy: it cannot take itself as the subject of awareness. Whatever I can be aware of, whatever I can notice or conceptualize, whether in the field of sense perception or intrapsychically, is always an object of my awareness—never awareness itself. I can become aware of being aware, but when this happens, what I have done is take this reflexive awareness as an object of experience. *What I cannot do is be aware of the source of awareness in the act of being aware.* In other words, I cannot directly observe my observing self. If I try, it recedes each time I turn to observe it: I never catch "it"; I only turn the act of awareness into another object of awareness in an infinite regression. To use Mitchell's phrase again: "I" am *never* my "self"—today or any other day. The "self" that I can represent, the "self" that I can know or grasp, cannot be "me." The eye that sees, Zen says, cannot see itself. Finally it dawns: detaching our "self" from awareness in order to observe it is impos-sible because we *are* that awareness.

In this sense, awareness is not simply an ego function, like the psychoan-alytic notion of the "observing ego." As Arthur Deikman (1982) and Suler (1993) point out, psychoanalysis tends to assume that the observer and the observed are phenomena of the same order. They are not. Awareness itself can never be objectified, can never be grasped as an object, can never be identi-fied with the contents of consciousness, can never be represented as "this" or "that." It is of a fundamentally different nature: without qualities, limitless, without boundaries, no more affected by what it observes than a mirror is by what it reflects. In essence, I am not anything that can be named or thought, represented or denied, found or lost. "Who you are," Sri Nisargadatta Maharaj (1982) says, "is indefinable and indescribable." Subjective awareness is what makes experience possible, but it itself is not an experience. It is always present but easily missed, because, like the water the fish swims in but never sees, it is the *condition* of all experience. Full realization of this is non-dual awareness as one's natural state. Identification with any representation or activity of a separate self as "me" or "mine" becomes impossible.Examples of this approach in the Advaita Vedanta tradition are Ramana Maharshi's practice of meditating on the question "Who am I?" and Sri Nisargadatta's meditation on "I am." Koans serve this function in Rinzai Zen. The classical practice of *shikan taza* ("just sitting") in the Soto Zen school has the same effect. The explicit or implicit demand by the Zen teacher in every *dokusan* is, "Show me this 'who' who thinks, who acts!" Tibetan Buddhist *dzogchen* trains the student to relax into our already present innate awareness, to "rest in natural great peace" (Nyoshul Khenpo).

This approach to practice proceeds from the assumption that non-dual awareness is our natural mode of functioning. Practice simply calls attention to it, grounds us in it, and allows our natural functioning to function naturally. These traditions therefore tend to nonlinear or "discovery" models of practice (Klein 1995): we are "already enlightened" from this point of view. The task is to discover our natural state.

The second approach is to direct awareness to the moment-to-moment manifestations and experiences of self. This is the basis of all forms of Buddhist mindfulness practice: vipassana in Theravada Buddhism (Goldstein and Kornfield 1987) and Mahamudra (Brown 1986; Namgyal 1986), the other great enlightenment practice in Vajrayana Buddhism. Enlightenment tends to be viewed as a goal and outcome of practice in this approach: something we become rather than something we already are—though once attained, the practitioner comes to the same realization of no-self. Models of practice in this approach therefore tend to be linear and "developmental" (Klein 1995): a sequence of progressive stages toward this goal.

Discovery and developmental models of practice only appear contradictory. Both are true, depending on the practitioner's point of view. If you imagine yourself standing on "this shore" of the river, as the early Buddhists did and as is natural for goal-oriented Westerners to do, the goal is to get across to the "other shore"—to somewhere you are not. If you imagine yourself already standing on the "other shore," the goal is to realize it. The goal in both cases is the intensely practical one of ending self-generated suffering by ending "clinging to self" *(attavadupadana)*. Consistently taking either approach does that, though their metaphysics appear contradictory.

The basic instruction in vipassana meditation, for instance, is to attend to every object of consciousness, without preference or selection—a thought, a feeling, a body sensation—as it arises in awareness moment by moment. This approach proceeds from the same assumption that Kohut made when he refused to give a definitive meaning to the term "self" because he believed its essence was unknowable: "We cannot by introspection and empathy penetrate to the self per se; only its introspectively or empathically perceived psychological manifestations are open to us" (1977, 310–11). Mindfulness meditation differs from psychoanalytic inquiry in that the *contents* of consciousness—the specific representations of self and other and their configurations—are not attended to or analyzed. Instead, by directing attention to the *process* whereby all manifestations of self arise and pass away, are constructed and deconstructed, moment by moment, irrespective of content, mindfulness leads to insight into the nature of all representations of self and reality as constructions only and as ungraspable in any real or definitive sense.

Trained moment-to-moment attention to the flow of psychophysical events with a minimum of reactivity will trigger a deautomatization (Gill and Brenman 1959; Deikman 1966) of the psychological operations that register, select, organize, and interpret perceptual and conceptual stimuli by reinvesting them with conscious awareness. As this occurs, psychological functions that were once regulated automatically, without conscious awareness and control, become accessible to awareness. I described earlier how previously repressed or dissociated self and object representations are typically accessed via memory, fantasy, or thought. But, much more important, the practiced meditator can become aware of the very processes and operations that contribute to the construction of the perceptual and representational world. Accessing these requires a degree of disciplined concentration and equanimity that is completely different from the self-observation required in therapy. From a platform stage of "access concentration," when attention can be held steady and completely nondistractable for extended periods of time, without censorship or reaction, the meditator actually begins to *retrace the stages in the representational process itself* as it occurs moment by moment (see Brown 1986; Engler 1983b, 1986). The *ñanas* or "stages of insight" in vipassana practice actually represent progressively earlier stages in the entire sequence of information processing, pattern recognition, and conceptualization by which we bring a self and a representational world into being each instant.

In this process, the singular, continuous "self" is discovered to be an illusion, a construction only, the byproduct of not being able to perceive the more microscopic level of events—much as the tachistoscopic flicker-fusion phenomenon produces the illusion of an "object" when discrete and discontinuous images are flashed too quickly for normal perception to distinguish. No enduring or substantial entity, observer, experiencer, or agent can be found behind or apart from these moment-to-moment events, only a discrete moment of consciousness and its object arising and passing away in awareness, nanosecond by nanosecond.

When this "coming to be and passing away" *(udayabbaya)* is experienced as the complete, total, and irrefutable reality of each moment of experience, there is a profound understanding of the radical impermanence *(anicca)* of all that I have taken to be "me." Not only do I no longer perceive any enduring "objects" of perception, but I witness the processes of thinking, feeling, sensing, and perceiving as a series of discrete and discontinuous events, each arising and passing away without remainder. In this experience of complete and discontinuous change, a Copernican revolution occurs. "Things" disappear. What is apparent is only events on the order of milliseconds. Not only is everything changing all the time; there are no "things" that change. Any notion of an enduring or inherent self, a solid body, a durable perceptual object, even a fixed point of observation like an "observing self" becomes completely untenable. The practitioner comes to understand the lack of intrinsic existence anywhere; he or she grasps in direct moment-to-moment experience the no-self *(anatta)* or empty *(shunyata)* nature of mind, body, external objects, and internal representations.

Furthermore, at this level of experience, normal affective and motivational bases of behavior—pleasure-principle functioning and object-seeking itself—are experienced as sources of great suffering. This becomes particularly clear in observing the painful effect of normal reactive tendencies in this state of awareness. Any approach/avoidance response to pleasure and pain, no matter how "normal" in everyday experience—the simplest responses of attraction and aversion, wanting and not wanting, preferring pleasure and avoiding pain, wanting this and not wanting that—irrespective of their particular aims and objects—is experienced as an extraordinarily painful and misguided effort to block the natural flow of events. Such desires are now seen as futile attempts to deny and resist the process of change—to perpetuate this experience and avoid, block, stop, or get rid of that. Any attempt to constellate a separate and continuous representation of self, or to preferentially identify with some self-representations as "me" and extrude others as "not-me," is experienced as an equally futile and painful attempt to interrupt, undo, or alter self-representations as a flow of moment-to-moment constructions.

But insight into this process is not enough. As in therapy, these insights need to be worked through. In meditation as in therapy, the deepest working through also involves confronting loss, the deepest possible: the loss of "self" as this unique, singular, separate "me," this "entity residing within." Buddhists are fond of saying that actually nothing is lost; something that never existed in the first place cannot be lost. One only discovers the way things have been from the beginning, all along. What is lost is a mistaken representation, not anything real. This may be true ontologically, but before this discovery leads to the freedom and liberation of enlightenment, it is usually experienced as terror and misery (the sixth and seventh "stages of insight" in vipassana). Representations of "self," particularly this most cherished representation, have a psychological and emotional reality; they are not surrendered without profound grief-work. This most cherished experience of self in particular has never felt like a "representation"; it has either felt like something real (neurotic or normal organization) or something missing or defective that I am desperate to find (psychosis, personality disorders). And so insight inevitably sets in motion a process of mourning in vipassana as it does in therapy, if the practitioner allows it and can bear it. The higher ñanas in fact embody the universal stages of mourning (Engler 1986, 1999). "Enlightenment" occurs when all grasping at self and objects, even in their subtlest forms, is relinquished and all reactivity in the mind is exhausted. Only then is identification with this representation of self surrendered and the mind awakened to a way of being not organized around consolidating and protecting a separate self.

As I outlined earlier, in Buddhist vipassana practice there are four distinct enlightenment experiences before this kind of awakening is completely secure. The "unwholesome mental factors" (akusala cittas) said to be extinguished at respective stages of enlightenment can be looked at as different psychological operations involved in constructing the sense of a separate self, and they are only confronted, worked through, and surrendered gradually.

Any description of the resulting self-state can only be partial at best. To describe it as "no-self" captures one aspect of it. It is not that one is temporarily unselfconscious simply because the anxiety that makes us self-conscious is absent. This is not a "glimpse" of freedom from anxiety and fear. The "self" as we normally experience it has been seen, in the deepest marrow of one's bones, to be a construction only, and the potentials for reconstructing it as an "entity residing deep within" are first diminished and then permanently extinguished.

Nor is it a unity or oneness experience like a state of absorption. First of all, it is not an "experience." Any experience is transient, temporary, bounded in space and time, dependent on circumstances and conditions. This is the way things fundamentally are. Whether one calls it Self (capital *S*) as Hinduism tends to, or no-self, as Buddhism does, who I am is discovered/realized to be atemporal, without beginning and without end—in traditional language, "unborn," "deathless," "uncreated," not dependent on causes and conditions. Second, it is not the momentary "being one with" one's actions or "being one with" that which one knows or loves that we experience in states of complete attention and attunement. Who I discover myself to be is "both subject and object, and neither, and beyond" (Nisargadatta 1982).

Out of this nonidentification with a separate sense of self comes a natural equanimity, contentment, joy, and compassion for all beings. Also a rightness, freedom, and spontaneity in action that Theravada Abhidhamma denotes with the term *"asangkarika citta"*: literally, "unmotivated action"—action that arises spontaneously, in response to the need of the moment and is free of attachment to the intended result, so that one is free to act again in response to the need of the next moment.

Two very brief personal descriptions of this state of consciousness follow, one from each approach to accessing no-self. The first is from a letter of a contemporary Western woman, a fellow practitioner of vipassana, to our mutual Indian teacher. Carol had endured considerable suffering in the course of her life: an abusive childhood, the Nazi occupation of her country, torture by the Gestapo as a secret agent in the Dutch resistance, two failed marriages after the war, eventual blackballing by the oil industry where she later worked as a geologist, a lifelong struggle with recurrent depression, and finally three suicide attempts, the last of which eventually led her to India and meditation practice. This letter was written following her second period of practice in India, after she had returned to Australia for good:

Sometimes I meditate intensely and sometimes I don't meditate at all. But you see, in a way my whole life is one total meditation, because I live every minute of the day in full mindfulness and awareness. It is living on two levels: the outer level will make conversation with people and say the right things at the right time [asangkarika citta]. And under that is the second level, where there is a core of untouched and untouchable stillness and quiet attention and peace. Because somehow, life is so simple, uncomplicated, and all those upheavals were after all just of my own making. (Kornfield, reprinted in Walsh and Shapiro 1983 pp. 330-31).

The second is from a response of Sri Nisargadatta Maharaj to a question from a student about the nature of his experience after realization:

Having realized that I am one with and yet beyond the world, I found myself free from all desire and fear. I did not reason out that I should be free—I found myself free—unexpectedly, without the least effort [i.e., following a number of years of uninterrupted meditative self-inquiry in accordance with his teacher's instructions]. This freedom from desire and fear has remained with me since then. Another thing I noticed was that I do not need to make an effort. The deed follows the thought without delay and friction. I have also found that thoughts became self-fulfilling; things would fall in place smoothly and rightly. The main change was in the mind. It became motionless and silent, responding quickly but not perpetuating the response. Spontaneity became a way of life, the real became natural and the natural became real. And above all, infinite affection, love, dark and quiet, radiating in all directions, embracing all, making all interesting and beautiful, significant and auspicious.

Both these methods pass through the final bedrock that Kohut said psychoanalysis could not pass through: the ontology of self. The meditative traditions would agree that the ontology of self is not analyzable: it is not directly accessible to empathic introspection; only its products and manifestations are. But they see the ontology of self as accessible to a different kind of inquiry: into the nature of awareness and subjectivity; and into the nature of the self's "products and manifestations," including its own representations, as moment-to-moment constructions.

The Relationship between Self and No-Self

Alternating Self-States?

Rubin (1997), Suler (1993), and others have proposed thinking about self and no-self as essential types of self-experience with healthy psychological functioning requiring an oscillation or balance between the two.

Rubin (1997) argues, for instance, that what he terms the "non-self-centric" mode of subjectivity is as essential to good functioning as "self-centric" subjectivity. He faults psychoanalysis for ignoring the first and Buddhism for evading the second; each psychology, he claims, overvalues one mode at the expense of the other. The general point of his argument is well taken, but the "non-self-centric" experiences he refers to are within normal self-experience. They are primarily absorption states, states of unselfconsciousness, not the no-self of the enlightenment traditions: liberation from "that entity residing within."

Suler (1993) questions whether the experience of no-self may be another type of disintegration experience that seems to be an essential aspect of growth and creativity. In processes of integration-disintegration-reintegration, representations of self are constructed, modified, deconstructed, reconstructed. Suler cites suggestive parallels in the earlier psychoanalytic literature (Kris 1952; Schafer 1958; Van Dusen 1958; Loewald 1960). Winnicott (1971), for instance, describes the patient's immersion in a "stage of hesitation"—a state of nonbeing and nonthought where nothing can be said or done—which becomes the catalyst for a breakthrough into new insight and subsequent new constructions of the self.

That processes of disintegration and reintegration are essential to healthy psychological functioning is indisputable. But the instances of this Suler cites are experiences of psychological disintegration in which self-representations dissolve, collapse, are undone, but in the service of reconstructing an enriched, expanded sense of self. None of them liberate from separate selfhood. Identification with a sense of self that is still singular, continuous, and self-identical remains, however expanded, revitalized, and enriched. The experience of no-self is not a new construction of self.

Self and no-self are not simply alternating states of selfhood in normal processes of psychological integration/disintegration, nor simply polar opposite modes of subjectivity that exist in healthy tension in the psyche, any more than they can be thought of as hierarchically or developmentally ordered "stages," as I first suggested.

Non-Separation of Self and No-Self

This is a difficult notion to grasp, but I think it is the key to a clearer understanding of the structure of self-experience and why we represent ourselves to ourselves as we do: why "I" am so determined to be "me."

The core of the no-self notion is actually a simple idea: that all things are interdependent, including the self. This is enshrined in the core teaching of all Buddhist schools regarding "dependent origination" *(paticcasamuppada)* or "dependent co-arising": all things arise dependent on causes and conditions, and pass away when those causes and conditions change. Psychologically, there is no difficulty acknowledging this as long as it simply points to the fact that I, you, all of us, are interrelated in a thousand complex ways. In states of loneliness and grief, this feeling brings consolation and relief. And indeed it is becoming an increasingly popular and powerful notion—culturally, politically, ecologically. Within it, however, are the seeds of a much more radical and subversive realization.

If I press the notion further, which is what Buddhist psychology and meditative inquiry do in their respective ways, I can't find anything I can call a "thing" at all—not a single entity with an independent existence of its own. I find only an ongoing flux of momentary events that "exist" in the infinitesimal fraction of a moment between coming to be and passing away. What I perceive as an object with a reality of its own is actually only a momentary pattern or configuration. Buddhist psychology uses the term *rupa,* "form," to denote the boundedness of phenomena, the visible shape that distinguishes one "thing" from another, because it avoids any connotation of substantiality or independent existence. This is analogous to the quantum mechanical idea of matter as simply "frozen" or "bound" energy, without inherent substance (Ferris 1998). This is the sense in which Buddhism speaks of all things as "empty"—empty, that is, of inherent or substantial existence. To use Whitehead's (1929) pregnant term, "things" appear as a temporary "concrescence" of certain conditions and that is all they are. That does not mean that things don't exist or that I don't exist—they do and I do, but dependently: as a form, a patterning, that is nothing more than the totality of our relation with everything else in this moment. They are no-*thing* apart from these relations.

By the same token, "emptiness" cannot be known directly; it can only be known through the absence of inherent existence (Klein 1995). It can be known only by knowing "things" as "form." Both insights are brought together in the famous formulation of the Heart of Perfect Wisdom Sutra: "Form is exactly emptiness; emptiness is exactly form.'

However, it is one thing to acknowledge the emptiness of "things," quite another to acknowledge emptiness of self, and still another to actually *experience* emptiness of self moment to moment and be faced with accepting its irrefutable truth. This is exactly the situation the practitioner of mindfulness faces. Even apart from formal meditation practice, when I am silent and attentive I can sense directly how I cannot truly possess anything in or outside myself—certainly not things, others, or careers, and not even my thoughts, feelings, moods, and the functioning and sensations of my body. All of these events that I take as my own and that feel like "me" actually arise, change, and pass away by themselves, neither possessed nor directed by my consciousness or my desires (Kornfield 1993). When attention becomes refined in the ñanas, the advanced stages of vipassana practice, I can observe how individual, discrete moments of consciousness and their "objects" arise and pass away together, are constructed and deconstructed moment by moment *without remainder*—without any "subject" or "self," even an observing self, existing apart from the process, enduring behind it, or carrying forward into the next moment.

But "emptiness" or "dependent co-arising" means still more. Continue to press the inquiry and even intellectually it is quickly apparent that there is no way to arbitrarily limit the temporal or spatial radius of conditions affecting this present moment. The tiny electric charge caused by the beating of a butterfly's wings in the Caribbean can be catalyst enough to transform a tropical storm passing through the Straits of Florida into a devastating hurricane in the

Gulf of Mexico (Larson 1999). Changing the spin of one paired photon here will instantaneously change the spin on the other photon light years distant (Ferris 1997). Each conditioning factor affects and is affected by every other.

This present occasion literally and holographically reflects, manifests, and embodies the entire network of its relations. As a discrete momentary occasion, it is nothing but the sum total of its relations converging and interacting in this moment. Again, this realization has a profoundly different impact when it is directly experienced as true of "me," not just of electric charges or photons. My form, the shape of "me" in this moment—biologically, physically, and psychologically in every way—is this particular manifestation here and now of all that is happening in the entire universe and has no separate existence or substance of its own apart from that. There is no ontological core. This too the meditator grasps directly in the third ñana, "knowledge of conditionality" (Mahasi Sayadaw 1965).

In this sense, Buddhism says, the self both *is* and *is not*. It *is*, in the sense that this particular configuration that is "me" has a momentary reality of its own in the ongoing flux of change and transformation. And that reality is real ("real in a relative sense," Mahayana Buddhists would say). I recall once hearing His Holiness the Dalai Lama interrupt a conference participant who had started to preface his question with what he imagined was a typical Buddhist disclaimer, "Of course I know the self doesn't exist." His Holiness jumped in: "Wait! Your self is very real! If you don't respect its reality, you will cause a lot of suffering to yourself." On the other hand, the self *is not*, in the sense that it is not some "thing" which inherently exists. Self and no-self, form and emptiness, not only co-exist but are identical or, better still, not different.

So my experience of selfhood exists interpenetrated with an experience of no-self. My experience of being "me" inevitably reverberates with the sensed experience that this "me" does not exist in the way I think it does or want it to.

When I take myself to be that separate, ongoing "entity residing within," that singular self with which I identify so profoundly, any realization of this self's inherent emptiness as a representation, a moment-to-moment construction only, can only be profoundly disturbing.

Psychoanalytic theories of representation actually agree with the Buddhist view that the self-representation, even the representation of self as singular, separate, and enduring, is not a fixed entity or engram but a temporal succession of discrete and discontinuous images. Each is a new synthesis of past and present in the present moment of experience, a new situation- and need-specific construction that is always a construction of the moment (Schafer 1976; Rizzuto 1979. But the logic of psychoanalytic theory makes it difficult to view experiential insight into this state of affairs as therapeutic or liberating. On the contrary, the few psychoanalytic thinkers who have tried to incorporate this sense of nonbeing underlying existence into their theory have only been able to conceptualize it as a condition of "catastrophe" (Bion 1963, 1970): a nameless condition of oblivion, meaninglessness, and terror from which the self emerges and evolves and into which it dissolves. Michael Eigen (1993, 1986) can only describe it as a "zero point," a "null dimension" that exists as the "psychotic core" within each individual.

The Nature and Function of the Separate Self

If the sense of separate selfhood is illusory, a way of organizing experience that is not reality based and inevitably creates anxiety and conflict, why do we repeatedly and persistently construct experience around it? This returns us to our original question.

Those psychoanalytic thinkers who acknowledge the illusory nature of continuity in self-experience have as much difficulty with this issue as Buddhist traditions. The logic of psychoanalytic theory inevitably leads to viewing this representation of self as a necessary illusion because it seems essential to integrated functioning. Western cultural assumptions about the self make it necessary to find some theoretical legitimation for representing it this way. There also seems to be no other way in psychoanalytic theory to account for the invariants in experience that self-cohesion seems to require.

Buddhist psychology, of course, is much clearer about the illusory nature of this self-construction than psychoanalytic theory. In fact, it makes it an explicit target of inquiry. The technical term *sakkaya-ditthi* is an exact equivalent of "misrepresentation of self" and denotes "delusion" in the clinical sense: a belief that is not in accord with reality. But Buddhism not only doesn't elaborate on how this sense of self is constructed, it doesn't address *why* we construct it if it only creates suffering.

If all psychological structures emerge in response to a need, this must be true within a Buddhist perspective as well. Is there a way to understand the emergence and function of this particular self-representation that sees it as an adaptation consistent with its own inherent emptiness, that accounts for its pervasiveness and its resistance to meditative inquiry and insight, and that nevertheless does not view it as a necessary illusion? I believe there is. The key is Fingarette's (1958) notion that it is anxiety that calls the self into being.

We can account for all these apparently paradoxical attributes and functions of the self, and for its adaptive aims, its maladaptive solution, and the unintended suffering it generates, if we view the singular, constant, separate self of normal experience as a *compromise formation* in the psychodynamic sense: a psychological structure that emerges to confront a "danger situation" by binding anxiety and warding off unwanted and unwelcome knowledge and the aversive feelings that knowledge evokes, that nevertheless unconsciously reveals the very thing it attempts to conceal, and that thereby betrays its origins in unresolved conflict that it actually perpetuates instead of resolving.

The "danger situation" against which this sense of self is erected is the most fundamental anxiety of all: that we do not exist in the way we think we do. This is not the fear of death or mortality, both of which are second-order anxieties and only arise as a result of identification with the separate self. Death and mortality only elicit fear when "I" identify with the activities of mind and body as "me," as someone separate from their arising and passing away. The root fear is the fear of emptiness *or no-self. No-self or empiness can only apear empty and void when experience is organized around the representation of a singular, separate, ongoing core "self".* Then selflessness can only be experienced as a "null dimension" of horror (Eigen 1993) and "catastrophe" (Bion 1970) instead of freedom. One falls into emptiness as the negation of an existent self instead of embracing it as liberation from the illusion of a separate self.

It is this identification with a separate self that makes the confrontation with selflessness or "emptiness" in the higher stages of meditative practice so terrifying, in direct proportion to the tenacity of the identification. It will then be experienced as a "great doubt" (Zen), a "dark night of the soul" (Christian contemplation), a "knowledge of terror, misery, and revulsion" (Theravada Buddhist vipassana). We attempt to bind this anxiety by organizing ourselves around a sense of continuity and singularity, by creating the illusion that "I" exist, will continue to exist, and have a privileged position in existence. Constructing and continually reconstructing this "I" defends against the unwanted awareness of no-self and the dependent and interdependent nature of all individual constructions of self.

But this way of representing myself to myself cannot help but reveal what it tries to conceal. It is painfully evident in the anxious insistence on "me" and "mine" whenever this "I" is threatened. In states of "injured innocence," when I feel that I have been wronged unjustly and am owed reparation for my injury—and in my anxious insistence on my innocence and what is owed me—that particular I-sense can be captured in full cry.

It is important not to confuse this with clinical narcissism. Organizing experience around a separate, ongoing self has nothing to do with attempts at grandiose autonomy or mystical fusion as forms of self-repair for narcissistic injury. These are desperate attempts to repair the damaged, undervalued, under-mirrored psychological self. The identification with a separate self is an altogether different type or level of narcissism, which may not even be the right term here, because it is a way of organizing all experience, normal as well as pathological, around a construct of self as separate, constant, singular, self-identical.

Odd as it may sound to psychodynamic thinking, we do not need the illusion of continuity and sameness to be fully awake, alive, aware, loving, and effective human beings, or for experience to have structure and coherence. In fact, to the extent that we cling to and operate out of this illusion, it will inhibit and constrict all these ways of being, as compromise formations always do. We do not need this illusion to smooth over our multiple organizations of experience, or to prioritize our goals and motives. We need it, or so we think, to ward off intimations of emptiness and freedom, of who we really are.

Calling this representation an "illusion," as psychoanalytic writers are forced to, or a "delusion" (moha), as Buddhist psychology does, overlooks the fact that this is not a simple case of not knowing. As in all compromise formations, this is a dynamically charged and culpable ignorance: an anxiety-based, determined, and willful ignoring, an unconscious effort not to know because I do not want to know. As always, psychic suffering is the unintended outcome. The attempt not to know is never fully successful: I still do not feel myself to be quite who I am. "I" am never "myself" today, or any other day. This too marks the separate self as a compromise formation that can be submitted, along with the motives behind it, to scrutiny and investigation. This is the path of practice.

Commentary

SOMEBODIES AND NOBODIES

STEPHEN A. MITCHELL

Jack Engler is right to say that he and I have been struggling with some of the same questions—very, very difficult questions—and it has been a distinct pleasure (although not, I hope, a pleasure of an illusory nature) to accompany him by reading along as he tries to sort out different kinds of experiences of self and no-self and to puzzle through their interrelationships. I particularly enjoy the way he is able to keep open the enormously dense conceptual problems he is attempting to solve, for the result is an enrichment and increasingly textured complexity. In this brief commentary I will note several points he makes that are congruent with my own experiences and that I found especially illuminating, and I also express some reservations about his conclusion.

The issues Engler writes about here have been interesting to me for a long time; they came into focus during my undergraduate years in the mid-1960s when, like so many of my cohorts, I became fascinated with Eastern philosophy and meditative experience through the writings of Alan Watts, D. T. Suzuki, and others. In many ways, some conscious and some not, the exposure to these modes of thought had a deeply formative impact both on my life and on my approach to psychoanalytic thinking and practice. In my early reading of Erich Fromm, I came across the account of his meetings with Suzuki to explore the relationship between psychoanalysis and Zen. David Schechter was a participant at a conference in Mexico where Suzuki was asked if schizophrenics, who presumably have no sense of self, had a head start on the way to the no-self of enlightenment. Suzuki's response, as Schechter related it, was very much like Engler's controversial position: you have to have a self to lose the self. This position has always made great sense to me, and I appreciate Engler's efforts in his essay to refine just what sort of self (functions) are maintained, even cultivated, in meditative practice and what sort of self (representations) are transcended. But there were troubling moments for me as well in this essay. I remember a coffee hour I had been invited to, along with some other students, with a very well-known historian and public figure. One of the other students, a devotee of Eastern thought, kept interrupting the discussion with statements like "It all comes down to your ability to confront the void," which made it impossible for us to learn anything about our guest's experiences. I felt that there was something about his interjections that was compelling, but also something terribly wrong with his inability to experience and respect life, his own and others, with more complexity. And then there was the disconcerting phenomenon of renowned gurus of the sixties who would speak so persuasively about the no-self doctrine to adoring throngs of admirers. These experiences had always puzzled and bothered me. So, I find Engler's study of Westerners' encounters with Buddhist thought interesting and helpful. He points to the complexity of motives that different people bring to meditative practice, the confusion of ontological "emptiness" with psychological emptiness, and the unrealistic hopes that meditation will solve all problems, both philosophical and psychological.

I found it interesting to reflect on the similarities between the ideal of spiritual practice that is supposed to eliminate all mental suffering and the traditional ideal of technically correct psychoanalytic practice of neutrality, abstinence, and anonymity that is supposed to eliminate all countertransference participation. The "needless self-accusation and guilt" Engler describes in students of meditation who find themselves still with problems reminded me of the sense of shame generated in generations of psychoanalytic candidates by the classical ideal of an immaculate technical posture. Similarly, I found Engler's remarks on teacher misconduct very thought provoking. Condemning wrongdoers as not truly enlightened preserves the ideal that someone, somewhere, is so enlightened as to be immune from temptation and the pushes and pulls of the human condition.

In his struggle to refine his earlier position on being somebody before being nobody, I found Engler's more general point about the unevenness (in terms of levels of functioning and psychopathology) of practitioners of meditation very relevant to current psychoanalytic thought. We function discontinuously, he is suggesting: perhaps enlightened in some contexts, caught in neurotic struggles in others. Rather than locating states of mind and illumination on a linear developmental continuum, Engler now presents us, in a fashion that is quite consistent with recent analytic contributions (Mitchell 1991; Bromberg 1998; Davies 1996; Pizer 1998) as multiple and variable. In analogous fashion, I have been increasingly impressed, in recent years, by the unevenness and inconsistencies in modes of functioning and degrees of organization in both patients and therapists. The traditional structural approach to development and diagnosis, where more "advanced" versions of self and levels of organization are assumed to replace and transform earlier, more "primitive" versions of self and levels of organization, has long outlived its utility.

The brief discussion here of the Buddhist approach to desire was also of particular interest to me. One feature of the version of Eastern thought that disturbed me in the 1960s is the view that desire is the root of suffering. It seemed to me, and this may have been partially a product of my own misreading at the time, that a state of renunciation of all desire was being promoted, and I had (and still have) too many desires that I am not interested in renouncing and that provide much more pleasure than suffering. Mark Epstein suggests in his book *Thoughts without a Thinker* that in Tibetan Buddhism, in contrast to Indian Buddhism, the goal is not the elimination of desire but the capacity to embrace and relinquish desires over time. Engler elaborates this approach here, referring to the "desire for sense pleasure" and "ill will" as conditioned behaviors, not drives. I have argued that sexuality (Mitchell 1988) and aggression (Mitchell 1993) are more usefully understood as responses to external and self-generated stimuli rather than as endogenously arising instinctual drives, in the way Freud portrayed them. Some people have had trouble grasping this notion, but it is consistent with and illuminated by the Buddhist distinction between desire, which is contextual and responsive, coming and going, and craving, both sexual and aggressive, which is the product of an addictive, self-reinforcing cycle of repetitive, anxiety-driven behavior. This ought to be graspable by anyone who has radically altered their diet and found themselves with little taste for particular foods, like chocolate or red meat, which they had previously craved.

Another feature of Engler's essay I found extremely interesting was his description of what he terms the third type of self-experience, that involving transitory states in which self-consciousness is suspended. Engler is right to note the lack of attention paid to these states within psychoanalytic theory, with its reliance on structural concepts and its portrayal of the self as having properties like "permanence" and "constancy." But Sullivan, who regarded the self essentially as an anti-anxiety system, pointed toward, although he did not elaborate on, such experiences. In an evocative passage (1950), Sullivan suggests that in a situation with no anxiety there would in fact be no self-system at all. It is interesting that this position got Sullivan into a lot of trouble with theorists who believed very much in the importance of a unique, core self. Because Sullivan was suggesting that the function of the self is to steer clear of and handle anxiety, he was accused of regarding people as purely conformist and adaptation oriented. What these critics miss is that Sullivan was arguing, like Engler, that the self (Engler's conceptual self, Sullivan's self-system) is a fundamentally narcissistic structure that disappears if there is no need for self-protection. That allows for something quite different to appear in experience. Unfortunately, Sullivan didn't elaborate on what such a no-self state would be like. Leslie Farber's contributions on the will also speak directly to these concerns. Farber distinguishes will from willfulness. The latter is the narcissistic effort to exert an impossible omnipotent control over areas of experience that simply cannot be controlled. Farber also describes states in which the will is in the background, seamlessly congruent with other motives and actions, where one acts without self-consciousness and self-protection. These descriptions are similar to Engler's accounts of transitory no-self states and activities.

I'd like now to turn to how Engler proposes to resolve the issues he grapples with in this essay. He describes four basic categories of self-experience. The first two are drawn from my work: the self as multiple and discontinuous and the self as integral and continuous. The second two involve no-self experiences, both a transitory loss of reflexive consciousness and a more continuous experience of no-self.[1] Engler regards both of the first two kinds of self-experiences as illusory, because, it is increasingly clear, he regards any sense of self as fundamentally illusory, regardless of whether it is viewed as singular and continuous or as multiple and shifting. No-self, whether fleeting or continuous, is our "natural state," the "complete, total, and irrefutable reality of each moment of experience," "the way things fundamentally are." Engler then raises what seems to me to be a very fruitful question: If the sense of a singular, separate self is an illusion, why are we so consistently taken in by it? What does it do for us? And his answer is that like many psychological phenomena, the construction of a singular, separate self is a compromise formation whose major purpose is to protect us from a particular danger situation, the "root fear" in this case being the fear of "emptiness."

I like Engler's adaptational approach to the first two kinds of self-experience. What are they good for, he is asking. What function do they serve?

After several years of observing and participating in discussions about theories of singular versus multiple selves, I have come to the conclusion that the argument about which of these theories is right is fruitless. Who would know? How could we ever decide? Theories, like selves, are constructions, useful for some things and obstacles in the way of others. Rather than deciding whether the self "really" is singular or multiple, it seems much more useful to ask: What are the consequences of viewing the self as singular? What are the consequences of viewing the self as multiple? There are lots of consequences, both philosophically and clinically. Adherents of a singular self (e.g., the synthetic ego of the Freudian ego psychologists during the 1950s) promote a certain type of experience as the richest available to us humans; adherents of multiple selves (e.g., today's postmodernism-influenced analysts) are promoting a different type of experience. These differences are reflected in the way clinical material is handled. Believers in a singular self necessarily tend to encourage the patient to work toward the capacity to contain conflictual experiences in consciousness at the same time, working toward a tolerance of ambivalence and an experience of the world not in blacks and whites but in shades of gray. Believers in multiple selves necessarily tend to encourage the patient as much as possible to suspend concerns with continuity and integration and pursue the vividness of experience at the moment. These differences clearly reflect the analyst's own life experience, preferences, and values. But they are generally disguised as claims about what the self really is like.

So, I think it is very helpful for Engler to be asking what the idea of a singular, separate self is used for, and his notion that one of its functions, perhaps its major function, is that it protects us from the dread of emptiness is compelling. But Engler applies a double standard when it comes to his second pair of categories of self-experience, those involving transitory and stable experiences of no-self. These, he argues, are not constructions or compromise formations. They are reality rather than illusion. On what grounds can he make such a claim? It seems to me he is offering us an argument partly based on reason and partly on a certain kind of experience. Engler argues with other authors (e.g., Rubin) who regard self and no-self as alternating states. Grasping the constructed nature of all experience, Engler suggests, is itself not a construction. "The experience of no-self is not a new construction of self." Although I think I know what Engler means by this, I am not wholly convinced. To grasp the constructed nature of all experience seems to boost us up to a sort of meta-level. It reflects a kind of transparent self-consciousness, a consciousness skilled at observing its own processes, and I think Engler is right to implore us not to regard it as equivalent to any other old self-representation. But do we really want to regard it as an unmediated grasping of things as they are? A direct route to fundamental reality? Do we really want to embrace no-self as the only natural state against which all others are measured as illusions?

Maybe, but I'm not convinced. For one thing, I've become very dubious about any claims to anything as "natural." (See Coates 1988 for a history of the enormously complex concept of "nature" and Phillips 2000 for a very thought-provoking meditation on the aesthetic, moral, and political implications of concepts of nature in Darwin and Freud.) Second, given current developments in epistemology, staking out claims for "reality" and "illusion" is a very hazardous business. I think some postmodernists have overdone it in their debunking of any claims about "reality." For example, I'm willing to argue with some degree of certainty that the levitation act of a stage magician is an illusion. But the construction of a separate, singular self is much more complicated; if it is an illusion, it is certainly not the same sort of illusion.

Third, Engler's descriptions of meditative practice, which are so rich and interesting, convey a sense of just how cultivated a no-self state of mind is. This state of mind is the product, as he has shown us, of the arduous development of ego strengths of various sorts and the collaborative result of centuries of cultural development and sophistication. It seems a little strange that it would take all that effort, experience, and accumulated wisdom to get back to what things are simply like naturally. Like all other theories about the human mind and experience, this view of the mind seems to be promoting, on aesthetic and moral grounds, what its practitioner wants it to be.

So, on logical grounds, I think it would be more consistent for Engler to approach his second two kinds of self-experience as constructions among other constructions and then ask what functions they serve and what they are good for (which is clearly quite a lot). But I think there is a whole other dimension to this essay that needs to be addressed—the experiential basis on which Engler's argument clearly rests. I have worked with several patients who have had different kinds of mystical experiences of various sorts. In the old days, analysts could assume they understood what generated those experiences by reducing them to psychodynamics. That practice seems abhorrent to many of us now. Yet, addressing such experiences in the analytic situation is very complicated. They tend to become the basis for the patient's deep convictions concerning the nature of human beings and what life is about. If these encounters with what we might loosely call the "supernatural" are "real," everything else becomes revalued as either illusory or of lesser importance. "Do you think they are real?" the analyst is inevitably asked.

I have struggled a lot with these issues. If I have not personally had some sort of encounter with the divine, for example, how would I know whether it is real or not? I cannot say the patient's experience is "unreal" (ontologically, not subjectively), but I also cannot say it is "real." I am not in a position to make a judgment. I can help them explore its possible contributing factors and implications, which can be very important. And I have told them that if I had experienced some of what they had, it would undoubtedly reorient my own sense of realities and illusions.

Underlying (or rather accompanying) Engler's main argument, that no-self states ought to be regarded as having greater reality than self states, must be the many years he has spent cultivating no-self states. I have had some experience of various sorts of transitory no-self states, but Engler's fourth category of such states is certainly outside my repertoire. Had I had some of the experiences I imagine Engler has had, I too might be impressed by the fundamental naturalness of those states and regard other forms of self-experience as ultimately illusory. Although I don't feel in any position to make that judgment, I can say that I have found Engler's efforts to make sense of his experiences extremely thought provoking and inviting. They illuminate some of the deeper mysteries of human experience.

Reply

CAN WE SAY WHAT THE SELF "REALLY" IS?

JACK ENGLER

I was delighted when Stephen Mitchell agreed to provide a commentary to this chapter. His thinking about theoretical and clinical issues over the years has produced some of the liveliest and most original contributions to contemporary psychoanalysis. *Hope and Dread in Psychoanalysis* (Mitchell 1993) in particular was a springboard for me in trying to rethink these difficult questions about the nature of the self and self-experience. I wasn't aware of his earlier involvement with Eastern thought and meditative experience or the formative influence he says it had on him. But this is clear in his spirited, thoughtful, and insightful commentary. He has put his finger on the key issues and has been forthright in saying where he agrees and where he doesn't.

I appreciate his opinion that the conceptual issues are enormously dense. I don't remember writing a more difficult piece. At times I despaired of completing it. So I'm glad he found the final result an enrichment and an increasingly textured complexity rather than the muddle it often seemed to be. If Mitchell has reservations about my conclusion, that the representation of a singular, separate, continuous self is a compromise formation with defensive aims, so do I. I proposed this view as a hypothesis that might fill in some of the gaps I see in both Buddhist and psychoanalytic thinking. My hope was that it might stimulate further thinking, like Mitchell's commentary does.

I want to start by responding to his main reservation: that I seem to be applying a double standard by claiming that the second two types of self-experience, one involving transitory and the other stable experiences of no-self, are *not* constructions—that grasping the constructed nature of all experience is itself not a construction. He wonders if it wouldn't be logically more consistent to approach these second two kinds of self-experience as constructions among other constructions and then ask, not what the self "really" is, but what the consequences are of viewing the self in one way or the other. This goes to the heart of the matter. The key issue is whether the experience of no-self is a construction like others. If it isn't, then I don't think there is any logical inconsistency in what I'm proposing. The question is whether we can decide this issue. Mitchell says he has come to the conclusion that we can't.

From a Buddhist perspective, it is critical that we do. Ameliorating and ending our self-generated suffering ultimately depends on our primary self-identifications—who we take ourselves to be. This is not a theoretical matter. If we investigate the consequences of each view of self, just as Mitchell recommends, we will find that some lead to the end of suffering while others only create more suffering. So all views about the self are not considered equal. Our well-being depends on our being able to discriminate which is which. The most important difference is not whether the self is singular or multiple, as in the recent psychoanalytic debate, but whether experience is organized around the sense of self or no-self.

This is because the root of all self-generated suffering in the Buddhist view is *attavadupadana*, clinging to self or identifying with the construct of a singular self with its own separate or inherent existence, with all the anxiety, conflict, and underlying alienation that follows. The great difficulty is that this self-construct seems so self-evident in everyday experience. It is embedded in the most deep-rooted characteristic of human thought and perception: the tendency to regard every object of experience or perception as a separate entity or "thing" having its own separate concrete existence and identity and only secondarily related to other "things." Jeremy Hayward (1987) calls this mode of perception and thought "thing-thinking." But "thingness" or "inherent existence" is actually an imputation or attribution, not a characteristic of "things"—an instance of what Whitehead (1959) called the "fallacy of misplaced concreteness." As the Buddhist scholar Anne Klein puts it: "Things simply look, smell and taste more solid, findable and inherently available than they actually are" (1995, 139). Unfortunately, thingness is the most powerful, central, and consequential mental imputation that we can make, especially when we make it of the self: "The strong tendency to experience *anything* as independently existing …rather than any particular personal history is what most fundamentally predisposes one to experience suffering or impose it on others" (130). This "unthinking attribution of inherency" to oneself and others is the "lived ontology that underpins all other experiences of selfhood, including the modern psychological selves" (129), and especially the partly conscious, partly unconscious representation of self as that singular, unique, separate "entity residing deep inside us."

Long before postmodernism, Buddhist and other great yogic-meditative traditions evolved methods for deconstructing this construct of self, not so much to decide a theoretical or philosophical issue about "reality" but to liberate oneself from what today we would call pathogenic beliefs or dysfunctional cognitions. The underlying assumption is that we *can* make this discrimination, in much the same way we assume our patients can make similar discriminations—to become aware of their unconscious beliefs about self and others, examine their consequences, and distinguish "reality" from wish, fantasy, and illusion. We, like our patients, must then mourn the giving up of limiting attachments and identifications that previously seemed just who "I" am.

The problem here is that it isn't possible to prove the nonexistence of something directly: "You can't point to the absence of some inherently existing thing to which the word 'I' refers and say, there you are, I told you it didn't exist!" (Hayward 1987, 68). This is the parent's classic dilemma: when my daughter wakes up crying that there is a monster under the bed, I can't find the nonexistent monster and show it to her. I can only ask her to show me the monster and each time show her that what she thinks is the monster is actually something else. Likewise with the separate, independent self: we can only look closely at everything we think might be evidence of it and see whether an existent "I" is really necessary to explain what we're looking at or whether there is a simpler explanation.

When we inspect our everyday experience this way, what we find are not permanent objects or selves, but perceptual elements—"dharmas" in Buddhist terminology—out of which we construct the objects and selves that we "perceive." These "dharmas" arise and pass away moment by moment as we continually construct our experience. They themselves are not "things" that really exist, any more than atoms or particles are "things." They are the fundamental perceptual-cognitive-affective *events* that go into the moment-by-moment making of our "reality." They are all we can directly experience. Buddhist psychology groups these events into five categories called *skandhas*, literally "heaps" or aggregations: form, feeling, perception, mental formations (including both cognitions and emotions), and consciousness. If we analyze every moment of experience, we will find that it consists simply of constantly changing configurations of these five categories of "reality"-constructing events. Repeatedly looking for but being unable to find either an "I" or "things" among these fundamental constituents of experience is one route to the realization of selflessness and impermanence.

This is the method of "dharma-analysis" in the Buddhist schools: looking at everything that might be evidence of an existent self and finding a simpler and more straightforward explanation for it. The goal is heuristic rather than philosophical. The idea is not to come up with a better description of "reality" but to come to an understanding and then conviction—at least intellectually—that the self, like any "thing," is nowhere to be found among the fundamental constituents of experience.

Cognitive science has recently come to the same conclusion (Hayward 1987). But it makes all the difference in the world *how* you come to it. If you come to it as the result of scientific inference by taking the mind as an object and researching perceptual processes "objectively," it won't affect you much personally. I remember an Australian friend relating her first experience with an electron microscope. She described the awe she felt watching the solidity of the world dissolve under that level of magnification. But she said her sense of self wasn't changed by what she had seen. She still thought and felt in terms of existent selves and "things" that her scientific observation and inference said were illusory.

On the other hand, if you come to this realization by analyzing your own direct experience, your understanding isn't about the world "out there." What you're seeing is *you,* and it affects how you hold yourself and conduct your life. It is one thing to understand that the concept of "I" or "myself" *is* merely a concept; "it is another thing entirely to realize that *this particular* concept referring to *this particular* 'me' is merely a concept"—a representation—"and has nothing corresponding to it" (Hayward 1987, 69). Nothing corresponding to it?!

Dharma analysis is used this way in the living traditions of Theravada and Vajrayana Buddhism. Students are asked to note each passing moment, first in meditation, then in daily life, and to note which "dharmas" they observe entering into that moment. All possible states of experience and consciousness can be mapped out in this way (cf. Nyanatiloka 1971). Of course, this requires considerable training. But as the student's attention becomes more finely tuned, he or she begins to see the world not in familiar terms of "things" and "selves" but in terms of impermanence and absence of "thinghood" or "selfhood." Ideally, this understanding gradually becomes personal and direct rather than merely intellectual or theoretical.

To the extent that this realization remains largely conceptual—is held as an intellectual understanding or conviction, or simply as a belief—it is still a construct, still a theory of self. Here Mitchell is right. No-self can certainly be held as one construction among others. Buddhism even has a term for this, *ditthi,* which means "view" or belief (Narada 1975). And as a view or belief, no-self does not ultimately have transformative power. Nevertheless, the view one holds of self does matter. As a basis for practice, "right view" of self *(samma-ditthi)* directs the inquiry, instructs you to inspect experience for evidence of an existent self; "wrong view" of self *(miccha-ditthi)* blocks inquiry by assuming a self-referent that isn't there. One leads to the end of suffering, the other to more suffering.

No-self only has the transformative effect I've tried to describe when it becomes a lived experience—a "reality" in this sense: when you discover first-hand that this is true of "*me*"! Mitchell is absolutely right when he says that my argument rests on an experiential basis.

This is where practice enters in. For most people, the stable transformation of functioning I've called no-self is normally attained (the Theravada model) or discovered (the Mahayana model) through a long and challenging process of self-inquiry and observation of moments of psychophysical experience as these arise and pass away in the stream of consciousness. This is essentially the same dharma-analysis, but brought to bear on finer and finer levels of observation, much like amplifying the level of magnification, so that one sees more and more features that are not apparent to normal observation.

As I tried to say, what comes into view when you do this is something remarkable: you see *the actual stages in the conceptual-perceptual process by which we dualistically structure our experience in terms of self and objects, impute "thingness" and inherent existence to them, and thereby literally bring a self "in here" and a world "out there" into existence moment by moment*. It was the great discovery of the yogic-meditative traditions, no doubt through long trial and error, that, with the right kind of training, *we can actually retrace the stages in this process experientially*—experience them as they occur. The great traditions have always claimed that once a certain point of advanced training is reached, yogic-meditative practice unfolds sequentially in discrete, recognizable stages—much more so than therapy does, for instance. One reason for this is that these classical stages of practice—the so-called stages of insight (ñanas) in vipassana, for instance—are the stages of perceptual and conceptual processing in reverse. Each "stage" is the experience of a progressively earlier step in this process of reality construction.

Dan Brown (1981) was the first to propose this, first for Tibetan Mahamudra practice and later for Hindu Raj Yoga and Theravada vipassana meditation (Brown, 1986). Hayward (1987) has subsequently detailed the convergence of the Buddhist model of cognition and perception with experimental findings in contemporary cognitive science. The most important of these findings is that the division of experience into "inside" and "outside," "self" and "object," "self" and "other," "self" and "body" arises within the perceptual process itself, from the patterning of the first input to the final stage in which we become conscious of our perceptions and weave them into a framework of meaning.

It is remarkable that we can observe this at all. Ordinarily we are only aware of the end products of this process: thoughts, concepts, percepts, feelings, and sensations that make up our ordinary experience. The stages of the process itself are preconscious and normally outside awareness because they occur within fractions of a second. At the level of magnification that meditative training makes available, however, we can observe the moment-to-moment way in which we bring these elements of our ordinary experience into being. Meditation allows us to get back inside the first half-second of perception where all this occurs, much as the ability to look deeper and deeper into the universe allows us to see what normal vision cannot: how the universe looked in the earlier stages of its evolution. This is the "meta-level" of "transparent self-consciousness" Mitchell wondered about. It's possible to directly see the constructed, momentary, and interdependent nature of self and "reality" by actually experiencing the steps in their construction. Deeper and deeper layers of conceptual presuppositions are discovered and seen through until the entire projection process of perception and its imputation of inherent existence to self and things is directly grasped (Hayward, 1987).

What is missing from a purely cognitive-perceptual model, however, is the affective side of the process. The traditional "stages of insight" in vipassana actually describe the same process of insight, working through, mourning, and acceptance that we are familiar with in therapy. And as in therapy, working through and mourning turn out to be much more important for transformation than insight, no matter how profound. This is the dimension I tried to add to Brown's cognitive model (Engler, 1983).

Discovering that there is no ontological core to consciousness or self that is independent and enduring and no stable "objects" of perception, just the basic qualities of experience (Khandas in pali or skandhas in sanskrit) out of which our thoughts, sensations, feelings, percepts, and representations are being constructed and deconstructed moment by moment, like virtual particles bubbling up in a quantum vacuum and immediately vanishing again, with no "I" or "thing" enduring across the gap between the disappearance of one construction and the arising of the next—this is a profound shock. It is experienced as a free fall into a looking-glass world where, as the Mad Hatter tells Alice, "Things are not as they seem!" It so turns our normal sense of self and reality on its head that, as Niels Bohr once remarked about quantum physics, another window on the micro-universe, if you don't get dizzy thinking about it, you haven't understood it.

Seeing the absence of inherent existence and accepting it are two very different things however. There is an immense sense of increasing loss along the way, both of the solid, stable "thingness" of the perceptual world and the normal sense of self as "that entity within." As in therapy, these losses are extremely difficult to accept, even if what I have lost is a cherished belief rather than some "thing" that never existed in the first place. Again as in therapy, the real challenge is acknowledging and eventually surrendering to what you now see. There can be enormous resistance: evasion, avoidance, denial, flight. Each stage only comes into view when the experience of the previous one has been sufficiently "worked through" and fully accepted. This involves the emotions and will even more than the understanding. In other words, as in other transformational processes, insight necessitates the work of mourning. At each "stage of insight," a perceptual-cognitive shift initiates one of the phases and tasks of mourning work: from acute grief, through disorganization and withdrawal, to a reorganization around a very different sense of self and world (Bowlby, 1969, 1973).

Mitchell asks why "it would take all that effort, experience and accumulated wisdom to get back to what things are simply like naturally." Because here as in other areas of life we make things difficult for ourselves with misattributions, dysfunctional beliefs, painful reenactments, wishful thinking, and unsatisfying attachments. We fight to hold on to what we have and resist any challenges to entrenched positions that feel familiar and secure, especially challenges that can awaken primitive terrors. Why does it take so much effort, experience, and wisdom to see myself more clearly in therapy? No different here I think.

There can be risks in this discovery of no-self. Until there is some experience of it, at least glimpses, it can only be thought about conceptually. And this thinking is invariably from the viewpoint of a separate self. To this "self," no-self is a pessimistic, self-denying, life-denying, nihilistic idea. This is the way it appeared to early European scholars like Weber who lacked the experiential context, the way it appeared to Freud and Alexander and many psychoanalytic thinkers since, and the way it can still appear to some contemporary commentators. It can even appear this way to practitioners of yoga and meditation until they have some direct experience of no-self. Largely for this reason, as Klein (1995:127) points out, "questions about whether the self exists are typically not raised until Buddhist practitioners have been well imbued with the importance of ethics, the power of mindfulness, and the significance of compassion, a vitally important context that is often overlooked in Western discussions of 'selflessness.' Emptiness (no-self) is a topic only for those whose religious and cultural identity is secure." Otherwise the notion of selflessness can undermine a sense of personal agency and moral responsibility. As I pointed out, it can rationalize avoidance of normal developmental tasks around love and work as Mitchell noticed. At worst, it can exacerbate identity problems in self disorders.

A final comment on the question of "reality" versus "illusion," which I agree is a hazardous business given current developments in epistemology. Mitchell's nuanced reflections on this issue stimulated me to rethink it, and I would take a slightly different approach now. A chain of associations led me back to a seminal paper by my earlier collaborator, Dan Brown.

In his comparative study of perceptual-cognitive change in three major systems of meditation (Hindu Raj Yoga, Tibetan Mahamudra, and Theravada vipassana), Brown (1986) points out that although the perceptual changes reported at each stage are structurally similar in all three—all retrace steps in the perceptual process—the way these changes are experienced depends on the approach the system takes toward the fundamental problem of continuity and discontinuity in experience. This influences the viewpoint from which one observes during meditation and therefore the way the different stages will be experienced.

All three systems acknowledge the essential discontinuity of awareness and manifestation in immediate experience. They agree that psychophysical events are in a process of incessant change. However, the practitioner of each system experiences the nature of the change differently. From the dualistic viewpoint of Samkhya philosophy, moment-to-moment vicissitudes of mental and physical events are experienced in Hindu Raj Yoga as a continuous transformation of the "same stuff" *(ekatattva)*. From the viewpoint of selflessness and dependent origination in Buddhist practice, change is experienced as a succession of "momentary" *(ksanika)* and discontinuous discrete events. Events unfold in a *continuous* manner for the practitioner of Raj Yoga and in a *discontinuous* manner for the Buddhist meditator. How about it? Is "reality" continuous or discontinuous? It may be both, depending—as quantum physics has taught us—on how we set up our "experiment." In other words, as Brown says, this paradox may be inherent in yogic-meditative practice.

The same paradox seems to run like a thread through Western physics and the social sciences: field theory versus particle theory in quantum physics; continuous versus discontinuous models of mental health and illness in the social sciences. Depending on our point of observation, that is, how we construct our experiment, light reveals itself to be either wavelike (continuous) or particle-like (discontinuous). What is light "really"? Our mind wants it to be this or that. Calling it a "wavicle," as some physicists like to do, seems just another attempt to turn it into a unitary "thing" with specified properties.

So in rethinking this issue, it may be that a particular meditation system does not disclose what "reality" is. It may only reveal how we construct it given our perceptual bias or the point of observation from which we start. But what all these disciplines do is take us back through the process of self- and world-construction itself. Not so much to come up with a "true" description of reality, though they often claim to do so—as I may have as well—but to show us firsthand, in our direct immediate experience, that any representation of self is just that, a construction. The point is to loosen the anxious grip we have on ourselves and initiate the mourning and grief work that will finally allow life and experience to flow unimpeded by maladaptive fixations about who "I" am. That which observes in silence and wonder—"with infinite affection"—the moment-to-moment constructions of self and world is not, cannot be, the result of constructive activity itself.

QUESTIONER: When there is no "I," who is free?

SRI NISARGADATTA. The world is free of a mighty nuisance. Good enough!

I want to express my appreciation to Stephen Mitchell again for once more stimulating me to think beyond what I thought I knew.

Note

1. Emmanuel Ghent (personal communication) has suggested that Engler's view of the illusory nature of the self and the ultimate reality

of no-self derives from meditative practice in which the experience of selfness at any particular moment is so ephemeral as to render any sense of self illusory. In a sense, it is the extreme of multiplicity, where the utter impermanence of moment-to-moment consciousness is observed so closely that the thinker of the thought disappears—no self. Language becomes very difficult here, because one then becomes very "centered" and "whole." Who, then, is the one who is centered? Is this not a version of self? But on a less abstract level, the sense of no-self is closer to the divestiture of narcissism, the total absence of defensiveness. If there is no self, there is nothing or nobody that needs protection.

References

Aaronson, H. 1998. Review of *Psychotherapy and Buddhism: Toward an Integration,* by Jeffrey Rubin. *Journal of Buddhist Ethics* 5:63–73.

Alexander, F. 1931. Buddhist Training as an Artificial Catatonia. *Psychoanalytic Review* 18:129–45.

Bion, W. 1963. *Elements of Psychoanalysis.* London: Heinemann.

———. 1970. *Attention and Interpretation.* London: Tavistock.

Blanck, G., and R. Blanck. 1974. *Ego Psychology: Theory and Practice.* New York: Columbia University Press

———. 1979. *Ego Psychology II: Psychoanalytic Developmental Psychology.* New York: Columbia University Press, 1979.

Bromberg, P. M. (1998). *Standing in the Spaces: Essays on Clinical Process, Trauma and Dissociation.* Hillsdale, N.J.: The Analytic Press.

Brown, D. 1986. The Stages of Meditation in Cross-Cultural Perspective. In *Transformations of Consciousness,* ed. K. Wilber, J. Engler, and D. Brown. Boston: Shambhala.

———. 1993. Affective Development, Psychopathology and Adaptation. In *Human Feelings,* ed. S. Ablon, D. Brown, E. Khantzian, and J. Mack. Hillsdale, N.J.: The Analytic Press.

Brown, D., and J. Engler. 1986. The Stages of Mindfulness Meditation: A Validation Study. Parts 1 and 2. In *Transformations of Consciousness,* ed. K. Wilber, J. Engler, and D. Brown. Boston: Shambhala. Reprinted from *Journal of Transpersonal Psychology* 12, no. 2 (1980): 143–92.

Brown, G. 1981. Mahamudra Meditation: Stage and Contemporary Cognitive Psychology. Doctoral Dissertation. University of Chicago.

Buddhaghosa. 1975. *The Path of Purification (Visuddhimagga).* Trans. Nyanamoli. Kandy: Buddhist Publication Society. Reprint, Boulder, Colo.: Shambhala, 1976.

Coates, P. 1988. Nature: Western Attitudes since Ancient Times. Berkeley: University of California Press.

Cohen, A. 2000. *What Is Enlightenment?* 17 (spring/summer):94–101.

Davies, J. Davies, J. M. (1996). Linking the "Pre-Analytic" with the Post-Classical: Integration, Dissociation, and the Multiplicity of Unconscious Processes. *Contemporary Psycholanalysis,* 32, 553–556.

Deikman, A. 1966. Deautomatization and the Mystic Experience. *Psychiatry* 29:324–38.

———. 1982. *The Observing Self: Mysticism and Psychotherapy.* Boston: Beacon Hill Press.

Eigen, M. 1986. *The Psychotic Core.* Northvale, N.J.: Jason Aronson.

———. 1993. *The Electrified Tightrope.* Northvale, N.J.: Jason Aronson.

Engler, J. 1983a. Buddhist Satipatthana-vipassana Meditation and an Object Relations Model of Developmental-Therapeutic Change: A Clinical Case Study. Ph.D. diss., University of Chicago.

———. 1983b. Vicissistudes of the Self According to Psychoanalysis and Buddhism: A Spectrum Model of Object Relations Development. *Psychoanalysis and Contemporary Thought* 6:29–72.

———. 1986. Therapeutic Aims in Psychotherapy and Meditation: Developmental Stages in the Representation of Self. In *Transformations of Consciousness,* ed. K. Wilber, J. Engler, and D. Brown. Boston: Shambhala.

———. 1999. Practicing for Awakening. Part 2. *Insight,* spring, 31–35.

Epstein, M. 1989. Forms of Emptiness: Psychodynamic, Meditative and Clinical Perspectives. *Journal of Transpersonal Psychology* 2:61–71.

———.1995. *Thoughts Without a Thinker.* New York: Basic Books.

Farber, L. (1996). *The Ways of the Will: Essays Toward a Psychology and Psychopathology of Will.* New York: Basic Books.

Ferris, T. 1997. *The Whole Shebang: A State-of-the-Universe Report.* New York: Touchstone.

Fingarette, H. 1963. *The Self in Transformation.* New York: Basic Books.

Freud, S. 1930. *Civilization and Its Discontents.* In *Standard Edition,* 21:55–145.

London: Hogarth Press, 1961.

Geertz, C. 1979. From the Native's Point of View: On the Nature of Anthropological Understanding. In *Local Knowledge: Further Essays in Interpretive Anthropology*. New York: Basic Books.

Gill, M. M., and M. Brenman. 1959. *Hypnosis and Related States: Psychoanalytic Studies in Regression*. New York: International Universities Press.

Goldstein, J., and J. Kornfield, 1987. *Seeking the Heart of Wisdom: The Path of Insight Meditation*. Boston: Shambhala.

Harvey, P. 1995. *The Selfless Mind*. Surrey, England: Curzon Press.

Hayward, J. 1987. *Shifting Worlds, Changing Minds: Where the Sciences and Buddhism Meet*. Boston: New Science Library, Shambhala.

Herrigel, E. 1971. *Zen in the Art of Archery*. New York: Vintage Books.

Kakar, S. 1970. *The Inner World: A Psychoanalytic Study of Childhood and Society in India*. Oxford: Oxford University Press.

Kapleau, P. 1979. *Zen Dawn in the West*. New York: Anchor Press/Doubleday.

Kernberg, O. 1976. *Object Relations Theory and Clinical Psychoanalysis*. New York: Jason Aronson.

Klein, A. 1995. *Meeting the Great Bliss Queen: Buddhists, Feminists and the Art of the Self*. Boston: Beacon Press.

Kohut, H. 1971. *The Analysis of the Self*. New York:

————.1977. *The Restoration of the Self*. New York: International Universities Press.

————.1984. *How Does Analysis Cure?* Chicago: University of Chicago Press.

Kornfield, J. 1993. *A Path with Heart*. New York: Bantam.

Kris, E. 1952. *Psychoanalytic Explorations in Art*. New York: International Universities Press.

Larson, E. 1999. *Isaac's Storm: A Man, a Time and the Deadliest Storm in History*. New York: Crown.

Levinson, D., et al. 1978. *The Seasons of a Man's Life*. New York: Knopf.

Loewald, H. 1960. On the Therapeutic Action of Psychoanalysis. *International Journal of Psychoanalysis* 41:16–33.

————. 1978. *Psychoanalysis and the History of the Individual*. New Haven: Yale University Press.

Mahasi Sayadaw. 1965. *Progress of Insight*. Kandy, Sri Lanka: Buddhist Publication Society.

Mahler, M., Pine, F., and Bergmar, A. 1975. *The Psychological Birth of the*

Human Infant.

Mitchell, S. 1988. *Relational Concepts in Psychoanalysis: An Integration.* Boston: Harvard University Press.

———1992. True Selves, and the Ambiguity of Authenticity. In N. J. Skolnick and S. C. Warshaw (eds.), *Relational Perspectives in Psychoanalysis* (pp. 1–20). Hillsdale, N.J.: Analytic Press.

———. 1993. *Hope and Dread in Psychoanalysis.* New York: Basic Books.

Namgyal, T. T. 1986. *Mahamudra: The Quintessence of Mind and Meditation.* Boston: Shambhala.

Narada. 1975. *A Manual of Abhidhamma.* Kandy, Sri Lanka: Buddhist Publication Society.

Nisargadatta Maharaj. 1973. *I Am That.* Durham, N.C.: Acorn Press.

Phillips, A. 2000. *Darwin's Worms: On Life Stories and Death Stories.* New York: Basic Books.

Pizer, S. 1998. *Building Bridges: The Negotiation of Paradox in Psychoanalysis.* Hillsdale, N.J.: Analytic Press.

Rizzuto, A., 1979. *The Birth of the Living God.* Chicago: University of Chicago Press.

Roland, A. 1988. *In Search of Self in India and Japan: Toward a Cross-Cultural Psychology.* Princeton: Princeton University Press.

Rubin, J. 1997. Psychoanalysis Is Self-Centered. In *Soul on the Couch: Spirituality, Religion and Morality in Contemporary Psychoanalysis,* ed. C. Spezzano and G. Spezzano. Hillsdale, N.J.: Analytic Press.

———. 1996. *Psychotherapy and Buddhism: Towards an Integration.* New York: Pelenum.

Schafer, R. 1958. Regression in the Service of the Ego: The Relevance of a Psychoanalytic Concept for Personality Assessment. In *Assessment of Human Motives,* ed. G. Lindzey. New York: Rinehart.

———. 1976. *A New Language for Psychoanalysis.* New York: International Universities Press.

Sterba, R. F. 1934. The Fate of the Ego in Analytic Therapy. *International Journal of Psychoanalysis* 15:117–26.

Stolorow, S., B. Brandchaft, and G. Atwood. 1987. *Psychoanalytic Treatment: An Intersubjective Approach.* Hillsdale, N.J.: Analytic Press.

Suler, J. 1993. *Contemporary Psychoanalysis and Eastern Thought.* Albany: State University of New York Press.

Sullivan, H. S. 1938. The Data of Psychiatry. In *The Fusion of Psychiatry and the Social Sciences.* New York: Norton, 1964.

———. 1950. The Illusion of Personal Individuality. In *the Fusion of Psychiatry and the Social Sciences.* New York: Norton, 1964.

Suzuki, D. T. 1956. *Zen Buddhism: Selected Writings.* New York: Doubleday/Anchor.

Vajirañana, P. 1975. *Buddhist Meditation in Theory and Practice.* Kuala Lumpur: Buddhist Missionary Society.

Van Dusen, W. 1957. Zen Buddhism and Western Psychotherapy. *Psychologia: An International Journal of Psychology in the Orient* 1:229–30.

———. 1958. Wu Wei, No-Mind and the Fertile Void in Psychotherapy. *Psychologia: An International Journal of Psychology in the Orient* 1:253–56.

Walsh, R., and Shapiro, D. (Eds.). 1983. *Beyond Health and Normality: Explorations of Exceptional Psychological Well-Being.* New York: Van Nostrand.

Watts, A. 1957. *The Way of Zen.* New York: Vintage Books.

———. 1958. *The Spirit of Zen.* New York: Grove Press.

Whitehead, A. N. 1929. *Process and Reality.* New York: The Free Press.

Winnicott, D., 1958. The Capacity to Be Alone. In *The Maturational Process and the Facilitating Environment.* New York: International Universities Press.

———. 1960. Ego Distortion in Terms of True and False Self. In *The Maturational Process and the Facilitating Environment.* New York: International Universities Press, 1965.

———. 1971. *Playing and Reality.* London: Tavistock.

Yalom, I. 1975. *Theory and Practice of Group Psychotherapy.* New York: Basic Books.

CHAPTER 2

Tibetan Buddhism
and a Mystical Psychoanalysis

MARK FINN

*This paper is dedicated to the memory of Phillip Aranow
Ph.D., who contributed much to the dialogue between
Buddhism and psychoanalysis.*

For almost 2,500 years of Buddhist history, psychological and spiritual discourses have been inseparable. Our present predicament of living in a world where they are seen as separate and as requiring a rhetorical bridgework is quite recent. The purpose of this essay is to show how traditional Tibetan Buddhist narratives present the simultaneous duality and inseparability of spiritual and psychological life. Since Buddhism is a path of psychological growth, I will suggest that this "not one, not two" stance, to use Shunryu Suzuki's (1970) phrase, is at the center of the Buddhist practice. It is my hope that psychoanalytic readers will see that almost a thousand years ago Buddhist teachers were representing, in narrative, such basic psychoanalytic discoveries as Oedipal dynamics, transitional space, object relations, and transference. Tibetan Buddhism will be shown to have been practiced in relationships that look like psychoanalysis in a traditional, non-Western religious context. Lastly, I will reflect on how these stories are also implicit fables about the endlessly recurrent psychoanalytic issues of authority and diversity in practice.

Before turning to the Buddhist texts themselves, I would like to state my own purposes and sense of our current situation. Adam Phillips (1995) advises that the central question for a psychoanalyst is not, What theory do I embrace? but, What kind of person do I want to be? What kind of world do I want to live in? Speaking for myself, I very much want to be a responsible and ethical psychotherapist. A seemingly modest statement in a way, but a clarifying one. I once heard the Dalai Lama describe himself as a "Buddhist monk—no more, no less." I don't want to be a monk or a guru, but I do want to live in a world where something that gets referred to as the mystical is a real experience, not a philosophy. As I work toward these goals, I am duly reminded that the conversation between Buddhism and psychoanalysis is really a version of an older and larger tension between science and religion.

When I become submerged in this argument, I have found it helpful to remember that Buddhism posits a version of multiple determination. Buddhism teaches that in any moment, any thing, any matter, has an enlightened and a neurotic possibility. Nothing is always enlightened; nothing is always neurotic. There is then some madness and some wisdom in anything we say, think, or feel. With that view in mind, let us consider the heuristic notion that the conversation between Buddhism and psychoanalysis seems to take three recurrent forms. Rubin (1996) has made an elegant and extensive presentation of these issues. The first view, usually credited to or blamed on Freud, regards spiritual practices as either regressive, pathological, or both. It's either sentimental nostalgia, dreamy cowardice, or outright mental disorder. There is both a psychoanalytic and a biological version of this view, frequently characterized as "reductionist." However, if we didn't take this skeptical view of religious and spiritual life seriously, there wouldn't be a need for this dialogue at all. I can't get through a clinical day without considering the defensive purposes to which spirituality is put or the reality of mental illness. The interesting discovery for me has been that the closer I get to the spiritual traditions themselves, the more apparent it is that they have sophisticated psychological understandings of the neurotic purposes to which spiritual practice and ideas can be put. The Tibetan doctors I have spoken with seem to have a diagnostic knowledge of schizophrenia, bipolar disorder, and childhood autism. As a psychotherapist, I felt empathy and amusement when the American Zen teacher John Daido Loori told me about the narcissistic rage he occasionally faces when he has to tell aspiring students that they need more psychotherapy before continuing Zen training. It seems that in some segments of the Buddhist community psychotherapy is seen as at best a remedial project, like being told one has to repeat a grade in school.

The second major view is best represented by transpersonal psychology, which has rescued spirituality and religion from reductionistic contempt, ironically by studying meditation scientifically (Wilber, Engler, and Brown 1986). Would Jung be pleased to see psychoanalytic candidates trooping off in significant numbers to meditation retreats? Our present cultural movement is interesting because post-psychedelic researchers and scholars located in whatever is left of a counterculture find themselves in the company of evangelical Christians and Mormons, all recruiting behavioral and laboratory data to show that religion is good for us and has more to do with maturity than regression. This is not just an ironic postmodernist observation, because the Buddhist-psychoanalytic dialogue is not independent of the Buddhist-Judeo-Christian dialogue. Perhaps Buddhism is of special interest to psychoanalysts because it allows us to have a spiritual life and seemingly sidesteps the traditionally embarrassing question of belief in God. As I survey this landscape and my own feelings, I appreciate the precision of R. D. Laing's (1967) phrase "the politics of experience." Who is on top? Who is entitled to categorize now? The problem with this transpersonal view, as Rubin points out, is that there is a tendency to idealize spiritual practices, and things Asian in general. I recall a roundtable of leaders in the psychospiritual community, and like all roundtables it got somewhat competitive. One solution to that problem became the fantasy that Tibetans did not need psychotherapy because their parenting practices were so perfect that they could launch themselves directly into the higher spiritual realms. The Americans all nodded sadly and wisely about our tragically dysfunctional families. Unfortunately, this reassuring mood of unanimity was disrupted by the only actual Tibetan in the room—Gelek Rinpoche. He chuckled ruefully and remarked that Tibetans would be only too glad to complain about their parents to their spiritual teachers except that it would be considered bad manners.

The last group I will call integrationists for want of a more felicitous phrase (see Epstein 1995, 1998; Finn 1992, 1998; Suler 1993; Rosenblum 1999). This is currently the most fashionable view and represents a maturation of the Western experience of Buddhism. Western therapists have found meditation psychotherapeutically useful in their own lives and in the lives of their patients. In addition, there is a recognition that psychoanalysis at times seems like a spiritual practice for both patient and analyst. Subscribers to this view feel that the transpersonalists have neglected the spiritual depths of psychoanalysis as much as the Freudians failed to respect the psychological acumen of contemplative practice. Hans Loewald (1978) is the mainstream psychoanalyst most often cited because he argued that Freud had found his way to the mystical place of eternity beyond time and space, and turned away because of personality and cultural context. Loewald concluded that the religious dimensions of personality may be as repressed in our day as sexuality was in Freud's. While more controversial, Wilfred R. Bion (1970) put the mystical at the heart of psychoanalysis. The overlap between psychoanalysis and spiritual practice in general, and Buddhism in particular, is that they are both strategies for the deployment of attention. All spiritual practices require different uses of attention, and all psychotherapies direct attention to different aspects of psychological life.

When I was in college, I had a woman friend who was practicing Zen by counting her breath. She decided she wanted to explore spiritual practice in a more matriarchal environment, so she arranged to do a retreat at a contemplative convent. In her first interview, she informed her spiritual director that she did not know how to pray, that she had only been trained to pay attention to her breath. The sister who was directing her asked if she thought there was really any difference. Are spiritual practices "folk" psychotherapies? Is psychoanalysis a spiritual practice posing as a treatment? The first clinical psychologist in Japan, Hayao Kawai (1996), recalls that he was eighteen in 1945 when he saw the horror that World War II had inflicted on Japan and the world. He felt that Japanese religious culture, including Buddhism, had supported the violence of the war effort. He repudiated all things Japanese, especially Japanese religion. He came to America and became a psychologist. However, in the years of doing psychotherapy he found himself coming back to Buddhism because the discipline of therapy demands a simultaneous focus and openness of attention. He modestly concludes that he has become just a vague Buddhist, but he recommends having a certain confidence in that vague Buddhism. This vague Buddhism that Kawai advocates is appealing to those wary of religious zealotry and orthodoxy, but is criticized by some Buddhist teachers who are concerned that this type of synthesis of Buddhism and psychotherapy could result in a dilution of spiritual discipline (Merzel 1994).

To summarize, as a meditating psychoanalyst I live in a complex world, balancing on a razor's edge. Do Buddhist teachings offer any help? In many places of Mahayana Buddhist practice the Heart Sutra is recited daily. It is very short—usually less than a page long. Buddhism can be long-winded, but it is often marvelously brief and pithy. In the Heart Sutra, the Buddha and his disciples are meditating together when Shariputra asks Avalokitesvara how to practice the transcendental knowledge called in Sanskrit *prajnaparamita*. The answer is as complete and satisfying a statement of everything that I have ever encountered. Avalokitesvara tells Shariputra that form is not other than emptiness and emptiness is not other than form. There is no purity and no impurity. There is no ignorance and no end of ignorance. There is no old age and no death, and no end of old age and death; there is no suffering, no origin of suffering, no cessation of suffering, and no path; there is no wisdom, no attainment, and no nonattainment. Therefore there is no obscuration of mind and no fear.

"Form" is all that is dual: time, space, my feelings about my childhood, etc.—all that is psychological; "emptiness" is eternity beyond concept, time, and space. But form is also form, and emptiness is also emptiness, obviously; and yet form is emptiness and emptiness is form. We live in a world where psyche is psyche, spirit is spirit, but spirit is psyche and psyche is spirit. But why stop there? God is God, Jesus is Jesus; Jesus is God, God is Jesus. Another less spiritual, but often more pressing discourse is gender. Male is male and female is female. Male is female, but female is also male. Or in clinical terms, there's the real relationship, and there's the transference. But the real relationship comes from the transference, and the transference comes from the real relationship. No single proposition is privileged over another. It is the simultaneity that moves us to transcendent wisdom. All of this is very mystical, all of this is very practical. Many years ago Stephen Pepper (1942) said there are four "world hypotheses" in Western science: formism, mechanism, organism, and contextualism. All four are contrary and mutually exclusive. The only solution is a post-rational eclecticism, as he calls it. Is that another way of saying prajnaparamita?

While the Heart Sutra articulates the Buddhist view that absolute spiritual truth and relative psychological truth are both separate and identical, one can still ask how this works out in practice. Because meditation is a solitary activity even when done in a group, the discussion of the psychology of meditation has been that the process of change in meditative practice is a "one person" psychology. I believe this is a serious misreading of Buddhist teaching and practice. Even the Heart Sutra is a dialogue. If meditation is practiced within the context of a relationship with a teacher, the parallels to psychoanalysis become even more apparent. Tibetan Buddhism has elaborated the relational aspect of Buddhism in a rich biographical literature and in meditation techniques involving visualizations of various spiritual beings. James B. Robinson (1996) observes that biography and history are more characteristic of Tibetan than Indian Buddhism, and that Tibetan accounts of Indian teachers are the most accurate. I would add that the Tibetan emphasis on history and biography also distinguishes it from Zen. Robinson recommends that the biographies of Tibetan saints be analyzed along what he calls vertical and horizontal dimensions.

The vertical dimension of myth allows the saints to "humanize" the transcendent; they make the status of an enlightened being accessible to the human level. They give living focus for devotion. They exemplify spiritual triumph in ways understandable to those who still struggle. They give hope in the sense that if they were able to achieve their goal, so might the aspirant who makes the requisite effort. And the symbolic levels of the stories reveal how such a transition may take place. This value is transcendent in the sense that it does not depend upon historical accuracy.

> But the horizontal dimension of history is not to be ignored. The claim of these stories to historicity anchors this vertical linking of spiritual success and the ordinary life. The saints represent continuity; they bind the great figures of the past to our own history-bound humanity. They are links in the chain of enlightened beings going back to the Buddha himself, the source of highest wisdom and the supreme teacher in the present day. By their insight and success, the Indian saints guarantee the value of the Dharma and preserve the purity of transmission. They legitimate lineages of spiritual masters living in times closer to our own. The fact that these masters link the present with the sacred past makes their historical existence very important. The alternative is a

rupture in the tradition. So this genre derives its value
not just from doctrine but also from its affirmation of the
sacred in the process of history in which we all live.
(Robinson 1996, 67)

For the psychoanalytic reader, it should be emphasized that these Tibetan
biographies are stories of relationships. These are the links in a chain of relationships going back over centuries. One person helped another who helped
another down to the present. Greek myths have been traditionally used by
psychoanalysis to narratively represent psychic process (e.g., Oedipus and
Narcissus). The Tibetan stories go further in that they offer narrative representations of relationships wherein psychological and spiritual transformations take place. There is no single, exclusive path of transformation, because
there are many stories, even if they are all Buddhist. Each story represents a
different model of the helping relationship, and each story represents a different successful personal transformation. The stories taken together are a
collective narrative representation of a genuine eclecticism. Some saints get
married, others become monks. Some become respectable, some become
outrageous. Discovering the no-self of Buddhism and one's authentic idiosyncratic creative self are not separate goals. Perhaps it is this emphasis on
the individual messy personalities and the historical nature of the Tibetan
narratives that makes them seem so related to psychoanalysis. In a recent
popular book titled *The Gifts of the Jews,* Thomas Cahill argues that Judaism
broke with other religions by positing a linear history (with past and future),
as opposed to a cyclical view of time, and by privileging the unique individual over the group identity. Such a view of Judaism supports the view of
the Jewish roots of psychoanalysis. Cahill argues that Buddhism and Hinduism are traditional cyclical religions lacking a sense of the past and future
and of the individual. What I am arguing is that the Tibetan narratives meet
Cahill's criteria of history and the importance of the individual. Tibetan
Buddhism is elaborating a view and set of practices that regard history and
personhood as inseparable from mystical eternity. Certainly they are not the
only traditions to do so, but I hope these stories demonstrate the importance of their contribution.

I have examined the stories of Naropa and Milarepa in depth elsewhere
(Finn 1992, 1998). What I would like to do here is acquaint the non-Buddhist

reader with the early Kagyu teachers and then reflect on some general propositions that emerge. The Kagyu lineage begins in Buddhist India with Tilopa
(Situpa, 1988; Gyaltsen 1990). Tilopa, while regarded as mystically related to
the historical Buddha, achieves his awakening without a human teacher. His
method of meditation was to grind sesame seeds into oil for a bordello where
he was employed. There is little known of his early life, but it is mentioned
that his practice would allow him to transcend "his family's arrogance"—a
tantalizing detail for a psychoanalyst and suggestive that issues of character
and familial emotional climate were not irrelevant to his spiritual path. The
Tibetan Buddhist mystics were given to singing spontaneous songs of realization called *dohas*. Tilopa sang:

> *Sesame oil is the essence.*
> *Although the ignorant know that it is in the sesame seed,*
> *They do not understand the way of cause, effect and becoming,*
> *And therefore are not able to extract the essence, the sesame oil.*
> *Although innate coemergent wisdom*
> *Abides in the heart of all beings*
> *It is not shown by the guru*
> *It cannot be realized*
> *Just like the sesame oil that remains in the seed*
> *It does not appear.*
> *One removes the husk by heating the sesame,*
> *And the sesame oil, the essence appears.*

> (Trungpa 1980, 128)

Several foundational assumptions of Tibetan Buddhism are contained in
this song. The inseparability of the absolute spiritual from the relative psychological as described earlier underlies the song, but with the addition that
purposeful efforts in the relative are required to release the innate absolute.
Tilopa is also a classic tantric yogi. Tantra is a tradition of spiritual attitudes
and practice originating in India, where it developed in both Hindu and Buddhist forms. Tibetan Buddhism has been called tantric Buddhism because
its incorporation of tantric practices distinguishes it from Zen or Theravada
Buddhism. The term *tantra* is difficult to define but translates as "thread" or
"continuity." It is a radically experiential approach. The Tibetan teacher

Trungpa Rinpoche says: "In the tantric notion of indestructibility, there is no ground, no basic premise and no particular philosophy except one's own experience which is extremely powerful and dynamic. It is a question of being rather than figuring out what to be, how to be" (Trungpa 1981, 27). This approach excludes nothing: our ideas about what is spiritual serve as an insulating buffer to the raw experience of the spiritual. Tilopa gains his realization working in a whorehouse, not a monastery. In tantra, nothing is excluded, and the whole tendency of the mind to exclude is challenged.

I recall that at the first Tibetan ceremony I ever attended I noticed all this strange-looking food on the altar. At first I took it to be unusual Tibetan offerings, but then I realized that American junk foods were being sanctified. It was explained that offering junk food is an expression of confidence in the transformative possibilities of meditative practice. Psychoanalysis, I am suggesting, has a tantric aspect. The directive to exclude nothing, however repellent, establishes a "thread" and "continuity" without limits. Introductions to tantric teachings warn of the dangers of an unconditional approach; "crazy wisdom" has its risks. The lack of conceptual reference points puts sanity and morality up for grabs. These hazards are mitigated by a relationship to the spiritual teacher. Devotion to the teacher reduces pride. The relationship "contains" the intense experience of the student, and the teacher offers both guidance and interpretations.

The paradox of Tilopa is that he recommends having a human guru but accomplishes the path without one. The lineage that begins with him continues unbroken to this day. This lineage, which regards devotion to the guru as essential to practice, starts by offering an example of a person who completes the journey without one. The teacher-based system with its inherent hierarchical structure rests on the subversive foundation of a founder unconnected to any hierarchy. Like Freud, Tilopa stayed close to the ordinary and to sexuality, and made his discoveries outside organized academia. While most of us benefit from teachers and analysts, both Tilopa and Freud serve as examples of the solitary and more autonomous basis of our self-exploration.

In the Tibetan tantric practice of Guru Yoga, one is instructed to visualize a buddha, in some cases to visualize the person of one's teacher as a buddha, and, after an elaborate construction of mental imagery, one visualizes becoming that which one has visualized. Why should one have to work so hard to claim our essential nature? The Japanese master Dogen

(Tanahashi 1985), who founded the Soto school of Zen, regarded grappling with this paradox the basis of spiritual practice. If we are already a buddha, why must we meditate? A student asked a Zen master, "If the nature of wind is unborn and undying, why do you fan?" The master replied, "You know nothing of wind or fanning." Tilopa tells us the seeds must be ground. The stories of his successors suggest that that grinding is related the experiences observed in psychoanalysis.

Tilopa's most famous student was the Indian prince and scholar Naropa. Naropa's parents wanted him to continue their royal line and demanded that he marry, which he did. But he defied them by never consummating the marriage. After eight years of his sexual standoff, Naropa was free to pursue Buddhist studies in a university setting. He was a very successful scholar and achieved a position of leadership in the academic community. One night he had a disturbing vision of an old woman who told him that he understood only the words of Buddhist teachings and not their inner sense. Naropa accepted this challenge and went in search of Tilopa, whom the old woman had mentioned. Naropa's concepts of spirituality were shattered in his attempts to reach Tilopa. He came upon diseased animals and people and tried to avoid them only to discover that these resulting images were manifestations of Tilopa. He encountered people performing antisocial acts and violating various Buddhist precepts. Each time he tried to avoid involvement, it always turned out Tilopa was at work. Each time he resolved not to be ruled by his prejudices, he always failed. He was exhorted to look within to the dakini within him. (The Tibetan psychospiritual world is densely populated with not only familiar-looking Buddhas but fearsome, monstrous, or erotic representations of our potential for psychological awakening. Some of these representations seem to derive from Indian tantra, others from the indigenous pre-Buddhist religion of Bon. The pantheon of representations is as ornate as any European cathedral. These representations, like the guru in Guru Yoga, are understood to be both inside and outside.)[1] The dakini that Tilopa directed Naropa to attend to is a female representation of enlightenment in the form of anger and lust. His practice was to regard enlightenment as identical with sex and aggression. This is not an easy practice, and Naropa became suicidal before Tilopa agreed to engage him more directly.

The penultimate teaching required Naropa to remember the moment of his conception and feel hatred toward his father and longing toward his

mother. Tilopa cautioned him that some meditators may become too frightened of an original primal scene to proceed. (It is frankly remarkable that the
discovery of the importance of the Oedipus complex by Indian Buddhists
has received so little attention from psychoanalysis.[2] Of course, the Greeks are
the source of its myth and drama, but the Tibetans give its imagery a central place in techniques of psychological transformation.) The result of this
"working through" by Naropa was a new experience of his body and sexuality. He consummated a relationship with a young woman and went on to
become a teacher living in the forest. Although many conventional practitioners once considered him disreputable and unsavory, Naropa is now
known as a great master.

The Tibetans appear to have worked out a flexible relationship to the
Oedipus complex. The resolution of oedipal anxieties is clearly central to the
journey of Naropa, and the inclusion of similar directed imagery in the *Book
of the Dead* suggests a universal applicability consistent with classical Freudian
theory. However, oedipal issues are not even mentioned in the stories of
Naropa's descendants, who struggle with dynamics more easily correlated
with post-Freudian psychologies.

Naropa's most famous student, and the first Tibetan of this lineage, was
Marpa (Tsang 1982). Marpa was born to prosperous farmers. His parents
were concerned about his hot temper and stubbornness from an early age. So
they encouraged Marpa to pursue religious studies in the hope that meditation would tame him. He was a single-minded student who also had a talent
for languages. After studying with Tibetan teachers, he wanted to get closer
to the source by going to India. He overcame his parents' objections and
contacted Naropa in India. If the account has a distinguishing feature, it is
that Naropa frequently directed Marpa to study with other masters. In one
memorable episode, Naropa sent Marpa to study with Kukuripa (Tibetan:
Shiwa Sangpo). Kukuripa lived on an island in the middle of a poisonous lake
with many wild dogs. When Marpa told the wild-looking teacher that Naropa
had sent him and requested instruction, Kukuripa denounced Naropa as a
fraud. Kukuripa then asked him if he was angry at his criticism of Naropa.
Marpa admitted his anger. Kukuripa responded that Marpa's anger indicated
that Naropa was his root or primary guru.

Upon completing his training with Kukuripa, Marpa returned to Naropa.
Naropa asked if he had completed his mission. Marpa replied yes, whereupon

Naropa began denouncing Kukuripa as second-rate. Marpa wondered if it was in the nature of these teachers to be so competitive. Naropa then asked if Marpa was angry. Marpa said no and Naropa declared that this indicated that he, Naropa, was truly Marpa's primary guru.

Given the emphasis on Marpa's temper in every text, does this story point to some working through? Naropa was able to contain and tame Marpa yet also establish that he, Naropa, was not the only source of teachings. Naropa established a relationship but subverted a narrow definition of his own authority by recruiting another teacher. Again, hierarchy was both established and challenged.

Marpa made several trips to India and spent almost twenty years there. He eventually established a life different from that of the academic monks or wild forest yogis. He married a woman with no shortage of will herself, established a family, and managed a prosperous agricultural estate. In portraits he appears as a large, physically powerful man with a crewcut. I imagine him as a combination of Zorba the Greek and Prospero. The story of his relationship with his most important student, Milarepa, is the most famous of these narratives and the first of a Tibetan guru working with a Tibetan disciple in this lineage.

Milarepa's biography (Lhallungpa 1982) is one of the great works of world religious literature, richer in detail, style, and scope than any of the other Kagyu narratives (for a more detailed examination of Milarepa, see Finn 1992). Early life was very difficult for Milarepa. His father died when he was young, and the estate was left to an aunt and uncle who treated him, his mother, and his sister as slaves. Milarepa's mother became possessed by vengeful rage and demanded that Milarepa learn black magic and murder the aunt and uncle. When Milarepa hesitated, she threatened suicide if he refused. Given this terrible threat, Milarepa complied. He learned sorcery and used his magic to cause the collapse of his aunt and uncle's house. All the aunt and uncle's children were killed in the disaster but Milarepa's aunt and uncle survived. Milarepa realized that having committed murder, he was in a desperate spiritual predicament, and decided to seek training with Marpa.

Marpa's biography gives us some access to Marpa's experiences as a teacher. Marpa had dreams that alerted him to Milarepa's arrival and his importance as Marpa's spiritual heir. He also knew he would have the painful job of withholding his blessing and subjecting Milarepa to various ordeals because of the seriousness of Milarepa's burden as a mass murderer. Marpa's treatment of Milarepa was so harsh that Marpa's wife, Dagmema, became very angry and demanded that Marpa soften his approach. Marpa refused, and Milarepa despaired. Following an extended period of more routine training with Marpa, Milarepa went to the mountains for solitary meditation practice. During this period, the most important (or most often cited) experience of his journey took place. While looking for firewood, he collapsed from exhaustion and, in despair, called out to Marpa. Marpa appeared on a cloud and with characteristic brusqueness asked, "What's the problem? You know how to practice. Get to it!" Encouraged by this rough coaching, Milarepa returned to his cave, which had been taken over by demons. He was initially quite frightened and tried to drive them off with magical techniques like special gazes and secret chants, but this only worked with the smaller demons. He then recalled Marpa having taught him that all phenomena are of one's mind.

He then invited the demons to stay, offering them tea, beer, and conversation. The more confident and welcoming he became, the more enraged the demons became. Finally, they became one enormous demon and Milarepa blithely stepped into its mouth. The demon disappeared in a rainbow. As a result of this experience, Milarepa eventually became a great teacher and perhaps Tibetan Buddhism's most significant poet.

In psychoanalytic terms, he was finally able to confront his own terrifying internalization of his enraged mother and his equally terrifying identification with her: she had threatened to kill herself and he had killed many children. No longer intimidated by an unhealthy internal object and his own aggression, he was able to rejoin human society. If the story of Tilopa and Naropa has similarities to Freudian psychoanalysis both in content (oedipal and sexual) and in form (Tilopa is distant and neutral in the manner of a classical analyst), the story of Marpa and Milarepa looks more like an object relations/interpersonal model. Marpa is much more of a "real person" than Tilopa. He is not serenely detached but engaged in forming an authentic relationship with his student. Sullivan, a difficult man like Marpa and interested in difficult cases, is reputed to have said, "God save us from smooth treatments." These stories are not smooth, they are fraught with risk, rupture, and misunderstandings. The teachers are sometimes supportive, sometimes brutally confrontational. For all of the Buddhist emphasis on the emptiness of the self, powerful, unique, creative personalities emerge from these teachings.

Later in his life, Milarepa was encouraged to marry, as Marpa did. He declined the advice, responding, "Marpa was a lion, I am a fox. If a fox jumps like a lion, he can hurt his back" (Gyaltsen 1990).

Before Milarepa left Marpa, Marpa cautioned him that in the future most students would require gentler treatment. Milarepa's dharma heir was Gampopa, and their relationship exemplified this friendlier approach (Stewart 1995). As a young man Gampopa followed his father in the career of physician. His life was shattered when his wife and children died in an epidemic and he was unable to save them. He resolved to pursue spiritual practice and achieved great success in meditation. He began to dream of a green yogi dressed in rags. (Milarepa was reported to turn green when he subsisted only on nettles.) Gampopa reported his dreams to his fellow monks, who warned him about dreams of wild yogis who might pull him away from monastic discipline. Gampopa ignored their cautions and sought out his green yogi. Milarepa knew from his own dreams that Gampopa was coming and would be his spiritual heir. Gampopa's vulnerability was pride—he was almost too good at meditation. Milarepa embraced Gampopa as his spiritual son from the outset—a dramatic contrast to the earlier stories. He did so with heartfelt expressions of gratitude and affection. Milarepa softly undermined Gampopa's pride by taking a very relaxed response to Gampopa's reports of wondrous visions in meditation. Milarepa usually said that whatever has happened was neither good nor bad and gave him some small suggestion about meditation technique. At one point, Gampopa reported a vision of his mother dying of thirst. Perhaps this was related to the traumatic loss of his wife, but unfortunately details of Gampopa's early life are unavailable. But, again, the integration of feelings and imagery related to early objects is central all along the contemplative journey. There is no dramatic spiritual escape from our parents and our feelings about them in the Tibetan biographies. Gampopa was able to relax his rigidity and his pride and was able to assume a position of leadership. He was the first in this lineage to build a formal organization with hierarchies and larger groups of students. He established a training situation with 51,600 monks and an elaborate bureaucratic structure (Trungpa 1980). All the monks kept close to the rules except for three yogis from the Kham district of Tibet. These yogis were in a bind. Although they wanted to comply with the rules, they remained loyal to the wilder foundations of the lineage established by Naropa, which included sacramental feasts with alcohol, singing, and dancing. Such activities were in violation of the monastic order. Because they refused to comply, they were expelled by the monk delegated to enforce discipline. Meanwhile, up on the mountain, Gampopa had a vision that benevolent spirits were leaving. He understood the vision to mean that the three yogis from Kham must be called back. There is a marvelous text of responsive songs as Gampopa called to the yogis, "Sons, don't go further down, come back up, come back up." The yogis eventually heard him and they responded with their own song, "We're coming back, we're coming back." When they finally got there, everyone danced. The legend is that their footprints can still be seen in the rocks.

Who are the mad yogis of psychoanalysis? Who are the mad yogis who will revitalize the conversation between Buddhism and psychoanalysis, now that such dialogue has reached the brink of respectability? Why have a conversation between Buddhism and psychoanalysis at all? All of these tales that I have recounted could be seen as a precocious folk psychoanalysis of comparative and anthropological interest only. Clearly, my goal is less dispassionate. I have recruited these texts to show us the potentials in psychoanalysis for pluralism and individuality. But even that doesn't go far enough. I want a psychoanalysis that admits the mystical, however impossible that is to define. I think these stories model what Loewald was hoping for: the wildness of the Freudian unconscious without the repression of religious experience. I think that for some, the the mystical seems interesting but not necessary. For others, it is a necessity of life. I don't know how that happens. Recently a patient quoted Thomas Merton to me. We need prayer, Merton said, the way a drowning man needs air. I am not sure that *we* means everyone, but for those it includes, I hope these old tales provide a few fresh breaths.

Commentary

PSYCHOANALYSIS AS A SPIRITUAL QUEST

NEIL ALTMAN

Mark Finn's chapter argues, contra Freud and many others in the psychoanalytic tradition, that psychological and spiritual discourses are not incompatible with each other. In fact, he claims, from a Buddhist perspective, they are "inseparable." First, he demonstrates that to be a Tibetan Buddhist does not exclude psychological concerns. He demonstrates that Buddhist teachers keep the psychological health of their students in mind, may advise them to seek psychotherapy, and implicitly regard "neurosis" as an obstacle on the spiritual path. Finn warns against an idealization of Tibetan Buddhists that entails believing that they are, unlike us, spiritual creatures free from the psychological hang-ups characterizing the ordinary Westerner. He quotes Gelek Rinpoche to the effect that if Tibetans felt free to talk about these matters, we would hear many of the same psychological complaints from Tibetans as we hear from Americans. In his book *Cutting through Spiritual Materialism,* Chogyam Trungpa Rinpoche warned of the temptations, for Tibetans as well as for Westerners, of taking egoistic pride in one's spiritual accomplishments. In the tantric tradition, Finn finds evidence that Buddhists seek spiritual growth not only in rarefied places like the Himalayas but in the rough-and-tumble world of sexuality and aggression, the domain more familiar to psychoanalysis. Through Tibetan narratives of how spiritual transformation takes place, Finn demonstrates the centrality of the teacher-student relationship and its vicissitudes, thus forging a link to psychoanalytic concepts of transference and countertransference and countering any notion that spiritual transformation is entirely a "one-person" phenomenon. Finn finds evidence for an openness to spiritual experience in psychoanalysts such as Loewald and Bion, and in the current receptivity to meditation as a supplementary therapeutic modality. Altogether, then, he sees no reason why there shouldn't be a two-way street forming between Buddhism and psychoanalysis, even as psychoanalysis moves toward a more interpersonal focus. In my reading, however, there is the basis for a more fundamental argument in Finn's essay: that contemporary psychoanalysis, along with postmodern Western thought in general, has bumped up against the limitations inherent in the dichotomies endemic to modern Western thinking (scientific versus spiritual, rational versus irrational and emotional, subjective versus objective, past versus present, self versus other, male versus female). The thinking—both deconstructive (e.g., Dimen 1991; Goldner 1991; Harris 1991) and dialectical (e.g., Benjamin 1998; Hoffman 1998)—that has characterized much recent psychoanalysis is quite consistent with the Buddhist tradition of undermining such dichotomies. What is at stake here is more than the next step in theory building; there are therapeutic issues as well. As psychoanalysis just begins to explore the therapeutic potential inherent in the process of trying to free ourselves, and our patients, from the constraints of overly rigid, polarized, thinking, we might well draw on the centuries-old tradition in Buddhism of developing the liberatory potential of their version of this process.

I will begin with some of the theoretical issues, then turn to the therapeutic ones. Finn alludes to one of the conundrums into which dichotomized thinking has forced us as psychoanalysts. Is the analytic relationship a real, current relationship, or simply a repetition of past relationships? We have had to conclude that it is both, and simultaneously! This seems like a conundrum because of two embedded dichotomies: we want the present and the past to be distinguishable, and we want the patient and the analyst to be distinguishable. Here we encounter another conundrum: present and past, analyst and patient are distinguishable and not distinguishable. We seem to have generated experiences as analysts that force us to set aside the logical structure of thought on which we were raised, the Aristotelian basis of Western philosophy. Did Freud somehow set us out on a path that has, through a number of twists and turns, joined up with that of the Eastern spiritual seeker?

I will illustrate with a brief clinical example: a patient, Mr. C., a man in his late thirties, is trying to terminate analysis. It has been unclear from session to session recently whether the current session will be the last. Impatiently, I have been trying to get him to focus on a termination date, ostensibly so that he and I will be prepared emotionally when he does leave, but it has increasingly come to feel more and more like a power struggle. It seems relevant that Mr. C. did not leave his parental home until his late twenties, and then to live with an older, "maternal" woman. In terminating, it seems that Mr. C. is trying to leave "home" but is having trouble. At some point in the present session, he decides that this will indeed be our last session. Then, he asks whether I have a patient immediately after him. I ask why, and he says he was wondering if he would have to leave immediately at 10:30. I say: "What does it matter? When you leave, no matter what time it is, we will have finished." The patient replies: "That is so like you to be rigid about endings!" Then he interpreted: "I'm not going to stay all day, you know." At this moment, it occurred to me that Mr. C. was trying to leave on his own terms, and that I was standing in his way by trying to have the ending occur on my terms.

Consider now the paradoxes that arise when we think about this vignette. Who am I? Shall I think of this sequence of events as a here-and-now inter-action, or a replay of a pattern based in the past, with me playing the role of a parent? I am myself in a very familiar way trying to manage the separation in somewhat obsessive-compulsive fashion, trying to be in control, and so on. But, as I look at myself through this man's eyes, I can also see myself as representing his parent(s) of the past, making it hard for him to leave home. In trying to control his leaving, even if I am ostensibly trying to get him to just *leave already*, I am holding on to him. One might say that, at first, he has induced me to become the controlling parent of his past whom he cannot leave; one can equally well say that he has found a preexisting part of me that fits with his need to rework unfinished business with a controlling parent. All this becomes clear (provisionally, of course!) only once we have found a way to break out of the impasse, so that Mr. C. can leave. So I am both myself cur-rently, and as I often have been long before I met Mr. C., and I am the rep-resentation of Mr. C.'s historical parent, freshly inducted into the role. These are the dialectics or paradoxes that have become very familiar to contempo-rary analysts; we have been led there as Freud's concepts of transference and countertransference have been developed by current generations of analysts trying to focus simultaneously on the here-and-now and the there-and-then, as well as on the inextricability of transference and countertransference. In the words of Roy Schafer (1982, 81): "Thus, in considering psychoanalytic knowl-edge, we confront this triple circularity: conventional distinctions between subject and object, between observation and theory, and between past and present, no longer hold."

Historically, analysts have had difficulty with these paradoxes. Their dif-ficulty is reflected in emphasizing either past or present, either transference or countertransference. The extreme of such either/or thinking appears in regarding transference as entirely transferred from the past onto a blank-screen analyst. The opposite extreme would be regarding transference as entirely derived from veridical perception of the analyst as a person. Of course, contemporary analysts of all schools do not subscribe to either extreme. But how to take account of the inseparability of self from other, of past from present? There have been a variety of strategies for doing so. Mer-ton Gill (1982), in a trailblazing effort, believed that transference, with roots in the past, always found a plausible basis in the actual behavior of the analyst.

Irwin Hoffman (1983) went an intersubjective step further in claiming that transference amounts to expectations of the countertransference. Hoffman now sees polarities, such as the ones we are considering, as dialectically organized: each pole exists only in relation to the other. A dialectical point of view preserves the integrity of each pole: self and other, past and present are distinguishable on one level of abstraction, but on another level they constitute each other; they "create, inform, negate, and preserve" each other, Thomas Ogden writes (1986, 208). In Hans Leowald's work (1980, 1988), distinctions between self and other, past and present, and so on, belong to secondary-process thought; they are absent in primary-process thought. According to him, psychological maturity resides in having access to both modes of thought and experience. The idea of paradox, on the other hand, has to do with simultaneity of seemingly incompatible states, such as there being a self and there being no-self. Buddhist as well as postmodern, deconstructive writings and teachings sometimes build on paradox and dialectic to destabilize the reader's/seeker's mind through negation of a habitual mode of thought or experience.

Consider the opening lines of the the Heart Sutra, which constitute a paradox, or perhaps a dialectic (recall that the poles of a dialectic constitute one another): "Form is emptiness and emptiness is form." I believe that this statement seeks to induce confusion, to the point that someone might be ready to start from the "beginning" without preconceptions and constraints of logic and language.

This approach to traditional categories is like the deconstructive strategy in postmodern thought (Derrida 1978) which seeks to transcend categories, such as gender, altogether. Judith Butler (1990, 1993), for example, sees gender as having only performative reality, no substance beyond that illusory substance that emerges from reiteration through performance. Gender's existence depends entirely on our acting as if we believed it exists. I imagine Buddhists might say the same about the individualized self.

Dialectical thinking is one way of "resolving" paradox, by showing how seemingly opposite poles actually are part of a larger whole. Emmanuel Ghent (1992) took a different tack, relating paradox to an underlying process. For example, with respect to early developmental needs, Ghent noted that clinically there are times when one could well say that the patient is a baby, while also noting that the patient is a full-grown adult. Clinically, one might claim that a patient (who is actually an adult) is asserting infantile needs for defensive, regressive purposes. An underlying process might be that the patient has a need, but camouflages it with clinging, demanding behavior, and "neediness," which pushes people (such as the therapist) away and makes them insensitive to the need. In such a case, there is a need, and there is no need, and the two are related by a false-self camouflage of need with neediness.

D. W. Winnicott, the psychoanalytic pioneer in the realm of paradox, insisted on not resolving paradoxes but rather on living with them. Is the transitional object, for example, the toddler's "blankie," the most precious thing in the world, or is it a dirty old blanket? Obviously it is both. In subjective reality it is the former, in objective reality the latter. But subjectivity and objectivity are themselves paradoxically (or dialectically) related. In the Winnicottian tradition in psychoanalysis, efforts to resolve paradox are likely to do violence to the complexity of the situation; for example, the analyst who claims *only* that the patient is a baby, and the analyst who claims *only* that the patient is an adult, will have a one-dimensional view of the patient. Those who speak dialectically, speak of the dangers of collapsing the dialectic into one pole or the other rather than sustaining the tension between them (Benjamin 1998).

So, has psychoanalysis taken us to a place where we have had to adopt, according to the dialectical point of view, a less linear, less polarized, more complex view of basic categories such as "self" and "other," "male" and "female"? Or has it taken us to a place, namely, the deconstructive postmodern point of view, where we are hamstrung by our conceptual system and need to transcend altogether such categories that we have inherited? How radical a shift do we need to make? Here is where we might look to Buddhism, which has been dealing with this dilemma for centuries; indeed, this dilemma is at the heart of Buddhist teaching and practice. For example, is a concept of unique selfhood a necessary precondition of love, compassion, and compassionate action toward other people? The Western liberal, humanistic tradition takes for granted that individual human beings exist, have value, and suffer; that the source of this suffering lies in material deprivation, social injustice, and oppression; and that this suffering can be alleviated. The idea that we might eliminate the notion of suffering and of the individualized self makes the humanistic liberal worry that we thereby remove the raison d'être of compassionate social action—clearing the way for unfettered injustice and oppression. On a more personal level, our deepest loving attachments to family and friends and lovers rest on a sense of the uniqueness of each individual person, or self. These bonds, to many people, are the major sources of meaningfulness in life itself.

The Buddhist, by contrast, might point out that these bonds are equally the source of our greatest suffering, as they are impermanent and subject to inevitable, yet unpredictable, disruption and loss. The Buddhist might also point out that the individualized self is equally the source of the greed and hatred that cause injustice and oppression. For the Buddhist, compassionate social action arises from enlightenment, from the loving identification with all people that becomes possible from surrendering ego and egoistic attachments.

I conclude with some thoughts about aims and techniques in Buddhism and psychoanalysis. First, relational analysts (e.g., Mitchell 1997) tend to work within the interaction between patient and analyst in order to effect changes in the (internalized) attachment system. At first blush, this goal may seem inconsistent with the Buddhist emphasis on surrender of attachment. However, one might define the "clinging" element as inhering in the "internalization" of interpersonal patterning, that is, in the rigid expectation of, and need for, the perpetuation of early interpersonal patterns of relating. The goal of relational psychoanalysis might be defined as the use of the analytic relationship to free oneself from this attachment to primary objects. The paradox of the analyst as a simultaneously "new" and "old" object might be thought to unsettle the patient's preexisting internalized attachment system, much as the gurus described by Finn unsettle their disciples.

As Finn points out, the evenly hovering attitude advocated by Freud looks a good deal like the meditative state described by Buddhists. The patient's free association is also similar insofar as what is required is a surrender of "memory and desire" (Bion 1988) tantamount to a surrender of ego. But this analytic stance appears to be inconsistent with the pragmatic aims and desires (e.g., symptom relief) that the analyst may adopt, or with the analytic aim of fostering insight through not only remembering the patient but understanding his or her dynamics. There appears to be a paradox or dialectic here: we must remember the patient, and forget him. We must forego all desire, and aim for a better life for the patient. But we could not forget the patient unless we had first remembered him, and we cannot renounce desire unless we had first desired. There is a big difference between remembering the patient with a readiness to be surprised and remembering the patient in a way that defensively forecloses on the unpredictable flow of events and experience. This latter form of remembering the patient constitutes a form of clinging to one version of the patient in a way that fosters false-self compliance on the patient's part. There is a big difference between having desires and goals with self-reflectiveness and having fixed desires and aims that constitute a straitjacket for the patient and ourselves.

In asking us to free-associate and to listen with evenly hovering attention, Freud set us out on a path that leads to a confrontation with many of the same paradoxes brought out in Buddhism. Somehow between Bion and Winnicott (both Englishmen of colonial days, influenced by the East) some loose threads in Freud's psychoanalytic vision have been picked up and woven into a psychoanalysis that begins to resemble a spiritual quest.

Reply

The Persistence of Spiritual Shyness in Psychoanalysis

Mark Finn

Fifteen years ago, I was a postdoctoral fellow at the New York Hospital, Westchester Division. The hospital was, in those days, directed by psychoanalysts. Encouraged by ambition and friends, I invited a distinguished Tibetan Buddhist teacher to speak. As the date approached, I became increasingly anxious. My worries became most acute and agonizingly specific as I fretted over the details of protocol and the etiquette of hierarchy for the visit. The hospital was a very hierarchical institution, and there were certainly many authority figures I feared. The Tibetan Buddhist lineages were at least as hierarchical as the hospital's. When several teachers were in attendance, each had a platform of cushions at different heights according to their place in the lineage. When teachers entered the meditation hall, we would all stand and do three prostrations, bringing our heads to the floor. The teacher I had invited to the hospital was one of the most important in the whole lineage. Like the Dalai Lama, he was considered the reincarnation of a great teacher who was, in turn, considered a reincarnation of a great Buddha. In the Tibetan theocracy, he was a prince.

Was I going to reveal my own naked religiosity to my psychoanalytic teachers? Was I going to ask them to defer to a man in exotic robes? Would I fudge the whole thing, insult everybody, and commit a sort of double suicide of my professional and spiritual lives? Help came from both sources. I was in analysis at the time. My analyst was a faculty member at the hospital, and our work was conducted under the most rigorous adherence to "classical" analytic formalities. As the day of the Tibetans' visit approached, he pronounced, during a pause in my increasingly frantic associations, "Of course you think that I think that inviting the lamas to the hospital is too crazy for words." It was, as they say, an exact interpretation. I realized it was the possibility of being found out as mad that lay at the root of my fears. The phrase "too crazy for words" was especially memorable to me because it is those aspects of experience beyond words that somehow all our talk about spirituality points at. Naming my fear reminded me of my faith. I called my cousin, also a psychologist, who had arranged visits for his Indian yoga teachers to various conventional mental health settings. His advice was as direct and true as my analyst's interpretation: "Serve your teachers without hesitation." I called the monastery and requested instructions. I was told by the monastery that His Eminence's chair should obviously be the best in the room, everyone should stand when he entered and left the room, and, if possible, some soft drink in a crystal glass would be appreciated. I complied with these requests. His Eminence arrived with several attendant monks who arranged crimson brocades before I did as I was told and requested our distinguished faculty to stand for the young Tibetans. The talk was only a modest intellectual success, but everyone was pleased and heartened by the experience. Far from being censored, I was thanked.

In the years following, I organized conferences, gave presentations, and wrote papers on Buddhism and psychoanalysis. I have encountered almost no unfriendliness from the "conventional" psychotherapeutic and psychoanalytic worlds. Today Buddhism is a small but growing part of psychoanalytic culture.

Neil Altman's response to my chapter seems yet another instance when a "non-Buddhist" analyst finds little to disagree with in my argument. He notes that my discussion of the Heart Sutra is quite consistent with intellectual developments in contemporary psychoanalysis and postmodern thought. I think it was helpful of him to emphasize the point that paradoxes are not so much resolved as inhabited. I was hoping he would be more interested in the stories of the teacher-student relationship. He recognizes what I see in those stories but seems not to share my enthusiasm for them as analytic data. I think these narratives deserve more attention from psychoanalysis; they have much to recommend then.

Perhaps most importantly, they rescue the Buddhist-psychoanalytic dialogue from theoretical problems of definitions and terms. They engage the Western reader in the recognizable world of family difficulties while describing actual lives grounded in extraordinary experiences of mysticism. The mystical world is not something only ancient prophets can know. It is the basis for our own daily lives. The Heart Sutra declares the inseparability of relative psychological forms and absolute mystical formlessness. These stories locate what could be abstract philosophy in the personal struggle with psychological suffering. What makes them especially compelling to me as a psychoanalyst is that the psychological helping relationship is at the center of religious life in these stories, which convey the inseparability of the psychological and the spiritual. Aside from myself, I am only aware of Robert Paul (1982), an analyst and anthropologist, who has recognized the prominence of oedipal insights in Tibetan narratives.

I began this response to Neil Altman with a lengthy self-disclosure because I felt that despite his agreement and supportive ideas, somehow we could have made more contact. I began to think about where that feeling was coming from. It struck me that there remains in my chapter a coyness about spiritual matters that perhaps contributed to my feeling of our agreeing but not quite meeting. I had a sense he found Buddhst psychology generally acceptable but chose not to engage the mystical ground of that psychology. I believe part of the reason that Buddhism has proven so acceptable to psychoanalysis is that it is an empirical method of psychological change with spiritual overtones that can be pursued while the whole upsetting matter of religion can appear to be avoided. In my attempts to be a psychoanalytic apologist for Buddhism, I believe I have been guilty of a religious coyness. I noticed that Neil Altman used the word *spiritual* only at the very beginning and at the very end of his piece. Now there is probably wisdom as well as coyness in skirting the spiritual. We are walking so close to the vastness of theology that a little caution is not out of place.

Winnicott's positing of transitional space created a much less pejorative way of regarding less rational aspects of mental life like play, creativity, and religion. Winnicott's language is evocative and agnostic in the best sense, in that no special claims are made. On the other hand, Bion and Loewald are explicit in their belief that there is a mystical or divine aspect of the mind. Recall that Loewald redefines primary process as originating in the mystical experience of eternity beyond time. Michael Eigen (1998) deserves a great deal of credit for observing that Bion's mysticism, central to his theory, is often left out of psychoanalytic discussions of his work. With poetic eloquence Eigen explores the implications of a clinical practice defined by the mystical or the real. Eigen offers much appreciation for Buddhist practice, but he refuses to be spiritually hemmed in by an idealization of Buddhism and finds himself also drawn to the passionate expressiveness of Jewish prayer. God is not left out. Eigen has wonderful ways of portraying the complex interaction of psychological and spiritual dynamics in his patients. He empathically describes the psychological benefits of spiritual practices, particularly their capacity to contain terrifying destructiveness, as we saw in the Tibetan narratives. Spiritual truth has liberating, consoling, and shattering possibilities. Freud was worried that if spirituality were admitted to psychoanalysis, the door would be flung open to the whole world of the occult (Grosskurth 1991). Once we admit the spiritual, how far are we willing to go with the supernatural? Tibetan Buddhism is currently much in vogue, but I see an ambivalence. On the one hand, there is the inspiring kindness and clarity most publicly embodied in the Dalai Lama. On the other, there is a religious culture overflowing with the supernatural and the parapsychological founded on a view of "mind" that goes way beyond even "two person" psychologies into a world that could be called transpersonal. It may be useful to consider these issues historically.

Much of the current emphasis on relational aspects of psychoanalysis can be seen as reflecting the restoration of Sandor Ferenczi and his ideas to a more rightful place in the history of psychoanalysis. In a parallel fashion, in considering a larger context for my spiritual coyness in the world of psychoanalysis, I wonder if it doesn't reflect the continued exclusion of Jung from much psychoanalytic discourse. Recently, *Psychoanalytic Dialogues* devoted an issue to a discussion of a case of Stephen Mitchell's by contemporary Jungians (vol. 10, no. 3 [2000]). Mitchell and James Fosshage then commented on the Jungian writers. The tone was generally cordial and interesting. "Spirituality" was sometimes mentioned frequently and yet at other times ignored. No mention was made of spirituality and religion as central to the Freud-Jung rupture. Sometimes there doesn't seem to be any tension between religion and psychoanalysis, such as when the lamas came to the hospital. At other times the exclusion of spiritual discourse can feel overwhelming. It is my impression that contemporary psycholanalysis is more open to regarding spirituality in nonpathological terms than it once did. But it is not consistent in this respect. I think we are trying to create an atmosphere that is profoundly ecumenical. Do we fear that spirituality will interfere with this ambition—that it will bring along religion and the problems of authority, orthodoxy, and sectarianism from which psychoanalysis is emerging? Have we been using the sophisticated agnosticism of Buddhism to re-legitimize spirituality in psychoanalysis without mentioning the Swiss black sheep of the family? It is remarkable how little Jung I have read since college, long before my formal psychoanalytic education began. It is equally remarkable how rarely Jung comes up in so many conferences and panels on religion, spirituality, and psychoanalysis. I wonder if we need to revisit Jung and Freud to really understand our present context.

As I have grown older, less fearful of madness, less desperate for clear positions, I am more open to a felt sense of the supernatural. Clinicians have written on the need to stay open to being surprised by the patient no matter how hard this is to do. I find it hard but helpful to try to be open to being surprised by the world. That effort takes me further into religion than some friend and patients and not nearly as far as others. Part of the effort is to keep listening to everybody. Recall that the Tibetans teach the inseparability of relative and absolute truth. They define relative truth as everything that can be seen, categorized, or measured. Absolute is beyond space and time. Perhaps there are two reality principles then: one of relative truth and the other, never entirely decoded, frequently bewildering if not terrifying, of the absolute world. The Jung I recall had a real feel for the interweaving of the two, in a way that didn't require subscribing to a whole new set of confining "archetypes" or metapsychological categories.

I am grateful that Neil Altman found so much to agree with in my chapter. Both Buddhism and psychoanalysis can, from a certain vantage point, seem very sensible and down-to-earth. But they also call us to the wildness and vastness of our minds. I was hoping our conversation in print could have inhabited this space to a greater extent, but I was timid in expressing my own longing.

Once I asked the Tibetan lama mentioned at the beginning of this essay how one should go about finding a teacher. He encouraged me to be critical, observant, and cautious in initiating a relationship with a teacher. He went on to say, "You Americans always think there is only one right person out there. Consider that as you seek there could be a whole stadium of buddhas behind you and just outside your peripheral vision encouraging you with compassion." In this manner he pointed toward the vast space I have been trying to hint at here.

In the language of psychoanalysis, he was encouraging me to see the spiritual world not as a static "object" but as a living "subject." This is a real shift that undermines our authority about knowing our world. Sometimes dialogues about Buddhism and psychoanalysis lose sight of the stadium the lama referred to. One could ask whether this stadium is real or an act of creative imagination. But this question would miss the point, I think. Because Tibetan Buddhism has such a strong feeling for the constructed nature of all phenomena, this distinction breaks down. To paraphrase a famous incident: William Blake was asked the question, What if your vision of God were just your imagination? He replied that since his imagination was inseparable from God, the answer really didn't matter. The uncertainty of postmodernism can direct us not only to a multiplicity of perspectives but back into an experienced relationship with the whole, ineffable, living infinity we refer to as spiritual.

Notes

1. The Tantric deities inhabit a zone that is identical to Winnicott's notion of transitional space wherein no hard claims can be made about the psychologically interior or exterior. See Finn 1992 for further applications to Tibetan narrative, and Jones 1991 and Meissner 1984 for extended discussions of Winnicott's contribution to the conversation between religion and psychoanalysis.

2. Oedipal imagery is also included in *The Tibetan Book of the Dead*, which is a liturgy and guide for the stages of psychological change after death. However, *The Book of the Dead* is also understood as a guide for the living, in that we are in a sense constantly dying and being reborn and enduring the ambiguity of transitional states. See Fremantle and Trungpa 1975; Sogyal 1992.

References

Benjamin, J. 1998. *The Shadow of the Other.* New York: Routledge.

Bion, W. R. 1970. *The Psychoanalytic Mystic.* Binghamton, N.Y.: ESF Publications.

———. 1988. Attacks on Linking. In *Melanie Klein Today,* ed. E. Bott-Spillius, vol. 1. London: Routledge.

Butler, J. 1990. *Gender Trouble.* New York: Routledge.

———. 1993. *Bodies That Matter.* New York: Routledge.

Cahill, T. 1998. *The Gifts of the Jews.* New York: Nan Talese/Anchor Books.

Derrida, J. 1978. *Of Grammatology.* Trans. G. C. Spivak. Baltimore, Md.: Johns Hopkins University Press.

Dimen, M. 1991. Deconstructing Difference: Gender, Splitting, and Transitional Space. *Psychoanalytic Dialogues* 1:335–52.

Eigen, M. 1998. *The Psychoanalytic Mystic.* London: Free Association Books.

Epstein, M. 1995. *Thoughts without a Thinker.* New York: Basic Books.

———. 1998. *Going to Pieces without Falling Apart.* New York: Broadway Books.

Finn, M. 1992. Transitional Space and Tibetan Buddhism: The Object Relations of Meditation. In *Object Relations and Religion,* ed. M. Finn and J. Gartner. Westport, Conn.: Praeger.

———. 1998. Tibetan Buddhism and Comparative Psychoanalysis. In *The Couch and the Tree,* ed. A. Molino. New York: North Point Press.

Fremantle, F., and C. Trungpa. 1975. *The Tibetan Book of the Dead.* Boulder, Colo.: Shambhala.

Ghent, E. 1992. Paradox and Process. *Psychoanalytic Dialogues* 2:135–60.

Gill, M. 1982. *Analysis of Transference.* New York: International Universities Press.

Goldner, V. 1991. Toward a Critical Relational Theory of Gender. *Psychoanalytic Dialogues* 1: 249–72.

Grosskurth, P. 1991. *The Secret Ring.* Reading, Mass., Addison-Wesley Publishing.

Guenther, H. G. 1986. *The Life and Teaching of Naropa.* Boston: Shambhala.

Gyaltsen, K. K., trans. 1990. *The Great Kagyu Masters.* Ithaca, N.Y.: Snow Lion.

Harris, A. 1991. Gender as Contradiction. *Psychoanalytic Dialogues* 1:197–224.

Hoffman, I. Z. 1983. The Patient as Interpreter of the Analyst's Experience. *Contemporary Psychoanalysis* 19:389–422.

———. 1998. *Ritual and Spontaneity in the Psychoanalytic Process.* Hillsdale, N.J.: Analytic Press

Jones, J. 1991. *Contemporary Psychoanalysis and Religion: Transference and Transcendence.* New Haven: Yale University Press.

Jose, I. C., and R. Jackson, eds. 1996. *Tibetan Literature, Studies in Genre.* Ithaca, N.Y.: Snow Lion.

Kawai, H. 1996. *Buddhism and the Art of Psychotherapy.* College Station: Texas A&M University Press.

Laing, R. D. 1967. *The Politics of Experience.* New York: Ballantine Books.

Lhallungpa, L. P. 1982. *The Life of Milarepa.* Boulder, Colo.: Pranja Press.

Loewald, H. 1978. *Psychoanalysis and the Life of the Individual.* New Haven: Yale University Press.

———. 1980. *Papers on Psychoanalysis.* New Haven: Yale University Press.

———. 1988. *Sublimation.* New Haven: Yale University Press.

Meissner, W. 1984. *Psychoanalysis and Religious Experience.* New Haven: Yale University Press.

Merzel, D. G. 1994. *Beyond Sanity and Madness: The Way of Zen Master Dogen.* Rutland, Vt.: Charles E. Tuttle.

Mitchell, S. A. 1997. *Influence and Autonomy in Psychoanalysis.* Hillsdale, N.J.: Analytic Press.

Nalanda Translation Committee. 1970. *The Sutra of Heart of Transcendent Knowledge.* Private publication.

Ogden, T. 1986. *The Matrix of the Mind.* Northvale, N.J.: Jason Aronson.

Paul, R. A. 1982. *The Tibetan Symbolic World.* Chicago: University of Chicago Press.

Pepper, S. C. 1942. *World Hypotheses.* Berkeley: University of California Press.

Robinson, J. B. 1996. The Lives of Buddhist Saints: Biography, Hagiography and Myth. In *Tibetan literature,* eds. J. J. Cabezon and R. R. Jackson. Ithaca, N.Y.: Snow Lion.

Rosenblum, R. 1999. *Zen and the Heart of Psychotherapy.* Philadelphia: Brunner Mazel.

Rubin, J. 1996. *Psychotherapy and Buddhism.* New York: Plenum.

Schafer, R. 1982. The Relevance of the "Here and Now" Transference Interpretation to the Reconstruction of Early Development. *International Journal of Psychoanalysis* 63:77–82.

Situpa, T. 1988. *Tilopa: Some Glimpses of His Life*. Edinburgh, Scotland: Ozalendara.

Sogyal, R. 1992. *The Tibetan Book of Living and Dying*. San Francisco: Harper.

Stewart, J. M. 1995. *The Life of Gampopa*. Ithaca, N.Y.: Snow Lion.

Suler, J. 1993. *Contemporary Psychoanalysis and Eastern Thought*. Albany: State University of New York Press.

Suzuki, S. 1970. *Zen Mind, Beginners Mind*. New York: Weatherhill.

Tanahashi, K. 1985. *Moon in a Dewdrop: Writings of Zen Master Dogen*. New York: North Point Press.

Trungpa, C. 1973. *Cutting through Spiritual Materialism*. Boston: Shambhala.

———. 1980. *The Rain of Wisdom*. Boulder, Colo.: Shambhala.

———. 1981. *Journey without Goal: The Tantric Wisdom of the Buddha*. Boulder, Colo.: Prajna.

Tsang, N. H. 1982. *The Life of Marpa the Translator*. Boulder, Colo.: Prajna.

Wilber, K., J. Engler, and D. Brown, eds. 1986. *Transformations of Consciousness: Conventional and Contemplative Perspectives on Development*. Boston: Shambhala.

CHAPTER 3

The Dissolving of Dissolving Itself

ROBERT LANGAN

Dissolve me into ecstasies.

—Milton

As you start to read these words, if you pause to notice, you and I bear a peculiar relation. To some extent you place yourself—your *self*, the roiling fount of your present experience open to the whim of your possible choosing—in abeyance. As you choose to follow my words, you try on for size, so to speak, my being. You allow yourself to speak my words with your mind, to mind my words with your speech. Whose voice is it that occurs between us? You affiliate yourself, for the time being, with my meanings and meanderings. You allow yourself to flirt with my choices and choosings of what merits attention.

Yet there is a gap. You can lift your eyes from the page, and my words become silent ink on dry paper. I dissolve. Drop your eyes to these words once again, and I spring into being. You carry my being across the gap between us.

Let us say, out of interest, that our relation is psychoanalytic. Let us not say, just yet, who is psychoanalyst to whom. What we do, by agreeably construing our relation as psychoanalytic, is to focus on self—usually one self more than the other. We focus on the nature of our being in the world, and we do so with the assumption, or perhaps the hope, that it brooks improvement. Self needs help. Being alters (for the better?) when carried across the gap between us. I become, importantly if not totally, what you make of me. And you become mine. Our hope is to escape from a self too confining by borrowing possibilities intimated in the self of the other.

The gap makes the other. Other intimations remake one's self. The gap is between us, and as well, within oneself, between old and new, between what was and what can be. One discovers oneself suspended in a between, one's present self a dissolving of future into past, past into future. Awareness of this gap, this dissolving edge of being, is a perpetual invitation to the intentional alteration of self that entails letting self go, letting other be, altering being itself. This is the invitation of psychoanalysis.

Highfalutin talk, all these words. If I get to be analyst, you get to come and see me several times per week for several years, and you pay for it as well. We could set it up as an exploitation. But it would not be just an exploitation of you by me out of greed; it would be an exploitation of me by you out of fear. It would be an avoidance by both of us of the fear-fraught dissolving nature of being. An exploitation is knowable, its verdict made, blame cast, case closed. It affords the illusion of certainty. Why would we do this to each other? It could be that we would have to. Then our side-stepping analytic work would begin through examining how we had to. Our effort would be in undoing the imperative of "have to," the better to glimpse other possibilities and other selves. So we do that. (Not to mention: years pass.) Does the fear go away? Can any self, new and improved and flexible as it may be, face the facelessness of its own dissolving, face knowing, pointedly witnessing, that whoever I am, I am dying? Face Macbeth's "All our yesterdays have lighted fools the way to dusty death." Is there no dissolving of dissolving itself?

In a letter of 1926 to Ludwig Binswanger, Freud would answer, despairingly, no. Listen: "To me this child had taken the place of all my children and other grandchildren, and since [his] death, I don't care for my grandchildren any more, but find no joy in life either. This is also the secret of my indifference—it was called courage—toward the danger to my own life [through contagion during the influenza epidemic].... You are young enough to surmount your loss; as for me, I don't have to any more" (Binswanger 1957, 78–79).

Here is a have to: we have to die.

Toward the end of his life, Freud famously limited the scope of psychoanalysis to the supplanting of neurotic suffering by the suffering that is the common lot of mankind. No little part of this common misery is the certainty of death. Sickness and aging can erode vitality; death can corrode with meaninglessness all hope and love and valued purpose. In the face of death, resort to a religious certainty of the hereafter can seem, as it did to Freud, avoidant self-delusion. Yet resort to his stoic, scientific certainty that nothing lies beyond the grave can seem self-comforting arrogance, merely replacing one sort of certainty by another. Freud's veer toward despair neglected, in my opinion, two liberating and self-surmounting features of his psychoanalytic method: the admission of fundamental uncertainty, and the subversive assumption that even with what we have to do, we have some choice about how to do it.

Freud might see himself as the last claimant to any fundament of uncertainty. After all, he designed his psychoanalytic method to make the unconscious conscious, to replace id by ego, to solve the mysteries of neurotic behavior by providing the certainty of rational explanation. Yet the method hinged, and still hinges, on the ambivalent admission of uncertainty. Not only must the patient abandon the sensible certainty of known connections in order to say whatever comes to mind, but the doctor as well must abandon familiar expectations in order to be able to listen with free-floating attention (Langan 1997). Each participant in the analytic dyad should adopt what we might call a know-nothing mind, the better to open to uncertainty. Freud ventured into, then stepped decidedly back from, uncertainty, so as to establish certainly his psychodynamic etiologies. The psychoanalytic formulation was the truth.

If we venture further, past Freud's footsteps, what then? An openness to uncertainty more radical than Freud's begins to impugn the finality of any truth. We join Descartes, puzzled by the problem of establishing that one's self exists at all. Yet we cannot join him in his answer—I think therefore I am—if we open the stability of "I" to uncertainty. Contemporary psychoanalytic theorists (e.g., Mitchell 1993; Langan 1993; Phillips 1994; Stern 1997; Hoffman 1998; Pizer 1998) do just this, leaving self ungrounded, "standing in the spaces" (Bromberg 1998). Go further adrift. Dissolve yourself in space. By extension, even more radically, if we dissolve the fixity of self, do we dissolve, in some sense, death? If there is no fixed self, is there no one to die?

The Buddha would answer, quizzically, yes.

Buddhism's answers as to the nature of self and the dissolution of suffering are highly pertinent, I suggest, to contemporary psychoanalytic theory. Moreover, the Buddhist and psychoanalytic methods meant to provide answers (viz., meditation and analytic attention) show correspondences. For me, the one method leads, and has led, to the other. Each method lays open to view from a different angle the elusive nature of the dissolving self, and the revelatory power of disciplined attention.

But remember, dear reader, our peculiar relation. Attend not just to the content of the ideas I aver, but to how each of us hovers over this page, even now, attending to some things, forgetting others. This effort exercises our side-stepping awareness, common to meditation and to analytic attention. We are in the words, and at the same time, apart from them. The words spin out, spin us out, over a void. There, somewhere between us, some words form some answers for some time, allowing us more fully to live in the forgetting face of nonexistence, in the dissolving away of each other.

How we decide upon our answers, it appears, is up to us. Freud's assumption of free will—that even with what we have to do, we have some choice about how to do it—is an assumption shared by Buddhism. Free will demands responsibility for the course of one's life. We can deny free will, but then from the vantage of free will that denial is a choice for which we are responsible: we have chosen victimization. We cannot avoid responsibility for our choices, even our unconscious choices. Mikhail Bakhtin (Clark and Holquist 1984) construes this as "answerability" for our lives, unavoidable because there is "no alibi for being." No less than the givens of history and circumstance, our choices shape our own lives and the lives of those around us, for better and for worse. Likewise in Buddhism, the ineluctable chain of cause and effect—karma—binds us into our present predicament, but that predicament includes the necessity that in going on being we cannot help but willfully cause effects. What we do, by omission and commission, matters.

Psychoanalysis and Buddhism philosophically begin, then, with the fact of finding oneself alive in the world and faced with the question of what to do about it. Buddhism's answer rests on the Four Noble Truths, which truths, to my way of thinking, lend themselves more than superficially to a psychoanalytic framework. That perceived psychoanalytic framework, of course, is mine, idiosyncratically tinkered up and not strictly representative of a particular psychoanalytic school. And just as a century's bickering has not unified psychoanalysis, so 2,500 years of debate, exegesis, and scholarship have not produced a unified Buddhism. The Buddhism that I speak of here reflects my idiosyncratic understandings and misunderstandings of many speakers

in what remains importantly (like clinical psychoanalysis) an oral tradition.[1]
Here again, in the face of fractionating diversity, are some words forming
some answers—mine.

And what are these "noble truths" about your life and mine?

The First Noble Truth is the recognition of suffering, our human lot. Into
the happiest of lives must come sickness, aging, and death. Include with sickness any of the slew of psychopathologies, and so included is the raison d'être
of psychoanalysis. Understanding pathology implies understanding health;
likewise, living with sickness poses the question of what it is to live well, and
to live well in the face of inevitable suffering. Within psychoanalysis the
emphasis shifts from the reduction of pathology to the potentiation of a life
well lived. Freud's resignation to common misery stopped short of the transcendent hopes of theorists such as Erich Fromm (Fromm, Suzuki, and De
Martino 1960) and Donald Winnicott (1975), in whose hands psychoanalysis becomes a tool for liberation from bondage. Neurosis is a self-imposed
bondage—self-imposed even if one is unaware of how one has tied oneself up
in knots. Psychoanalysis proposes to undo some of the bonds by insight,
understanding, and new experience within the psychoanalytic relationship, all
contingent on shifts in attention. Buddhism, more radically, construes all
suffering as a self-imposed bondage open to transcendence, if only one can
attend to it appropriately.

The Second Noble Truth holds that the root of suffering is attachment.
The roots of attachment are consumptive (like greed, lust, gluttony, vanity—
the usual self-aggrandizing desperations), aversive (hatred, envy, simple
anger), and ignorant (shirking the responsibility of self-examination). A translation from moral terms to psychodynamic strategies is approximate but
telling: vanity may well imbue narcissism; gluttony and greed may mask
deprivation; lustfulness may shy from vulnerable intimacy; and hatred may
serve complacency. Whether and how such links apply to a particular person
at a particular time is open to examination, which is the dispelling of ignorance. In a way, the insightful and interpretive aspects of psychoanalysis are
an examination of attachments. Genetic work traces how past loves and fears,
and expedient shortcuts taken to handle them, linger in present strategies of
living. Dissociative self-states can be seen as constellations of attachments, of
cathexes, marshaled in an effort to keep oneself happy. When the effort fails,
the person wants change. Change is a revision of attachments (or "affiliations"

[Langan 1999b]), catalyzed by the quality of attachment to the analyst (or in a different vein, perhaps, the quality of attachment to the guru). If, however, the thrust of analysis is to make attachments less adhesive, the thrust of Buddhism is to dispel them altogether. Dispelling attachments does not mean necessarily abandoning the world, but rather living in it in a way not predicated on attachment. Just what this means poses a puzzle since, as the old monk is said to have said, "Before I was enlightened, I ate, I walked, I slept; after I was enlightened, I ate, I walked, I slept."

The Third Noble Truth embodies the puzzle: overcome attachment, overcome suffering. The puzzle arises reflexively, because overcoming attachment, seemingly, requires attachment to overcoming. And this "truth" appears nihilistic if one equates no attachments with no reasons to live. Is not love itself an attachment? Is not everything that matters, all hope and joy, purpose and meaningful effort, an attachment? From the vantage of Buddhism, the answer is no—or not necessarily, or (the kind of answer that drives children livid with frustration) yes and no. The question implies a duality, an either-or choice between attachment and detachment. The paradox of the Buddhist answer is captured in the Heart Sutra (Hua 1980): "Emptiness itself is form; form itself is emptiness." Attachments are attachments to forms, to the passing semblances of things. Recognizing emptiness in form, somehow, permits the dissolving of attachment.

This is a weighty and mysterious "somehow." Let us return to it momentarily with "self" as a case in point. What would it mean to give up my primary attachment to *me*, the one who appears to be at the center of my experience?

But first, how to overcome attachment? How does one ultimately realize that the paradox of emptiness-being-form-being-emptiness is itself the Fourth Noble Truth, that an Eightfold Path leads to the understanding of the paradox and the cessation of suffering? The Path's aspects are living with right belief, right aims, right speech, right actions, right livelihood, right endeavor, right mindfulness, and right meditation. If you see before you on the scholarly horizon tomes of explication and further numbered lists—the Three Jewels, the Twelve Perfections, the Ten Fetters—in their serried ranks, you are right. They are there to be read (see, for example, Waddell 1895; Das 1997; Thurman 1996). Here, however, simply notice the emphasis on *right*. One must manage by choice to live in the right way to diminish suffering—one's own and others'. And though prescriptions and proscriptions abound, the Buddha insists that one decide what is right on the basis of personal and direct experience, not on the basis of faith or obedience. The Buddha is a guide, not a god. The Path is pragmatic, not theistic. One is to judge it by its results in one's personal experience. One judges psychoanalysis likewise.

Psychoanalysis has its path: I come to realize I am not just who I thought I was. Yet Buddhism's pragmatic path leads further, to logic-stopping paradox. If emptiness is form, and form emptiness, what becomes of the form I know as myself? It is not just that I am not who I thought I was; it is just that I am never just who I think I am. Self is not-self, not-self self. There is a gap, a formative gap, between me and you, self and not-self, self and other than self. And simultaneously, gap implying form, there is no gap.

From this paradoxical perspective, the Dalai Lama (Gyatso and Shengyen 1999, 4) recasts the Four Noble Truths: "Know suffering, although there is nothing to know. Relinquish the causes of misery, although there is nothing to relinquish. Be earnest in pursuit of cessation, although there is nothing to cease. Practice the means of cessation, although there is nothing to practice." Pursue psychoanalysis, although there is nothing to pursue? Or more pointedly, who can psychoanalysis help if there is no self to help?

You either do, or you do not have, I suppose, a proclivity for such paradoxes. The Buddha (Mendis 1979; also Hua 1996; Nyanaponika 1949) led his first five disciples past proclivity to the necessity of illusory self by a process of logic. First is the premise of unsatisfactory impermanence: everything that arises passes away, and not just eventually, but moment by moment. A sentient being arises from the combinatory interplay of five heaps (*skandhas*) or aggregates: physical form, feelings, perceptions, volitional states (or thoughts), and consciousness. (Consciousness is a sixth sense, not superordinate to the other five senses.) Each of the aggregates is impermanent. Neither one nor all can give rise to an abiding essence in a sentient being. Ipso facto, there is no abiding self.

No self means no one to cling to, no one to defend. No self means acting selflessly, that is, acting toward others with generosity and kindness, so as not to increase delusive clinging to a world and a being-in-the-world that inevitably dissolves. The dissolving of all leaves nothing to dissolve; nothing to dissolve is the dissolving of dissolving itself. Dissolving does not mean that nothing matters; quite the contrary, everything, every action, every moment, matters utterly. Even now in the balance of this brimming moment between all past and all future is the beauty of the world, the preciousness of others, the opportunity to generate deep happiness, to quell the unease of greed and antipathy and ignorance, to open to the fullness of being. (Remember Basho: "The old pond / A frog jumps in / Plop!") The balance of this moment is continually ours to tip, one way or another. The realization of no self is the liberation from bondage.

But, the logician objects: if there is no one to liberate, there can be no liberation. Such logical objections assume plausibility by means of restricting the context—in this instance, restricting it to the set of operations wherein subjects act upon objects. The pragmatic William James (1904) confronted such logic in his paper "Does 'Consciousness' Exist?"—a neglected psychological counterpart to Einstein's 1905 theory of relativity. According to James, the fallacy lies in a too-ready assumption that a given point, say, can lie at one and only one point along a line. The assumption fails to consider that that point can lie at the intersection of two (or an infinitude) of lines. Think of lines of argument, or overlapping frames of understanding. So understood, consciousness, which can seem of necessity subjective in one context, becomes objective in another. Whether experience is thoughtlike or thinglike (or, I add, whether it is self or not-self) depends upon its relational contexts with other thoughts and things. Contexts relationally define reality, and contexts shift in relation to one another. James goes on to conclude that consciousness as an entity does not exist. Indeed, the stream of thinking, which indubitably does exist, is in essence the flow of the breath past the nostrils. Consciousness (and by implication self as the seat of consciousness) "*is fictitious, while thoughts in the concrete are fully real. But thoughts in the concrete are made of the same stuff as things are* [viz., 'pure experience']" (James 1904, 1158). It is hardly surprising that James, late in life, developed an interest in Buddhism.

The effort to come closer to "pure experience" (cf. Wolstein's [1994] "immediate experience"; also Epstein 1995) is, I maintain, common to Buddhism and psychoanalysis. The meditative effort in Buddhism is, in effect, the practice of stopping (or at least sidetracking) thinking so as to become more purely aware of awareness. One doesn't chase thoughts; one observes them as they, like the breath, come and go. One remembers to forget. The analytic effort to rethink thinking, that is, to understand oneself anew, requires first the subtle stopping of habitual, self-perpetuating thinking.

One must forget to remember. Meditation entails a remembering to forget; analysis a forgetting to remember (Langan 1999a). The two are complementary, like the medieval Christian mystic's cloud of forgetting and cloud of unknowing (Way 1986). Both unmoor the ego by venturing a less restricted immersion in the flow of experience. Experience subsumes everything: restriction and nonrestriction, self and not self, remembering and forgetting, thinking and unthinking, flow and stasis. All loop back and flow into one another and arise and subside and arise anew. Even stasis has its temporal flow. The upwelling flow of pure experience is what Schafer (1976) discerns, I believe, in his recommendation of an action language for psychoanalytic theorizing; and what Mihaly Csikszentmihalyi (1999, 825) styles the flow of "autotelic experience" wherein, as an interviewee of his puts it, "'You are in an ecstatic state to such a point that you feel as though you almost don't exist... . [As a composer] I just sit there watching in a state of awe and wonderment. And the music just flows out by itself." Ecstasy *(ex stasis)* is the standing outside of oneself. Meditation with its sidetracking of thinking, and psychoanalysis with its sidestepping commentary about what has just gone on, both invite the standing outside of oneself. Both, however hesitantly, touch on ecstasy.

Not a few psychoanalysts might shy away (or run in horror) from considering what they do, day in and day out, to be dabbling in ecstasy. Such a view of analytic change, hard enough to explain, can seem barely respectable, dangerously evangelical, or incomprehensibly distant from the "data" of the consulting room. Typical patients do not present themselves for psychoanalysis out of a desire for ecstasy. Or do they? If not in so many words, patients do come out of a desire to step outside ways of being that have themselves become straitjackets.

For some, respectability can be a straitjacket. And psychoanalysis, with its reputation as a science currently sullied, emerges more clearly as an art of potentially radicalizing interchange: "It is not possible for an art form, however precise its descriptive methods or systematic its collation of findings, to be respectable. The reason is clear. An art form must be highly individual and its oeuvres unrepeatable. Its arbiter of value ...must be aesthetic, and its impact ...must vary with the receptiveness of its recipient. There can be no arguing, only evocation" (Meltzer and Williams 1988, xii). What is or is not evoked out of the "data" of the analytic situation depends entirely on its participants. A too respectably assiduous analytic examination of a patient's life could prove susceptible to the anti-analytic quip. "The examined life is not worth living." Or such an examination could represent a newfound competence to remediate a damaged dignity. One can judge its value only on the basis of personal experience.

If linking psychoanalysis to ecstasy becomes evangelical, how and why this might occur remains open to analytic inquiry. Such an inquiry, by definition, proceeds by a deconstructive sidestep to examine possibilities of suggestion, persuasion, avoidant compliance, and attentional myopia. You and I try to talk about what's going on. You be analyst. The asymmetry of the analytic dyad obtains. Your job is not to indoctrinate me with Buddhism, not to advise me to meditate, not to advise me at all, in fact, but alongside me to wonder about the flow of my experience, to wonder about the givens of my values, history, culture, and class, and to wonder about the given nature of my very self. You assume, and I may or may not believe you, that I can change some of these givens. You provide me the opportunity, we hope, to find out for myself. We can alter, I hope, *how* I approach my experience.

That Buddhism also alters how one approaches experience is theoretically relevant, but not necessarily personally relevant to any particular analysand. The givens of reality can become contents of consciousness subject to recontextualization by an active attention, but no analysand need necessarily explain this. It is hard enough to begin occasionally to do it, as the thoughts and the things of life stream ceaselessly along, buoyed by contexts already provided like ready-made boats.

And you and I sit on the riverbank, sporadically commenting on the waterborne traffic. Only as we sit there, hour after analytic hour, we may come to realize that the riverbank itself is a water-borne thought, and likewise in each other's ken float you and I. This is real experience, not a gossamer thought. Thought is thing. You blow your nose. I feel the boundedness of my body. Is the session over? When I walk out the consulting room door, do I leave alone, or do I carry you across the gap of physical distance between us?

Crossing the gap metaphorically assumes a separation between us. The commonsense givenness of this separation springs from assumptions so taken for granted in our time and culture that they appear obvious, if not unquestionable. Our bodies are separate. You cannot read my thoughts (though I hope you are reading some of them). We can keep secrets from one another. We can lie.

The crossover dimension is that we need one another in order to sense our separateness. That we are together allows us to be apart. If I lie, I need to lie to someone. My secrets are delivered from you, rendered secrets by your obliviousness. Even the separateness of our bodies can be lost in the physical experience of our interpenetration. You give me my self; my self dissolves in the connectedness of our giving. Winnicott famously said that there is no such thing as a baby—only a baby-with-mother. A Buddhistically informed relational psychoanalysis must conclude that there is no such thing as a self, only self-with-other, yet further and at the same time, no self, no other.

One hesitates to take this further step portending, as it does, no one to step. The dissolving of self seems dire, yet the ecstasy of mystical unity suggests itself: where there is no one, there is no other one, so all is no other than one. There is here. Place is someplace in mind (Langan 2000). Time is all at once.

A literary exposition of these ideas is woven through a story by Jorge Luis Borges called "The Aleph." The Aleph is the *hic stans* and *nunc stans* of Scholastic philosophy: the point that contains all points, the moment comprising all moments. The narrator of the story is led to its mundane location near the nineteenth step of dark basement stairs in a Buenos Aires house about to be demolished. He lies in the proper place, squints at the proper angle. It is there, a small iridescent sphere containing the universe, which in turn contains the Aleph. To describe what he sees,

> the central problem is unsolvable: the enumeration, even if only partial, of an infinite complex.... What my eye saw was simultaneous: what I shall describe is successive, because language is successive.... I clearly saw [each point] from all points in the universe...in an inner patio in the Calle Soler I saw the same paving tile I had seen thirty years before in the entranceway to a house in the town of Fray Bentos.... I saw a sunset in Querétaro which seemed to reflect the color of a rose in Bengal... (149–51)

Notice the dreamlike associational leaps, from the rose of the sunset to the Bengal flower, from the time and place and circumstance that long ago occasioned the narrator's entering a house with a peculiar tile, to the noticing of that tile now—or "now" for want of a better word when now and then begin simultaneously to blend, dissolving one another. The usual self, unthinkingly assumed so obviously to exist, is like the linear selector of successive moments, the "I" who remembers when I got up and forms expectations as to when to be abed, the "I" who places me here and you there somewhere beyond the opaque screen of this written page. The unusual self, reflexively imagined, undoes itself, finds itself simultaneously suspended by and suspending its own associational matrix. The associational matrix is no other than the relational connectivity of all experience, whereby all past is present, everywhere here in the perpetual unfolding of pure experience which includes the experience of perpetual unfolding. It includes as well the experience of no experience: my dreamless sleep, my having forgotten so much, my inability to converse in Aramaic. It contains contradiction and duality. It is all here at once, where "here" loses meaning. From this vantage, lying in the proper place, squinting at the proper angle, the Aleph is the self.

"Of course if you don't see it, your incapacity in no way invalidates my testimony," says a guide as he leads Borges's narrator to the Aleph (1966, 148). There can be no arguing, only evocation. I can lay no claim to being your guide in this mysterious matter of how self is no self. How can dissolving dissolve itself? I, too, sit back knit-browed and scratch what I confidently take to be my head. Buddhism provides some guidance in these matters, but guidance is like a map for a psychological territory so complex it can never be the same twice over. Each analysis is unique. Yet each analysis, from this vantage, to the extent that it essays to change self, must encounter at least indirectly the conundrum that there is no self to change. The easier path, theoretically, has been to presume a positivistic truth underlying a linear development in life. Patients were treated like cars, in for repairs after a crackup. The easier path came to a theoretical dead-end. The theory itself cracked up.

Current theorizing shifts toward a psychoanalytic understanding that is relational, contextual, and constructivist. Self becomes fluid and multifarious. Extend the fluidity, I suggest, and self dissolves. Extend the dissolving into Buddhist parameters, and find the dissolving of dissolving itself. There is no self; neither is there no self. No self becomes something like the square root of minus one, a number so unacceptable for five centuries of mathematics that it was impugned as "imaginary" and derogated as obvious nonsense until required by necessity to solve real problems in the real world (Nahin 1998). The doctrine of no self, according to Buddhism, solves just such problems: real suffering in our real world. Just so, in psychoanalysis it clarifies the interpersonal action of therapeutic change.

What the assertion of no self pushes into the theoretical foreground is psychological response to loss, and in particular, to the ultimate loss of self that is death. The chatter of each analytic session occurs over the abyss of mortality. Irwin Hoffman (1998) draws attention to a dialectic between meaning and mortality that he sees as fundamental in the analytic situation. How can life be meaningful in the face of the grave? Avoidance and denial and the casting of blame are stopgap strategies to answer the question. A psychologically mature response is manifest among the parents Hoffman studied who had to undergo the death of a child. He found that "the parents' sense of growth was reflected in a changed temporal orientation [toward living in the moment], in a greater empathic identification with and tolerance for the limitations of others, and in an enhanced sense of resiliency and capacity to endure suffering. All of these changes had at their root the experience of loss and the associated confrontation with mortality" (62).It may be that what psychoanalysis (implicitly) and Buddhism (explicitly) most share is their function as *memento mori*. As Mark Twain put it, nothing quite so focuses a man's mind as knowing he will be hung in the morning.

The result of that focus, tellingly, generates ethical decisions about how to live, not just alone in the solitary trajectory of one's life, but with others. One may find more value in the moment, and better endure suffering, but it is with and through others that the meaningfulness of life is most accessible. Stephen Batchelor's (1983) application of Buddhist thinking to Heidegger's existential philosophy puts the change in a nutshell: instead of leading a life in the mode of being-with-others, one lives in being-for-others. What living in the mode of being-for-others means to a particular person is worth investigation, if one only recognizes the worth of the person—what it is, despite flaws and errors and transience, that can make a person matter. Analyst and analysand can allow each other to matter, can make their interchange meaningful and, in so doing, can enact a modally different way of living life that extends outside the consulting room to all the human world.

A patient of mine died recently. She had come back to me after her cancer metastasized. It was supposed to have been all better, allowing her to continue living as she always had. Then it wasn't better. She couldn't walk well. Her hair fell out. She could no longer continue living as she always had. She felt, of course, anger and grief and fear, but what she came to focus on was how she wanted to live. She no longer wanted to live as she always had. She had led a life where her art came first, and such mundane matters as money and men second. As she reevaluated her past and her present options, she began to feel that she had avoided deeper personal commitments out of a self-indulgent fear she now scorned. With others she began to speak what was on her mind, what she felt and wanted. She wanted her boyfriend to be there for her. In important ways, because of who he was, he could not be. She called it off, then let it be, as she found herself able to accept him for who he was, with all his limitations and all his ordinary, compensating charms. Worse things happened. What we talked about in the therapy, again and again, was how her limitations and lapses did not have to define her; she was able still to choose with courage and dignity to live in her own way, whatever the circumstances.

The next to last time I saw her she couldn't raise her arms from the hospital bed, which bothered her because she wanted to hug me. (We had never so much as shaken hands.) She asked me to rest my hand on her forehead and was glad that it felt cool from the outside air. There was nothing more to talk about, in particular. Talk didn't seem to matter. I asked if there was anything I could get her, and she said to get strawberries and vanilla ice cream. I went out and found perfectly ripe strawberries and the ice cream. When I fed them to her, small mouthfuls on the tip of a plastic spoon, she held my eyes with hers as she tasted and swallowed and relished what she could relish. We said good-bye. When I left I felt that she was all right—perfectly all right—and that remarkably, she had taken care of me so that I could feel all right, too. It wasn't just her giving me something to do so that I could feel useful. It was that she actively extended herself, that she was there for me.

It is an experience hard to put into words. I can say that she dissolved the gap between us. Or, perhaps, that for the time being in the fullness of her presence (which is here still, even as you read about it) she dissolved the dissolving between us.

And so recall, reader, I have written this for you, without knowing in particular who you are. I suppose it is a gesture, however feeble, toward being for you, and in selfish hopes of your being for me. Are you, to me, someone but no self? Am I the same to you? You have more clues than I do. It could seem plausible to you that I was an only child, more of an introvert than an extrovert. But you would need to ask, and to ask, it would have to matter to you, even if just a little. And so in this psychoanalytic relationship we have entertained, we matter enough to wonder what comes next, to follow the trail of words. We hold each other in imagination, the selfsame place where we each hold a self and everything else, everyone else, who matters. Again as ever, all of the past and present, the myriad entirety of whatever each of us has experienced in life, hovers now between us as your eyes now skim over this page. Now, like the frog in the pond, *plop*.

Imagine me up in a tree a twelve-year-old boy in his tree house. It is not a house, however, nor even a platform, but several 2 X 2's roughly parallel lashed and bolted twenty-five feet up in the Chinese elm where the big branches bifurcate into smaller, where the shimmering leaves enclose the empty space at the center of the tree in an orb of dappling green. This boy had discovered that he did not need a floor, that he could lie with a 2 X 2 under each shoulder blade and snug against his pelvis, his legs and arms dangling in the air, the back of his head against the rough bark of a leg-thick limb gently rocking his head with the breeze. The bough gently rolled his gaze side to side among the sun-dappled breathing leaves, leaf-sized bits of blue sky sparkling through, sparrows like thoughts flitting here and there, his body secure in warm mid-air swaying with the tree for hours. Imagine him up in a tree. Imaginary me.

Imagine a walker on a ramshackle bridge. It is a rope bridge with hand-spun ropes for handrails and ropes supporting narrow boards for the footpath. It sways only a few feet above the shallow ripple of the Vishnumati River, a wide river cupping Kathmandu to the east and to the west footing the singular temple hill of Swayambu Nath, where gilt depictions of the Buddha's eyes gaze unblinkingly in four directions, seeing all at once. The walker stops. Overhead the first stars are out. The half-moon rising over the jagged mountains at the rim of the high mountain valley casts shadows. Shafts and pools of dark lie in the moonlit dark the sun has left. Upriver glow the charcoal pyres of the crematory burning ghats, smoke-shrouded corpses in the shadows. The river carries ashes, half-burnt bones. From the Swayambu side, at first far off, then nearer, comes fitful barking, snarling: a roving pack of scavenger wild dogs, dangerous to meet at night. The walker stops, listening, suspended.

Imagine the twelve-year-old boy, high in a Chinese elm. Imagine the walker on a ramshackle bridge. Imagine me. And you? Imagine you?

Commentary

IMAGINING LANGAN: A TRANSCENDENCE OF SELF

STUART A. PIZER

Robert Langan offers us the quintessentially Buddhist haiku by Basho:

> *The old pond.*
> *A frog jumps in.*
> *Plop!*

"*Plop!*" We are meant to experience the dissolving of old images (sameness) on the still surface of the pond as the frog's "plop" sends out ripples, breaking up and redistributing the pond's reflections. In order to dissolve the dissolving between Langan and myself, I am required to sustain "plop-mindedness" (see Goldstein 1983). I believe that is precisely what Langan invites us to do, and inducts us into doing. Perhaps in psychoanalytic terms plop-mindedness might be referred to as "courting surprise" (Stern 1997), or a version of "evenly suspended attention" (Freud 1912), or the relinquishment of "memory or desire" (Bion 1970). Langan seems to emphasize—at times, even to reify—a dissolving of self and to pose the dilemma of no-self. *Plop.*

Yet, consider another quintessentially Buddhist haiku, also by Basho (in a version told to me by a patient):

> *In the deep autumn air,*
> *I sometimes wonder*
> *Who my neighbor is.*

As I read (and reread and again reread) Langan, I wonder who Langan is. Indeed, finding myself (or losing myself) in Langan's protean prose, I also wonder who I am. My certainties (my preconceptions? my prejudices?) dissolve in a Borges-like labyrinth of nonlinearity (perhaps at times circularity). I am disoriented, disquieted. For me, approaching Langan's chapter is like being a novice confronted with a Zen master's koan bearing an aggressive challenge to the mind. And the dizzying challenge lies in the requirement of a sudden encounter with paradox that spins the mind around, bedeviling its efforts to hang on, to grab hold of certainty or comprehension. Like a koan, Langan's chapter feels "solvable" only by an act of surrendering to its unsolvability since, like the Aleph, it appears to contain all of life from all directions and, thus, dwarfs the mind's efforts at a complete encompassing of complexity and contradiction. Again, we must cultivate plop-mindedness.

The acceptance of paradox is essential to an immersion in bare experience, which is ever paradoxical (Pizer 1998). Where we think Langan is there, he is not. Plop. And just when we think Langan is not there, he is. Plop. He's elusive, with a purpose. Langan writes in a way to assure that he remains "other" for the reader. His elusiveness and allusiveness place him beyond my omnipotence. He might call this a gap. I would call it a potential space in which the medium is the message. I could dismiss Langan or I could use him. I can't so readily appropriate, or even grasp, him. Hence, in my surrender toward accommodating what I cannot facilely assimilate, I may to some degree "escape from a self too confining."

Here is how Langan is choosing to "be-for-others"—in this instance, for me as reader. How can I be for Langan? Perhaps by making what I make of his writing, by my own opening of mind toward an act of recognition laced with misrecognition (as Benjamin [2000] might put it—which seems apt because, in a way, Langan is locating our hope in some version of intersubjectivity). Langan asks how we carry the other across what he calls the "gap" between selves (how do we wonder who our neighbor is). He also asks how we can bear the knowledge that, whoever we are, we are dying. For Langan, these two questions are central and interrelated. I take his implicit answer to both questions to be through acts of "being-for-others" that hold the other, with deep respect and high seriousness, in our imaginations.

So Langan imagines the reader, and a relationship between himself and the reader, and he invites me as reader to imagine his self and also to imagine myself. These "acts of meaning" (Bruner 1990) require that I suspend ("dissolve"?) my comfortable, reliable categories of thought along with my own personal stencil of meaning categories, so that I may discern emergent possibilities for the creation of meaning jointly with Langan (see Stern 1997).

Such a joint creation of meaning is just what Langan and his dying patient accomplish, poignantly, in their penultimate visit. Langan visits her in the hospital to sustain their ongoing therapeutic sessions in the face of her imminent death. They both know that therapy talk no longer serves or honors the integrity of their mission or their human connection—indeed, to cling fixedly to an attachment to "therapese" would now be no therapy. Langan asks what he can give her. She asks him for strawberries and vanilla ice cream. Langan gets some ice cream and wonderful strawberries and spoon-feeds her. In this creative act of "no-therapy," this resourceful woman and her devoted therapist paradoxically sustain the heart of the therapy to the last. Strawberries and ice cream, spoon-fed, replace (and reconstitute) the good feed of free association and apt interpretation. As the boundaries of standard therapeutic technique dissolve between them, the dissolving of their dissolving therapeutic journey itself dissolves. For the moment, they remain who they can be, with and for each other. And, thus, instead of mutually suffering an awkward attempt at a ritual non-therapy, they dissolve for this moment the suffering of their losses in the transcendent sharing of basic reciprocal human caring in a transformed and transformative version of their essentially ongoing therapy. This present experience cannot be alive and awake if it is like previous experiences. Nor can this intimate and tranquil moment exist for Langan and his patient if they dwell fixedly and obtrusively on the moment they both know is soon to come. There is only now. And there is only now, and what is made of now, holding it all together.

I recall a tranquil and intimate moment between my brother and me when I was about seventeen and he twenty or twenty-one. At seventeen I was rather obsessionally constricted, living all too much in my head. My brother, Ronnie, was a gifted pianist and composer whose more undisciplined style was leading him toward an emergent career in jazz. Throughout childhood, some of our most loving exchanges, when it seemed as if we truly existed for each other with mutual recognition, occurred when Ronnie took me in hand to introduce me to music appreciation. On this particular occasion, during my first visit to Ronnie's first apartment of his own, he put on a recording of Ravel's string quartet, and, as he pantomimed conducting the music as a way of guiding my attention, he offered me this knowing advice: "Only listen to the notes being played now. Don't hold on to the previous notes or anticipate the next notes. All the music is always in the notes you hear now. Just stay in the present moment, with the note you hear now, and you will hold all the music together."

In retrospect, I think that's probably the only way a performing musician can play music, holding on to the integrity, the architecture, and the continuity of an entire piece by letting go of everything but the note he or she is playing now. Ronnie, as a young performing pianist, seems inherently to have understood the concentration, the presence, and the freedom of "bare attention" (see Goldstein 1983), and perhaps also the heart of attuned analytic listening as Langan and his patient movingly embody in their therapeutic improvisational duet.

Joseph Goldstein (1983) tells the old story of a hermit in the woods whose sitting meditation is suddenly interrupted by the growling of a large tiger. The hermit, fleeing the tiger, falls over a cliff and breaks his fall by grabbing hold of a vine. Looking up at the pursuing tiger that watches from the edge of the cliff, the hermit becomes aware of another tiger below, waiting for his next meal to fall. Just then the hermit notices that two mice have appeared, and they begin to gnaw on his vine. "At such a moment," Goldstein asks, "what would be on *your* mind?" And then, Goldstein continues, the hermit looks to the side and notices a strawberry growing out of the rock. He reaches for the strawberry and eats it, and he says, "How delicious!" Goldstein suggests that the tiger above and the tiger below represent our birth and death, and that the mice are always gnawing at our vines. How, then, shall we experience the present moment? Goldstein commends the Buddhist practice of "bare attention" or, as Krishnamurti called it, "choiceless awareness." In the face of our existential plight, many an analyst might prescribe free association; attention to one's desire, conflict, frustration, or anger; self-reflection (Langan's "side-stepping awareness"?); a tolerance for uncertainty; grieving and renunciation; and the location of authentic personal agency—all facilitated in the potential space of an empathic, inquiring, and mutually engaged relationship. As Hoffman (1998) suggests, the problem of meaning and mortality may be faced with a combination of making the unconscious conscious and making the conscious unconscious: expanding ironic self-awareness and diminishing anxious self-preoccupation.

Langan offers us another alternative in our struggle to reconcile existence with death. He wants us to make room in ourselves for paradox, contradiction,

and uncertainty (as in the continued presence of his absent patient). But paradox is deucedly difficult for any of us to bend our minds around, and, at least
in places, I think Langan himself lapses from the realm of paradox and enters
the realm of legerdemain. Consider this instance:

> An openness to uncertainty more radical than Freud's
> begins to impugn the finality of any truth. We join
> Descartes, puzzled by the problem of establishing that
> one's self exists at all. Yet we cannot join him in his
> answer—I think therefore I am—if we open the stability
> of "I" to uncertainty. Contemporary psychoanalytic the-
> orists ...do just this, leaving self ungrounded, "standing
> in the spaces." ...Go further adrift. Dissolve yourself in
> space. By extension, even more radically, if we dissolve
> the fixity of self, do we dissolve, in some sense, death? If
> there is no fixed self, is there no one to die? The Buddha
> would answer, quizzically, yes.

I find several problems in this line (or squiggle) of argument. First, the
Buddhist problem: In the words of Mark Epstein (1995, 63), when asked
point-blank whether there was or was not a self, "the Buddha remained 'ther-
apeutically' silent.'" The Buddha later explained to his attendant that "there
was no way to answer the man's question without reinforcing some erroneous view of self." As Epstein further elaborates:

> If the Buddha had answered that there was a Self, he
> would have reinforced his questioner's grandiosity, that
> is, the idealized notions of possessing something lasting,
> unchanging, and special. If he had answered that there
> was truthfully no Self, he would have reinforced his
> questioner's sense of alienation and hollowness, a
> despairing belief in personal nothingness. When asked
> the ultimate narcissistic question by another follower—
> "What is the nature of the self?" the Buddha responded
> that there is neither self nor no-self. The question, itself,
> was flawed, the Buddha implied, for it was being asked

from a place that already assumed that the self was an entity. (65)

The Buddha evidently chose to preserve an unresolved paradox in order to foil inclinations toward foreclosure and reification. (It pleases me to consider in this an analogy to my definition of analytic neutrality [Pizer 1992, 1998] as the analyst's responsibility to keep the paradoxes of potential space optimally open for ongoing negotiation.)

Nina Coltart (1992, 1996), in her personal and cogent essays on psychoanalysis and Buddhism, takes up the challenge of *anatta* ("that all things ultimately are without self" [1992, 170]), and the ways it boggles the Western mind. She considers her own grasp of anatta, after many years of meditation, to be a "liberation of the spirit." She adds: "It also opens the door to the appreciation of a great cosmic joke about our work, which I might now express as something like '*of course* one has to know one's Ego is strong and understood before there is a chance of seeing that it doesn't exist.' As I have said elsewhere ...our work is full of paradoxes, and this is the most radical and delightful of them all" (170–71). Elsewhere (1996, 139), Coltart elaborates further:

> The paradox that is perfectly viable is that the Buddha taught the sorts of practice, including moral discipline, that can strengthen a healthy or a healing Real Self, awakening out of neurotic False Selves, yet at one and the same time would be teaching that there is no True Self in the sense of an unchanging identity. It is the notion of a central solid soul that the Buddha was trying to combat—a soul that is always recognizable to the self and to God and not only persists through this life, but moves over, unchanged, retaining identity, either into eternity ...or into the next incarnation.... Of course, in psychoanalysis we behave as if there is a self that recognizably continues, suffers, hopes for treatment and happiness, struggles for changes, knows itself often quite deeply, and experiences degrees of self-realization. But then so do we in Buddhism. It is what gives depth and meaning to life.

facility at handling, and even playing with, paradox. Psychic reality exists as the bridging of separate islands of subjective experience, an infinite latticework of causeways that span the islands of affect, memory, desire, introject, representation, word, metaphor, idea, mood, fantasy, and vision that constitute the multiple components of self-experience. Thus, psychic reality can be viewed as the mind's integrative process, yet not an integration; a bridging process, but not a bridge. And our psychoanalytic model of the mind needs to account for the universal presence of dissociation—or complex, nonlinear organizations— in health as well as in illness. We need a model of the self that is decentered and dimensional; a self that, as Whitman put it, contains multitudes; a *distributed* self.... . Our creative potential lies in the preservation and exploration of transitional spaces between otherwise dissociated elements of the self—in this sense, the creativity of everyday life, or of a psychoanalytic process, does not differ from the creative process of the painter or poet. Wellness lies in the capacity to straddle paradoxes within the self. Creativity lies in the fresh negotiations of paradox within the self as well as between the self and the material and relational outside world. As Bromberg (1993) has written, "health is the ability to stand in the spaces between realities without losing any of them. This is what I believe *self-acceptance* means and what *creativity* is really all about—the capacity to feel like one self while being many."

I am not speaking here of multiple personality disorder when I assert that we are all inherently multiple selves. Pathology reflects the failure to contain, tolerate, or mediate multiplicity—and, thus, the degree of dissociation, fragmentation, or foreclosure of internal potential space.... Neurotic defenses, and character defenses in analysis, can be seen as the foreclosure of internal potential space by coercing a solving of paradox within the self; requiring the repudiation of contradictory self-experiences, the eclipsing of inner conflict.... In contrast, the creative process *plays* with the paradoxical nature of a multiple self and its multifaceted relationship to the external world. The creative artist sees, hears, or names the paradoxical welter of experienced living.

Now I can declare that Langan's gift to us in his chapter lies in the creative artistry with which he plays with multiple perspectives, contradiction, and paradox. By a brilliant tour de force, he writes us into a journey within a world of nonlinearity. As readers, we find ourselves invited to dwell in the rippling moments of each of Langan's thoughts and images, only to find ourselves bobbled and lifted by the next (contradictory) ripple of thought, continually set down in a new place, and then lifted again by Langan's next ripple. Langan requires us to open our minds afresh. Plop. He reminds us, as he names it, of the paradoxical welter of experienced living—if, through bare attention and choiceless awareness, we allow our pond to remain open to the frog's leap. Ultimately, for Langan, this means allowing each other to matter.

Langan quotes the narrator of Borges's "The Aleph," who says, "What my eye saw was simultaneous: what I shall describe is successive, because language is successive." Elaborating on this Lacan-like view, Langan articulates something of his Buddhist perspective:

> The usual self, unthinkingly assumed so obviously to exist, is like the linear selector of successive moments, the "I" who remembers when I got up and forms expectations as to when to be abed, the "I" who places me here and you there somewhere beyond the opaque screen of this written page. The unusual self, reflexively imagined, undoes itself, finds itself simultaneously suspended by and suspending its own associational matrix. The associational matrix is no other than the relational connectivity of all experience, whereby all past is present, everywhere here in the perpetual unfolding of pure experience which includes the experience of perpetual unfolding. It includes as well the experience of no experience.... It contains contradiction and duality. It is all here at once, where "here" loses meaning. From this vantage, lying in the proper place, squinting at the proper angle, the Aleph is the self.

Langan joins this perspective with a current "relational, contextual, and constructivist" psychoanalysis that sees the self as "fluid and multifarious." With the dissolving of the monadic self, as Langan sees it, "the dissolving of dissolving itself" may be achieved. "There is no self; neither is there no-self." What there is, at least in psychoanalysis, is the potential for "the *interpersonal* action of therapeutic change." In dialogue "over the abyss of mortality,"

Langan tells us that "analyst and analysand can allow each other to matter"—as his clinical vignette so aptly depicts—and that in such a duet two people "can enact a modally different way of living life."

To reciprocate Langan's gift, I would like to illustrate his ideas as I have seen them embodied in the unfolding of an analytic process. Here I will share a few moments from the termination phase of the analysis of "Donald," who, years earlier, had entered treatment in a profound state of schizoid disconnection and emotional remoteness and had asked for my help in learning how to enrich his life. Here is how I have previously described these moments of Donald's "modally different way of living life":

> Donald mused about his initial therapeutic goals—information, insight, and explanations—and how, as we negotiated a process between us over time, his awareness had awakened to the importance of involvement in relationship, experience of affect, and attention to inner states. He marveled at how he could now sense what it was to be himself with another person and to sense feeling in the other person as well. Donald made the following remarkable statement to me: "I thought I'd come here to fix my life. The only way I could think was in a kind of linear, logical, problem-solving way. Now, it's like my mind works differently, at least sometimes. Now my mind is more like the scent of a spring day."...
>
> During the spring of Donald's termination year, he joined a cooperative gardening group in a country town. One Monday he came to our session eager to tell me of an experience from his weekend at the garden. He had been traversing the path into the garden, "grown over like a meadow with purple flowers," when he encountered a huge swarm of bees and was stung. "Well," he said, "the stings are really nothing. The big thing was suddenly seeing all those bees in the air over the path. It was ...like ...right there in focus, and yet beyond comprehension. I don't know if I can explain it clearly ...although, I may be easy to understand now. But, when I started here, I think

I was certainly not a person that could be easily understood. And …that's the paradox! I don't really understand myself now. I don't even think I ever could really understand myself …where I came from, how I got here, what this process has been. Like all those bees in the air—it's there, but beyond comprehension. But now I feel more understandable. Like the meadow full of bees …sometimes the thing to do is not to intellectualize, but just to step back and observe and enjoy the beauty of it." "Donald," I said, "today you are my teacher."

Again, within a week of this encounter with the bees in the meadow, Donald entered a session eager to share with me a moment of novel personal experience that had felt to him like the signal of a threshold. He was attending a workshop and driving to a restaurant during a lunch break when his car ran out of gas on the highway. He walked to the nearest exit and found a service station. Carrying a can of gas, as he walked along the shoulder of the highway back to his car, Donald had what he now happily called "an uninterpreted experience." Suddenly, Donald said, he found himself aware of the sloshing fluid inside the can, both the feeling and the sound, and the feeling of his own walking on the pavement beside the road. It was like a "click" [a plop?] inside him, an enjoyment of the freedom of experience. And he thought, "This moment is also a part of the workshop," and, instead of feeling anger, he felt alive. Then he thought, "I am a mess." Telling me his story, Donald said, "Mess was not bad. It felt rich. Complex. The emphasis was on am. The word am—me—being me. And then I thought, 'good,' and then my tears came freely." And so did mine. (Pizer 1998, 204–5)

I do picture Langan, a twelve-year-old boy, high in a Chinese elm. I imagine how a couple of 2 x 2's under the shoulder blade and pelvis became, for him, the sufficiency of his tree house. I agree with him that what we have for making meaning at the vertiginous edge of mortality's abyss is our imagination, our attention, and our relatedness. We all, in analysis, in the words of the Beatles, "take these broken wings and learn to fly." While honoring Langan's high-seriousness, I would also like to honor his playfulness by closing with a poem by Hughes Meanes:

> *As I was sitting in my chair,*
> *I found the bottom wasn't there.*
> *Nor legs, nor back, but I just sat*
> *Ignoring little things like that.*

Reply

A Saturated Solution

Robert Langan

> *Yesterday upon the stair*
> *I met a man who wasn't there.*
> *He wasn't there again today.*
> *Oh, how I wish he'd go away.*
>
> —*Anon. (appropriately)*

I am delighted that Stuart Pizer took my essay as an invitation to come out and play. The game under way, of course, is hide-and-seek. It behooves me to let evaporate some of what Pizer has found, the better to seek it anew.

He has found several problems in my "line (or squiggle) of argument." The particular line he seizes is my invitation to "Dissolve yourself in space.... do we dissolve, in some sense, death? If there is no fixed self, is there no one to die? The Buddha would answer, quizzically, yes."

Not so, counters Pizer, and he recounts the hoary tale of the Buddha answering the question as to whether there is self or no self not by a simple yes or no, but by silence. We might say that the Buddha answers with no answer, casting us back onto paradox. The quizzical aspect lies in "yes" being equivalent to "no" because each simple answer is equally irrelevant (and relevant) in the face of a subtle enormity of being that overwhelms our faltering approximations of reality. We need to be taken aback to be reminded anew of the illusory nature of me and you.

How necessary is the illusion? I agree with Pizer "that it is the inherent capacity to tolerate and bridge paradox that is central to the development and *growth* of the personality" (1998, 90). And I agree with Bromberg that "health is not integration. Health is the ability to stand in the spaces between realities without losing any of them ... the capacity to feel like one self while being many" (1998, 186). How could I disagree with Epstein's (1998) Buddhist valuation of, in his apt phrase, "going to pieces without falling apart"? The central paradox opposes one against many, continuity against fracture, a bridging toleration against an unbridged dissociation. The ontological paradox is not resolved but sustained. Sustaining (breath by breath) perdures through time, so to create its own sort of unity. That unity takes the psychological form of a me and a you, sustainedly here and now and with each other. Sustaining yields sustainers. Like Minoan bull dancers, we leap between the charging horns of our paradoxical dilemmas. And yet, I aver, there is something more.

Being-with must yield to being-for. A transcendence of self, I suspect, opens an experience of being wherein we dance for one another, our leaps and somersaults of such beauty as to take the breath away. Let me try to clarify my metaphor.

A model of psychological health that stops with the bridging of disparate self-states stops short of considering more fully what ends bridging might serve. If a capacity to tolerate paradox becomes merely a psychological strength, like capacities for creativity or empathy, the model of the psyche merely provides another hook on which to hang more bells and whistles for our fully outfitted psychological fashion plate. We end up with a bespangled morris dancer rather than a naked Minoan. Paradox loses its power for becoming too blandly knowable, just another head-scratching instance of life's endless dualities. Yet the power of paradox is to unseat knowability.

Pizer provides a sterling example of bridging self-states and of how such bridging might occur in the context of one person (mother) being for another (child). Imagine the toddler staggering those first few steps toward mother, in accomplished delight. Trip, fall, scowl; then up and reassured and bipedal to toddle again. And so,

> the transition from "mastery of walking" to "tumbling downward," and onward to "up and at it," has been accompanied by parental ego-coverage that helped to hold the moment together and negotiated a tolerable mediation of unthinkable anxiety at the brink of "going to pieces" ...the child has experienced not only the daily repetitions of sequence, but the repetitions of the transitions between sequences ...the experience of bridging.... We come to trust the experience of getting from here to there without yet knowing how. Hence, by internalizing the affective experience of state transitions, we form the basis for our ability to bridge, to straddle, paradox without a disruption of our sense of self, although we may be cognitively or affectively strained. (Pizer 1998, 91)

Pizer is utterly plausible in his argument that the ability to experience bridging, learned with another who is there for you, is crucial to the development of a continuity of self. And the ramifications for psychoanalytic treatment follow accordingly. When his terminating patient Donald has his epiphanic moments with the swarm of stinging bees and the sloshing can of gasoline, those "uninterpreted experiences" bear the hallmark of paradox, as well as what I have called elsewhere "the emergence of the present" (Langan 1993).

And yet, is there nothing more? If, as the Heart Sutra has it, "Emptiness is form, form emptiness," Pizer comes down on the side of form (not that he rests there), while I am making the case for emptiness. As his brother advised, Pizer listens, with a deepening enrichment he can so well convey, to each musical note in its singularity before him. I follow the composer John Cage, who was more struck by the silences between the notes. Is there nothing more? There is more: nothing. In other words, a paradox unresolved is still a paradox, a nameable conundrum we can lasso conceptually by bridging. That's too safe. When Descartes reassures himself of his existence by reasoning that he is indubitably doubting, he constricts the panoply of experience to that of an essentialist self-as-thinker. (See Lakoff and Johnson 1999, esp. 400–404.)

As these thoughtful words bridge one paragraph to another, as my ongoing "I" bridges multifarious self-states into an ongoing identity, as that identity reveals itself to be an altered and altering iteration of what has gone before and what follows, nothing stays the same. Everything changes; nothing stays except nothing. Even while time alters all, aging bridges and islands and self-states alike, even while no moment is ever repeated or repeatable, nothing stays the same. Emptiness is form.

The bridges are always, so it seems to me, illusions, both there and not, swaying delicately over an incomprehensible void. Pizer feels I reify that void and the bridges: "I would prefer more dynamic terms.... Space itself can be the location of processes of bridging or interconnection." If obliged, I should rather stand upon a bridge than a process (which requires space?), but we had best avoid the endless permutations of metaphor and the mercurial flux between nominative and transitive. The power of paradox is to rip open reality, to make it all go to pieces, while, at the same time, not. A capacity to tolerate paradox, to sustain bridging, can enrich and amplify life, but it leads (perhaps developmentally) toward the dark prospect of sustaining the unsustainable span from gasping life to certain death. The bridges, the thoughts, the self-states so various and new, all evaporate in a void.

Let us do be careful not to reify that void. The Buddhist commentator Garma C. C. Chang (1989) can assist:

> At this point a few words on "Voidness" may be helpful. When we say "That house is empty," we mean that it contains no occupants; but Buddhist "Voidness" does not mean absence. When we say, "That whole block is now empty," we mean there were houses in the block before, but none exist now; but Buddhist "Voidness" does not mean extinction. Voidness is difficult to define and describe. We can say a great deal about what Voidness is not, but very little about what it is. Voidness denotes the relative, flowing, undefinable, and ungraspable nature of all things. Philosophically it represents the illusory and dream-like nature of phenomena; psychologically it signifies a total liberation from all bondage. (8 n. 2)

And further:

> The patterns of thought of sentient beings are of a limited or finite nature. When one realizes the truth of Voidness (Shunyata), the limitative patterns of thought are fundamentally transformed. Using Buddhist terminology, they "dissolve" into the Dharmadatu—the absolute, universal, and interpenetrating state of all the different aspects of existence in the light of the Void. (36 n. 14)

What we are faced with, philosophically, is what we cannot know. Knowledge seems of necessity to be built upon knowledge, the chattel of words. We discover ourselves thrown into a world of duality—of here and there, before and after, you and me, pleasure and pain, health and sickness, life and death. What we ultimately both need and fear is not more knowledge of that world, nor even more adeptness at negotiating the paradoxes of that dualistic world. What we need and fear is for the bottom to drop out of the world. We need the dissolving of the dualistic dissolving and resolving of experience: we need the dissolving of dissolving itself.

Philip Bromberg comes close to this precipitous view by way of his conceptualization of psychoanalytic treatment as a royal road riddled with potholes, that is, with failures on the part of the analyst to share experientially the patient's reality. When the patient's reality includes experience of potentially annihilating trauma, a pothole can become an abyss. Then, "until the analyst is forced [to] deal with a patient's experience as something that gradually permeates its way into his soul in spite of his theories and his logic, the iatrogenic threat of potential retraumatization escalates.... Because the abyss is subjectively an abyss to an aspect of the patient's self that feels it as 'really real,' if we are to personally live with and know that part of who our patient is, the abyss must become a "really real" experience for the analyst too" (Bromberg 2000, 13–14). Knowing about such an abyss is no substitute for being in it, since only being in it can provide the "safe surprise" of new experience rather than retraumatization. One risks going beyond what one can know only to discover that one can know anew.

The experience of changing personhood becomes analogous to the transformation in chemistry of a saturated solution (or more properly, a supersaturated solution). So much of a salt, say, is invisibly dissolved in solution, that the dissolving of a minuscule amount more precipitates out an unexpected quantity. Likewise experientially, one faces the prospect of dissolving only—out of the void—to form unexpectedly anew.

Form arises from emptiness. In the framework of psychoanalysis, the experience of oneself as a person (alone and yet not, and particularly with your analyst there for you) can open to the unknown. This conceptualization of psychoanalytic change becomes, in a Buddhist framework, a self-allowed opening to the interplay of form and emptiness whereby each is seen as an aspect of the other. The paradoxical equivalence of form and emptiness cannot be resolved—it remains a paradox—but can, in a sense, dissolve. It dissolves not into some oceanic unity, because unity implies duality, one enmeshes many. Such a dissolving requires a not knowing, a fundamental transformation of "limitative patterns of thought," a leap into the abyss, an eviscerating somersault between the horns of the charging bull.

The trauma we all share lurks in the suspicion that at one time we did not exist, and that soon enough, same story. The duality that ultimately seizes us is life and death. The Buddha's Middle Way steered historically between the despair of nihilism and the passion for perfection of eternalism's everlasting soul (see de Silva 1975), but as well it steers experientially into the *between,* between life and death. I want to conclude with a brief consideration of a Buddhist view of death, because I believe it sheds an interesting light on the nature of psychoanalytic "bridging" as discussed by Pizer (1998) and on the "standing in the spaces" Bromberg (1998) felicitously poses.

White Tara, whose name literally means "Savioress," is a Tibetan deity known for her salvific powers and ability to bestow long life. "Tara was born from a lotus blossom that sprang from a tear shed by Avalokitesvara, the bodhisattva of compassion, as he surveyed the suffering universe"(Lopez 1997, 548). To complicate matters, although she is the mother of all Buddhas, Tara is commonly depicted as a sixteen-year-old beauty (if seven eyes don't mar your sense of beauty); yet she can also appear in at least twenty-one manifestations, including green and red, wrathful and benign. A rococo universe of possibilities opens up. To stick with White Tara, however, she can be visualized along with the following traditional invocation: "If, foreseeing signs of premature death, may I, by a clear vision of White Tara, subdue the Lord of Death, attaining the *siddhi* [power] of immortality. By this merit, having quickly attained the state of noble Tara, may I establish every sentient being, without a single exception, to that state." How can the Tibetan school of Buddhism, a nontheistic religion, have such a panoply of deities? And how can Buddhism entertain a promise of immortality? The deities can be regarded in a variety of ways. At the simplest level of understanding, they are outside spiritual entities capable of intervening in one's life. Tara, from this perspective, is something like Catholicism's Virgin Mary. At a deeper level of understanding, the deities are less entities in themselves than they are visualizations of the meditator, rendered in eidetic detail by years of practice. At a deeper (or more sublime?) level still, the deities are less visualizations than they are empowered ways of being created and experienced by the meditator. The deity is not a picture, but an ontological envelope that one's consciousness occupies. The deities are learning aids on the path toward an enlightened understanding of consciousness and reality. They are gods inasmuch as one can think of them that way; they are not gods so much as permutations of consciousness.

And what of the siddhi of immortality? Fairly well known in the West is the Buddhist idea of reincarnation: one is chained to a wheel of rebirth, reborn life after life into better or worse circumstances depending on the karmic consequences of one's actions. Reincarnation does not, however, entail an everlasting essentialist soul; instead, the process is likened to a flame passing from one candle to another. One does utterly die. Death is a destroyer.

Immortality, then, requires escaping the wheel of rebirth. *The Tibetan Book of the Dead* (Thurman 1994) describes how. When one enters the *bardo*, the between state manifest upon dying, one feels still embodied, still present to oneself. The rub comes out of attachment to that self. As a parade of benign presences becomes more wrathful, fear arises, terror of dissolution. The easy recourse is to flee, in effect, to another womb, another rebirth. The boddhisattva's recourse, perhaps with the aid of a sustained clear vision of White Tara, is to realize that the body is a manifestation of consciousness, that form is the void itself, so there is nothing to fear. The terrors, like the pleasures, are at base hallucinations, forms of the void, and voidness cannot harm voidness. Therein lies enlightenment, and freedom.

Immortality, accordingly, does not mean living forever. It means being unshackled from life and death, even time and space. This is not to deny life and death, but to know them differently.

From the Western point of view that embeds consciousness in the body, this whole after-death scenario is bizarre. One need not subscribe to it wholly, however, in order to recognize certain emphases pertinent to the nature of psychological change. The first is the power of visualization. The second is an altered attitude toward the reality of oneself. For the Tibetans "healing transformations basically take place in the spaciousness *between* the 'place' one is in and the 'place' one is projecting oneself into.... simply *visualizing* oneself as being [some other being] is, experientially, the *same as being*...that other being...there is no ultimate *metaphysical* difference between the being one projects or dreams and the being one is" (Levin 1981, 262–63; see also Govinda 1969; Blofeld 1974).

Is it not the case that the psychoanalytic dialogue (an interplay of two beings) can be construed as a kind of verbal visualization, a trying on of ontological possibilities? The treatment's success occurs when certain of those possibilities become realities, empowered states of being. The "bridging" of self-states entails *petits morts*—little deaths—of a non-orgasmic variety: from the arcing vantage of the bridge, who one took oneself to be dies—or can never be known in quite the same way again. "Standing in the spaces" entails recognizing oneself as space, a void given form after form after form by the play of consciousness. It's bizarre, really.

Note

1. I thank, in particular, Chogyam Trungpa Rinpoche, Kyabje Gelek Rinpoche, Robert Thurman, Larry Rosenberg, Alan Ginsberg, Mark Epstein, Joseph Goldstein, and Stephen Wilder.

References

Batchelor, S. 1983. *Alone with Others: An Existential Approach to Buddhism.* New York: Grove Press.

Benjamin, J. 2000. Intersubjective Distinctions: Subjects and Persons, Recognitions and Breakdowns. Commentary on paper by Gerhardt, Sweetnam, and Borton. *Psychoanalytic Dialogues* 10:43–55.

Binswanger, L. 1957. *Sigmund Freud: Reminiscences of a Friendship.* New York: Grune and Stratton.

Bion, W. 1970. *Attention and Interpretation*. London: Tavistock Publications.

Blofeld, J. 1974. *The Tantric Mysticism of Tibet: A Practical Guide*. New York: Causeway Books.

Borges, J. L. 1966. *A Personal Anthology*. New York: Grove Press.

Bromberg, P. 1993. Shadow and Substance: A Relational Perspective on Clinical Process. *Psychoanalytic Psychology* 10:147–68.

———. 1998. *Standing in the Spaces: Essays on Clinical Process, Trauma, and Dissociation*. Hillsdale, N.J.: Analytic Press.

———. 2000. Potholes on the Royal Road: Or Is It an Abyss? *Contemporary Psychoanalysis* 36:5–28.

Bruner, J. 1990. *Acts of Meaning*. Cambridge: Harvard University Press.

Cavell, M. 2000. Self-Reflections. *Psychoanalytic Dialogues* 10:513–29.

Chang, G. C. C., trans. and ed. 1989. *The Hundred Thousand Songs of Milarepa*. Boston: Shambhala.

Clark, K., and M. Holquist. 1984. *Mikhail Bakhtin*. Cambridge: Harvard University Press.

Coltart, N. 1992. *Slouching towards Bethlehem*. New York: Guilford Press.

———. 1996. *The Baby and the Bathwater*. Madison, Conn.: International Universities Press.

Csikszentmihalyi, M. 1999. If We Are So Rich, Why Aren't We Happy? *American Psychologist* 54: 821–27.

Das, S. 1997. *Awakening the Buddha Within*. New York: Broadway Books.

de Silva, L. A. 1975. *The Problem of the Self in Buddhism and Christianity*. New York: Harper and Row, 1979.

Epstein, M. 1995. *Thoughts without a Thinker: Psychotherapy from a Buddhist Perspective*. New York: Basic Books.

———. 1998. *Going to Pieces without Falling Apart: A Buddhist Perspective on Wholeness*. New York: Broadway Books.

Freud, S. 1912. *Recommendations to Physicians Practising Psycho-Analysis*. In Standard Edition, 12:109–20. London: Hogarth Press, 1958.

Fromm, E., D. T. Suzuki, and R. De Martino. 1960. *Zen Buddhism and Psychoanalysis*. New York: Harper and Row.

Goldstein, J. 1983. Bare Attention. Talk delivered at the Insight Meditation Society, Barre, Massachusetts, May 27.

Govinda, A. 1969. *Foundations of Tibetan Mysticism according to the Esoteric Teachings of the Great Mantra OM MANI PADME HUM.* New York: Samuel Weiser.

Gyatso, T., and Sheng-yen. 1999. *Meeting of Minds: A Dialogue on Tibetan and Chinese Buddhism.* New York: Dharma Drum Publications.

Hoffman, I. 1998. *Ritual and Spontaneity in the Psychoanalytic Process: A Dialectical-Constructivist View.* Hillsdale, N.J.: Analytic Press.

Hua, H. 1980. *The Heart of Prajna Paramita Sutra, with Verses without a Stand and Prose Commentary.* Trans. R. B. Epstrin. San Francisco: Buddhist Text Translation Society.

————. 1996. *The Shurangama Sutra: The Fifty Skandha-Demon States.* Burlingame, Calif.: Buddhist Text Translation Society.

James, W. 1904. Does "Consciousness" Exist? In *William James: Writings 1902–1910*, 1141–58. New York: Library of America, 1987.

Lakoff, G., and M. Johnson. 1999. *Philosophy in the Flesh: The Embodied Mind and Its Challenge to Western Thought.* New York: Basic Books.

Langan, R. P. 1993. The Depth of the Field. *Contemporary Psychoanalysis* 29:628–64.

————. 1997. On Free-Floating Attention. *Psychoanalytic Dialogues* 7:819–39.

————. 1999a. What on Closer Examination Disappears. *American Journal of Psychoanalysis* 59:87–96.

————. 1999b. Coming to Be: Change by Affiliation. *Contemporary Psychoanalysis* 35:67–80.

————. 2000. Someplace in Mind. *International Forum of Psychoanalysis* 9:69–75.

Levin, D. M. 1981. Approaches to Psychotherapy: Freud, Jung, and Tibetan Buddhism. In *Metaphors of Consciousness,* ed. R. S. Valle and R. von Eckartsberg, 243–74. New York: Plenum Press, 1989.

Lopez, D. S., ed. 1997. *Religions of Tibet in Practice.* Princeton: Princeton University Press.

Meltzer, D., and M. H. Williams. 1988. *The Apprehension of Beauty: The Role of Aesthetic Conflict in Development, Violence and Art.* Old Ballechin, Strath Tay, Scotland: Clunie Press.

Mendis, K. N. G. 1979. *On the No-Self Characteristic (Anatta-Lakkhana Sutta).* Kandy, Sri Lanka: Buddhist Publication Society.

Mitchell, S. A. 1993. *Hope and Dread in Psychoanalysis.* New York: Basic Books.

Nahin, P. J. 1998. *An Imaginary Tale: The Story of the Square Root of Minus*

One. Princeton: Princeton University Press.

Nyanaponika. 1949. *Abidhamma Studies: Buddhist Explorations of Consciousness and Time.* Reprint, Boston: Wisdom, 1998.

Phillips, A. 1994. *On Flirtation: Psychoanalytic Essays on the Uncommitted Life.* Cambridge: Harvard University Press.

Pizer, S. 1992. The Negotiation of Paradox in the Analytic Process. *Psychoanalytic Dialogues* 2:215–40.

———. 1998. *Building Bridges: The Negotiation of Paradox in Psychoanalysis.* Hillsdale, N.J.: Analytic Press.

Schafer, R. 1976. *A New Language for Psychoanalysis.* New Haven: Yale University Press.

Stern, D. B. 1997. *Unformulated Experience: From Dissociation to Imagination in Psychoanalysis.* Hillsdale, N.J.: Analytic Press.

Thurman, R. A. F. 1996. *Essential Tibetan Buddhism.* New York: HarperCollins.

———, trans. 1994. *The Tibetan Book of the Dead.* New York: Bantam.

Waddell, L. A. 1895. *Tibetan Buddhism, with Its Mystic Cults, Symbolism and Mythology, and in Its Relation to Indian Buddhism.* Reprint, New York: Dover Publications, 1972.

Way, R., trans. 1986. *The Cloud of Unknowing and the Letter of Private Direction.* Wheathampstead, Hertfordshire, England: Anthony Clarke Publishers.

Winnicott, D. W. 1975. *Through Pediatrics to Psycho-Analysis.* New York: Basic Books.

Wolstein, B. 1994. The Evolving Newness of Interpersonal Psychoanalysis: From the Vantage Point of Immediate Experience. *Contemporary Psychoanalysis* 30:473–99.

Chapter 4

An Analyst's Surrender

Sara L. Weber

Wanting to grasp the ungraspable,
you exhaust yourself in vain.
As soon as you open and relax this tight fist of grasping,
infinite space is there—open, inviting and comfortable...
Nothing to do or undo,
Nothing to force,
Nothing to want
and nothing missing.

—*Venerable Lama Gendun Rinpoche*

When I was a child I often experienced equanimity—a sense of profound peace—when I was sick. If I had the flu and a fever, all was somehow at rest in the world. Though uncomfortable, throwing up, or congested, I was somehow safe—held in a state of grace. My bedroom seemed filled with soft, cooling sunlight. My mother was calm, loving—seeming to bestow upon me the feelings of love one has for a sleeping, amazingly angelic, vulnerable child. She felt secure in her role. Somehow all the evil and terrifying forces in my home were safely away. I had nothing to protect myself from, nothing to strive for, nothing to struggle with. The flu had its own course to follow, and though clearly I was taken over by it, intensely focused on every awful sensation, afraid that any minute the next one would overtake me, some aspect of me and of my mother that made discomfort into suffering was off duty. There was serenity, even a kind of bliss, in the midst of, or possibly at the core of my being.

My mother was holding me. She took my temperature, held a cold cloth to my head, brought me juice, called the doctor. But most importantly, she allowed me to be ill, for things to take as long as they needed to. She felt safe, able to know how terrible and frightened I felt, yet simultaneously sure both of us would survive. She was exquisitely sensitive to my subjectivity, yet aware of her own.

This mood was different when I was ill in other ways—sick with terror over my mother's suicidal wishes, sick with fear of the dark and evil forces that my undiagnosed manic-depressive older sister's presence evoked in the house, sick with anxiety and humiliation over my inability to concentrate at school, sick with the heavy-heartedness that prevented me from playing with my peers. I tried to stay home sick with these ills, but it didn't work. For these illnesses I felt no equanimity. I had no capacity to learn what was wrong, no real intimacy. There were only defensive reactions to the terror, a deeply shameful clutching and rejection.

In a reverie about holding I see before me an image of Michelangelo's *Madonna della Pieta*. Michelangelo, when he was fifteen years old, carved this statue of the Virgin Mary supporting the dead Christ on her knees. In his vision Mary holds her lifeless son with an amazingly light touch. Her only effort is in the arm that holds him. Could this little be enough? His lifeless body seems ready to slip off her lap, and yet it does not. She sits effortlessly erect. Only her head bows to the dead body, but with deep kindness and grace, not with angst and suffering. All else is lax, surrendered though not collapsed, flowing gracefully into and out of the stone from which the figures are carved. Perhaps what is solid here is not life or death, but some ephemeral quality best known as grace.

Michelangelo's Christ is graceful, glowing even in death with holy beauty. Perhaps it is not so difficult to look with open-heartedness upon the death of someone so wondrous. A more disturbing view of the martyred Christ is found in the painting of Hans Holbein the Younger entitled *The Body of the Dead Christ in the Tomb*. In *The Idiot* Dostoyevsky through the character of Ippolit describes the painting thus:

> The picture depicted Christ who was just taken from the
> cross.... there was no trace of beauty. It was a faithful rep-
> resentation of the dead body of a man who had undergone
> unbearable torments before the crucifixion, been wounded,

> tortured, beaten by the guards, beaten by the people, when
> he carried the cross and fell under its weight, and, at last,
> suffered the agony of the crucifixion, which lasted for six
> hours.... there is still a look of suffering on the face of the
> dead man, as though he were still feeling it. In the picture
> the face is terribly smashed with blows, tumefied, covered
> with terrible, swollen and bloodstained bruises ...the open
> whites of the eyes have a sort of dead and glossy glint. (Dos-
> toyevsky 1955, 236)

When another character in the novel, Prince Muskin, looks at the picture, he exclaims, "[S]ome people may lose their faith by looking at that picture" (237). Indeed, how can anyone believe, faced with the depth of pain, wounds, depression, ugliness, and fear of death that we all carry, that we can survive being alive—much less become fully alive? And yet if we cannot tolerate our pain and suffering and fears, can we be truly present in our lives? Is it not the case that this sort of equanimity lies at the elusive core of psychodynamic experience?

*   *   *

In this chapter I explore the exquisitely subtle and yet simple state of mind—or being—that allows one more fully to experience oneself and thus the suffering of others, without doing anything to escape that suffering and without being destroyed by it. The state of mind entails "willing-not-to-will" (Langan 1997). I shall describe how, late in a long psychoanalysis, I stumbled, meditatively, across that state of mind into the space of willing-not-to-will I had known when I was a sick child. Much was very painful in that state, but there was some great peace. The patient's attacks stung, yet somehow I was unhurt, undefended, not wondering about "me." I felt completely safe, held, while our hearts ached and storms raged. Time, memory and desire were suspended (see Bion 1970). In Emmanuel Ghent's (1990) terminology, I had "surrendered," and she followed suit. There was nothing to do. I was not the holder, nor was I holding back any part of me. I myself was held, floatingly.

D. W. Winnicott defines holding as *"not only the actual holding of the infant, but also the total environmental provision, prior to the concept of living with ...[And it] includes the management of experiences that are inherent in existence ...determined by the awareness and empathy of the mother"* (1965, 43–44).

The infant's psychosomatic world is dependent on this state of being characterized by the "psyche indwelling in the soma" (Winnicott 1965, 44). On this indwelling rests not just one's actual being but one's own personal complex psychological sense of "being." For Winnicott the infant is unaware of the other/mother. Recent advances in infant research (Stern 1985), however, seem to indicate that the infant has an awareness of the other at least from birth on. Perhaps, it is a state of being in which experiences that originate from some inner cause, like hunger, and those that originate from some outer state, like the emotional being of one's caretakers, are all present in the soup of earliest existence. Certainly we all know from experience that one's inner state will predominate when it is extremely uncomfortable, but no one—not even a very sick baby—is in distress all the time.

For multidimensional reasons inherent within each of us, including psychosomatic state, psychodynamics, cognitive structures, and capacity to tolerate discomfort, we may attend to any of a multiplicity of these experiences. We may block out the other, or we may become completely involved in the other; we may notice our hearts pounding in our chests, or we may notice our mother's, father's, or lover's heart pounding. We may move gently from one experience to another, or we may get traumatically pinned down, compelled to live in one state. It may be more in keeping with current thinking to conceptualize "holding" as a state of mind that does not preclude the capacity to know of the existence of others, but that is characterized by the discounting of the other, perhaps "ruthlessly" (Winnicott 1965, 24) privileging one's own psychosomatic awareness.

The need to access the "holding" state of mind is omnipresent in life, alternating with the state of "living with," in which one is privileging or at least compromising with others who comprise one's "object relationships." Indeed, Winnicott (1965, 44) speaks of the importance in healthy development of retaining "the capacity for re-experiencing unintegrated states" inherent in holding. These states are dependent on the existence of reliable care created by the mother-baby pair or memory of it. These states are the fodder of what Winnicott (1958, 212) calls the true self (a concept akin to the Buddhist notion of selflessness [(Tarab Tulku 1999, 20)] and creativity). In fact, intimacy with another is only possible with the capacity to surrender to ourselves.

The alternative to the experience of holding is called impingement. Winnicott (1965) describes an infant who is being breast-fed. He says that it is impossible for the observer, and perhaps even for the mother, to know whether this infant is getting a good feed, that is, being "held," or whether he or she has been seduced into this feeding and feels impinged upon. Under the common circumstances of having to do something on someone else's terms, the supplies are not satisfying. We cannot ignore or discount the other's irritating, unwanted and controlling presence and live our own experience fully. Although we may be able to behave to some extent differently than we feel, any successful coercion to feel other than we actually feel—even a coercion to fit some preferred version of ourselves—will keep us at distance from our true selves. It will result in little personal evolution, and mere defense building.

Freud recommended that the analyst use a unique kind of attention when listening to patients in order to minimize impingement from their defenses and allow what is in their minds to be revealed (to make the unconscious conscious). Psychoanalysts, he admonished, should listen with "evenly suspended attention" during which the critical faculty is suspended, allowing for "impartial attention to everything there is to observe. He should simply listen, and not bother about whether he is keeping anything in mind" (Freud 1912, 111–12). In an attempt to evoke the same state of mind in his patients, he instructed them to "free associate" without censorship. Further, he forbade them from making any major changes in their lives, so as to leave the door open for unexpected and as yet unknown answers to their concerns.

These goals became colored by the zeitgeist of the times. For psychoanalysis to be accepted, it had to be seen as a science. The psychoanalyst was a cold, distant observer wearing the psychological equivalent of a white lab coat and observing the patient as a specimen, or perhaps he was a surgeon necessarily dissociated from his own feelings. In today's zeitgeist, the relational model has returned the psychoanalyst to a more human position, and the goal of psychoanalysis to one of mutuality. But how do we then see the role and use of "evenly suspended attention"? And more pertinent to my not-so-hidden agenda, who among us is actually able to give truly impartial attention on a regular basis? What is such attention anyway?

Freud's goals may have had something in common with those of mindfulness meditation (also called *vipassana*, or insight meditation): a cultivation of a moment-to-moment awareness of changing perceptions in a neutral, impartial way. A basic tenet of Buddhism is that it is healing simply to pay open, neutral, gentle attention to one's perceptions, thoughts, emotions, and somatic experiences. Neutrality here does not mean perching equidistantly between ego, id, and superego, or being indifferent to or distant from any emotion or pain. It means seeing things as they are, fully aware of one's perceptions, from a foundation of equanimity and deep acceptance, including physical and emotional pain and even evil.

There are different forms of mindfulness meditation, arising from different teachings of the Buddha. In general, the practitioner of mindfulness meditation practices attending to deeper and simple aspects of perceptions, starting with breathing, and ending with the impermanence of all things and the lack of separation between one's self, others, and the world (Kornfield 1993). During these practices the meditator is instructed on how to sit in stillness, attending but not reacting to the many distractions in the body-mind. The meditator as well can maintain and practice mindfulness while walking, eating, and doing chores.

One highly structured form of mindfulness meditation is based on the Buddha's Anapanasati Sutra. In this sutra, organized into sixteen contemplations, one's breath is the focus of attention (Rosenberg 1998). First one meditates until one is fully and steadily aware of the breath, its qualities, and its manifestation in the body. Then partial, simultaneous awareness is given to somatic feeling states, then to mental states, and then to the impermanence of all things.

Another form of meditation called "choiceless awareness" (Rosenberg 1999) sounds more like Freud's "evenly hovering attention." In this form of mindfulness meditation one pays attention to "whatever momentarily arises in the body mind," says Lama Gendun Rinpoche (Gendun 1995), without identifying with it, without becoming attached to it and without passing judgment upon it or upon oneself.

What does it mean not to identify with a thought or pain or sensation or whatever arises? In an intermediate way, it means being able to feel compassion for the person who hurts you because of your realization that it is from pain and ignorance. (This does not mean passively to allow others to harm you.) More radically, it means genuinely not thinking of *my* foot moving, *my* hunger, *my* pain or anger, or *my* rights and needs. One is existing choicelessly, like a leaf falling or the grass growing. One is aware, when it arises, of the heart beating, of anger welling up and fading, of sexual feelings waxing and waning, of the breath coming and going. This awareness is not about changing narcissistic hurt into healthy narcissism. The Buddha is advocating a radical end of narcissism.

Attachment, in the Buddhist sense, may be even harder to get our psychologically oriented minds around. Nonattachment is not about being aloof. It is about, for example, loving and accepting your child's behavior when it does not gratify your sense of how *your* child should behave. It is about your having genuine acceptance, even though you are a college professor, of your son's decision to become an auto mechanic—no ifs, ands, or buts. Or, to give a more difficult example, it is about sustaining compassionate equanimity while your child goes through the throes of manic depression. Are you able to do what you can without deluding yourself that there is nothing wrong with your child, because you can't handle knowing the truth? Can you act without suffering the shame of having a child who is so "inappropriate" and "dysfunctional"? Nonattachment even means not feeling pride if your child gets into Harvard. Imagine life without shame or pride. For the Buddha, many paths through life each offer the possibility for enlightenment. All that we are attached to is impermanent—so there's nothing to get ruffled about.

Issues of attachment can be observed even more subtly in our attitude toward thoughts, sensations, and feelings. We are directed not to push away unpleasant thoughts or sensations, nor to elaborate on pleasant ones or on ones that gratify or justify our egos. One particular example of how attachment can play itself out in our minds is highly illustrative of a major difference between Freud's suggestions for the process of healing and the Buddha's. The process of dwelling on the pain caused by, say, a friend's insensitivity— of associating this pain to other similar slights one has suffered and then connecting it to pains suffered in the past—is seen as rife with attachment. Corrado Penza, an Italian pscholanalyst and Buddhist teacher, calls it "proliferation." Penza (2001) points out that the object of observing these "proliferations" or "free associations" is to become free of them, not to use them to explain or understand anything. When one notices one's thoughts proliferating, one remembers to return one's attention to the breath and to more immediate perceptions of the here and now. In doing so one's "free associations" are soon noticed to be anything but free. Soon one is, perhaps, amused at how repetitive, boring, and empty they are. There can be a profound loosening of the grip your past has on you.

The final part of the directive in choiceless awareness, and a crucial part of all mindfulness meditations, is to pay attention to perception without passing judgment upon it or upon oneself. There is a clear distinction between judgment and discernment. When we see that a certain act stems from anger and ignorance, we should do what we can to avoid the creation and consequences of such acts, but not judge the person. We suspend the thousands of judgments that inhibit further knowledge and acceptance. Our perpetual criticism of ourselves and others is exchanged for observation, generally through the practice of compassion or loving-kindness meditation. This exchange is a gradual process, and far from the simplistic *Don't Worry Be Happy* we see on T-shirts. We must notice the many judgments we make, including that we should not have any judgments. Far from repressing judgments, we gradually replace them with compassion for our suffering and bring about a diminution of their arising.

Greater awareness of attachment, identification, and judgment alter experience. An itch can be noticed as hot or cold, or as a tingly feeling that gets intense, moves, and disappears—but never gets scratched. A hot, throbbing, stabbing pain in the heart can lead to a release of tears of joy and gratitude, without associating to any cognitive content. A need to "do something" about an irritating person in one's life can lead to a feeling of fundamental terror normally defended against, or to a feeling of hatred and lack of acceptance for the same characteristic in oneself, or perhaps to love for the bothersome person, or to a reluctance to allow such persons to be who they are and to go through what they need to go through. Or the need to "do something" may lead simply to related bodily sensations. More fundamentally, this sort of mindfulness leads to an awareness that all these perceptions arise and pass away.

Mark Epstein sums it up nicely: "Instead of running from different emotions (or hanging on to enticing ones) the practitioner of bare attention becomes able to *contain* any reaction: making space for it, but not completely identifying with it because of the concomitant presence of nonjudgmental awareness." And: "Thoughts and feelings, stripped of their associated pride or shame, gradually lose their charge and come to be seen as 'just' thoughts or 'just' feelings" (1995, 111, 124).

This mindfulness, prescribed by Freud and even more radically by the Buddha, is at once ordinary and difficult to attain and sustain. Mindfulness meditation offers a method. By this method one grows more able to "hold" those greater degrees of discomfort that might otherwise be experienced as impingement. Walls between self and other become more permeable, while the self is known more fully.

At times controlled holding is crucial for development. The patient cannot tolerate anything less, and will perceive the subjectivity of the other as insulting. However, by itself controlled holding ultimately leaves patients feeling ashamed and dependent, unable to believe themselves, to know themselves, have faith in, or give credence to themselves. By contrast, the surrender of holding permits the *analyst and the patient* simultaneously to give up external control for a holding that exists beyond the person, the self, and especially the ego of both analyst and patient. Neither analyst nor patient knows where things will go. The analyst is deeply in a state of free-floating attention, not *having* to say anything, do anything, or hold anything, even in mind. In keeping with W. R. Bion, "What matters is the unknown and on this the psychoanalyst must focus his attention." The analyst uses a "disciplined space that should remain unsaturated by any form of preconception" and shows a "faith unsustained by any element of memory or desire" in which truth can manifest (Bion 1970, 69, 41, 32). In a phasic development, analysis first recognizes and acknowledges how analyst and patient both hold tight to ego; next it allows a surrender of that tight hold. The real holding environment is faith—a most difficult accomplishment.

*   *   *

Let me illustrate the clinical play of mindfulness with a psychoanalytic case study. In this case, the passage was from a holding environment characterized by control of self and other to a holding environment characterized by surrender to the vast and ever changing experience of the psyche-soma—a state permitting greater creative experiences of being.

The patient was an extremely intelligent and perceptive woman who was often in excruciating mental and physical pain. She had developed masochistic self-sacrifice and suffering to a sophisticated and impactful level. Her presence was often raw and sore, like the sores she picked at. Her world was peopled by those who sadistically, pitifully, and righteously took advantage of her. By profession, she aggressively and effectively fought for the rights of the downtrodden. She kept legislators, lawyers, and mayors busy maneuvering.

Yet always she ultimately lost. She felt unable to know what *she* really wanted at any given moment. She hated her work. Though alienated from and secretly disdaining everyone she worked for and with, she nonetheless felt great compassion for their pain. Her compulsion was to fix them, to help them avoid the consequences of their own behavior.

At the beginning of therapy she had just run away from a dangerous and abusive relationship that was both professional and romantic. She still allowed her former lover to control her every move, even though he was living a thousand miles away. He called several times a day. She felt that she had to be there, had to be supportive of him, could not change her phone number, tell him no, tell him off. She was terrified about how he might retaliate if she did. She was unable to take any of the very good advice of friends who had *her* interests in mind. In fact, she was so far from her true self that she could not even say where she wanted to eat, or what movie she wanted to see. Every inner feeling, desire, and surge of anger was checked and double-checked— denied, withdrawn, deemed unacceptable. She felt alternately self-righteous and then dishonest about her stance toward others. Although she seemed to be in training to be Mother Teresa, she felt fraudulent deep in her bones.

Yet from the first day I met her, I was impressed that she could distinguish personal truth from fraudulence when she encountered it. She brought me works of literature that spoke to her authentically. She longed to find her own true voice, relentlessly striving for it. At the same time she could not believe that her life could be hers. She was able to destroy, negate, or belittle any signs of her own being when she accidentally found them. She had nightmares of self-sabotage. Nonetheless, she courageously struggled to fix herself so that she could allow herself to live.

Early in the therapy she brought me a videotape of herself on her second birthday. She was the only one shown in the video, but you could hear her parents and sister off-screen. She was watching her parents to try to ascertain what they wanted her to do. Her parents didn't register her predicament. They carried on with her as the focus of the film. But she was not their focus. They were thinking about what good parents they were for making this film. She did not really exist for them. Not surprisingly, she looked completely lost. They chatted away, completely wrapped up in their own narcissistic haze. Her sister understood her predicament and handed her a toy, but she could not play with it. Although I knew facts of her history that explained her difficulty in owning her life, I was still awed by the power of a world that could render a two-year-old unable to play. She was to develop into someone who *must not* have her own subjectivity. In the video she seemed to feel it was compulsory that her parents be the center of attention even though they were off camera, ostensibly making a movie about her.

During graduate school I saw some films of babies and their mothers that Margaret Mahler had made. These babies were in their rapprochment phase, which occurs in the second year of life. In one film, all the babies are happily crawling or toddling around, going back and forth between play and their mothers, except for one. This baby's mother is hiding behind a newspaper, not engaged with the other mothers or with her baby. This baby sits—already depressed—next to her mother and looks longingly on while the others live. This child has not failed to survive—she "goes on being" in the literal sense of the word. Like my patient, failures in the holding environment have left her unable to have her life, her creativity, her going-on-being that makes life worth living. She can only watch the world with envy.

Like this girl in Mahler's film, it seemed my patient could only watch others live, and at best envy them and submit to them. So she lived watching all those who represented her parents, including me. This extremely powerful, intelligent woman searched me, sought to charm me, needed me to tell her what to do. Often I was seduced, especially in the beginning of therapy. It felt truly necessary that I support her, allow her to idealize me as someone who knew how to be alive. She had dreams of my leading her through the birth canal. She felt unborn. I became convinced that she needed me to be the one person who could lead her somewhere different, healthier. I felt a powerful impulse to convince her that her subjectivity should be respected. I felt that I had to do so by being intensely focused on her and her subjectivity to the exclusion of my own.

For years we functioned within this kind of "holding" relationship. It felt as though there was no other way to be with her. Our work from within this all-encompassing but "false-self" dependency actually seemed to help her to disengage from several horrifying, humiliating, and dangerous personal and professional relationships. She even married someone who encouraged her to have her own pleasure, and with whom she could allow herself fiercely to represent her own point of view. She also found ways to work with others that better preserved her integrity. This happened progressively and slowly.

Nonetheless, she still suffered and felt particularly unable to be free of her sado-masochistic issues at work. It became obvious to her that, although she had left home many years ago, it was *she* who was creating her own deadening existence. She, miserably, though now subtly, perched between abandonment and sado-masochism. She was unable to stop trying to hold the world together with her considerable efforts.

In the next phase of treatment, although she came to know some of her desires and was no longer at the mercy of sadistic others, she was still unable to have her own creative life. She either felt like she didn't know how to express creativity or became terrified that if she realized her own considerable gifts she would be attacked. Every comment I made—even those that were simply reiterations of what she had said, repeated so that she would take her own thoughts seriously—she turned into thoughts from outside, directive suggestions for how to live her life, or judgments about her failure to live her life. Often she ascribed these thoughts and opinions to me, becoming awed by them or afraid that I would judge her badly for not being able to live up to them. Intelligent, perceptive, she could do this turnaround subtly and smoothly. For a while it seemed to be good personal insight, but slowly we became dissatisfied. Her idealization of me shifted more dominantly to envy. No longer was I rescuing her. I became someone who lived in a big, beautiful house, the likes of which she could never hope to have. We were caught in a stale dance in which she evacuated her goals and perceptions—her very being—into me and then envied me for having something she believed she could never attain.

I was increasingly aware of my frustration. How could I help this woman hear herself, have faith in her own being? Concomitantly I noticed that I lacked free access to my own subjectivity. I felt my every thought was controlled by her and that I must watch her very closely, never miss a word, never fail her, and never neglect her, *especially* for myself. I must not be the neglecting, angry, narcissistic mommy or daddy. I must be the completely self-sacrificing "good" person who loved her, respected her, admired her, yet ironically constantly regarded her as the "sick" one. I must never have an independent thought. In retrospect, I realized I felt just like her, secretly furious and powerless. Without any aggression or separation, we had to fix her great difficulty trusting me and herself enough to live. I presented this case to some very perceptive colleagues, one of whom was Dr. Jack Engler, who had come to my analytic institute to share his experience with mindfulness meditation. Dr. Engler is a psychologist, one of the founders of the Insight Meditation Society in Barre, Massachusetts, and a longtime practitioner of mindfulness meditation (he's also a contributor to the present volume). All my colleagues had wonderful ideas—more ideas of where to lead her, what to ask her. Each one meant to help my patient connect to herself at a deeper level—but each question embodied a model of how people are organized, ignoring her deep evasion of self-contact. I had fallen into this trap for many years. My patient used any idea—no matter how subtle—to keep primary experience at bay by organizing a plan for how to react to the world. Engler, the formal case discussant, sat quietly, had little to say, but I felt his presence. He was just there. That seemed to be the most helpful thing, reminding me that I had, perhaps like psychoanalysis itself, become overly involved in ideas and models, forgetting the ground of being.

I resolved to *stop trying* to help, to stop trying to undo the considerable wrongs that had been done her, to stop trying to follow her every nuance. I resolved instead to be there, to pay attention to myself more, to let myself be more alive in the sessions. Further, I resolved to speak only if I was sure my words would not be turned into something she could *do* about her problems—her "Ms. Fix-it" mode, we called it. That left me little to say. In effect, I began more to follow Freud's rules with regard to free-floating attention, or, more deeply, the instructions of mindfulness meditation. I thought to attend to the thoughts in my mind, not to judge them, or to hold on to them, and to abstain from doing anything about them.

Everything changed. Out came a tirade of rage and humiliation. Out came her sense of abandonment, terrifying loneliness. Out came her sense that I was purposely attacking her. An occasional remark indicated that she understood that I cared about her, even if impotently. For example, when noting that she couldn't swim—a metaphor meaning that she couldn't trust—she said, dripping with hostility, "Bless your heart, you can't teach me." She was furious with me, berating me for humiliating her, judging her, neglecting her. Mostly, she was terrified.

I was aware of feeling much closer to her and to myself. Somehow I felt free to think, to feel whatever happened, including my impulses to respond in the old ways. I watched the desire to comment in my usual ways rise and ebb. I felt my muscles tense, especially my back and shoulders, when I first set out to control myself and not answer. Then I noticed my stomach clench as I felt myself denying her urges and demands for me to react in our familiar pattern. But then my tightness passed, and I noticed the pattern the light made on the wall. I felt my breath move in and out, changing pace with my urges for mobilization. I noticed the beating of my heart, the ache in it and in my stomach. I noticed her tone of voice, the judgments that arose and faded and, then more primarily, the sick and frightened way it made my body feel.

Her sense of abandonment moved me deeply but no longer mobilized me. It was a feeling that came and went. She blamed me for it. Oddly, I felt completely unscathed, not guilty—a little astonished that when I experienced myself as more truly available to her I was being blamed for abandoning her. Later, long after the session, I thought that in a way she was right. I had left her. I had left my subtle involvement with the defensive, frightened part of her. But in the session I felt comfortable, untroubled, in my own experience. I felt no judgment, no defensive clinging (perhaps, in the Buddhist sense, no attachment) to the pain or suffering. I was allowing it to flow, not having to worry about it, to say anything "important," to understand it, or to remember anything. I was just being with her and myself.

The next appointment began with the immediate shock of having done something very wrong when I realized I remembered nothing of the previous session, except that it had been very different. I felt ashamed that I had stopped doing something I was obliged to do. Remembering my previous resolve, I tried to calm down and follow this new set of feelings and thoughts. While I was struggling with my expectations, she was in a great mood.

What followed for her was a period of joy and a sense of well-being. For the first time in her entire life she was free of migraine headaches. Surprisingly, since she had experienced great difficulty in conceiving, she also became pregnant. (Both her migraines and her infertility had been diagnosed as symptoms of an autoimmune disorder). She looked different, more at ease, relaxed. She was floating in her own life.

Of course, her state of wellness did not last. The old modes of control, directiveness, and rules returned. Unable to have faith that she could create new life, or herself be more deeply alive, she returned to her infertility specialist. He put her on huge amounts of medications that had to be injected into her legs, causing severe black-and-blue marks. She lost the baby. Severe disappointment and rage followed. Unable to stay with her feelings, she fell back on her tendency to inhabit a world defined by others. The migraines returned, as did the practicalities of trying to manage some deeply rageful and painful feelings that were bubbling up.

Having tasted some freedom, I wanted more. Over time there were more forays into this newfound mental space in which I "willed not to will." I stopped colluding with her defensive need to fix everything and opened to possibility, even for very "bad" possibilities. Each time I did so she was more angry, more bitter, more potentially destructive. She was convinced that she was murdering the babies inside her, unwilling to let them have a life if she couldn't have one. She tried to convince me that she was so psychologically damaged that she could never hope to find her creativity. I rode the waves of despair and terror, sometimes able to stay in my meditative state, allowing myself to be aware of what arose, sometimes scared that I was making a big mistake and that she was really falling apart. Then I'd return to the old safe way. Yet there was a difference in that we were also discussing the issues that were coming up during the periods of more intimate awareness. Then she would tell me she was ready for more, either by an acceptance of some not so attractive part of herself or by an expression of her desire to be really alive. Though both of us were unsure where we were going, I felt simultaneously, oddly, safe. She claimed that she was sure she was not safe; but she kept reporting spontaneous improvements in her life.

The darkness deepened as her fear and rage grew uglier. For a time, perhaps through some subtle unconscious communication, I grew aware of stinking, putrefying smells in the room (there were none). I shared this rather bizarre experience with her. She was not surprised. She had held her putrefied self in check until then. They stayed with us for some time while she came to reveal the sources of these odors: the humiliating exhibitionistic, filthy, primitive anal and oral displays her father had subjected the entire family to. He had made every one of his bowel movements a preoccupation of the entire family, sharing every detail and leaving soiled paper and enema bags everywhere in the bathroom. He also spat repeatedly, leaving sputum-soaked tissues all around his chair in the living room. His terror about his own health was forcibly made the concern and obsession of the entire family, including the two little girls. Her experience of this, and of other acts that crossed appropriate boundaries, had an effect similar to sexual abuse, in that she felt sullied by them and responsible for them. She revealed many things she was ashamed of, increasingly aware that she was her own worst judge and that she had been attributing these cruel judgments to me.

Surprisingly, the more miserable she was, the fewer migraines she had. Between bouts of rage, she began honoring herself by keeping a journal. She started writing a book, and, most astonishing to her, for the first time in her life she stopped compulsively picking at her sores. She was living, creating, and getting more of what she wanted. When she returned from her summer vacation she reported that she had had the first vacation in which she had been free of headaches and had felt the joy of real creativity. She was more aware of her own difficulties with faith, and with staying true to her own perceptions.

For this patient, dramatic psychological and physiological changes resulted from the change in the way I related to "holding." I switched from holding her "true self" by listening to it, advocating for it, and, subtly trying to "fix" it, to a holding characterized by a surrender of myself to deeper, more unknown areas of her and of myself.

Allow me to give a somewhat mundane example of the difference between the two kinds of sessions.

Sitting very stiffly on the analytic couch, my patient reports that she is really tired. She relates how stressful the visit by her sister and her family had been over the weekend. Her body conveys her anger, agitation, and inability to relax, which she complains about. Interspersed among the complaints about her sister's extreme passivity, and her brother-in-law's passive-aggressive attempts to ruin things of theirs that he envies, are statements of self-recrimination like "I'm so disappointed that I feel so alienated from my sister—I should be used to that by now. Had a big headache by the end of every night" or "I didn't do a very good job of staying relaxed." These statements stir my guts and sadism up, for I feel her masochism at work, grounded always in the denial or derogation of her more primary feelings.

In the pre-surrendered state I would make some comment about her saying these things—comments I have made about her disconnection from herself and her ceding her subjectivity to others. These comments would often engage her in a somewhat intellectual discussion of what she *should* do. Instead I note the anger and impatience grinding in my stomach, and wait to see what happens next. Silence ensues, I feel anxiety and think that she is angry that I have not rescued her from her uncomfortable feelings by talking. She sits up stiffer and pulls her knees into her chest. I feel my stomach and neck relaxing as I accept the feelings this is evoking in me, watching these old friends come and go. She says, "I have this huge need to be taken care of and disappointment with myself that I can't take care of myself." I feel guilt—I should be taking care of her—making her relax, but only I am relaxing. I wonder why she won't join me. She responds joltingly, "I can't relax—relentless, so fucking relentless." The agitation this arouses makes me want to act by speaking, but I control myself and feel like I'm going to jump out of my skin. But I know action will not help. So I am quiet—soothing myself with my breath. Her body, still stiff, knees pulled in, relaxes subtly. She talks about how her computer hasn't been able to save her work for over a month, but she keeps trying to make it do so. Just like her life, trying to make things work that won't. "Every time I get burned." She talks about how her desire to matter, to be taken care of, agitates her but is checked by her compulsion to take care of others, to protect them from the consequences of their behavior. This is exactly what we have been living out together. Only I escaped, by not being identified with the feelings.

The next session the patient reports a dream: *She is in Paris, having a wonderful love affair. She is happy. One evening she goes to a comedy club, where a woman—doing a one-woman show—is shooting the telephone repeatedly as it reels off messages. She is laughing with glee. Soon a man is trying to murder her.* So her compulsiveness to respond to the unrelenting demands for her attention, and to be involved in the chaos, psychosis, and anxiety of others, is based on a fear that some man will murder her if she does what she wants to—shoot the phone, i.e., destroy his access to her—and enjoy love and sex with another man. In this analytic process, I had disengaged from her compulsion to react, making it more available to further exploration.

A prolonged tantrum about abandonment, long suppressed, followed. All the while, far from being abandoned, my patient was more fully known and held. Rather than addressing ourselves consciously to the repair of her mistaken reactions to others, as though the harm embedded in these reactions was dangerous, this new state allowed her reactions to move to center stage without reactivity. A very perceptive woman, who brutalized herself for doing any minor harm to others, she knew she was doing me no harm. Convinced she had not harmed me, she discovered that she was not her rage. She was even free to have me fail as her therapist—a really novel experience for both of us. She was simultaneously free to try every tactic she had in her repertoire, as she had in the previous session, to get me to abandon my position. Each effort dissolved into an awareness of fear: fear of revealing her shame, fear of revealing her hostility, and fear of the unknown—thus exploring her terror of living her *own* life. I could not pretend to be able to be nonjudgmental, unhurt, unafraid of her brutality; I was sufficiently there. If she had gone into these dark spaces under conditions of pretense, of my neutrality, she would have been truly abandoned. Perhaps equally crucially, she was able to contain herself sufficiently so that others in her world were not compelled to react. If we had tried to go there when therapy began and she was living with others who would do her real harm this could not have happened. Both Freud and mindfulness emphasize the importance of nonreactivity to what comes into awareness. It is clearly crucial at a profound level. Any reactivity would have made this situation traumatic.

The case demonstrates, to my mind, a shift in the nature of holding.

$$*\quad*\quad*$$

Of course, Winnicott's term "holding environment," used to describe an important aspect of the mother-child relationship, has become a useful metaphor for the analyst-patient dyad. Winnicott seemed to be saying that the mother takes an active role in "holding" the infant; the "maternal care enables the infant to live and develop in spite of his being not yet able to control, or to feel responsible for, what is good and bad in the environment" and in himself or herself. And yet soon enough she needs "to not know—not be such a 'good mother' anymore—to allow for separation—not to know so much" (1965, 37, 51–52). Of course, mothers have to "do" a lot to provide either form of the holding environment. Much remains open to interpretation as to what kind of emotional state the "holding" communicates to the infant. Holding can range from physically restraining a child, who might fall or disintegrate emotionally, to a state of dreamlike grace. Even the holding of the screaming or very sick child might range from an emotional franticness to a holding that is physically effortful, emotionally aware, but totally free from clutching to the suffering. Winnicott speaks to this issue when he says the "alternative to being is reacting, and reacting interrupts being and annihilates" (47).

How does one act without reacting? What a paradox! Good parenting and analyzing require myriad ego controls, yet mothers, fathers, and analysts must also sensuously communicate the experience of unimpinged-upon *being.* To gain the ability to live one must develop the experience—maybe even the discipline—of feeling without interference from the *need to do,* in order to know when and what one *is doing.* Perhaps only when I was able to be with my patient without letting her impinge on my being was she able to experience my not impinging on her.

Joyce Slochower makes a compelling argument for the importance of a period of "holding environment" in which the patient experiences an *"illusion of analytic attunement"* (1996, 323; her italics). She describes a case in which her own subjectivity was allowed little or no presence in the consulting room. She felt that the patient needed her to hold her own subjectivity in check. As Slochower told me, she felt like a mother who is so involved in taking care of her sick baby that she doesn't realize how badly she has to go to the bathroom until the baby finally falls asleep. In situations like this, the patient's worldview holds the analyst in a fierce grip. Outside the consulting room and in the absence of the patient, other feelings related to the patient can be known. Only when a baby/patient does not need her does the mother's/analyst's subjectivity gain its full power. Slochower reminds us of the importance of allowing this experience to play itself out in an analysis. She defines this *period of illusion* as "holding" and drops the notion of holding when the analysis moves into a period of greater mutuality, becoming an "intersubjective dialogue." Here the patient and the analyst seem to have dropped their mutual need to hold, or individual need to be held.

This conceptualization is unsatisfying. They have indeed stopped holding each other in some death grip, but have they stopped holding? Slochower (1996) notes that there are times in which the holding stance allows the analyst more space to think her own thoughts. Perhaps at these times when the analyst is free to be with herself, a different, less defended, less frightened kind of holding is going on. Impingement has ceased and holding exists in its cleanest, "truest" form. Only then can one recognize a "true me" and a "true not-me" and be able to have creative experiences (Kakar 1991). Only then is one able asymptotically to approach living "with all one's heart, with all one's soul, and with all one's might," as Michael Eigen remarks (1981, 109), quoting a Jewish prayer.

One of my patients related to me that once when she was asked how her daughter was, she was surprised to hear herself answer, "Just perfect!" because in spite of all their struggles that was how she felt about her daughter. That was how she wished someone felt about her. When people want or feel the need to be held, they are hoping for an experience of a freedom just to be, although they will defend against it. We may behave so as to get the other to restrain, rule, or control, but what we really seek is a nonjudgmental, unattached, noncontrolling space in which to be safely. Ghent described "the centrality, despite its buried secrecy, of a longing for the birth, or perhaps rebirth, of the *true self*" (1990, 110). As terrified as we are to let go of an idealized other, a right way to do things, or some concrete way to fix our problems, what we long for in our souls is a sense of faith in our own growing beingness.

There is an important balance between structure and freedom, which may seem on the surface a paradox. Both psychoanalysis and meditation provide fairly rigid structures, in order to produce deeper internal freedom, but they are far from advocating that we let it all hang out. Structure is crucial to reduce the traumatic, and thus defense-building, effects of being-in-the-world. The structures one uses and chooses are important. My patient was trapped by the structure her family had created to reduce the negative consequences her very disturbed father's behavior had on his and their world. He was the youngest child of a woman whose three previous children had all died young. He and his mother were locked in terror of death, and consequently terror of life. Mindfully not reacting to perceptions and sensations that do not need a reaction allows space for knowing without fear or harm.

Holding is an aspect of human existence the need for which never disappears, but which undergoes developmental, characterological, situational, and qualitative changes. Those qualitative changes occur along the dimensions of degree of control, breadth of support, and depth of internalization. Perhaps the more concrete and literal the control necessary to sustain a sense of being held, the more frightened the individual. Conversely, the more symbolically elaborated the "holding," the more one may have come to deeper levels of faith. Feeling held in a less concrete way may be no "illusion." The choice is to surrender (Ghent 1990) to living and being, despite death and the multitude of other horrors, despite the temptation to submit to being held by control of another. The choice is to move toward being, living, and having faith that one may as well live, so that one may discover how to live well. The choice is to be held in the "area of faith" (Eigen 1981).

The need to be held does not stop at three months of age. It goes on through-out childhood and adulthood, changing manifestations, increasingly becoming symbolically elaborated. It does not manifest in only the most severe periods of regression. During periods of acute or chronic distress it may be more difficult to access, and so can require a great deal of effort by an analyst to reach it. The need to be held is the essential underpinning of transitional space and play. Such playful work does not require any compulsive effort and may be seen as the metaphorical playground of "mutuality."

People need others to act as mirrors, to reflect profound self-knowledge. The more intelligent that reflection is, the more one can know oneself and one's effect on the world. But as Jacques Lacan (1949) reminds us, there is always an element of illusion in any organized meaning we frame for ourselves. The formulated understanding of who one is always has a slightly false ring to it, like the odd experience of looking at a photograph of oneself. What may balance that disso-ciated experience is a capacity to hold our models rather loosely, and to allow ourselves to be in flux. Others can teach us about the state of being that allows us to become beings in process, whose inner truths manage our lives. Like water, the process holds you up only if you surrender yourself to it by a kind of floating. One is not aware of doing anything. The great contribution of the relational model to psychoanalysis is its emphasis on the nature of the relationship and the uses of the analyst. I suggest that our regard of our role as "the holder" is insufficient unless we see it as a special case of that more profound faith in being that is temporar-ily embodied in ourselves, ever passing through our person. Mindfulness medi-tation is one way to find how better to hold ourselves in faith.

Commentary

A CONTEMPLATIVE RESPONSE

NEVILLE SYMINGTON

The mood of this essay is set by a serene beginning. The author is in the mid-dle of hectic activity when suddenly she is struck down with illness and there she is in bed. The shocking tyrant that drives her has been given his march-ing orders, having to be satisfied with the joy of seeing her ill, but what he does not know is that this young child is turning it to good account.

This serene mood, the theme song of the essay, is a therapeutic tool par excellence. It is a state of mind that Sara Weber defines as "Not wondering about 'me.'" As one reads further it is elaborated into a state of mind where she is not preoccupied with her own sensibilities. So when the patient gets furious with her, she remains calm, does not defend her own hurt self. She calls this state of mind "choiceless awareness" and "mindfulness." When she adopted this state of mind the patient's life became more creative and fruitful; when she allowed her mind to become agitated the patient's life degenerated.

It is the psychotic part of the personality that sends out the vibes that provoke an agitated state, so the first step toward containment of the psychotic part of the personality is the development of a state of choiceless awareness or mindfulness meditation. Any interpretation made when the analyst is in an agitated state, under pressure from the psychotic part of the personality, only inflames the patient further. I think therefore that Sara Weber's technique is spot on.

This state of mind that she recommends is also one of observation. It is scientific observation of the most accurate kind. She stresses the need for detachment from judgments. She does not say this but I think implies that many judgments flow from "me-*itis*"—a pathological wondering about "me." What interferes with observation is emotional woundedness, a state of agitation. When she disparages the way psychoanalysis clothes itself in scientific garb, it is not science she is condemning but rather a coldness that must ultimately be born of a primitive hatred rather then love. She stresses that observation needs to be coupled with sympathy. Choiceless awareness is scientific observation. She observes the effect that this attitude of hers had upon her patient.

The only aspect I should have liked to see developed in the essay is how this observational method elucidates the specific ways in which the mind works. For instance, when she mentions of her patient that "of course, her state of wellness did not last," it would have been instructive to hear why and what it was that brought in the damaging state of mind. It seems that there were two states of mind in this patient: one of faith or confidence and one in which there was an absence of faith. What shifted her from faith to absence of faith? Some agency within the personality was, no doubt, responsible for it. The way that the state of choiceless awareness engages with insight and understanding to produce elucidation of the mind's processes is psychoanalysis at its most fruitful.

Another way to think of this might be to say that the state of *choiceless awareness* is the presence of a functioning mother, that *interpretation* is the functioning father, and that the two need to be in harmonious intercourse if the child (patient) is to flourish.

I want to finish with a question. Sara Weber recommends this state of mind, but how does someone bring it about? What I mean is that I don't think it can be brought about just by following a recommended practice. It has to be desired. I think it is the inner desire that brings it into being. The outer practice, postures, breathing, etc., do not do it alone. The state of mind is generated by desire. It cannot be forced. Desire has its own time schedule. It will not be hurried.

I think the emphasis of this essay, on the effect of the analyst's state of mind upon the patient, is crucial. The healing factor in psychoanalysis is the analyst's state of mind. Words are the messengers of the state of mind and unless they reflect *mindfulness* they will not heal but will worsen the patient's state. This patient illustrates this truth very clearly.

Reply

SWIMMING LESSONS

SARA L. WEBER

I want to thank Dr. Symington for his sensitive and gentle-hearted reading of my chapter. Clearly, he knows and understands the state of mind I am working to infuse more deeply into my work and my life. I appreciate his capacity to put the experience into words. Since he has reminded me of the importance of words and of interpretation as "the messengers of the state of mind" implied by the term "choiceless awareness," I shall try to verbalize some of the ways I see mind working in relation to faith.

Faith has a magical quality: now you see it, now you don't. It is both robust and fragile. My patient and I shared a desire to live more honestly and with greater vitality. We also shared a conviction and a faith that this desire was attainable. But how was this attained? When she brought her suffering self to therapy, she brought with her this conviction, along with a capacity for trust and an enormous energy. Masochistically, she had placed this profound capacity for faith over and over again in the wrong people—surrendering it to people who were more lost than she, submitting to their insanity and sadism.

Dr. Symington describes the patient as having two states of mind: faith and an absence of faith, the latter characterized by an agitation that he calls the "psychotic part of the personality." Although I believe that her experience does have this binary quality—sometimes life flowing forth, fully experienced, sometimes anxiously dammed up, at a distance—I am uncomfortable with the binary exclusion from faith of agitation, shame, and even the psychotic part of the personality.

In her most agitated moments she had faith—or nascent hope—that there was a way out, but little faith in her own ability to find the pathway. Whenever she surrendered she would find in some guise her uninterested, disabled mother or her seductive, self-absorbed father, yet she had the faith to surrender. Until recently, when she began to live more from her own creative juices, she maintained by faith what she knew to be fantasy: that my life was abundantly flowering from creativity and that my well-lived life was free of pain. Despite her illness and the impact of her troubled parents, she was able to allow herself acts of faith, just as I in childhood allowed myself the freedom of being ill with my own mother. She was so concerned with being a good person who did not inflict harm that misbehaving in my office, telling me I was failing her, was an act of faith. Among the "good," being "bad" is an act of faith.

I should like to believe that deepening faith permits reduction of agitation and a clear-sighted "scientific observation," but I am not so sure. Each step forward entails faith that one will survive the subsequent profound agitation, that one will survive the increasingly painful, anxiety-provoking periods of blindness that are part and parcel of the experience of "knowing." Perhaps the periods of serenity between are deeper. Perhaps one can move forward only when one has deepened one's faith in the ability to survive. Perhaps she surrendered to me to allow, within the sessions, the full-blown episode of her lack of faith that I truly felt we would survive, together and independently. For the first several weeks of analysis presented in my essay, my patient was profoundly angry, agitated, and apparently desperate in her sessions, yet she reported an increasing sense of well-being and productivity outside. Within a few months she became pregnant. The anxiety about maintaining the pregnancy and the ensuing loss precipitated the end of well-being outside the sessions. Within the sessions angst deepened as a battle against the experience of loss ensued.

When she read what I was writing about her she, too, felt the most important issue addressed was faith. Until then, I felt my work with her was a steady approach toward faith in her own being, but our work thereafter resulted in a leap forward in her capacity for finding faith more independently—in short, for ownership of her faith. Looking back, the change was probably due to my profound faith (not an intellectualized belief) in her capacity to "swim" on her own. I had stopped shoring her up. I had the faith that she had had enough experience with the deep faith she projected into me and into the health I represented that she could find it in herself. That act of trying to find one's own way constitutes an act of faith in and of itself. The experience of that act of trying can, for a time, be one of deep faith underlying great agitation.

Upon finding a way to reside in one's faith and being, one is free of a certain aspect of agitation, although physical pain, sadness, confusion, even terror and agitation may be present. I am reminded of a Buddhist description of suffering. Imagine that you have been shot by an arrow. You experience the physical sensations of the arrow penetrating your body—the depth, the heat, the dullness, or sharpness. You see the blood, and assess whether it has pierced something important. Perhaps you even seek immediate help. But then you start to mull it over and say to yourself, "Oh my God, I've been shot by an arrow!" Panic mounts, emotions run rampant, you are profoundly aware of your vulnerability, you get defensive, you pursue fantasies of revenge. This reaction itself is a second and unnecessary arrow. You should, of course, think very clearly about how to take care of yourself (and how to get the guy with the bow and arrow off the streets), but forgo the extra thoughts ("If it had been one inch to the right I might have died," or "I'd like to kill that S.O.B.!"). Separating the appropriate, necessary response and the panicked elaboration is something that few of us can manage. The physical pain of the arrow's penetration can be nothing compared to the pain of knowing it.

Buddhist teachers often teach loving-kindness meditation alongside other sorts of mindfulness meditation. One prays for happiness, freedom from pain, freedom from suffering, and peace of mind. Freedom from pain and suffering does not mean that you are without physical pain, illness, and painful feelings. It means that you have a freedom from that second arrow—more distance and less identification with the pain. Any feeling becomes qualitatively different when underwritten by mindfulness. There can be a fuller flowering, a clearer knowing, and a quicker passing. There is a greater sense of spaciousness. One might notice, amid the pain, the singing of birds.

The period of my patient's life I wrote about was significant for her. She was trying to procreate. Before she even began to try to become pregnant, she went to a doctor who specialized in difficult pregnancies. She had no faith in her ability to have a baby. Was her infertility—or more specifically her inability to maintain a pregnancy—due to a psychological lack of faith, to a biological disorder (autoimmune disease), or to a desire to create herself without the interference of a baby? We will never really know. If she had a biological disorder independent of psychogenic causes, perhaps going to the doctor early was unconscious self-knowledge—in fact, an act of faith. If the autoimmune disease was an expression of her self-sabotage, of some deeply buried murderous part of her, could becoming aware of such rage have been part of growing faith? Or could the infertility have been an attempt to process her grandmother's trauma of multiple dead children and siblings? Whatever the root, she had to live with it, regret and all. In the process she had to explore dark aspects of herself, and frightening, ugly facts about her family and her experience of them, including and especially her experience of abandonment by her mother. All this blocked her surrender to her grief about miscarriage and her loss of hope for a child.

Both choiceless awareness and psychoanalytic attending allow room for very uncomfortable states of mind—rage, terror, and physical pain—and for great joy, freedom, and beauty. Both are choiceless. When life's inherent pain or terror or disappointment arise, it is common to want to run away. The belief that "doing it right" can make life stop hurting sorely tries one's faith, like the impact of the second arrow. We all want to run to someone who can help end the pain. Sometimes we can get help. Sometimes we cannot. It is important to learn to discriminate between the two sorts of times, to allow oneself room to assess which is which. Suffering comes from the fearful effort to escape our pain in nondiscriminating ways. Suffering comes from deluding ourselves, from dragging our pain into the minefield of the mind where we try to make deals to escape our pain.

The choiceless awareness my patient and I allowed served to spotlight the minefield. Her state of wellness did not last for two reasons. One, it never lasts. There is always something to deal with. It gets too hot or too cold; your body wears out; friends or family members die. And two, because she had not been able to make her own the process of finding her safe place, she angrily panicked that I wasn't taking over for her. I seemed just like her mother and father, incapable of really caring about her. She had to face a fact: there is only one way to be truly safe, and that is to find yourself. Just as she said, I could not teach her how to swim. Of course, she had literally and figuratively taken swimming lessons, but she needed an act of faith to use those lessons without the water wings.

So why the silence on my part? As I sat in choiceless awareness, I was open to say anything I thought would be fresh or truly helpful. I was aware she would use anything I said as a scaffold to get out of her own water. She would become blinded by me, like a deer in headlights. Her habit of turning toward the impinging one was so deeply ingrained, as was her habit of turning me into an impinging one. She could not be alone in my presence, unless I was silent. Perhaps my silence was an interpretation. Perhaps, I was silently waiting for her to find a real foundation of mothering, not the disturbed mother and father she was used to. Her mother had had many untreated "breakdowns" and seemed to focus on only my patient's father. Her father, a minister, had been known for his inspiring sermons. She felt seduced and sullied by the inspiration she drew from them, because of who he really was. Perhaps only when I stopped my "sermon" could she find me and herself. Eventually, I did say something about why I was silent—that I could find nothing more useful to say to her than saying nothing. When we began to discuss the sources of her deep shame I began to ask questions and to speak from my experience in descriptive, neutral terms. Somehow, my words then seemed to be less blinding to her. They no longer evoked shame or the need to escape. They opened space anew for deep mourning of the babies that could not be born and the little girl whose parents were too ill to be present for her.

Dr. Symington, perhaps making reference to Bion's paradox of desiring not to desire, asked how one brings about this state of mind of choiceless awareness. If we believe that it can be brought about only by the desire to obtain it, then we have a contradiction. I am not particularly bothered by its paradoxical nature. One learns to ride a bicycle by being aware of things you must let go of to ride freely. But it is not "being without desire" that one desires. In fact, giving up desire and its satisfaction is an obstacle to obtaining choiceless awareness.

What one desires is an end to suffering. The end of desiring, the end of one's precious self-consciousness may be a byproduct, albeit one difficult to accept. Further, one can only desire this state of mind after some experience of it shows its value, the value in tolerating being alone with oneself. This state of mind is not initially desired. It happens accidentally and effortlessly. Perhaps it exists prenatally or in our infancy. Perhaps it happens while we are walking in the woods, or learning to play baseball or to ballet dance, or perhaps during sex, or in a house of worship or a museum, or on one's sick bed or analytic couch. If we notice that momentarily we felt some relief, we may begin to desire it, even begin a lifelong search for it—unclear what it is, where it is, how to attain it, looking for people who seem to have it (sometimes misled by charisma). As analysts we become enough aware of its power to advocate for it, as I am now. As a result we may become caught in desire for it, an effortful process for an effortless state of being. Paradoxically, we often need the urgency and compulsiveness to reach that desired state of mind, to combat our own powerful ambivalence about giving up our neurotic selves, familiar habits, self-absorption, well-known misery, and the pleasure of the satisfaction of our desires. That effort is both necessary to success and part of the problem. Fortunately, as Bion points out, desire loses its urgency and its compulsion to act when one succeeds in reaching choiceless awareness. One has the effortless feeling of being.

As Neville Symington reminds us, choiceless awareness cannot be hurried, but access to it can be helped or hindered. Meditation helps me recognize when I am there and when not. Sometimes in my mind I come upon a familiar doorway and then slip in.

References

Bion, W. R. 1970. *Attention and Interpretation.* London: Karnac.

Bromberg, P. 1998. *Standing in the Spaces.* Hillsdale, N.J.: Analytic Press.

Dostoyevsky, F. 1955. *The Idiot.* Trans. David Magarshack. New York: Viking Penguin.

Eigen, M. 1981. The Area of Faith in Winnicott, Lacan and Bion. *International Journal of Psychoanalysis* 62:422–29.

Epstein, M. 1995. *Thoughts without a Thinker.* New York: Basic Books.

Freud, S. 1912. *Recommendations to Physicians Practising Psychoanalysis.* In Standard Edition, 12:111–12. London: Hogarth Press, 1958.

Gendun Rinpoche. 1995. Free and Easy: A Spontaneous Vajra Song. In *Nat-*

ural Great Perfection, Dzogchen Teaching and Vajra Songs, by N. Khenpo, trans. Surya Das. Ithaca, N.Y.: Snow Lion Publications.

Ghent, E. 1990. Masochism, Submission, Surrender: Masochism as a Perversion of Surrender. *Contemporary Psychoanalysis* 26:108–36.

Kakar, S. 1991. *The Analyst and the Mystic: Psychoanalytic Reflections on Religion and Mysticism.* Chicago: University of Chicago Press.

Kornfield, J. 1993. *A Path with Heart.* New York: Bantam Books.

Kristeva, J. 1987. *Black Sun: Depression and Melancholia.* New York: Columbia University Press.

Lacan, J. 1949. The Mirror Stage as Formative of the Function of the I as Revealed in Psychoanalytic Experience. In *Ecrits: A Selection.* New York: Norton, 1977.

Langan, R. 1997. On Free-Floating Attention. *Psychoanalytic Dialogues* 7:819–39

Mahler, M., F. Pine, and A. Bergman, 1975. *The Psychological Birth of the Human Infant.* New York: Basic Books.

Penza, C. 2001. Talk at Insight Meditation Society, Barre, Mass.

Rosenberg, L. 1998. *Breath by Breath.* Boston: Shambala.

———. 1999. *Choiceless Awareness: A Quiet Passion.* Wendell Depot, Mass.: Dharma Seed Tape Library.

Slochower, J. 1996. Holding and the Fate of the Analyst's Subjectivity. *Psychoanalytic Dialogues* 6:323–53.

———. 1996. *Holding and Psychoanalysis.* Hillsdale, N.J.: Analytic Press.

Stern, D. N. 1985. *The Interpersonal World of the Infant.* New York: Basic Books.

Tarab Tulku 1999. *Nearness to Oneself and Openness to the World.* New York: Jewel Heart Transcript.

Winnicott, D. W. 1958. *Through Pediatrics to Psycho-Analysis,* New York: Basic Books.

———. 1965. *The Maturational Process and the Facilitating Environment.* New York: International Universities Press.

CHAPTER 5

Moments of Truth—Truths of Moment

JOSEPH BOBROW

And you shall know the truth, and the truth shall set you free.

—John 8:32

> *Not the intense moment*
> *Isolated, with no before and after*
> *But a lifetime in every moment*

—T. S. Eliot, "East Coker"

In a wildly popular song, Tina Turner belts out the lyrics "What's love got to do, got to do with it? What's love but a secondhand emotion?" In our postmodern mindset, could we say the same for the notion of truth in psychoanalysis? Don't we know that it is constructed, not discovered, negotiated rather than interpreted? Why raise an old warhorse from the scrap heap?

The ideas in this essay developed out of two psychoanalyses, one with a patient I call Martin, and the other with a severely dissociative patient. They also emerged from an ongoing effort to integrate, within my own thinking and practice, thirty years of practicing psychoanalytic therapy and Zen Buddhism. I hope they can provide a lens for looking at the experience of doing psychoanalysis, our day-to-day work.

In the film *Billy Elliot,* Billy's father is a stern, bitter, and hard man, a miner, from whom Billy hides his interest in ballet. Somehow, despite himself, the father softens, and ends up taking Billy to class. On the way, he is confronted by his elder son, who is identified with the father and their shared struggles for economic justice. Sensing a powerful, betraying turnaround, this son implores and begs his father not to take Billy to ballet class. The father exclaims: "He's only just a kid!" The transformation reflected in his words astounds us. We know of course, that Billy is a kid. It's obvious. But father and viewer together realize this ordinary truth for the first time.

Michael Parsons (1986) captures this in his paper "Suddenly Finding It Really Matters." He describes an analysis with a woman who brought them both "rather sharply against the realization that distinguishing fantasy from reality really matters." This is a truth every analyst knows. But their work together made him realize it for the first time. In Zen, too, it is the ordinary that astounds when viewed from a new perspective, scales fallen from the eyes. This is captured in a dialogue from the film. Billy and his father are riding in the bus on the way to London for the ballet competition. Billie asks: "So how's London?" "Dunno," says his father. "Why?" continues Billie. "Never been," father replies, "no mines there." Billy says, "Is that all you think about?" Trapped in the tunnel vision that comes from the over-determined habit of seeing only that which is "mine," not only did the father not know London, he could not recognize Billie's distinctive humanity.

In this essay I explore an elusive but fundamental dimension of human life—truth—and the activity of discovering it for oneself. I believe it is an inner willingness to directly know one's truth that determines how and to what ends experience is made use of. It is truth that nourishes and sets us free.

I am not referring to positivist or ecclesiastical truth, received from on high, truth with a capital *T*, but rather with a small *t*, the truth of the moment, which by nature carries a sense of moment, of psychic gravitas. I will not attempt to define it, since that would be like reheating good coffee. But I will explore, describe, and perhaps evoke it. I suggest that truth involves authentic experience, with two people in intimate attendance, or one person in intimate relation to an "other": animal, vegetable, or mineral, sentient or not. It comes unbidden, without fanfare and whistles, but often with a start, and is simultaneously emotional, gnostic, and mutative, reflecting and giving shape to an inner shift that has already happened. We want such experience, yet struggle against it. Truth, as I am using the term, is less a fixed place we get to once and for all than a moment-by-moment unpredictable emerging that is created as we discover it, and which, by nature, authenticates itself and carries a sense of conviction. The means are not separate from the ends—it develops in the doing. Thinking and feeling, knowing and doing, experiencing and being here do not oppose or exclude each other. Truth is an underlying motivational force and core value inherent in, and given living form through, being human. This capacity grows during the course of a genuine psychoanalytic process and authentic Zen practice.

Intrinsic to it is an inner, unconscious "turning toward" or surrendering, which is simultaneously an act of giving. This implies a turning away, disidentifying, or detaching from narrow, protective, unconscious conceptual and perceptual self-structures. Analyst and patient give of themselves through a joint giving over to free-floating attention and free association, to the painful and joyful moments of realization, and to the widened horizons that emerge. This is liberating, and this freedom co-arises with an ethical turning.

I will briefly review the philosophical debate relating to truth in psychoanalysis in light of several epistemological questions. I will explore, in an interweaving manner, the experience of truth, what fosters and impedes it, and its activity. I will touch on the nature of unconscious communication, the presence and quality of attentiveness of the analyst, and the ethical dimension of the analytic process, including the notion of psychic responsibility. I will weave in ideas from Zen Buddhism and will look at how psychoanalysis and Zen speak in distinctive yet mutually potentiating voices about core human dilemmas, values, and potentials with which they share common ground, such as truth and freedom.

*   *   *

Martin declares during an analytic hour, "This is my time and I can do with it what I want." This assertion can represent a discovery, a newfound sense of freedom. Or, as I experienced often with him, it can also mean that he had completely erased all trace of emotional impact that my prior statement might have had. Discriminating between omnipotence and freedom is important here. The question is: To what use is experience being put? What is the capacity we use to discern this? Is it something like what a non-therapist colleague many years ago called using our "lizard brain" (something neuroscience is articulating more and more clearly)?

Wilfred Bion called it intuition; Donald Winnicott described it as the mother's capacity to sense and adapt to the infant's needs, which arises from primary maternal preoccupation; Freud called it *zich zu Ubergeben,* the analyst's giving himself over or surrendering to his own unconscious activity in order to "catch the drift" of the patient's unconscious; Eric Rayner thinks it involves an "aesthetic judgment"; John Klauber, an "unconscious assessment"; and Thomas Ogden, "listening for something human." The Hebrew word *teshuvah* means "repentance," but more fundamentally refers to a turning toward truth. The act of taking refuge, in Buddhism, may likewise be translated as "I turn toward," or "I find my home in." As parents we use this instinctive capacity to tune in to our infant and distinguish the quality and meaning of his cry, which informs our response.

Each of these ways of thinking about such activity implies, I believe, an unconscious or preconscious apperception and assessment of the authenticity of the patient's communicated experience. The word *human,* after all, can refer to a wide range of activities, including deception. Gilbert and Sullivan wrote, "Skim milk masquerades as cream." So Ogden's "listening for something human" implies listening for something genuinely human. Likewise for the notion of aliveness. The manic defense can appear to be aliveness; a thief might say he felt quite alive after a successful heist. I think it is through a discerning resonance in truth that something is perceived as truly human. I believe real aliveness must co-arise with truth.

The word *Trieb* has been translated as "instinct" though many think "drive" better fits the original German. Freudian drive theory has fallen into disrepute these days, but *pulsion,* the French translation of *Trieb,* may reveal another dimension. While *pulsion* may be translated as "impulse," there is a pulse in impulse. As analysts we wonder, What is going on here? What is "driving" the communication? In ordinary speech we may ask, Where is he coming from? From an energic point of view, we might ask, What is the psychic fuel operating? What is pulsing through one's psychic veins, so to speak, through this moment together? It is in the reverberations, the echo, that we may put our finger on the pulse.

One idea crystallized out of work with patients where dissociation predominated. Here play was more like a shell game, the obstructive barriers protective but also prickly, keeping life out and others off guard and unaware of the truly empty shell. When I felt overwhelmed, lost, or confused in an hour, I found myself quieting inside, attending to breath and body, sitting in the midst of the confusion, continuing to listen. I slowly came to see that something else was also going on, but metaphors for it took many months to emerge. It was as if I were activating a kind of global locator system. When there were particularly big gaps between what a patient was saying, how he appeared to be feeling, and how I felt in his presence, I would imagine myself as a resonance chamber, receiving the verbal and nonverbal data from without and within and taking a sounding of the whole of it.[1]

It felt like putting out tendrils, something metaphorically akin to affective sonar, beneath the threshold of words, and noticing what came back and how it resonated. A chord was struck—what were the individual notes that comprised it? What were the overtones and the harmonics? It was like dropping a pebble into a pond; ripples spread out, which continued well past the analytic hour. Strange as it sounded, I wondered if the metaphorical tendrils were something like truth sensors. With this type of patient, where multiplicity could be a mind-scrambling defense, this activity seemed to help me survive, to maintain the capacity to recognize and make use of my internal responses, and continue on in a somewhat useful fashion.

For the first year or two of analysis, Martin would complain frequently that I gave him nothing and was only clinical with him. Quite often, however, just as I began to speak, he would interrupt me. It took him some time to see this, despite my trying to bring it to his attention, inviting us to look at it together, and interpreting along varied lines. I felt alternatively frustrated, erased, and detached and disconnected. After weeks of this, in one hour something occurred to me all of a sudden. The next time he interrupted I said, "When I'm about to say something, it's like my idea is something creative of mine, a connection I've made between things, but it feels like I generated it without you, like when parents have a baby, and a brother feels left out. And you cut it, you cut me off." He responded, "Yes ... and I love cutting the links." This was before I read Bion's paper "Attacks on Linking," but here it was. He continued speaking of cutting links, "like sausage links strung together out of the package."

In a sense he was continuing his associations to my interpretation, a sign that the analytic process was working. But in the overtones there was a manic quality. It seemed that he was not really letting in the impact of what had been said, but spinning anxiously away from it. Later, we came to see that this was one way he would "deconstruct" things. This word *deconstruct* emerged out of a dream he had in which he was the boss of a construction company and dismantled projects at will. He deconstructed anything I said, often glee-fully. This activity also had various fantasy meanings and attendant anxieties, including those related to forging intimate attachments, which we explored as much as possible.

It was eye-opening to see how Martin would associate richly to and develop an idea, while in the same breath distorting it beyond use and so missing the opportunity for learning. When I pointed out what I thought he was doing, he would listen, sometimes recognize it and agree, then spin off again, saying with scorn, "I do it because I can." It slowly became clear that to accord me a place in the room, a place and a voice in his psyche, was ter-rifying. The club Martin wanted to belong to had to have only him as a mem-ber. How unfulfilling his deconstructions were, how hollow and false the "freedom" he exercised in indulging his "exultant vengefulness." There were continuing stories about how his behavior would alienate bosses, lovers, and longtime friends and family. Very slowly we became able to look at the truth of this together. Since this was also how he knit himself together, the process was quite painful.

The capacity to turn toward and so generate this kind of emotional truth seems central. Patients differ in their willingness and their capacity to actu-ally do this, irrespective of the diagnostic picture. Some, despite profound cumulative trauma and severe deficits in ego capacities, are like psychoana-lytic troupers, pilgrims even, who seem motivated by a thirst for truth and the willingness to go as deep as it takes. Adrienne Applegarth calls this quality "having guts." I think of it as what we make, from one moment to the next, with the cards we are dealt.

Epistemology

The scientific age was in part a reaction to what were viewed as the unsub-stantiated and arbitrary claims of religious revelation. Positivism meant that you could be certain about something. Truth was decoupled from magic and became able to be tested, proved, and replicated. It did not come down from on high, nor derive its authority from papal or other decree. Freud developed his groundbreaking ideas in an age where the positivistic outlook dominated.

The search for objectivity in matters of the human mind and heart has grad-ually given way to an appreciation of the subjective elements in the analytic process. Psychoanalysis is presently in an identity crisis. It is variously described as a science, a natural religion, an art, a meaning-making hermeneutic endeavor, a form of poetry, and a meditation à deux. What is the nature of the beast? "What," asks Charles Spezzano (1993), "is the ground on which psychoanalysis stands?" As Victoria Hamilton (1996) has shown, such questions and the theories we develop to respond to them do not exist in a vacuum, independent of the preconscious clusters of beliefs, values, and experiences of the psychoanalysts who pose them. So the questions, "What is our true nature? and What is the fundamental ground we stand on?" become quite relevant.

While Owen Renik writes of the "irreducible subjectivity" of the analytic endeavor, completely jettisoning the idea of an objective observer, others, like Glenn Gabbard and philosopher Marcia Cavell, are reintroducing the idea of objectivity in ways different from the positivistic approach of nineteenth-century science. One of Cavell's main ideas is that there is a shared objective reality "out there," which is not the same as the individual's subjective "sense of reality," and which is knowable, but not completely or for certain. Rather, this concept of an objective truth external to private reality makes possible our subjectivity and our internal experience. The latter needs the former; one can't exist without the other. The concept of an objective reality that is shared, external, and public is, paradoxically, necessary for us to think, to become subjects with complex and unique internal worlds, able to intersubjectively interact with the private worlds of others.

Gabbard reminds us that there is an object in the word *objectivity*. The person of the analyst, by virtue of his position as external to the patient's subjectivity, gives him a crucial vantage point from which to convey impressions different from the patient's own reality. Becoming a "subject," some feel, inevitably involves an encounter with "otherness," becoming the object lived, so to speak, by unconscious processes. Lewis Aron and Sheldon Bach speak of the importance of developing the capacity to move and hold the tension between subjective and objective experiences of self.

Epistemology deals with how we know what we know. Those privileging subjectivity tend to think that the best knower is the one closest to the data. Gabbard and others speak for the value of a stance external to the patient's internal world.

For Bion, and James Grotstein, who has creatively developed some of Bion's ideas, the ground of psychoanalysis is "O," an unsaturated sign he uses to refer to truth, ultimate reality. "O" encompasses but is not identical with the Unconscious, the ground of psychic reality according to Freud and others. Also referred to as emotional truth, psychic truth, and the psychoanalytic object, "O" cannot be known or understood directly; it must be "been." Unless transduced for the infant through a sacred covenant, says Grotstein, by an attuned and metabolizing other [the parent], "O" is equated with profound anxiety, nameless dread, and disorganizing chaos. It operates silently and we can make ourselves receptive to it by an attentiveness akin to a mother's reverie whereby she tunes in to and dreams her infant. Similarly, by abandoning memory, desire, understanding, and "the irritable searching after certainty," the analyst may dream his patient. Elizabeth de Bianchedi (2001) recently said that this "dreaming" [Bion's dream work alpha] implies "mind to mind contact.... really being able to feel in one's mind what the other is feeling …the activity of intuition. Not simply nighttime dream activity, it is a mental function that operates passionately, through which we transform raw perceptions into images to be stored." The analyst, open to the patient, takes the patient in, creates the patient's emotional experience anew, and conveys it in a usable way. This activity builds the capacity to tolerate and represent heretofore inexpressible and unrepresentable experience.

Bion says that, although we embody "O," we cannot know it directly but only through its transformations or transductions, via a K or knowledge link. This is reflected in the selected fact, that which "floats up," for example, in the analytic hour. This fundamental and ineffable truth is not of a sensual nature, but we can put ourselves in attunement with it through intuition, which Bion also sees as non-sensual. Minus K refers to actively not knowing, destroying the capacity to know, or lying.

When we genuinely practice Freud's advice to the analyst to maintain evenly suspended attention, we come to hear from the self in ways we hadn't anticipated, says Christopher Bollas (1998). In such a state, we echo with the unconscious of the other. Although Freud, in certain ways, represented the Western intellectual tradition par excellence, in this instruction and in his discovery of free association he subverted our Western epistemological tradition, founded on the pursuit of knowledge. Grotstein says, "Understanding is overrated; 'O' is transduced after the fact in a realization of something we already knew or were" (personal communication). It is not only Kleinians who are interested in this dimension. Karl Menninger would speak about the "willpower of desirelessness," and Stephen Applebaum (1999) writes, in a beautiful paper on evocativeness, that "something uncontrolled is going on here."

Many of the debates in psychoanalysis today, however, still evidence a split between subject and object. Whether psychic truth and the analytic process themselves are constructions or discoveries is one such example. Dialectical thinking helps, but even the most elegant contemporary formulations retain some measure of dualism, similar to what we might call the "commuting" model where we oscillate between the subjective and objective modes of experience described by Aron and Bach.

Buddhism

What can Buddhism contribute to these discussions? Buddhist meditation practice and mindfulness in daily living help us enter intimately into the moments of living, no matter what their content, and maintain mindful, nonjudgmental awareness in their midst, even under great strain and anxiety. We develop the capacity to observe very closely our feelings, thoughts, breath, and bodily sensations, as they are, and as they interact, one with the other, to create all manner of pleasurable, unpleasurable, and "neutral" states of mind and being. We cultivate wholehearted or bare attention to the present moment, just as it is. When we drift off, we recognize where we are and return to our focus. In the beginning this is usually our breathing. We "turn" and re-turn, again and again, attending devotedly to our immediate experience.

Let's look at the Buddhist notion of the *three wheels*—the knower, the known, and the process of knowing. While most of us take these for granted—they are in fact at the heart of our intellectual tradition—in Zen practice we come to discover that they are empty; not vacuous, but without fundamental substance. As we become able to attend, to settle body and mind, we may find that we are no longer thinking of attaining any particular state; we are no longer a subject trying to achieve an objective, such as mindful breathing. We are simply breathing. We allow ourselves to become receptively absorbed.

A capacity for deep, nondualistic knowing develops as fixed conceptual structures based on subject-object duality drop away, as we become intimate with our "object" of study. Truth, or true nature, is not something "out there," not a "position" that allows us to maintain a detached perspective. Insight comes about when the three wheels as discrete entities fall away, and we touch life as it is, as it pulses through us. "To study the self is to forget the self. To forget the self is to be awakened by all beings," wrote Dogen, a pivotal thirteenth-century Japanese Zen teacher. It is surprising that the quality of awareness here is not some kind of blurred amalgam but is vivid and discerning.

Now these are unusual ideas: observation without a discrete observer and object, action without an actor and something acted upon, and knowledge without a knower and a known. There is no juggler here doing a balancing act between his subjective and objective sides. Yet differences are not collapsed.

In Zen, the fundamental ground of our lives, our true human nature, may be called generative emptiness charged with potential. The many beings distinctively present it: the bird sings it, our child whines it, the wind blows it, our stomach growls it; the extraordinary is not apart from, but part and parcel of, ordinary moments of living and dying. Sleepwalking through life, leading secondhand lives, we miss it. Once, when the Buddha was teaching, he twirled a flower. One of his disciples, Mahakasyapa, smiled. He directly realized something simple, lucid, and precious, yet not esoteric at all. This story is often used to describe the process of transmission from master to student in Zen. What was "transmitted"?

It is not embodied, sensual experience itself that creates and perpetuates the cycle of unsatisfactoriness and anguish; rather, it is "chasing out through the five senses," as Meister Eckhart called it—grasping after, attaching to, identifying with, and manipulating and thereby exploiting sensory experience. We cannot find serenity or encounter truth through such grasping and clinging, or through its opposite pole, aversion. But when, neither grasping after nor pushing away, it takes us unawares and bursts forth in a living moment, what we see, hear, smell, taste, and touch is unfathomable reality itself, in contrast to Bion's formulation, which requires a transduction and is non-sensual. We are incarnate creatures after all. This direct knowing is a passionate affair and we do well not to repeat the early tearing asunder of flesh and spirit that brought in its wake the body-mind split that we are only now revisioning.

Because the self has no absolute, permanent identity, we find fundamental, libidinal affinity with our fellow beings. Because we are empty, we "interare" with one another. The situations, people, and inner phenomena I encounter, just as they are, are nothing but ultimate reality itself. Standing up, sitting down, laughing, weeping—these are jewels we don't recognize as our own treasure. This is not an abstraction, not a credo to rally around or debate, but a perennial human experience, arising from a falling away (distinguishable from falling apart), which is simultaneously a falling together.

So truth is public and shared in a profound, experiential sense, not as an abstract concept, as in Cavell. It is unknowable and inaccessible through the senses, as Bion writes, but only if we mean dualistic knowing, as a subject knows an object.

"Post-modernists have seized on the uncertainty principle as a fetish," writes Margaret Arden (1999). In Zen, the concept of not-knowing is not the alpha and omega, but rather represents getting stuck in emptiness. The psychoanalytic counterpart would be a theoretical overvaluing of the "deconstructive" aspects of the analytic process. We can make use of not-knowing just as we do knowing—in growth-promoting and in obstructive ways. Notknowing is quite in vogue these days, and we tend to speak about it more than we actually do it.

Free association, for example, is a great leap. When we actually do it, we really don't know what will emerge next. It subversively undermines ordinary experience and certainty. But we reify and privilege this aspect at the peril of disowning our capacity for direct, transformative, nondualistic knowing. "Take a step from the top of a hundred-foot pole," a Zen koan urges us. A true word, please. A gesture of truth. Parading the deconstructionist banner, we cannot do this. It is not esoteric at all. The point is that tolerating ambiguity, complexity, and not-knowing, we come to know things about ourselves we were unaware of. We realize very ordinary truths, including the limits of our knowledge, nondualistically and quite intimately. This knowledge is not discursive. Lived afresh in each moment, it is provisional and only slowly and partially integrated, but it can have great weight, great "moment." Evocativeness, the expression of profoundly resonant experience, arises when dualistic notions of subject-urgently-pursuing-object drop away.

In Zen, our true nature can't be fathomed by thinking about it or figuring it out, but it is embodied in each moment of ordinary experience. We have only to let the scales fall from our eyes and wake up from our dualistic slumber. As Layman Pang (Sasaki, 1971), a revered and down-to-earth Zen practitioner in T'ang period China, wrote:

My daily activities are not unusual,
I'm just naturally in harmony with them
Grasping nothing, discarding nothing
In every place, there's no hindrance...
[My] supernatural powers and marvelous activity—
Drawing water and carrying firewood.

In Buddhism this miraculous and simultaneously ordinary "things as they are" is sometimes referred to as "suchness" *(tathata)*. Tathata can be thought of as intimacy with what is, with that which arises and passes. Marion Milner describes something similar when she speaks of encountering the "sheer thusness, the separate and unique identity of the thing" (1987, 281–82).

We humans are at once empty, unique, and in intimate relation with the world. "Every point of thought is the center of an intellectual world," wrote Keats. This echoes the Buddhist metaphor of Indra's Net, where every being is like a mirror at each point in a vast, dynamic web, reflecting and containing all the other points. How can we be simultaneously a distinctive point and the center of a world? We don't know, but we are. It is so. Is this subjective? Is it objective? Both? Neither? Is it transitional experience? Probably closest to the last of these, it is not adequately captured by any category. As Bion wrote, it must be "been."

The Buddha was not a god but a man, and the truths he lived and taught were not esoteric and abstract. He told inquirers, "Don't take my word for it, don't take it on faith; go have a look for yourself." In this spirit, let's examine the conditions that facilitate the emergence of truth, and the ethical dimension in psychoanalysis and at the heart of our lives.

The Analyst's Presence

The attentional activity I am describing requires something akin to one's complete presence, or, if you will, one's being. Paradoxically, this attentiveness depends on what Keats called "negative capability." It draws on unconscious communication and makes use of, but is not equivalent to, projective identification. It resembles not so much the intrusive, destructive, and controlling variant, so well described by Melanie Klein, as the communicative version described by Bion. Yet it cannot occur, I believe, between two discrete "containers" into and out of which various contents are passed. Winnicott's notion of intermediate or potential space, the overlapping of two play areas, is closer, but these terms can give a misleadingly abstract and "spacy" impression.

Rilke wrote: "Someone who is ready for everything, who doesn't exclude any experience, even the most incomprehensible, will sound the depths of his own being." Taking a sounding—resonating with self, other, with life itself—is not simply empathy or containment. It has a discerning, fathoming quality that helps us know more profoundly and truly. It brings a breath of freedom. It involves two bodies, two brains. Reverie is a resonating process. The mother, using all channels, knows the infant's state within the matrix of her entire being. Her intuitive responses co-arise with, and are not separate from, this knowledge. A living, vibrating emotional field takes shape. Not unlike Indra's Net, this field of emotional interconnection stimulates the growth of neural connections in the brain essential for affective life and creative thinking. Body and mind work seamlessly together.

A clinical vignette: Jeremy is a patient who was so fragmented and plagued by dread that he could not speak of what troubled him. It was palpable. Without conscious aim, I found myself settling deeply, trying to find my breath, and focusing on this splintering feeling of growing terror inhabiting my body. Slowly, it began to melt away and I found a deep breath and began to relax. I glanced over at Jeremy, and, remarkably, he looked at me as if he too knew that something unusual had happened. His face, expression, and affect had shifted, and the dread and fragmentation had eased. Not a word had been exchanged. In time he began to find words to describe his experience.

I began to realize that things like this happen not infrequently. I am reminded of Marion Milner's essay "The Concentration of the Body" (1987) and her book *The Hands of the Living God* (1969). Milner describes how she experimented with attending in a meditative way to her bodily sensations while doing analysis with certain patients. She found that, with these analysands, classical interpretations sometimes were not useful. Rather, an inner focus on her own breath and physiological states, while simultaneously maintaining contact with the patient, seemed to help these patients develop the capacity to fathom their own internal realities and eventually make use of symbols and words to represent and communicate them.

Such experiences are not tricks; they flesh out the meaning of the term "holding environment." Patients in analysis often come to the point where they feel faced with the prospect of placing themselves in the analyst's hands. "Am I in good hands?" they ask, with varying degrees of anxiety. Peter Fonagy and his coworkers (1995) have identified a critical component of children's capacity to "think." It has to do with developing an internal image of an attentive "other" who holds the child in mind as someone with an internal world. But development is not only mental, as Freud reminded us when he wrote that the first "I" feelings were of a bodily "I." The first contact the infant has is with mother's unconscious via her internal chemistry, sounds, and smells, and later, upon emerging, via the quality of her touch.

We don't physically touch our patients, but emotionally we do—in the way we "hold" them, not only in our minds, but in our bodily attentiveness. *Kokoro* is a Japanese word that means "heart-mind." I think we read, know, and "hold" our patients with an embodied heart-mind. We don't provide emotionally and then know, contain and then interpret; it is one movement.

I think this activity promotes the emergence and the transformative potential of truth. We become like primal objects, the fundamental elements of life itself: earth, water, fire, and air. If one's heart-mind is an ocean, sounds, words, and feelings will resound deeply, freely. If one is like fertile earth, seeds take root and grow, differently. The patient recognizes and responds to such a climate but often can't accept or make use of it. While we work toward recognizing, symbolizing, and expressing in words our internal experience of the intersubjective process that is psychoanalysis, silence itself can be a catalyst.

Another vignette: Sandra is grappling with letting go of a relationship. "Cutting him loose," she says, recognizing his freedom as she takes possession of her own, would be hard. She would grieve and be tempted to drink. There is quite a long silence. In the silence I have a daydream about a TV commercial in which a teenage boy doing his homework is drawn to an image on TV where a woman is undressing. The boy looks to see if anyone is around and then hones in. The accompanying music has an erotic beat, singing that "the heat is rising." As the woman is about to take off her slip, the boy's mother appears, switches the channel, and asks. "What are you doing?" "Ah … nothing," he says, caught and flustered.

As I slowly realize that my attention has wandered, I see Sandra smiling a nervous smile. (Strange as it sounds, I wasn't at that time aware I had been daydreaming and hadn't registered the sexual nature of the daydream.) I ask about the smile, and she says she doesn't know. We discuss things rather gingerly, and after some time I suggest that sexual feelings may have been present. She thinks she was "just feeling caring. If the feelings were sexual, they were out the door," she says.

This resonates for me anew, re-sounds, in a timed-release manner, and I really access the daydream I had. This is similar to Freud's notion of *Nachtraglichkeit,* the retroactive attribution of new meaning; I wake up to something I thought I already knew. I suggest that if sexual feelings were there she might throw them out the door. She laughs and begins to talk about a new excitement she felt about leaving her current boyfriend, with whom she had not had sex and where control and power conflicts seemed to dominate, and maybe finding a new love. Yesterday she was looking at old pictures of herself with a former boyfriend with whom she did have a sexual relationship. She was amazed to see that, once upon a time, she was able to feel that way. Then she looks at me and says, "Yesterday I thought to myself, 'I've got to get me one …tomorrow [the day of our present session].'"

I wonder, Is she urgently warding off fragmenting or depressive feelings by eroticizing? Are real sexual feelings emerging in the transference? If so, how are they being used? I don't exactly know yet, though I have hunches. I do not want to interpret it quickly as defensive erotization because Sandra seems dead sexually and we'd never really been able to talk about it. Emotion and thinking, containment and insight, are both contained within this movement of unfolding truth. It is not simply a matter of "coming from the gut."

Sandra becomes more able, during the ensuing hours, to talk about the shame and disgust associated with sexual feelings, about her teenage years, about current incidents at work (where she saw couples hugging and strong feelings were stirred), and about the ways she copes with conflicts and intense desires, such as by craving and eating lots of chocolate. We are able to speak about what is coming to life in the transference. It's embarrassing and painful for her. Extratransference material folds in. She describes coming home late from work and finding her dog depressed because she has been so busy, irritable, tired, and drained, that she didn't play enough with it. I say, "You respond with the part of you that wants someone to play with you, listen to and pay attention to you, and give you a hug." Tears well up in Sandra's eyes and her hard expression softens remarkably; it is a powerful moment. Desire and pain come alive in the room.

In the next hour she relates a dream that leads to a memory of seeing her parents nude. Each paraded around nude as a matter of course, and Sandra would pretend she felt nothing, that it was normal. She would freeze over and numb out. In subsequent hours, she continues to rework teenage conflicts, and examine relationships with women, and with her mother in particular, in more depth. Past and present are contained within this movement. She realizes profoundly and poignantly that there is "something missing" in her, which makes her feel exquisitely vulnerable and ashamed around others. I can feel the emptiness and recognize the level of the "basic fault," now more bearable and thinkable.

I cite this example to illustrate several points. First, silence can be generative, not simply depriving or frustrating. Living through this—from which she urgently wanted relief—led to a useful unfolding for Sandra. When she could let whatever arose resonate within the silence on multiple sensory channels, it could find its way into our dialogue, and then ripple out into (and condense) aspects of her personality, including loving desires of all kinds and the conflicts and terrors associated with them. "Dwelling nowhere, let the mind come forth" is a Zen koan. When two can dwell in fertile silence, useful and usable truths emerge.

Second, a profoundly accepting, inclusive attitude toward all our internal experience, a nonjudgmental approach, is a hallmark both of the analyst's free-floating attention and of Buddhist mindfulness. What is overlooked as ordinary, or discarded as obstructive, can, if allowed to develop, prove a fruitful way into subtle dimensions of the patient's internal experience and complex tangles in the transference-countertransference matrix. Zen and psychoanalysis are reclamation projects in which we harvest the ordinary (Bobrow 2000).

Third, the case example illustrates what we actually do in our everyday work as analysts. There is already a meditative element in clinical psychoanalysis. While a meditatively attentive analyst need not practice Zen in order to make use of his reveries, an interest in and capacity for using this pathway to construct or discover usable analytic truths is helpful. Meditation practice may help us manage the powerful anxieties inherent in working with seemingly impossible states of mind (not to mention the most ordinary ones). With enhanced analytic attentiveness, we plumb them with care and creativity.

Ethics

Receptive and responsive attentiveness to conscious, preconscious, and unconscious experience is not an isolated skill that exists in a vacuum. Intrinsic to it, I suggest, is an inner "turning toward" truth that is simultaneously an act of giving, a letting in of the other. This attentiveness implies becoming aware of and turning away or detaching from narrow, protective, unconscious self-structures. In our attempts to survive, to not know painful truths, our "solutions" create their own problems and, in some cases, become malevolent. Freedom to know ourselves in action co-arises with an ethical turning. In this final section, I examine the relationship between attentiveness and ethics.

In response to trauma, the infant either chooses or repudiates an internal object, which Neville Symington (1993) names "the lifegiver." In choosing it the infant creates it and, with it, a source of creative emotional life. In repudiating it, he unconsciously identifies with fragmented aspects of traumatizing situations and people and encloses himself in a narcissistic envelope, much like an autistic encapsulate. This is akin though not identical to Winnicott's precocious constellation of a false self (Winnicott 1975) and Esther Bick's tough second skin (Bick 1967). The latter choice Symington calls the narcissistic option and he sees it as the crux of much psychological disturbance. He does not subscribe to the notion of good or healthy narcissism and bad or destructive narcissism, most eloquently put forth by Otto Kernberg. Rather the narcissistic option is set in contradistinction to the creative, life-giving, truth-affirming internal choice.

Repudiating the lifegiver is rooted in anxiety about the devastating potential of psychic pain. In describing this process, Symington is in accord with Bion that the capacity to tolerate frustration is key. Attributing intentionality to the infant, as do Klein and Bion, Symington emphasizes the unconscious dimension of this choice, and speaks of evading or turning away from. This formulation does not neglect the role of the emotional surround in the etiology of trauma; rather it speaks to the infant's participation in his unfolding development. What we make with the cards we're dealt, which is psychic responsibility, begins earlier than we might think. When we decide to turn away from pain, we may turn away from life as well. While this can be reactive and survival-driven, the protective structures we develop take on a life of their own. They can become quite obstructive, even malevolent, and are forces to be reckoned with.

I have been impressed by the frequency and power of patients' reactions, not only to my mistakes—ineffective provision or inadequate interventions or presence—but rather to the good interpretation or the containing presence:

for example, when something I say or the way I am strikes a deep chord and touches them. I do not subscribe to the theory of constitutional destructiveness and envy, although I do recognize their presence and power, in part as byproducts of the kind of repudiative unconscious choice I am speaking about. Neither do I think humans are innately good. Rather, we are intrinsically capable of good and evil, but neither is written in.

The choice of the life-giving other creates a space inside for an other to exist. The obverse of narcissism isn't an arbitrarily mandated "reality" that we passively resign ourselves to, but the creative source itself, with all its thrills and agonies. I have found these ideas clinically useful. Let me give a few examples.

Trying to fathom what might be going on with another patient Steve, whom I sense is dissembling, I make a comment that strikes a chord. He is moved to tears. Automatically he changes the subject or "goes away." I point this out. Gradually, painstakingly, he becomes able to report some of his actual internal reactions. I notice the words he uses: "I can't give you that much," he says. And later, "I can't give you credit."

We hear it in ordinary language. A host to a show invites the audience to "Give it up for" the performer he is introducing, meaning "Let's recognize and welcome him." There are variations: "giving in" or submitting, "giving up" or relinquishing, and of course "giving over to" or surrendering. The word "integrity" implies both wholeness and ethical fortitude. The French expression for becoming aware of something in a profound and immediate way, *prendre conscience,* literally means taking hold of conscience. I think there is an act of conscience implicit in understanding, "becoming conscious of," which relates to assuming responsibility for our psychic lives.

This process involves giving up and giving. In a sense it is relinquishing omnipotent control of the object, according it autonomy and therefore accepting that it has something to offer, a considerable developmental achievement, needing to be continually remade, like fresh bread. As Grotstein once said to me, "We are what we have done [in fantasy] to the object." This implies that we can derive from the object only that which we accord it. Such an object—freed to be—can have a place as an other in our inner world, rather than, let's say, adhesively pasted on, addictively amalgamated, or automatically split off. Of course, it might not follow one's wishes or respond to one's needs, might let one down, or drop one. Truth is a key and often overlooked ingredient in the development of a sense of safety, trust, and therapeutic alliance.

Nonetheless, this "setting free" still engenders profound anxiety. No doubt the surround plays a key part, but so does the patient.

Our intrinsic roots in mutuality and dialogue, as Rene Spitz called them (1963, 174), hinge on this unconscious choice. Attendant on this leap into unknown waters is the capacity to mine life's psychic riches, in contrast to walking through minefields; to play in the gap rather than plastering over gaping holes; to creatively "space out" rather than falling forever through the cracks into bottomless space. Freedom to free-associate implies freedom be deeply "associated" with our psychic sources, to recognize and take pleasure in intrinsic "associatedness."

Consider Carla, a bright, attractive, cooperative patient whom I am seeing at a reduced fee. She accrues a large bill. We explore some of the dynamics and meanings involved. She is inducing in me the experience of deprivation and helplessness that she experienced with her mother. As I wrestle with and learn about this firsthand, a shift occurs, which I don't fully understand, but which I recognize as I bring up the issue in a new way for our mutual consideration. As we explore her reaction to my beginning to interpret differently, it becomes clear that she recognizes what has been going on and that I have become more able to deal with it. Unconscious material shows, and through the interpretive dialogue she says that she perceives me as more capable than she is [and was] to deal with this dilemma constructively. And not just as having this capacity but actually using it. It also becomes clear that she begrudges me this learned capacity to do so. I should remain as helpless as she feels and not do any better at it than her. She wants to thereby make me and her internal others pay. She cannot "give me this"—not payment of the outstanding bill, which would follow naturally, but the fact that I somehow could find a "solution" in accord with my well-being whereas she, for the time being, could not. Bitter and envious of my ability, this "good" patient tries to spoil the analysis. Spite predominates.

Later, Carla confides that she sits dreamily with her new baby in the waiting room, after the hour has ended, looking to see who else comes to meet with me, but also taking in from afar, through "osmosis," something generative from me. It terrifies her to let this happen in the consulting room and unfortunately in her life as well. She doesn't want to "take anything from me that she hasn't put there herself."

Another patient, Martin, in one sense far more difficult to work with since he enacts extremely obstructive transferences, reacts differently to the above dilemma. After many rounds of exploring and interpreting his cutting me off, I spontaneously say, "My turn," as he begins his interruption. He is shocked, baffled. Then he laughs. Gradually he becomes able to play with it: Sometimes he jousts, "No, my turn." I laugh and continue. When he interrupts or obstructs, I repeat quietly but firmly, "My turn now." And usually he allows me to have my say. Turning toward "the lifegiver," he gives me my turn, my place. A tyrannical toddler, he is learning to take turns. The play of illusion needs truth as a marker; illusional play leads to realization of deeper truths; these in turn inspire creative uses of illusion.

I went through weeks and months wrestling with this, many cycles of getting lost and confused, thinking I saw some clarity, struggling some more, and getting lost again. My response arose spontaneously and was not defensive, although I was preserving myself and the analysis. Martin sensed a shift in me, which must have reflected an inner movement in him and between us as well. Perhaps we had each freed ourselves through a shift in truth. My statement and the playful new learning it set in motion followed naturally the breakthrough that had already happened.

In another example, Martin takes a tissue, cleans his glasses, and throws the tissue some distance into the wastebasket. He repeats this periodically. Many meanings of this activity develop, some we come around to, some not. Among them were breaking the flow of the session, distracting us, dissipating a painful or potentially painful moment, peeing into the basket and on our work, and playing at being Michael Jordan, "scoring" and having me adore his prowess. Once, after I remembered that I had, earlier in our work, cleaned my own glasses as he entered the consulting room, I saw that he was also identifying with me as being more interested in my clean glasses than in "giving it up for him" as he entered, and that he was giving me a taste of my own medicine.

This activity continued despite our exploring it and my interpreting. If he missed his "shot" he usually would get up, pick up the tissue, and place it in the basket. Once, he left it on the floor during the session and picked it up and deposited it as he left. He did this again another day. Then one day he did not pick up the tissue either upon missing the basket or as he exited the office. I felt rather soiled. The next time this happened, as he was getting ready to open the door to leave, I found myself saying, "It's okay for you to shit on my floor but it's not okay not to clean it up." He laughed in recognition, turned back, picked up the tissue, placed it in the basket, and left, shaking his head. I was not trying to be provocative; it turned out that the exchange was evocative.

Martin's reactions to my comments showed, I believe, that he was relieved that I responded as I did. How would I handle what he called being truncated? How would I manage feeling shit on, having my face rubbed in it, and having no help in sorting through it and making sense of the experience? Like his childhood experience of various early traumata. In some such instances, not every one, he surprisingly did not begrudge me the fact that I could survive, save myself, and navigate these straits more effectively than he did. He let me know that it was meaningful to him, and seemed to take in this capacity to some degree. He responded to my comment about the tissues by saying, "I'll give you this much, you stood up." Several months of intense and dense material regarding anality followed. I think Martin was learning to "give a shit," and through this, to "give and take."

A final example: Paul, a recovering addict, cannot let anyone get close or help him. He offloads emotions. Bit by bit, year by year, he discloses additional addictive behaviors like compulsive stealing and womanizing, episodes during which he feels completely entitled, vengefully self-righteous, and entirely without guilt or conscience. These disclosures bring in their wake the most intense shame. I begin to see that in such states he eradicates others and the effects of his actions. He painfully comes to see how self-centered he has been, and, for the first time ever, he cries as he begins to fathom the damage he's done. For each step he excruciatingly takes toward letting me in, toward letting himself experience the truth of his own emotions and actions and becoming a subject responsible for them—in inverse proportion he fights me, every step of the way, terrified of being controlled, of losing control, of having warm, loving feelings, needful longings. Exquisitely wary, he wants to terminate at a most vulnerable, exposed point. Somehow we are able to work through the anxieties, and he continues on.

After five years of intensive therapy, we agree to terminate. As we wind down, Paul says, "I will miss you." This carries a shocking authenticity. I feel the milk of human kindness rise in my breast and feel genuinely warm toward him. In our very last session, I am stunned when he gives me a book, *Tuesdays with Morrie* (1997). The subtitle reads "An old man, a young man, and life's greatest lesson." The lesson, it turns out, is saying good-bye.

But before he gives me the book, a visible giving that has impact only in that it embodies a not-visible, true, inner giving, he hands me a card. The title, on top in gothic print, which looks like a headline from an old newspaper, reads "Laugh in Time." The caption just below is "Lottery Winner says: It will not change my life." Below this, taking up most of the card's cover, is the picture of a dour, hard-looking peasant woman, clad in black with white babushka and apron, standing in the doorway of her simple dwelling.

For an instant I see his alcoholic, traumatizing, foreign-born mother, and his identification with her. I laugh aloud; it is a wonderful gift, a stunning admission. He joins in and we share a long, heartfelt laugh. After a while he says, "That's not me, that's what I was." I know this is only half true. What is most dear to me is his simultaneous recognition and expression of what he received, along with his consciously disavowed admission of the ongoing struggle to let change be, to "give me that," to give himself that. That was the real gift.

The psychoanalytic process offers an opportunity for an ethical "turning" or change of heart for both analysand and analyst. Symington once said that there was a difference between being selfish and being self-centered. This was a kind of psychoanalytic koan for me for years; I couldn't fathom it. In retrospect, I guess it had to be "been." One day, all of a sudden, it dawned on me. Of course. Selfish, like elfish, or reddish. Not just "like" red, but expressing red, expressing elf-ness. Being it. Expressive of self, true self-ish. One does not keep one's attributes all to oneself, but lives them expressively, thus giving them to others. One gives of oneself, "gives it up." Self-centeredness is indeed in stark contrast to this. This must have reflected an internal shift in which the perceived dichotomy between being myself and being in touch with others fell away. Ephemeral and needing integration, to be sure, this was nonetheless a freeing change.

Truth is not something we attain or patch on. It is something we realize with a start, as if we had always known it, as our self-protective delusions fall away, as we give them up.

> *At the source of the longest river*
> *The voice of the hidden waterfall*
> *And the children in the apple tree*
> *Not known, because not looked for*
> *But heard, half-heard, in the stillness*

Between two waves of the sea.
Quick now, here, now, always—
A condition of complete simplicity
(Costing not less than everything).

This joy asks of us "not less than everything," as T. S. Eliot (1971) writes. It is the gift inherent in the sacrificial yet enjoyable attentiveness of the analyst. It is this ongoing, engaged relinquishment, and the empty but fertile ground charged with potential that is its source. It provides the corrective to the analyst imposing his own problems and agendas on the patient—not forced neutrality, opaqueness, or self-conscious and often anxiety-driven self-disclosure.

Stephen Applebaum's words echo my own thoughts when he writes: "The heart of the ability to be evocative is heart. You have to be, not act to be. To care to engage one's feelings with those of another, to enter one's experiential world, to face the frightening warding off with determination and skill—all these are acts of love, and are experienced as such by the patient" (unpublished).

Acts of love co-arise with gestures of truth. As Martin helped me see, they pass through giving a shit to giving of oneself in creative abandon from the spacious ground of intrinsic affinity. Embodying this capacity is perhaps the most profound and elusive freedom of all. It opens the door to what Gerard Manley Hopkins calls "the dearest freshness deep down things."

Commentary

"East Is East and West Is West and Ne'er the Twain Shall Meet" (Or Shall They?)

James S. Grotstein

Introduction

Joseph Bobrow's moving contribution presents a thoughtful and carefully reasoned reformulation of the subjectivity-objectivity debate in current psychoanalysis as well as evocative proposals in which he more meaningfully recasts the debate by comparing Western psychoanalysis with Eastern Buddhistic practices. He presents the ontological and ethical dimensions of psychoanalysis for consideration and highlights "moments of truth" and "truths of the moment" as his instruments of investigation. In so doing, he reviews the development of psychoanalytic epistemology from a putatively "objective" science to one that is currently more "subjective" (and "intersubjective") and ontological in its orientation but which suffers from being dualistic (subject-object dichotomy). He then critiques the dialectical struggle between these points of view and opts for a third, that of the Buddhistic East, of oneness, a concept of being that seems to transcend the dialectics and dualities of the West.

He focuses upon the transient experience of the moment, especially as it is caught in the existential lens of Buddhistic thought and as it is virtually ignored in Western psychoanalytic practice, caught as the latter is, according to the author, between the poles of the selfobject dialectic. Perhaps the author's message is that Western psychoanalysis can gain from accepting the erasure of dualities of difference in favor of at-one-ment. While agreeing with the author and admiring his argument, I should like to play the (Western) devil's advocate for my discussion of this thought-provoking contribution.

What Is Truth?

I begin my discussion with a quotation from Pontius Pilate, "What is truth?" I was moved to recall this as I read the first clinical case that the author presented, that of "Martin." It occurred to me that Martin could not face one "truth" (the truth understood by the analyst) because of an interference by another "truth," the truth of a desperate inner ratiocination within him, his wondering (truthfully) whether or not he could survive the truth that the analyst held in trusteeship for him ultimately to reaccept. Put another way, the patient seems to be saying, "The truth of the matter is I do not know how much truth I can tolerate."

The Question of the Dosage of Truth

Here I am reminded of the applicability of Hooke's Law: Stress equals strain times the modulus of elasticity. Translated from physics, this means that the ability of any subject or object to withstand trauma (truth) depends on their inherent flexibility. *Symptoms, like falsehoods, are truth's merciful encryptions.*

Conclusion: Truth is complex, paradoxical, and ironic. It is as if falsehood is an encrypted truth that has a secret understanding with overt truth: both of them will work out an ongoing to-and-fro relationship, depending on the balance and safety afforded by circumstances. How much truth can the subject tolerate at any given developmental moment? Truth alone knows and must make allowances for its counterpart and often "loyal opposition," falsehood. Perhaps we can also say that Eastern and Western thought come together in regard to the quest to *achieve individual honesty in order to be able eventually to face the uncertainty of truth.*

Truth as a Philosophical and Logical Oxymoron (in Defense of Falsehood)

In psychoanalysis we run into this conflict between the two truths in primitive emotional disorders in which the defensive truth may be a weld of the patient's unconscious appraisal of his or her resilience in phantasy as well as an ineffably accurate and realistic appraisal of how far he or she can go at any given moment in tolerating existence. The critical issue in what I am stating is the consideration of the putative balance in one's mind in tolerating and anticipating, not truth per se, but the trajectory of truth—all the possible inferences, ramifications, auguries, and preconceptions that the arrival of the truth can conceivable evoke, launch, and ignite. Bion (1965, 1970) terms the end of this trajectory Absolute Truth, Ultimate Reality, "O." Heisenberg's (1930, 1958) "uncertainty principle" challenges Bion's notion of "Absolute Truth." Further, consider the "truth" of the rainbow, an illusion or mirage created by drops of water in the atmosphere, the appearance of which disappears as one approaches it. Does that not apply to truth?

Bion compensated for his idea of the Absoluteness of truth by the more credible notion of the "evolutions" of "O," that is, that "O," "Truth," is always evolving, transient, changing, is not a noun but a verb. Conclusion: May not truth, or even Truth, be but a mirage? May not honesty be an innocent (naive?) seeker for a truth that is always elusive? Let me express this in another way: Bion (1992) opined that man is born with a religious instinct to worship and needs to contemplate a deity in order to justify this craving. Yet paradoxically, this craving for the deity can never be fulfilled in actuality. In a similar vein Bion often quoted Marcel Blanchot as follows: "The answer is an embarrassment to the question." May this principle not also apply to the relationship between honesty and truth? May not Absolute Truth be an embarrassment to our honesty? In a recent contribution I suggested that the ineffable subject of the unconscious is the custodian of our honesty and "knows" the truth—as best as it can be known—or "become," in Bion's lexicon (Grotstein 2000). Thus, the attainment of honesty, not truth, is the virtue to which we aspire.

The truth of the matter is that human beings, with rare, very rare exceptions, can tolerate gradients of truth but rarely Absolute Truth. Ultimately, truth may be holographic, that is, holistic and implicate (particulate and dialectical) (Bohm 1980). Put another way, Absolute Truth makes allowances for half-truths and for the falsehoods that all the more pay homage to Absolute Truth's mercy as well as potency. Put yet another way, truth is defined by all the attempts to falsify it.

We know from infant development that infants must be protected from the premature arrival of Absolute Truth, a phenomenon that Bion (1965, 1970) also terms "beta elements" (un-mentalized phenomena, which correspond to Kant's things-in-themselves and noumena). The task of mother, father, and culture is to induce in the infant a state of mythic and phantasmal suspension of Absolute Truth until the infant is old enough and developed enough to come to peace with it. Yet, paradoxically, the infant demands that parents be truthful with them, emotionally.

Container/Contained, Primary Maternal Preoccupation, and "O"

The contributions of Wilfred Bion, multiply cited by Bobrow, constitute perhaps the most far-reaching efforts by a psychoanalyst to date to integrate the ineffable nature of the unconscious with the mystical nature that inheres in the reverie through which the mother (or analyst) apprehends—intuits or resonates with—and "becomes" the infant (analysand) in his or her emotional state. Formerly, analysts listened to their analysands in a stance that was characterized as "objective," which today would imply "left-hemispheric" listening: linear, didactic, decrypting. Today, more and more analysts listen with their subjective/intersubjective "third ear" more than with their more objective two ears. Bion helped to start this revolution with his discovery of the communicative aspects of projective identification. The mother, in a state of reverie, which is tantamount to meditation, is enabled to use her "dream-work alpha" ("alpha function") to understand her infant.

Likewise, Bion goes a step further and invokes the wisdom of the East as he does so. He suggests that, for the mother and analyst to obtain reverie, they must abandon memory, desire, understanding, preconceptions, and all the other forms of sensuous attachment to objects. He all but said "abandon ego," which suggests the surrender of one's claims to selfishness, pettiness, and desire itself—certainly the forfeiture of narcissism.

The question of the analyst's and parent's willingness to tolerate, not only the actuality and factuality of *objective* (symbolic) reality, but Absolute Truth, Ultimate Reality ("O") itself, having the unknowing but not blind faith to do so, constitutes their own "dark night of the soul." That is, they must have the faith in a coherence that they cannot know, yet whose existence they realize. Realizing is beyond knowing. It is virtually the same as *becoming*, in Bion's lexicon.

Undoubtedly, what he was getting at was the need to abandon all forms of imagery, both the sensuously derived and the symbolic, so as to free up the sense organ that is sensitive to internal qualities (Freud 1900). I wish that Bion had written "suspend" rather than "abandon," for the latter is too extreme. Here is where I also differ somewhat with Bobrow. The suspended sense organs (for external qualities) also serve in their silence. "They also serve who only stand and wait (Milton, "On His Blindness"). The point I am getting at here is as follows: The mind operates *holographically,* both in parts (dialectically) and as a whole. The act of psychoanalysis is, in my opinion, a testimony to the activity of the unsatisfied sense organs who, by their enforced unsaturation, are able to conjure the ghost (phantasies of the internal objects of their desire) for psychoanalytic explication.

In the subhead I also mentioned Winnicott's (1958) "primary maternal preoccupation." From my own observations of nursing mothers it is my impression that the state of mind that the mother enters when she is "preoccupied" is one that Winnicott termed "a normal psychosis," Bion "reverie," Bobrow (in terms of the analyst) "meditation," and I "a trance." I believe all these descriptions are congruent. What seems to characterize them is the idea of an altered state of mind, one in which the mother's preoccupation with the ordinary business of her life is transiently forsworn so that she can gain entry

into hidden potential states of higher, deeper, and more cosmic enlightenment—and the same with the analyst.

What Bion hinted at but failed to explicate (as was his wont) was that
the container capacity of the mother functions not only as a translator or
transducer of her infant's proto-feelings; it also functions as a protective
repressive or postponing barrier to premature or intolerable truths. In psychoanalysis this function is known as the *dosage* and *timing* of interpretations. In Bion's lexicon, this function would be known as "transformations
in 'L' (love) and 'H' (hate)." These correspond to Freud's (1911) concept
of the pleasure principle, whose task it is to keep reality at bay until the
individual is ready for secondary process (objective reality, truth). Phantasies and myths constitute protective blankets until the developing individual is ready to "allow Santa Claus to die" and ultimately come
face-to-face with truth. "Now through a glass, darkly; then face to face,"
in the words of St. Paul.

Bobrow states: "We cannot find serenity or encounter our true nature
through …grasping and clinging, or through its opposite pole, aversion. But
when, neither grasping after nor pushing away, it takes us unawares and
bursts forth in a living moment, what we see, hear, smell, taste and touch is
unfathomable reality itself, in contrast to Bion's formulation, which requires
a transduction and is non-sensual." Here the author touches on what I
believe is a problem in understanding Bion's conception of how the mother
employs her alpha function with her infant. The difficulty lies in the fact that
Bion seems to conflate two processes into one. The mother both (a) meditatively attunes, matches, symmetrizes with, and "becomes" the distressed
infant (transformation in "O") *and* (b) "translates" (transduces, reflects
upon) this experience so as to impart meaning to it so that it can become a
pragmatic realization in regard to the caretaking of her infant. Thus, Bion
suggests that the mother must employ the functioning of both cerebral hemi-
spheres, so to speak. And here is the question that I keep coming back to in
regard to the Buddhistic technique (dare I call meditation a technique?):
How are the results of meditation harvested? Are they harvested totally
unconsciously, or is there some kind of conscious reflection that occurs that
allows the meditator to be "let in" on what has happened? Is realization an
unconscious self-constituted and self-constituting function that renders
thinking redundant?

"The Stranger within Thee"

The author states, "I believe real aliveness must co-arise with truth." When I read this I could not help thinking of Heidegger's (1962) concepts of *Dasein* and of *aletheia,* the former meaning "be here" (in the imperative voice) and the latter suggesting "unconcealment." In making bridges between Western psychoanalysis and Eastern Buddhism, Dr. Bobrow wisely invokes the ontological perspective. Without his having stated as much, Freud strongly implied that psychoanalysis was a meditative technique, one that he understood in terms of sensory deprivation, in which the unconscious can be expressed. Freud missed the ontological and subjective nature of the unconscious, however, in his zeal to be affirmed a scientist.

Ontological considerations, consequently, have been noticeably lacking in psychoanalytic thinking, with rare exceptions. Yet the very purpose of psychoanalytic treatment is to permit the analysand "visitation rights" (and "rites") with him/herself through the analyst-as-channel. Psychoanalysis was conceived in the Zeitgeist of the "alter ego" or "second self," which played so prominent a role both in fiction and in the psychiatric studies of hysteria in the nineteenth century (Grotstein 1999). In the eighteenth century, an essayist, Edward Young, enjoined other authors to "Know thyself …learn the depth, extent, biass, and full fort of thy mind; contract full intimacy with the Stranger within thee" (cited in Cox 1980, 3). When Breuer and Freud (1893–95) studied hysterics, they found "double conscience" (really "double consciousness") as one of its invariant characteristics. Later, Freud rotated the axis of the two consciousnesses from the vertical to the horizontal, placed System *CS* above System *UCS,* later populated the latter with the id and its drives, and the concept of the second self, the "other ego" ("I") was lost until it was recovered by Lacan (1977) as "the Other," the unconscious as subject. Lacan assigned deprivation and desire to the subject (the Other) of the unconscious. This is the one who appears in psychoanalysis when the senses and desires are not gratified. I believe that this is also the subject in Buddhism. What I am really trying to say is the following: In his zeal to be a logical-positivistic and deterministic scientist, Freud all but buried the idea that the unconscious itself constituted an ego, albeit one of a very different, preternatural kind, one that completes the known ego and together with it comprises an ontologically superordinate subjective self (Grotstein 2000).

"Deconstruction" May Be Construction of Another Type

I was moved by Dr. Bobrow's description of Martin, the patient who "deconstructed" his analyst's formulations. His moving description of this "secret eater" evoked the possibility of an alternate view, one I adumbrated earlier, that can possibly illuminate the paradox of truth as it is revealed in psychoanalysis. The analysand who obstructs or "deconstructs" the truth as we see it in our interpretations may be revealing yet another truth in a different language system, that of pantomime, gesture, or sensory-motor-image posturing—all so as to *show* us a truth about a series of falsehoods he had to suffer as a child and now repeats. But the analysand does so as a prevaricator, in order to see if the analyst will persevere to obtain the buried truth in the analysand's deconstructions. He or she may have felt compelled to falsify, out of identification with parents who themselves could not face the truth ("O") and therefore passed on to their children the defaulted legacy that "real Truth is unfaceable!"

Put another way, the analysand never really lies because the lie is truth's betraying revealer! The truth is always present. That is why "liars" can be analyzed. Psychoanalysis is interested in the analysand's acceptance of his truth(s) behind the fortifications of falsehoods, the latter of which are "truths" of another order, albeit in need of rehabilitation.

Buddhism

Bobrow is at his best when he explicates the Buddhistic perspective. Here we can see perhaps the true hidden ancestry of psychoanalytic thinking when its subject-object dialectic is removed. Each discipline requires the subject to yield or surrender to process and thereby abandon (or suspend) pride, ego, control, mastery. Psychoanalysis is fundamentally characterized by a succession of two processes, however, the first of which is the activity of pure *experience* itself, and the second the *reflection upon* that experience. The very name "psychoanalysis" and the technical practice that underlies it valorize the former while dispensing most of its efforts on explicating the latter. Bion, perhaps more than any other psychoanalyst, has radically reemphasized the importance of attaining pure experience (transformation in "O") and also has reformulated the steps by which the psychoanalyst, once achieving this transformation in "O," then sets about conducting transformations from "O" to "K" (knowledge), by which he means a reflection upon the experience.

That Buddhist meditation may be superior to psychoanalysis in attaining this transcendent state of pure experience is a possibility that Bobrow seems to raise. What is left unanswered is what happens to the harvest, the reflection upon this meditative experience in Buddhism. One ironic possibility emerges: if one attains the state of pure experience—as defined in the coda of Buddhist meditation—does one really need to have that experience "analyzed"? Put another way: Is not enlightenment spontaneous—and even unconscious? If this be so, then is psychoanalytic "analysis," the second step following the attainment of the state of pure experience, redundant?

Parenthetically, while reading Bobrow, I suddenly and for the first time began to wonder about the near absence of psychoanalysis in the East. Are there cultural-geopolitical reasons why Buddhism and other similar disciplines are practiced there in comparison with psychoanalysis and psychotherapy? Is poverty a prominent reason? Can the psychoanalytic ambition to sublimate the subject's narcissism and "improve" his or her object relations be antithetical to Eastern self-abandonment? Is Buddhism a reincarnation of ancient Greek Stoicism? Is Stoicism the answer? May we not dialectically ratiocinate along Western psychoanalytic lines and, at the same time, enter into at-one-ment as part of a larger dialectic? These and other countless questions crossed my mind while reading this stimulating contribution.

❋　❋　❋

The author has written a cogent critique of Western psychoanalytic methodology and contrasted it with Buddhism. He makes it all too clear that the latter has much to offer the former: its philosophical outlook, its epistemology, and its unique ontology and ethic. The question I raise is: Does Western psychoanalysis have anything to teach the latter? The author also delves into the importance of truth in psychoanalysis. I should add that honesty, both with ourselves and with others, is our goal, if we have a goal. Truth is quite another matter.

Reply

EAST AND WEST ARE ALREADY MEETING—WHAT'S SHAKING OUT?

JOSEPH BOBROW

I am grateful to James Grotstein for his thoughtful comments on my essay and appreciate the opportunity they offer to clarify my ideas, enrich our ongoing discussions, and add to the deepening conversation between psychoanalysis and Buddhist meditative practice. Rene Spitz said that life begins in dialogue and that psychological disturbances are derailments of dialogue. Dialogue, perhaps more than any other quality, characterizes the psychoanalytic process and intensive Zen practice alike, as it does human development. When two people meet something happens. Bion called what happens an emotional storm.

Psychoanalysis and meditation, in particular Zen and other Buddhist approaches, have come increasingly into contact. Although analysts, anxious about "coming out" and facing criticism, have tended to disclose their meditative practice or interest in hushed tones, Grotstein has been a visible pioneer with his creative contributions on the spiritual dimension of psychoanalysis.

Grotstein writes that he agrees with my argument but wishes to play devil's advocate for purposes of discussion. I am not so sure about his agreement, however. I don't see myself in his characterization as "opt[ing] for …the Buddhistic East of oneness." My interest was to describe ways the two disciplines, psychoanalysis and Buddhism, can complement and enrich one another, and to illuminate methodological, theoretical, and foundational areas of *intrinsic* overlap, in particular, truth. Nor was my intended message that "Western psychoanalysis can gain from accepting the erasure of dualities of difference in favor of at-one-ment." Erasure of difference can be as big a problem in Buddhist meditation practice as in psychoanalytic work. Getting stuck here is called pernicious oneness in Zen. At any given moment, either discipline, dealing as it does in living intersections of oneness and difference, can be highjacked and put at the service of various unconscious motivations or "parts" of the personality. In Buddhist meditation practice, as in psychoanalysis, dualistic, either-or modes of experiencing are not erased; rather, over time, they no longer constrict experience as they become amenable to being held together, and occasionally fall away, making room for new modes of thinking, feeling, and being. When they inevitably return, they no longer exert the grip on us they once did; rather, we have a new, alternative experiential frame of reference to grow into.

Grotstein misreads the title of my essay as "truths of the moment" rather than "truths of moment": shared experiences of psychic gravity or intensity, where complex life truths take on immediate, experiential weight, accessibility, and impact, sometimes signaling, embodying, and leading to change. Finally, when he writes that "Bobrow is at his best when he explicates the Buddhist perspective," he seems to be implicitly calling attention to reservations about my portrayal of psychoanalysis. Perhaps I appeared to be criticizing psychoanalysis in my discussion of certain aspects of Western thinking. In Grotstein's view, psychoanalysis is a kind of spirituality, a particularly Western one, and I may have seemed to be giving it short shrift. If so, the question animating his comments would seem to be, What does Buddhism offer that psychoanalysis, in particular the Bionian version that Grotstein articulates and expands upon, doesn't already have? Put another way, So what's new?

I *was* critiquing certain ingrown assumptions of Western thinking that I think unnecessarily constrict current debates, but it was not my intention to undervalue psychoanalysis. Rather I hoped to show how it might be enriched through a consideration of other worldviews (some close to but subtly different from Grotstein's) of what it means to be fully human, and how aspects of psychoanalytic methodology, while distinctive and differently intended— let's say, simplifying for discussion purposes, integration of the personality in contradistinction to direct experience of our true nature and the meaning of our living and dying—are surprisingly similar to Buddhist meditative approaches. Psychoanalytic thinking and practice can make important contributions to Buddhism. I will discuss some of them below.

With "agreement" such as this, who needs differences—even if playfully couched under advocating for the devil or his Buddhist counterpart, Mara? I want to call attention to the differences, even the subtle ones concealed in apparent agreement—not erase or skim over them but explore them constructively—and distinguish areas of convergence and divergence: similarities with a difference and differences within similarity.

Grotstein's comments fall into four broad areas: first, the dialectical relationship between truth and falsehood; second, psychoanalysis as a two-step process (what is the "harvest" of Zen?); third, the nature of attention and truth with regard to sensory experience; and fourth, what psychoanalysis can offer Buddhism and how they may converge in a meta-perspective (can we, Grotstein asks, "dialectically ratiocinate along psychoanalytic lines and, at the same time, enter into at-one-ment as part of a larger dialectic?"). I will use these areas to organize my response, allowing for some detours along the way.

"Symptoms, like falsehoods, are truth's merciful encryptions." Here Grotstein turns the notion of falsehood on its head in a paradoxical reframing, creatively describing the interdependence of truth and falsehood, how each can be "the loyal opposition" to the other. Legend has it that when the Buddha was sitting under the Bodhi tree in one-pointed immersion in his question: Why is there suffering in the world? Mara came to him threatening to derail his inquiry with "his" temptations. Buddha remained steadfast and undaunted. But there is another story:

Once, Mara visited the Buddha. Upon his arrival the Buddha's attendants refused him entry saying that the Buddha wanted no part of him, that he didn't belong there. When the Buddha heard this, he scolded the attendants and warmly invited Mara inside, greeting him as an old friend and asking about his activities. "So how is temptation going? And the distractions, delusions and deceit? Is business good?"

Grotstein expands the notion of containment in describing the analyst as holding in trusteeship a truth the analysand is not yet able to face. Greed, hatred, and ignorance are the general categories for what obscures truth in Zen, though this may be a short list. Ignorance of the way things are, their essential nature, can likewise be said to be a "truth" the Zen teacher holds in guardianship as he works with the student. Of course it cannot fundamentally be "held" or "contained" by anyone for another, only *lived with* another, and the teacher cannot fundamentally give it (back) to the student or "enlighten" the student any more than an analyst can stand up and sit down or laugh and weep in place of his analysand, or a mother poop and pee for her infant.

Truth is unknowable and so, in Grotstein's view, absolute. It is "preternatural," super-human it seems, a reified "something" set apart from our merely human efforts to reach it, which he calls the capacity for honesty. It seems to me that, rather than unhitching the process from the aim, the struggle to be honest with ourselves can be seen as the *activity* of truth, truth-in-action. Can we think of our (ego) capacities for tolerating ambiguity, uncertainty, and creative not-knowing, developed in both meditation and psychoanalysis, as the investigative function and the activity of truth?

The one who says he knows does not know, as Lao Tse wrote two millennia ago, and Grotstein's view in part serves to drive home the danger of epistemological hubris that analysts have been intent on remedying in recent years. Grotstein once told me "God is the only atheist." The *idea* of God here functions as a corrective to the human tendency to self-aggrandize, imagining ourselves omnipotently as gods, only to inevitably come crashing down to earth. So Grotstein's view of Bion's "O," ultimate reality or truth, has two aspects: emotional truth, which is operative in the analytic process and relates to the effort at honesty, and absolute truth, which can never be known directly, or only by the few.

I agree when Grotstein writes that Eastern and Western thinking may come together in regard to the "quest to achieve individual honesty in order to be able to face the uncertainty" of what he refers to as absolute truth. In psychoanalysis, Zen, and everyday living itself, however, it is not simply that we have little tolerance for uncertainty, we also get snagged on our assumed and unarticulated (sometimes unconsciously repressed, sometimes unconscious but not classically repressed) beliefs, principles, and "procedures," and we expend tremendous amounts of energy not to know certain things directly. In the current psychoanalytic climate, I think not-knowing can itself become overprivileged, even fetishized, spoken about more than lived and practiced.

Grotstein's reframing of truth and falsehood rings true clinically and experientially. However, like all analysts, he is well aware of how arduous it is to do analysis when a patient is in the grip of rejecting the process of analytic inquiry itself, no matter how skillfully the analyst interprets and no matter how steadfastly he holds the patient and the truths the patient cannot yet bear. Here the analyst must himself discover, hold, and accept the truths that here is ignorance, here is envy, here is utter rejection of help. That is to say, the analyst must face his own limitations, fallibility, and powerlessness, and the limitations of the analytic process itself in which he has invested so much of himself, without necessarily giving up.

Grotstein equates truth with trauma and speaks of the gradient of how much we can take. That trauma and living go hand-in-hand was also presented 2,500 years ago by the Buddha as the First Noble Truth: there is suffering. The trauma of difference (sexual or not), otherness, the passage of time, the loss that comes with separation, independence, and growth—old age, illness, and death (three signs the Buddha's father is said to have wanted to keep him from seeing)—these are just some of life's inevitable, not to mention inflicted, pains. Michael Eigen, citing Lacan among others, believes we are born with capacities for experience greater than our ability to bear, make use, of, and enjoy the experiences, and this fact is itself a source, if not the chief source, of trauma.

However, it is not just primitive anxieties or a wired-in biological mismatch between experiential capacities and the "equipment" to use them that animates the reactive process—filled as it can be with envy, denial, repudiation, distortion, and hate—that meditation teachers and analysts alike know so well from their work. We are not simply God-fearing people, nor need the sacred dimension inspire fear. Our conflicted reactions and protective and sometimes malevolent constructions in the face of trauma are not only self-protective responses to uncertainty, not-knowing, and an inability to control and predict our lives. We also fear the vivid freedom of what Buddhists call "suchness," the "rightness" of life just as it is, closer than our own nose. We cling to our theories, the "certain certainties" about the way it is, and how it is supposed to be, afraid of springing free. As analysts, we know this as the fear of pleasure or the fear of success, but these don't quite capture this dimension.

Bion's "O," his vision of the basic ground of psychoanalysis, is comparable to what is called "essential nature" in Zen. "O" is often characterized as awe-some, with a sense of dread, of "uh-O." But when Bion writes that "life is full of surprises, all of them dreadful," this is only half of the story. The Kleinian and post-Kleinian worldview, and their descriptions of the nature of the infant and the tasks and possibilities of living, are helpful in that they present the awe-full side of human nature. Although sometimes characterized in Kleinian formulations as wired-in [innate envy for example], I see these formulations as innate capacities not predispositions. They help us face our afflictive emotions, our hate and envy, and integrate them. In the Bionian view, the infant's motivation is to communicate rather than simply discard unwanted contents. The horizons of human possibilities are expanded in Bion's vision of human nature and the creative development it receives in Grotstein's hands.

The fundamental ground in Zen is neither dreadful nor inviting. It simply is, empty of dualistic notions and absolute qualities and identity. Realizing this truth as it is *embodied* in everyday life situations is not only traumatic (a sword that kills our delusions) but liberating (a sword that gives life). This is so in a surprising way—as when we discover something we knew all along but now "get" for the first time. We might say it is a kind of (non-pollyan-naish) "'O'-kay!" So, the word Grotstein uses, the parental "covenant," is not a matter of transmuting into digestible chunks, taming for the infant what seems like a disembodied, externalized, inherently dreadful force, in order to ensure the infant's survival. Instead, the essential nature of our living and dying is seen manifesting *as* the intimate interplay of mother and infant dancing together as they become attached—what a miracle when it works well enough! There's a line from *the Song of Zazen* by Hakuin Zenji that we chant during Zen retreats: "Singing and dancing are the voice of the Tao." The capacity for this process to become derailed exists of course as well. When things break down, there is suffering; no need to posit a preexisting dreadful force.

Improvising on the First Noble Truth to fit a particular student, a Zen teacher said: "Suffering is not enough." We become ensnared by suffering, wearing it as a proud ball and chain, as any analyst knows, just as we become trapped by repudiation of psychic pain through the mindless pursuit of excitement at any cost. Here Bion's instructions regarding the analyst's technique, to renounce memory, desire, and understanding, might be revised as follows: be attentively aware of becoming snagged by *(attached to)* memory and the desire and compulsive need for (intellectualized) understanding.

Grotstein writes that "the answer is an embarrassment to the question." Easy cookbook answers, perhaps. In Zen koan study the teacher encourages the student to meditate by letting there be just that question—the koan itself—letting unrelated matters pass and returning to the question. By not aiming to solve it or find an answer, this investigative method facilitates, not an answer, but an unfolding realization of the question. Koans are metaphorical narratives, usually drawn from spontaneous, everyday encounters between student and teacher; they are the folk stories of Zen. The literal meaning is a "matter to be made clear," a "window that shows the whole truth but from a single vantage." It is one way to experience the intersection of the sacred in the particulars of daily experience, in a down-to-earth, everyday context. Bassui Zenji asked his students several centuries ago, "Who is the master of hearing that sound?" or "Who hears?" Students today use this koan to touch the true nature of the elusive subject. In form it is not unlike the question that serves as the title for Grotstein's collected writings, *Who Is the Dreamer Who Dreams the Dream?*

Disciplined, devoted, inclusive yet focused, not-knowing leads in Zen to a nondualistic realization that is enjoyed and relinquished (through not-knowing) to make space for further knowing. Tolerating ambiguity, frustration, psychic pain, and uncertainty are key capacities in both psychoanalysis and Zen practice, as they are in living itself. Of course, we can becoming enamored of this firsthand, direct knowledge (rendering it dry and lifeless) and begin to think we are quite special and not subject to the slings and arrows of mortal life, or worse, that everything we do, no matter how self-serving, cruel, and exploitative, is for the benefit, the "enlightenment," of the other.

The idea of the Truth with a capital *T* as unrealizable, "out there," only for the few, is akin to not being allowed to write or say the name of God. If there is a mystery, it is here: although we are unable to locate the truth anywhere or describe or grasp it, yet it operates as our sight, hearing, touch, taste, smell, the sensory pathways themselves; and, I would add, it takes the shape of the unconscious emotional field of intimacy. In a sense this realization comes only *after* long-term, intensive Zen practice. But fundamentally it is a discovery of something we never had to lose but always were. We wake, we sleep, we love, hate, laugh, and weep, and yet, when we look closely, we cannot identify the experiencer. But this does not mean we cannot realize directly for ourselves and vividly express (the nature of) "who hears," or for that matter "who dreams." It only means that it cannot be caught in the net of either-or thinking.

Psychoanalysis makes an essential contribution to the search for understanding, truth, and integrity in various ways, among them by describing in detail the kinds and levels of anxiety we are subject to, and how our adaptations often make for a solution worse than our original problem, an area often overlooked by Buddhist practitioners in their desire to leapfrog and transcend the world and their suffering into a state of everlasting peace. Whether called "affect modulation," "managing emotions," "containment," "holding," the "self-reflective function," or "mentalizing," this area is one in which Buddhism has both something to teach psychoanalysis and something to learn from it. At a recent talk by Thich Nhat Hanh, of the forty or so questions posed to him, over 90 percent had to do with how to manage affective states. People in droves are bringing emotional troubles to meditation teachers. And they are bringing their existential and spiritual concerns—Who am I? What is the meaning of my living and dying? What am I here for?—to therapists and analysts. (To play off Kierkegaard's and Winnicott's ideas, the "dreadful" has already happened!) As analysts and meditation teachers, exposure to the each other's worldviews, philosophies, and practices can thus be extremely useful.

Theravadin Buddhism, with its emphasis on mindfulness practice, can assist practitioners in managing emotions, whereas Zen, particularly insight-oriented Zen practice, usually involving koan study, has tended until recently to overlook the world of emotions. But meditation teachers typically know little about the unconscious emotional field, and though they may speak about transference, they seem not to grasp its ubiquity and operation. I don't think we can talk comprehensively about attention and awareness without an understanding of unconscious motivation, conflict, process, and affective experience.

Anxiety, like suffering, is not enough, however; it is not the whole picture, as psychoanalytic ideas like Hartman's conflict-free zone, Winnicott's aliveness, and Eigen's ecstasy suggest. In its view of essential nature, born of 2,500 years of practice, Buddhism expands the palette of what a human life can be. Although pain, suffering, and anxiety don't evaporate forever (despite classical Buddhist teachings such as "stream entering," "extinction," and the "end of suffering," which some take to indicate a permanent cessation of suffering in those at the highest level of attainment), Buddhism and psychoanalysis alike concern themselves with freedom, presupposing relief from, if not the absence of, suffering. One of the Four Abodes of the Buddha, character qualities of enlightened living that develop through practice, is equanimity, not unlike the quality of serenity Grotstein sees as the fruit of the "transcendent position." Contentment that is not vegetative deadness, complacency, or defeated resignation is an elusive fruit, barely more present at the end of certain analyses than at their inception. Being contented with simple, ordinary living is an achievement and an art: reading a book, having a conversation, going for a walk, eating a meal, taking a snooze—these are hardly mystical activities. However, enjoying them as the fruit of the sacred, with no stink of sacred-*ness*, is something else again, available not just to a few great mystics or reincarnated gurus but to everyone. Perhaps freedom, then, is the liberty to contact, bear with, and find joy in the ordinary. And, maybe, grasp its extra-ordinary nature.

This freedom is simultaneously the prerequisite for and the aim of each process. What then of the purposeful blinding of the senses as technique (captured by Grotstein's intriguing phrase "casting a ray of darkness") and the view of sensory knowledge as fundamentally obscurational and illusory? There is a logic here: if the fundamental ground, the unconscious for Freud, "O" for Bion, is nonmaterial, non-sensual, then we have to blind the senses. However, if we see the object of analysis as neither solely material nor immaterial but empty of all dualities and therefore interpenetrating both realms, then our technique need not be so blinding.

The denial of desire and of the senses was and to some degree still is part of various religions, including certain Hindu practices. Brahmanic traditions, with which Bion had contact while growing up in India, often teach that sense desire is the source of delusion and must be transcended in the realiza-tion of the Self, a trans-human entity that permeates everywhere. The Buddha's teachings arose in sharp contrast to this notion of a higher, reified Self, a "something" we melted into once and forever after transcending (rid-ding ourselves of) our human passions and desiring nature. The Buddha taught that there is no such Self, apart from or accessed through such tran-scendence. Combating desire and the senses is useless and counterproductive, as he discovered and demonstrated in his legendary turning away from near-fatal ascetic practices and accepting a bowl of milk and rice from a maiden. Rather, it is incisive, devoted, meditative awareness of the activity and struc-ture of our consciousness, how, moment by moment, we construct, protect, and defend a small illusory "I"—observation in action—that leads to libera-tion. In Zen we say "it" is neither Self nor not-Self, neither dual nor non-dual; "it" is empty of and so includes each. Liberating ourselves from the ingrained and unconscious habits of a mind and a heart in anguish is far more arduous than practicing austerities. Years ago in Hawaii, I knew a follower of the great Indian smiling sage, Meyer Baba. Although he had renounced speaking, as had his guru, the man never stopped "speaking": he was always scribbling on a chalkboard he carried around his neck!

Zen is also a step-by-step practice, of course: moment-to-moment atten-tiveness, focused and broadly directed, uncovering in the process how our mind, feelings, and bodily sensations interact to produce all manner of states that we pursue and cling to and avoid. As these patterns unfold and unravel, automatic, habitual modes are relinquished. We immerse ourselves in our particular practice on the cushion—breath counting, following our breathing, koan study, just sitting, bare awareness—and practice mindfulness of the activities of daily living. We muster the intention to understand and are not simply led along by following sense impressions and impulses. But we don't block them out; internal machinations are observed closely, nothing is ruled out of bounds. The cawing of a crow is not a distraction—it reminds us that we have gotten caught, mired in discursive or ruminative thinking, and returns us to our practice of attentiveness. More deeply, *caw caw caw* presents the truth itself.

Freud showed that the nature of unconscious experience was psychical and set it apart from the material realm. But the work of infant researchers, and in particular Anne Alvarez with her ideas on the observable shape internal fantasy can take in external behavior such as gait, is beginning to take the discussion further along, questioning these bedrock, seemingly mutually exclusive notions, rooted as they are in sharply separated categories of inner and outer.

In Zen we do speak of an absolute, but it is conceived of as empty of permanent, fixed substance, and identity. For purposes of discussion, it is called absolute, essential, or true nature. It is not barren however, but a creative wellspring, full of potential and energy. In contrast, there is the phenomenal side of our nature: coming and going, being born and dying, having height, weight, shape, color, texture, sex, ethnicity—all the particulars of our lives and the world itself. However, although there is a step-by-step progression and process of training in Zen (a gradual deepening not unlike Grotstein's description of the trajectory of the capacity to bear truth in the analytic process), training does not simply prepare us to better tolerate the uncertainty of an unknowable truth. Every step to truth is truth itself. The arriving is the doing. This is captured metaphorically in Yamada Ko'un Roshi's notion that each moment of life can be represented as a fraction: the denominator is empty infinity, the numerator is any phenomena. We can't have one without the other, can't detach one—spatially, temporally, or any other way—from the other. Each is needed for the other, and the whole moment, to exist. To realize this intrinsic state of things as they are: that the phenomenal world in all its particularity, in its goodness, badness, and ugliness, is itself the absolute, takes practice. However, it is not of the order of attaining or getting somewhere or something or becoming someone we are not.

I think this is a central difference between Grotstein's notion of truth and that of Zen. Any phenomena can trigger such a direct realization in Zen practice, the more ordinary the better. Any sound, smell, taste, touch, sight will do. The very pathways that in certain Hindu and other religious traditions, and partly in Bionian thought too, are usually seen as obscuring truth here are themselves the vehicle to, and the embodiment of, its realization. What is renounced, step by painful step, is not the senses, or the aspiration to understand, but the tendency to "rush out *through* the five senses" (Meister Eckhart), attempting to grasp in self-aggrandizing fashion the indescribable object of presumed satisfaction via the sensory apparatus.

When this often frantic and compulsive reaching out and away, complicated by the countermovement of aversion, comes to rest through repeated observation in action, the entire self-structure it is built on recedes, of itself. At rest, there is an experience of at-one-ment, everything is empty and we are at peace. While some spiritual paths stop here, this is not the case in Zen. A line from a koan points the way: "Take a step from the top of a ten-thousand-foot pole." We don't stay in empty oneness. What is the size, smell, taste, and touch of "it"? We must bring it home. Eventually there may be a breakthrough as all ideas about "it" collapse, and the sense of resting in empty oneness without distinctions gives way to a vivid awareness (characterized by a spaciousness that does not erase differences) of the ineffability and preciousness of each and every being, just as it is, in all its distinctiveness. This experience, too, is not kept for oneself. The Buddha walked the roads of India for decades, teaching. In the ten ox-herding pictures, a kind of metaphoric blueprint of the Zen process, the awakened one is shown mingling with the crowd in the marketplace, sharing of himself freely with those he meets.

So the unknowable can be realized quite directly and simply, always with a start, and conveyed, sometimes quite humorously. Koans are not meant to be frustrating mind-twisters; they can be playful. When the old teacher Yanguan asks his attendant to bring him the rhinoceros fan, the attendant replies that it is broken. Yanguan says, "Then bring me the rhinoceros." Young children can do this, but very smart grown ups might have some difficulty. Where is that rhinoceros? The poet Wallace Stevens captures this—self and other, the particular and the universal, the ineffable and the sensually human, inner and outer, mind and nature—pairs of what we usually take as opposites, in fertile intimate interpenetration:

> *I was the world in which I walked, and what I saw*
> *Or heard or felt, came not but from myself;*
> *And there I found myself more truly and more strange.*

It doesn't take a *kensho* or Zen realization experience to walk this path, although awakenings do occur, and not just in Zen practice. I think we wake up each time we turn toward truth and let ourselves contact our direct experience, affective, mental, somatic, conscious and unconscious, in an immediate and living way. This "turning" is at the deepest level of the personality, and not simply an act of will, though intention helps.

Here is a story of a Zen teacher playfully and unselfconsciously shedding light on the interplay of personal identity and no-self, knowing and not-knowing, truth and illusion. Yamada Ko'un Roshi, Robert Aitken Roshi's teacher and also a teacher of mine, came to the United States to lead *sesshin* (Zen retreats) yearly from 1971 to 1984. During what would turn out to be his final visit to the Maui Zendo, on the eve of his return to Kamakura, students gathered for tea and discussion following evening *zazen* (sitting meditation). After answering questions for well over an hour, Yamada Roshi said,

> Now I will say my last words. The "last word," you
> know, that is a koan. I will say the last word, ha! Earlier,
> Joe pointed to that picture over there [a picture of a much
> younger Yamada Roshi holding a flower] and asked if I
> knew that person. I asked him, "Do you know him?" Joe
> replied, "I do not know him." I too said that I didn't
> know him at all. I am afraid to have to tell you that what
> I have said this evening has been deceiving, that I have
> deceived all of you (laughter). And I must say that I have
> deceived myself too! (more laughter). But you know
> (pointing to his own head), I like him (even more laugh-
> ter). And we need him, we cannot do without him. This
> afternoon at Iao Valley, I was reading a poem of William

Merwin's (the poet, then a member of the Maui Zendo) in a book he gave to me. This!—is it the words I say, or is it the poem of William's? I do not know. It is like a dream. That is all. Sayonara. It is time to go to bed.

The purpose of Zen is not the erasure of the individual. The self cannot be erased, must not be erased. Each being, human and otherwise, is unique and precious. Yet what are we, really? Nothing but a dream, as we sang as children: "Row, row, row your boat…" The dream Roshi refers to—and speaks from—is described in the Diamond Cutter Sutra: "All things are under the law of change. They are a dream, a phantom, a bubble, or a shadow. They are like dew or a flash of lightning." There is a line from a pop song: "the secret of life is enjoying the passage of time." Easier said than done—and the perils are many. But, when we are able, we can enjoy the "merrily, merrily" part of the dream of life.

This dream relates to and arises from an understanding of who we are and what the meaning of our living and dying is. It is not identical to the Freudian dream, which arises out of repression. Analysts see the analysand's first associations as relating directly to a reported dream, others see the entire session as a dream itself. From session as dream to life as dream: evanescent, empty of permanent absolute identity, spirited, spontaneous, and "presentational" rather than abstract, a creative and liberating living of impossible-to-reconcile human contradictions, without recourse to a supra-human homunculus, arising out of intimacy with a spacious, interconnected ground of truth. We may call this the dream of Zen.

Who is the dreamer? For purposes of discussion, the absolute *is* unknowable, not because it is a secret, known only, let's say, to or as God, an entity inaccessible to our merely human apprehension. Truth is unknowable because, joke of all jokes, there is nothing (absolute) *to* know, and no solid someone to know it: no first cause, no fundamental identifiable basic particle. It can only be, to echo Bion's felicitous phrase, "been." But this is a living "been," not out of reach for ordinary people, reserved for the blessed few. Paradoxically, this spacious emptiness is the springboard to realizing our kinship with our fellows. Despite (we could say *because of*) our insubstantiality and interdependent nature, we awake, take the kids to school, are affected by others' behaviors and feelings, breathe the oxygen exhaled by the trees, laugh, weep, and live as a unique, richly complex node in a multicen-tered, interdependent world.

Knowing this directly, by one's own experience, and internalizing and liv-ing it can help us cultivate an open and free mind, feel connected, and develop compassion for ourselves and all things: animals, vegetables, and minerals, organic and inorganic, sentient and not. This process usually occurs with a "significant" other; that is, through give and take, an intensive and inti-mate relationship that both is a means to an end, and itself *embodies*, in form and activity, the content of the teachings.

Grotstein asks, What is the harvest of Zen? Singing and dancing, sitting down and standing up, laughing and weeping—there is nothing extra stick-ing to it, and nothing left undone. The sacred in the human, the ordinarily human as the sacred. It is not just the few great mystics, the spiritual elite, who get to taste this. It is our birthright as human beings. The Buddha said about practice: don't take my word for it, if you're interested, try to practice for yourself and see what happens. The teachings are pragmatic, and the teacher is a human, not a god. What are the implications of this for the notion of what the analyst is? Here too, the "meeting" between the two streams is already occurring. While the analytic relationship is not symmetrical, we ana-lysts, like Zen teachers, have more similarities to our patients and students than qualitative differences. We are not of another order of being. Our inter-pretations are not proclamations from on high, nor are they able to cure a patient with a single stroke. I remember how much I liked hearing my Zen teacher speak about Bodhidharma, our altar figure and the famous Zen leg-end who is said to have brought Zen from India to China, as "that old Buddha," as if referring to an old uncle, respected for sure, perhaps revered, but not worshiped as an idol, set apart from the human sphere. Analysts are more like senior helpers, having hopefully developed a deep and abiding con-viction about the usefulness of the analytic process through our own personal struggles and discoveries, our studies and work, able both to live it and to share the lived, internalized knowledge, including its inherent limits, with our patients, as well as to learn from them.

The harvest of Zen, though born of radical, devoted relinquishment, is very down-to-earth. It arises out of a non-goal-oriented immersion in what is. It accrues silently, comes unbidden, and is realized after the fact and mostly in what other people tell us about ourselves. Certain character qualities unfold: the four "noble abodes" of loving-kindness, compassion, joy in the joy of others, and equanimity. These are not the aim of Zen, but they develop out of authentic practice. The harvest of Zen, those very activities that seemed so unsatisfactory, boring, habitual, and pointless—sitting down, standing up, laughing, weeping, getting overwhelmed, talking to a friend, making cookies, doing the dishes, being born and dying—are rendered extraordinary by a change, a turning on its axis, of our relation to them.

This is in accord with the findings of empirical research on contemporary infant attachment paradigms. What engenders safety and security is not the content of an experience itself (pleasurable over painful, for example), but the form in which we make contact with it, our capacity to work with it, reflect on it fruitfully, represent it, such that it becomes meaningful. As Grotstein once said, thought is the taming of the sacred in its unmetabolized chaotic form. We might say that psychoanalysis and Zen practice help us develop a kind of meditative or analytic muscle. Confidence grows in our capacity to meet, understand, and accept the way things are: now joyful, now sad, now terrifying, now mixed, now gaining, now losing. Our outlook changes, we struggle less. Pain does not disappear, because transcending does not mean becoming suprahuman. Loss is part of living, but anguish is reduced, we wriggle and squirm less, go through it more, find ways for contact such that it becomes bearable and meaningful: which means that we can let it be as it is, and so it eventually passes. Samsara—what is disturbing, sorrowful, painful, traumatic, unsatisfactory, is transformed into nirvana itself, not by magic, not by a pollyanna-like rendering of it into glee, but by penetrating into the nature of the experience itself, and of the experiencer. The ending of suffering talked about as the third Noble Truth is not an extinguishing but a change from reactively fueled anguish to ordinary suffering. This may sound like Freud's idea that analysis helps transform neurotic misery into ordinary unhappiness. But it is not as grim as Freud's formulation sounds. There is joy, knowledge, acceptance, serenity, and, ironically, security in living in accord with the way things are. There is quiet contentedness in how(ever) things unfold, without being passive or submissive, come what may. Blake captures this: "He who binds himself to a joy / Doth the winged life destroy / But he who kisses joy as it flies / Lives in Eternity's sunrise."

The mutual contributions of psychoanalysis and Zen are already in progress. The title of the recent landmark conference sponsored by the American Psychoanalytic Association, "Beyond Interpretation" (which might have also been called "Before Interpretation"), points beyond how a good therapeutic alliance can help the patient accept, use, and grow from interpretation. What (else) does an analyst do? There is something elusive yet palpable about the responsive presence of the analyst and the Zen teacher alike and the intimate exchanges it fosters, which, as much if not more than anything we say, may facilitate the growth of the (capacities of) patient and student, as well as analyst and Zen teacher. The capacity for what Bion and Grotstein call dreamwork alpha—taking in and creatively transforming the experience of the other and then responsively sharing it in a mutually interpenetrating and fruitful exchange—is one version of this therapeutic presence. Another example of the meeting of psychoanalysis and Zen would be the relatively accepted "here and now" orientation of psychoanalysis as it has evolved from a rather "there and then" focus. In Zen the relationship of practice and insight to daily relational living in the world—living with others, in the body, with mixed and often unconscious emotions—is becoming significant. Meditation teachers are grappling daily with the activity and implications of transference and countertransference.

It takes another mind for one to discover one's own, just as it takes another's living truth to discover one's own. This is not just an operational statement: if you do this, this will happen. The discovering is in the doing, together. The relationship with another is not just an expedient, or a discrete variable. The dialogues of Zen masters and students are not just "enlightening." The give and take in them, the power of freedom in action, the intensity, intimacy, and emotional exchange, are not just a backdrop for, or a springboard to, a eureka experience. They are also the *embodiment* of interbeing: getting from here to there is in the doing, together. Method is separable from aim for discussion purposes only.

A monk asked Yunmen, "What is the most urgent matter for me?" The teacher replied, "The very you who is afraid that he doesn't know!" The monk said, "Though this is my most pressing concern, I cannot find any way in. Please show me a way in." Yunmen replied, "Just in your present concern there is a way" (App 1994). Here Yunmen was not simply suggesting a method *to* somewhere. In Zen we say that he showed his liver and guts, that is, he gave freely of himself, in accord with and in response to the monk's question and the obscuring underlying assumptions implicit in it.

An exchange with the Dalai Lama at a recent gathering in Northern California of 250 Western and Asian Buddhist meditation teachers from various schools and approaches around the world illustrates how crucial psychoanalytic thinking is to the development of Buddhist practice in contemporary culture and how this cross-fertilization can lead to a more integrated view of human psychological and spiritual development than is available using one or the other practice and worldview separately. A conference coordinator, seemingly anxious about the Dalai Lama's imminent departure from the conference, posed a rather long question, in what sounded to some like a whiny and affectedly plaintive manner, beseeching His Holiness for "suggestions, last words and blessings" for the Western teachers gathered, troubled by scandals and difficulties in their work with Western students. The Dalai Lama took it in, rocked from side to side, breathing deeply, waited quite a while, and then responded: "When I'm uncertain or distressed, I look inside and check my motivation. Motivation is key. If I am motivated by afflictive emotions, I work on myself. If I am motivated by wholesome emotions, if that is clear after careful inward looking, I don't care what anybody thinks [about me]."

What a breath of fresh air! In a sense this was a vividly expressed interpretation of the separation anxiety I sensed the conference leader was feeling but was unaware of and yet had conveyed emotionally despite the affected tone of his question. More centrally for our purposes, it spoke to the centrality of motivation, something we as analysts are intimately aware of.

What drives us? What fuel are we powered by? The French word *pulsion,* the equivalent of our "drive," has a pulse in it. What emotional fuel pulses through our psychical veins, animating our activities? Is it time to rethink the energy model? And how can we know this directly, know the truth of it without access to the unconscious dimensions of experience as well as conscious meditative practices? Meditative awareness, brought to bear during states of extreme anxiety or compulsive behavior, can reveal more than analysts imagine of the conscious mind's capacity for subtle observation-in-action of complex body-mind-feeling states and their rapid flux. This contributes to, of course, rather than detracts from, the capacity for free association. However, Buddhist meditators and teachers alike, with few exceptions, have yet to be convinced of the power of unconscious motivation and the necessity to cultivate friendly, skillful relations with our unconscious lives, and they tend to overprivilege and overestimate the powers of the conscious, meditative mind.

Integration implies distinctiveness; it is a coming together but not a melding. Psychoanalysis makes intrinsic use of human meditative capacities as intensive Zen practice harnesses our relational needs and capacities. What is shaking out of the storm arising from their meeting? A more nuanced, balanced, comprehensive, integrated view of the complex creatures that we humans are, in all our good, bad, and ugliness, and our potential for surprising ourselves and growing creatively in the midst of pain and suffering.

Note

1.   Concetta Alfano (1997) developed independently a similar idea, that of an echo chamber

References

Albom, M. 1997. *Tuesdays with Morrie: An Old Man, a Young Man, and Life's Greatest Lesson.* New York: Doubleday.

Alfano, C. 1997. *Echo and Space: Dreaming and Alternation States of Consciousness in the Anyalytic Hour.* Unpublished doctoral dissertation, Southern California Psychoanalytic Institute, Beverly Hills, California.

App, V. 1994. Trans, ed. Master Yunmen: *From the Record of the Chan Teacher "Gate of the Clouds."* New York: Koansha Int'l.

Applebaum, S. 1999. Speaking with the Second Voice: Evocativeness. Unpublished.

Arden, M. 1999. The Peacock's Tail and the Emperor's New Clothes. Unpublished.

Bianchedi, E. de. Case discussion at the Psychoanalytic Institute of Northern California, San Francisco, February.

Bick, E. 1967. The Experience of the Skin in Early Object Relations. In *Collected Papers of Martha Harris and Esther Bick.* Pertshire, England: Clunie Press, 1987.

Bion W. R. 1965. *Transformations.* London: William Heinemann.

———. 1970. *Attention and Interpretation.* London: Tavistock Publications.

———. 1992. *Cogitations.* London: Karnac Books.

Bobrow, J. 2000. Reverie in Psychoanalysis and Zen: Harvesting the Ordinary. *Journal of Transpersonal Psychology,* January, 32:165-75.

Bohm, D. 1980. *Wholeness and the Implicate Order.* London: Routledge and Kegan Paul.

Bollas, C. 1998. Lecture on differences between classical and Kleinian technique. Herrick Hospital, Berkeley, Calif., December.

Breuer, J., and S. Freud. 1893–95. *Studies on Hysteria.* In Standard Edition, 2:1–309. London: Hogarth Press, 1953–74.

Cox, S. D. 1980. *The Stranger within Thee: Concepts of the Self in Late-Eighteenth-Century Literature.* Pittsburgh: University of Pittsburgh Press.

Derrida, J. 1967. *Writing and Difference.* Trans. A. Bass. London: Routledge and Kegan Paul.

Eliot, T. S. 1971. *Four Quartets.* London: Harcourt Brace Jovanovich.

Fonagy, P. 1995. Paper presented at the Los Angeles Institute and Society for Psychoanalytic Studies and the Psychoanalytic Center of California, May 20.

Freud, S. 1900. *The Interpretation of Dreams.* Standard Edition, 4. London: Hogarth Press, 1953.

———. 1911. *Formulations of the Two Principles of Mental Functioning.* In Standard Edition, 12:213–26. London: Hogarth Press, 1958.

Grotstein, J. 1995a. Orphans of the "Real": I. Some Modern and Post-Modern Perspectives on the Neurobiological and Psychosocial Dimensions of Psychosis and Primitive Mental Disorders. *Bulletin of the Menninger Clinic* 59: 287–311.

———. 1995b. Orphans of the "Real": II. the Future of Object Relations Theory in the Treatment of Psychoses and Other Primitive Mental Disorders. *Bulletin of the Menninger Clinic* 59: 312–32.

———. 1996. Bion's Transformation in "O," Lacan's "Thing-in-Itself," and Kant's "Real": Towards the Concept of the Transcendent Position. *The Journal of Melanie Klein and Object Relations,* 14:109–42.

———. 1999. The Alter Ego and Déjà Vu Phenomena: Notes and Reflections. In *The Plural Self: Multiplicity in Everyday Life,* eds. John Rowan and Mick Cooper, 28–50. London: Sage Publications.

———. 2000. *Who Is the Dreamer Who Dreams the Dream? A Study of Psychic Presences.* Hillsdale, N.J.: Analytic Press.

Hamilton, V. 1996. *The Analyst's Preconscious.* Hillsdale N.J.: Analytic Press.

Heidegger, M. 1962. *Being and Time.* Trans. John Macquarrie and Edward Robinson. San Francisco: Harper San Francisco.

Heisenberg, W. 1930. *The Physical Principles of the Quantum Theory.* Chicago: University of Chicago Press.

———. 1958. *Physics and Philosophy.* New York: Harper and Brothers.

Lacan, J. 1977. *Écrits: 1949–1960*. Trans. A. Sheridan. New York: W. W. Norton.

Milner, M. 1969. *The Hands of the Living God*. London: Hogarth.

———. 1987. The Concentration of the Body. In *The Suppressed Madness of Sane Men*. London: Routledge.

Ogden, T. 1994. *Subjects of Analysis*. New York: Jason Aronson.

Parsons, M. 1986. Suddenly Finding it Really Matters. *International Journal of Psychoanalysis*. 67:275-88.

Sasaki, R. F., trans. 1971. *The Recorded Sayings of Layman P'ang*. New York: Weatherhill.

Spezzano, C. 1993. A Relational Model of Inquiry and Truth: The Place of Analysis in Human Conversation. *Psychoanalytic Dialogues* 3:177–208.

Spitz, R. 1963. *Dialogues from Infancy*. Ed. R. N. Emde. New York: International Universities Press, 1983.

Symington, N. 1993. *Narcissism: A New Theory*. London: Karnac.

Winnicott, D. W. 1958. Primary Maternal Preoccupation. In *Collected Papers: Through Pediatrics to Psycho-Analysis*, 300–305. New York: Basic Books.

———. 1975. Metapsychological and Clinical Aspects of Regression within the Psychoanalytic Set-Up. In *From Pediatrics to Psychoanalysis*. New York: Basic Books.

CHAPTER 6

Your Ordinary Mind

BARRY MAGID

For the past twenty-five years I have been practicing both psychoanalysis and Zen Buddhism. At first, these were two separate practices conducted in parallel. As the years have gone by, however, they increasingly converged, and I began to see them both as structured disciplines of moment-to-moment awareness and to evolve a common conceptual framework to describe the mechanism of character change within each. At the same time, I found myself in the unusual professional position of being both a psychoanalyst and a Zen teacher, and the people I work with likewise often find themselves in the dual roles of patient and Zen student. The convergence of these seemingly very different practices seems to me to be part of a larger social phenomenon. Practices that were formerly seen as purely religious or spiritual have increasingly taken on a quasi-therapeutic aspect in the public eye, and many people are drawn to them for many of the same reasons for which they might also consider entering psychoanalytic therapy. At a time when economic forces are at work pushing psychotherapy more and more in the direction of a medical model with managed care mandating specific diagnoses, symptom-focused treatment plans, and wherever possible, psychopharmacological solutions, spiritual practices of all kinds offer to address issues of identity, quality of life, well-being, and the role of values in contemporary life—questions that once upon a time psychoanalysis was seen to potently address. More and more of my patients seem to have had not only some prior psychotherapeutic experience but some interest in, or experience of, one form or another of spiritual practice, whether yoga, meditation, martial arts, or some new-age hybrid. The same seems to be true for more and more of my students, supervisees, and colleagues. Many currently augment whatever they are seeking through psychoanalytic practice with a personal spiritual practice of some sort, one that they may only very vaguely know how to relate to what is going on in their psychotherapy.

Roughly forty to fifty years ago, Zen and psychoanalysis went through another period of convergence, one that has been memorialized in *Zen Buddhism and Psychoanalysis,* a collection of essays by Erich Fromm, D. T. Suzuki, and Richard de Martino (1960). That collection grew out of a conference in Cuernavaca, Mexico, in 1957 sponsored by the Department of Psychoanalysis of the Medical School of the Autonomous National University of Mexico, which was attended by about fifty psychiatrists and psychologists, the majority of whom were psychoanalysts. This was a convergence that arose from *inside* the analytic community, under the impetus of some of its most prominent and innovative thinkers, such as Fromm and Karen Horney. These psychoanalysts, struggling to articulate an alternative to classical Freudian metapsychology, found in Zen a compelling method of radical personality change that seemed to operate on wholly different principles than those of the standard model. For Fromm, the crucial step was to move from a psychology of illness to a new psychology of well-being, which he called "humanistic" psychoanalysis. "If we stay within the Freudian system," wrote Fromm (1960, 86), "well-being would have to be defined in terms of libido theory, as the capacity for full genital functioning, or from a different angle as an awareness of the hidden Oedipal situation, definitions of which, in my opinion, are only tangential to the real problem of human existence and the achievement of well-being by the total man. Any attempt to give a tentative answer to the problem of well-being must transcend the Freudian frame of reference and lead to a discussion, incomplete as it must be, of the basic concept of human existence, which underlies humanistic psychoanalysis."

Zen offered that generation of analysts what appeared to be valuable new data about the nature of insight and human potentiality that could not be accounted for within the Freudian paradigm and thus served an important impetus for system building and paradigm change within this progressive faction of psychoanalysis. Today, the field of psychoanalysis is in very different shape. The Freudian hegemony having been overthrown, pluralism is the order of the day. Self psychological, intersubjective, and relational schools are thriving, and Fromm's battle, in part, has been won. But that victory, for most theoreticians, has meant that there is little current impetus to come to terms with Buddhist psychology. Western psychology is doing just fine now, thank you. The push has come, not from theoretical tensions within the field, as in Fromm's day, but, perhaps, from tensions from within the analysts themselves. Meditation, as often as further analysis, offers a way to deal with the stresses and strains of modern life and the realities of professional life. At the same time, psychoanalysis faces increasing competition from Eastern practices as a mode for the search for meaning in our lives. A growing public that could not name a single contemporary psychoanalyst is becoming more and more aware of the Dalai Lama and his teachings.

Having received my initial psychoanalytic training from teachers and supervisors who themselves trained with Karen Horney and her followers, I was exposed from the start to a humanistic and existentialist brand of psychoanalysis, one that was conducive to my ongoing interest in Zen practice. In those early years of my training, I went three times a week to my analyst and three times a week to the zendo. In 1996, after more than twenty years of Zen practice, my current teacher, Charlotte Joko Beck, formally gave me permission to begin teaching Zen myself, and I opened the Ordinary Mind Zendo in a space adjacent to my psychoanalytic office. Since then, a number of current and former analysands have joined a few others in an ongoing group practice of weekly meditation and regular all-day intensive sesshins. In what follows, I will try to give an account of what happens in Zen practice that is informed by my own psychoanalytic perspective from within self psychology and intersubjectivity. I will try to explain what is meant by such often-problematic Zen terms as oneness, emptiness, no-self, and enlightenment, and explore how I believe these ideas and the experiences they are meant to convey are understandable—or not—psychoanalytically. Finally, I hope to show how these two seemingly very different disciplines can be made to converge in a unified picture of the self and of practice.

Top-Down versus Bottom-Up

First of all, let me say a little bit about what one actually does when one practices Zen. As is the case with psychoanalysis, there are many schools of Buddhism, one of which is called Zen, and within Zen, there are many traditions and styles, in part corresponding to whether that style originated in Southeast Asia, China, Korea, or Japan. My own experience has been with different branches of Japanese Zen, but in general, the various practices can be roughly divided into two basic types, which I like to call top-down or bottom-up.

What I call a top-down practice is a concentration practice, such as working on the koan *Mu*. Traditionally, this is the first koan assigned in Rinzai Zen temples. The practice originates from the story of a famous encounter between a student and the Chinese Zen master Joshu. The monk asked Joshu, "Does a dog have the Buddha-Nature?" Joshu answered, "Mu." "Mu" literally means "no," even though it is one of the most basic tenets of the historical Buddha's original teaching that every sentient being possesses Buddha-nature. Generations of Zen students have been challenged to present to their teachers the meaning of Joshu's Mu. One practices with this first koan by concentrating all one's attention on silently repeating the single syllable Mu breath after breath after breath. Everything becomes this one sound Mu. I breathe Mu in and out; Mu breathes me in and out. Outside and inside disappear, the boundaries between the self and the world disappear, and there is only *this*. When we are nothing but *this*, there is no separation: no separate self, no separate object of experience. No *has* or *has not* Buddha-Nature.

I call this top-down practice because it is intended to induce a kind of peak experience that has been called "oneness." In traditional Zen terminology, we would speak of encountering "the Absolute," which is opposed to our ordinary "relative" world of dualism and differentiation. This way of practicing presumes that each time we have such an experience, the self we return to is subtly transformed, its boundaries not quite as rigid or well defended. The problem in this type of practice is always: How do we bring the experience of no-separation or oneness down into our everyday life? Having had such an initial realization, a student might be challenged by a traditional Zen master to show how he can "take a step off the top of a hundred-foot pole." The danger is that we can come to prefer the view from the top of the pole to doing the real work on the ground, because such a moment, no matter how profound, always ends, leaving the residual problem of how we transform our everyday lives to be in accord with the perspective such moments provide, rather than become subtly addicted to the "high" of peak experience.

A bottom-up practice proceeds from the other direction. This practice is sometimes called "just sitting" and is characteristic of the Soto Zen school. Here the premise is that zazen is already the perfect manifestation of the awakened way. We don't sit in order to become Buddhas, we sit because we already are Buddhas. Now, the fact is that most of the time we don't feel much like Buddhas—or rather, we can't believe that *this* is what it feels like to be Buddha. So any practice of "just sitting" immediately runs into this sense of resistance. And rather than attempting to induce experiences of oneness, we practice staying with the resistance itself. The two basic hallmarks of resistance in our lives are fear and anger. These emotions mark off what we don't want to accept or face, where the self feels it is not getting its way or not being treated the way it wants. It's at this level that Zen and psychotherapy practices dovetail. There is no psychoanalytic equivalent, as far as I am aware, to a top-down concentration practice specifically designed to induce "oneness" experiences. But a bottom-up practice of just sitting that focuses attention on resistance and on emotional and bodily tension leads to questions familiar to every analyst and analysand: What am I avoiding? What do I expect from others? Where did I get that expectation, and so forth.

In this practice, the student begins sitting with a simple focus on the sensation of breathing in and out. As thoughts come and go, we label them as "thought" and return our attention to our breath. (One good technique for labeling thoughts is simply to silently say to oneself, "thinking ...such and such" and repeating the thought to yourself. If this gets too wordy, we might use a simple label like "worrying" for a recurrent pattern of thought.) Gradually we learn to settle into the silence behind our thoughts. In that silence we simply experience the physicality of sitting. As we sit, we become attuned to the physical manifestations of fear and anger in our bodies. These will always be present in the form of bodily tension somewhere or another; they are the physical correlates of our psychological guardedness. When we sit, we bring the focus of our attention right to the boundaries of our experience of separation, right into the physical pain or tension that marks the line we don't want to cross. And that's where we sit, right on that line, right in the midst of that tension. Whatever boundaries the self habitually tries to set up in life, it will try to set up here and now in the zendo: boundaries of judgment of oneself and others; boundaries of how we think we're doing well or badly in our practice; boundaries of expectation regarding other students or the teacher. Whenever our fear or anger illuminates one of these boundaries, that's where we put down our cushion. Oneness is experienced as an all-inclusive "being just this moment." After years of mature practice, the distinction between the two directions, top-down and bottom-up, dissolves. Ultimately, both lead to simply being present and responsive to each moment as it is, including an awareness of our thoughts and emotional resistances as just momentary phenomena that we experience as they pass.

Zen practice is hard, both emotionally and physically. On the one hand, it should not be confused with any sort of relaxation technique or meditation that aims at simply quieting the mind and becoming calm. But on the other hand, too often in the past it has been the physical difficulty of practice that has been emphasized: the long hours of sitting and the intense physical pain that they can bring, as well as the austerity and asceticism that a monastic faces day in, day out. Too often students believe practice means mastering difficulties, as if Zen were a matter of cultivating toughness and endurance. This kind of approach can lead to a not-so-subtle elitism and pride in one's own capacity to handle any sort of pain or challenge that life throws our way. Not an inconsiderable accomplishment to be sure, but one that has more in common with the Marines than with psychoanalysis.

I vividly remember a Japanese Rinzai Zen teacher recounting to his assembled students the parable of the mother tiger and her cubs. The mother tiger, he said, throws all her cubs off a steep cliff when they are only a few weeks old. She will raise only those cubs that are strong enough to scramble back up the slope on their own. The rest are left to die at the base of the cliff. "Which kind of cub are you?" he asked. Not being Samurai material myself, I was pretty sure I knew the answer to that one.

My version of psychoanalytic Zen, therefore, has set up shop at the base of that cliff, ministering to those abandoned cubs, each according to its own needs. That Japanese teacher undoubtedly taught a valuable, rigorous, authentic Zen, one that had no qualms about its elitism and contained a not-too-subtle contempt for those who couldn't keep up. Ironically that same teacher became embroiled in a series of scandals, precipitated by his repeated sexual advances to his female students. Sadly, there seemed to be no avenue within his brand of teaching to acknowledge and work through his own personal weaknesses.

Unfortunately, this teacher was no isolated example, and the recurring inability of many teachers, from a broad variety of spiritual disciplines, to deal appropriately with eroticized transference and countertransference reactions has been one of the main sources of a growing appreciation among Buddhist communities for the experience that psychoanalytic training can bring to bear on meditation practice.

It is the explicit acknowledgment and working-through of the *emotional* difficulties of practice that has been the hallmark of a new American Zen, particularly in the Ordinary Mind School, founded by Charlotte Joko Beck. This style of practicing was born directly out of the failure of so many of the first generation of Japanese and American teachers here in the United States to adequately deal with their own emotional conflicts, transference reactions, substance abuse, and sexual behavior despite having completed traditional Zen training. Janwillem van de Wetering's (1999) memoir *Afterzen*, an insider's account of Rinzai training and koan study, recounts, often quite comically, the slew of emotional difficulties that dogged (and sometimes ruined) the lives of "enlightened" teachers, dedicated monks, and devoted lay students alike. Jeffrey Rubin (1996) and Michael Eigen (1998), analysts with strong sympathies for meditation practice, are among those who have documented case after case of experienced meditators whose practice not only failed to adequately address core conflicts and deficits but actually reinforced existing defensive patterns. Too often, it seems that both students and teachers have mastered their pain but succumbed to their impulses, experienced a oneness with all beings but remained in conflict with their families, discovered the emptiness of self but continued to abuse their authority, found peace on the their cushions but not in their lives. It is my hope that an understanding of transference and an appreciation of the role of empathy can transform the traditional student-teacher relationship. Good teachers of all persuasions, of course, operate with an intuitive feeling for their students' transferential needs and reactions, but they vary in their capacity to understand and deal with intense transference idealizations, eroticized transferences, competitive or conflictual reactions, and the disappointment, rage, and withdrawal that can accompany transference disruptions. Likewise, they may underestimate the extent to which an apparently devoted student may spend years stuck in a role of compliance, having formed a morbid dependency on the teacher or otherwise succumbed to some form of pathological accommodation, masochistically enduring a painful training solely as a way to maintain a tie to an idealized selfobject. Countertransferentially, coping with idealization, even when not erotically charged, is an ongoing challenge to the latent narcissism of any teacher. Empathy can ensure that a teacher will understand and respect the differing emotional needs, weaknesses, and strengths of different students and not impose a "one-size-fits-all" discipline.

ONENESS

I have referred to experiences of "oneness," and perhaps something more needs to be said about just what this means. Ever since Freud referred to a feeling of "limitlessness and of a bond to the universe" as the "oceanic feeling" (1930, 68), a lot of psychoanalytic ink has been spilled over this question. Inevitably, these attempts have tried to fit oneness experiences into some preexisting psychoanalytic schema, often resulting in the conclusion that "oneness" must involve some sort of regressed state, some kind of primitive loss of differentiation between self and other. M. Shaffii, for instance, wrote that "through meditation ...a profound but temporary and controlled regression occurs. This deep experience helps the individual regress ...to the somato-symbiotic phase of the mother-child relationship" (1973, 442). And the authors of *The Search for Oneness* (Silverman, Lachmann, and Milich 1982), even as they emphasize the psychological benefits of such experiences, assume that they can be understood only in terms of regression. Whether this state is to be conceptualized as an actual return to a developmental stage of childhood, or whether we think of regression in functional, not temporal terms, remains for these authors an open question. But even if we grant the existence and adaptive or defensive function of such states in other contexts, how relevant is this picture of oneness to what is called oneness or no separation in Buddhist practice? Are they identical? Analogous? Or are we talking about two fundamentally different states that have been metaphorically conflated?

Although most writers have focused their attention on single, intense moments of revelatory experience, we must remember that Zen is not primarily concerned simply with inducing such momentary experiences of "oneness" for their own sake but aims at the long-term changes in character and motivation that accompany the abandonment of a dualistic perspective.

If we only look at individual moments of experience, taking a top-down approach, we can easily conflate the religious experience with some regressive state. But it is the *functioning* from the perspective of oneness in our everyday lives that constitutes the real goal of practice, not some special or intense experience we have only while sitting on our cushions. And when we look at oneness from the perspective of functioning, then I think, the differences most clearly emerge.

A Tale of Two Meditators

Let us imagine two young analysts who have taken up meditation. Analyst A has been sitting at the local zendo for a few years now. One day, in the midst of counting his breaths, he gradually begins to feel like he is no longer doing the breathing but is *being breathed.* And then suddenly, he has the sense that he and everyone, everywhere, are part of One Body. The world is a living, unified whole, perfect just as it is. When he goes home at the end of the day, he is convinced he has had a great mystical experience, the kind he has always hoped to achieve as the result of his sitting. He feels different now, and special. He feels a certain condescension, even pity (which he calls "compassion") for his fellow meditators and analysts who have never had such an experience. With his own patients, because of his new insight, he is now more convinced than ever of the rightness of his interpretations and begins to believe that just being together with him in the room allows them to partake in some subtle way in his newfound feelings of openness and perfection. Convinced of his own essential goodness, he increasingly has trouble imagining that anything he does could have a negative impact on them, and blames their failure to improve on their own entrenched dualism.

Analyst B has also been meditating for some years but has never had a dramatic experience like the one Analyst A rushed to tell him about. His own sitting, instead of giving him any blissful sense of oneness, has only made him more aware of his own anger and anxiety. He has seen how much he tries to do everything perfectly in the zendo, and how frustrated he can get at his limitations. He's noticed how his shoulders always seem to tense up when he sits too rigidly, trying to be the model student and impress his teacher. Gradually he comes to realize that everyone in the zendo is struggling with the same problems and the same pain. Instead of feeling special, he begins to feel more like part of the group, supporting and supported by everything that takes place around him. With his patients, he had been prone to divide them into two camps—good analyzable prospects and difficult, if not impossible, borderlines. But now he seems able to empathically resonate with a greater range of human suffering and is more inclined to see whoever walks through the consulting room door as simply a fellow human being. The differences between himself and his patients no longer seem so profound or relevant. It was not that he became oblivious to their difficulties, just the opposite. He is becoming more willing and prepared to engage whatever arises in himself and others without pejorative labels or judgments. Differences have stopped making a difference.

In a way, it doesn't matter whether you call Analyst A's experience of oneness "regressive" or not. What does matter is that he immediately incorporated it into his previous self-centered view of things—a "special" experience that confirmed him as a special sort of person. Paradoxically, his realization of "oneness" only increased his sense of his own difference and his separation from everybody around him. Whatever sort of "oneness" this is, it isn't *functioning* to diminish separation or dualistic thinking in his life. Analyst B on the other hand, progressively became aware of the barriers he had habitually set up between himself and others, and as a result of his practice these barriers have gradually and undramatically begun to come down. He's never had a "mystical" experience, and his life, on the surface, doesn't look so different from that of his colleagues who never meditated. But he is *functioning* less and less from a self-centered, dualistic perspective.

What would *consistently* functioning from oneness look like? One hallmark of a nondualistic perspective is that *we no longer have any problems.* That is, we no longer divide our life into the good parts and the problems— there is simply life, one moment after another. Problems disappear not *from* our life but *into* our life. There needn't be anything particularly special or mystical about that disappearance. When we think of oneness in this way, as a nondualistic way of functioning, it is clearly not dependent on any regressive analogue, nor through such functioning are we returned to such a state. Analyst A's experience, had it taken place in a different practice context, might have served to challenge, rather than confirm, his self-centeredness. How we classify any given momentary experience is not what's crucial. How it functions in our life is what counts.

The Intersubjective View

Analytic theories that seek to explain religious experience by invoking analogies with an undifferentiated, symbiotic, or merged state of infancy are, in my mind, probably not only misrepresenting the subjective experience of the baby but, more importantly, looking at the wrong end of the developmental spectrum. The adult mind is just as intersubjectively embedded and co-determined by its contextual surround as that of the infant. Eigen's (1981) description of a Winnicottian transitional area in which "self and other are neither one, nor two, but somehow together make up an interpenetrating field" is, in fact, a description of the intersubjective reality that we all, as adults, inhabit. Robert Stolorow therefore has described intersubjectivity as neither a one-person, nor a two-person, but a "no-person psychology" (1997, 867). To nondualistically inhabit that reality does not involve regression, but constitutes true developmental maturity. Perhaps it's finally time for psychoanalysis to stop thinking that experiencing "oneness" means momentarily returning to the way things once *were,* and to recognize that it means seeing things as they *are.* Dualism, fundamentally a defensive, fantasized attempt to split off the self from a world of potential suffering, represents a developmental failure.

Emptiness

A similar confusion has surrounded the concept of "emptiness." Sometimes this word is used to describe a state of "pure" awareness, an alert mind that is momentarily empty of thoughts. James Austin (1998) has given a detailed account, both in terms of the phenomenology of the meditator's subjective experience and its various hypothesized neurological underpinnings, of a full range of levels of awareness and absorption, in which, to varying degrees, the mind is first quieted and then progressively emptied of any awareness of both external and internal sensory stimulation, including the usual awareness of time and space. These special states of "empty," concentrated attention are referred to as *samadhi* in the Buddhist literature. These states of consciousness represent the greatest *discontinuity* between Zen and psychotherapy practices, and different teachers vary in the centrality they assign to such states in producing lasting insight. In the Japanese Rinzai tradition they are seen as the necessary preludes to the sudden breakthroughs known as *kensho* or *satori.*

But there is also another sense of "emptiness." Traditionally, emptiness is another way of speaking about impermanence: according to the Buddha, all *dharmas* (things or moments of experience) are *empty* of any fixed or essential nature. The lack of any individual essential nature can also been seen as another consequence of oneness—all dharmas being aspects of a constantly changing, co-determined, interdependent whole. To speak of the self as empty is to remark on the transience of all experience, without positing any permanent *experiencer* or observer permanently set up in the background who watches it all go by.

Buddha-Nature

When emptiness is used to convey impermanence, there is no one psychological state that corresponds to the "feeling" of emptiness, any more than there is a state of experiencing pure "being."

If I say an apple is round and red, how many attributes am I listing? Does the apple possess *being* as a third attribute in the same way it possesses redness and roundness? Could it have just the roundness and redness, but not the being? To posit some intrinsic being or appleness alongside the apple's physical qualities of color, shape, and texture (all constantly changing, if ever so slightly) is to posit the sort of fixed unchanging essence that the Buddha's teaching denies. Likewise, the emptiness of the self is not an additional attribute in any way on top of, behind, or between the gaps of moment-to-moment experience. It is just a way of saying that all there is is that moment-to-moment experience. Jack Engler (1984) was certainly right to point out the confusion that results from equating the Buddhist use of "emptiness" with the pathological state of "empty" depression so characteristic of narcissistic and borderline patients. In Buddhist terms, an awareness of "emptiness" is simply a nonresistance to the flow and transience of our lives. In practice, we watch where we resist letting things come and go. These nodes of resistance are what Buddhism refers to as attachment. Nonattachment is an acceptance of impermanence. This way of understanding and practicing with emptiness—unlike the emptiness associated with samadhi—contributes to the *continuity* of Zen and psychotherapeutic practice. The analysis of our resistance to change, of our unwillingness to face, accept, or mourn the impermanence or limitations of our bodies, relationships, or understanding, becomes part and parcel of what we literally sit with in the zendo. Here we might draw an analogy to the practice of free association. Traditionally the analysand was told to simply allow his or her thoughts to freely come and go and to speak them aloud to the analyst, without editing or censorship. Of course, resistance to this seemingly simple basic rule quickly sets in, and the nodes of resistance become the focus of further inquiry. In Zen practice, we might say, we allow not simply our thoughts but life itself to come and go.

The "Buddha-nature" that Shakyamuni discovered we all possess (whether we realize it or not) turns out to be not some innate, immutable "spiritual" essence—nor even some innate potential for enlightenment—but impermanence itself. What would a life or a self that offers no resistance to its own impermanence be like? To fully accept the emptiness of experience, says Joko Beck, is to realize that "impermanence is, in fact, just another name for perfection" (1989, 110). And we might add, perfection is simply another name for full acceptance or nonseparation from life as it is.

Enlightenment

What relation do these moments of insight or experiences of oneness or emptiness have with the character structure of someone who is *enlightened*, when this is meant to describe a completely selfless individual, someone we would call a Buddha? Like the insights that occur in psychoanalysis or other disciplines, they offer us glimpses of a new way of being who we are. That way of being is one that makes none of our usual distinctions or separations: this transient moment, irrespective of its content, is perfect, just as it is. We might say, experiences of oneness give us a momentary experience of *no-self* in place of the usual self-centered organization of experience that usually defines us. In the traditional koans, we sometimes hear a story that ends with the words "with this, the monk was enlightened." The temptation is to imagine that this is the Zen equivalent of "and he lived happily ever after." But it's one thing to feel that a particular moment is perfect, and quite another to imagine saying that about any possible moment. But that is precisely how Joko Beck (1989, 115) describes enlightenment:

> If I am told ...you have one more day to live, is that OK with me?

If I am in a severe accident, and my legs and arms have to be amputated, is this ok with me?

If I were never again to receive a kind or friendly encouraging word from anyone, is this ok with me?

If I make a complete fool of myself, in the worst possible circumstances, is this ok with me?

Her list goes on and on. But what does "ok" mean here? Not, she says, "that I don't scream or protest or hate it.... . For these things to be ok doesn't mean I'm happy about them.... . What *is* the enlightened state? When there is no longer any separation between myself and the circumstances of my life, whatever they may be, that is it" (115–16).

Note that this absence of separation does not have any particular affect state associated with it. Okayness is not any feeling or affirmation added on top of the experience in question. She says she may hate it. There is no blissful glow of oneness here. When we're experiencing the undifferentiated perfection of a single momentary meditative experience, we can imagine how it might be accounted for by some model of regressive oneness. But an entire lifetime of engaged acceptance and functioning within the extremities of experience such as those that Beck lists is not explainable in any such way. No moment of regressive oneness can continue to bathe the whole rest of our life in a warm glow of sweetness and light, banishing any further discrimination or judgment or comparison. The "oneness" that is actualized in an enlightened life is not defined by a single moment of realization, no matter how intense or meaningful, but rather by an ongoing, engaged, wholehearted functioning. That functioning presupposes a cohesive structure of organizing principles through which it operates.

Any insight, no matter how profound, requires a long period of working-through for there to be real character change. Otherwise, we have simply had an intense experience, one that quickly gets reified *as* an experience and that we come to value precisely for its specialness and the *discontinuity* between it and our ordinary life. Part of the mythology of Zen, when I began my practice, was that enlightenment experiences somehow would spontaneously dissolve all neurosis and that one would emerge from them cleansed of all past conditioning. An infatuation with the intensity of such experiences for their own sake can be a particularly insidious form of Zen sickness. Rather than using their insights as a light to illuminate the whole of their lives, such individuals become Zen moths, uncontrollably and drunkenly drawn to their own light. Another, and I think more useful, metaphor for what happens in practice is that of going for a long walk on a foggy day. When we first set out, we may hardly notice the fine wet mist. But as we walk, hour after hour, we finally arrive at our destination thoroughly soaked. An old teacher once said, "Do not think you'll recognize your own enlightenment." He wanted us to understand that any experience we recognize has already become reified and has become something separate that we can define, possess, and even be proud of.

In some branches of Zen, the working-through process is formalized by means of koan study. The word *koan* means a public case, and you might say that koans are the Zen equivalent of clinical case presentations. The difference, however, is that a koan attempts to encapsulate a psychological or philosophical conundrum in the form of a simple story, dialogue, or riddle, usually within the context of a dramatic encounter between an old master and one of his students. These encounters are not studied or discussed by present-day students so much as reenacted; they are crucial questions that each student poses anew and resolves in his own way. As I discussed above, the koan of Joshu's "Mu" is used to induce an experience of oneness that then becomes the basis for further refinement and practice, traditionally by working through one after another of hundreds of koans. The particular virtue of Joko's style of bottom-up practicing is to focus attention precisely on the working-through of our conditioning, that is, our core beliefs or organizing principles that immediately spring back into place following any so-called enlightenment experience, negating its true import and all too often threatening to incorporate the experience itself into our preexisting mental habits.

True Self or No-Self?

All koans point to a perspective that is fundamentally nondualistic, anti-essentialist, and anti-transcendent. Should we achieve an experience of these states, koans challenge us to demonstrate what it means to function from within them. We have seen nondualism at work in "Mu." The anti-essential-ist perspective is illuminated by a koan such as "This very moment, thinking neither good nor evil, show me your original face before the birth of your par-ents" (*Mumonkan,* case 23). The koan is posed in such a way as to *join* with a naive assumption of an essential or true self, challenging the student to work through all their preconceptions of who, deep down, they really are. Having gone beyond dualism, beyond "thinking good or evil," is there an essential true self? Buddha taught that the self is "empty"—that is it has *no* fixed or essential nature at all. All there is is what the opening words of the koan itself tell us: Being this very moment *is* our true self. Our original face can be none other than this moment's face. Seeking for some pure or perfect inner essence only blinds us to the perfection of this moment. Eigen (1998, 34) mused that Donald Winnicott, Marion Milner, and Wilfred Bion "would like the Zen koan 'What was your original face before you were born?'" because they all "share a conviction that an original, naked self is the true subject of experience. Internalization processes are necessary for a fully developed, human self, but something originary shines through." Though Eigen normally is someone who celebrates a radical openness to the moment, here, I'm afraid, he and his men-tors may be searching for a chimerical true self that they imagine must be *behind* the moment and shine *through* it. Thomas Merton came much closer to the mark, when toward the end of his life, and looking back on his earlier writing about the "true self," he wrote in his journal,

> The time has probably come to go back on all that I have said about one's "true self," etc., etc. And show that there is after all no hidden mysterious "real self" OTHER THAN or "hiding behind" the self that one is, but what all the thinking does is to observe what is there or objectify it and thus falsify it. The "real self" is not an object, but I have betrayed it by seeming to promise a possibility of knowing it somewhere, sometimes as a reward for astute-ness, fidelity, and a quick-witted ability to stay one jump ahead of reality. (Merton 1997, 95)

Finding out that who you really are is nothing but being this moment may sound disappointingly ordinary or straightforward, but the moment of realization may be quite extraordinary. This is how the neurologist and Zen student James Austin (1998) describes discovering his "original face" while standing on a train platform in London:

> It strikes unexpectedly at 9:00 A.M., on the surface plat-
> form of the London subway system.... I am en route to
> the sesshin on a peaceful, balmy Sunday morning. I am
> a little absent-minded, and take the first train available.
> I wind up at a station where I have never been before.
> There, I submit to the reality of a slight delay...the
> empty platform is quiet.... I turn and look away from
> the tracks, off to the south.... This view includes no more
> than the dingy interior of the station, some grimy build-
> ings in the middle ground, and a bit of open sky above
> and beyond. I idly survey this ordinary scene, unfocused,
> no thought in mind.
>
> Instantly, the entire scene acquires three qualities:
> Absolute Reality, Intrinsic Rightness, Ultimate Perfec-
> tion. (Austin 1998, 537)

What happened? For a moment, there was only this scene and, as Austin reports, "no viewer." With it, he says, came the sense that this moment was perfect in itself, that there was nothing to do or fear. Only later did he per-ceive that this experience was itself the answer to his koan about his Original Face. Beyond thinking good or evil, all essential "self" fallen away, only this moment in the train station.

This actual, lived realization of nondualism (or oneness) and non-essentialism (or emptiness) demonstrates that there is a very real alternative to what Geroge Atwood and Robert Stolorow (1992) have called "the myth of the isolated mind." They have outlined three main areas of alienation from the essential embeddedness of life that are a consequence of this myth: First, *alienation from nature*, including the illusion "that there is a sphere of inner freedom from the constraints of animal existence and mortality" (8). Second, *alienation from social life*, including the illusion that each individual "knows only his own consciousness and thus [is] forever barred from direct access to experiences belonging to other people ...which ignores the constitutive role of the relationship to the other in a person's having any experience at all" (9). Third, *alienation from subjectivity*, including the "reification of various dimensions of subjectivity. These reifications confer upon experience one or another of the properties attributed to things on the plane of material reality, for example spatial localization, extension, enduring substantiality and the like.... Invariably associated with the image of the mind is that of an external reality or world upon which the mind entity is presumed to look out" (11).

This dualism—which has pervaded Western philosophy, as well as the psychoanalytic experience and literature in all the ways delineated by Stolorow and Atwood—is directly challenged by Zen practice. Whether gradually or in moments of intense realization such as Austin describes, Zen directly confronts and destabilizes our usual Cartesian presupposition of the essential interiority of the self, as well as any belief in a "true," "inner," or "essential" self or nature—all of which, I have suggested (Magid 1999), have been entangled with aspects of the myth of the isolated mind. The Zen alternative to a Winnicottian (1965) "false" self is not the discovery of an inner "true" self. Nor does it correspond to a Kohutian nuclear self, which Ernest Wolf (1988, 51) describes in this way: "At the time when an individual's self first comes into being as a singular and unique specific cohesive structure, the whole configuration of poles and tension arc being laid down is the core of this nuclear self. This unique core configuration gives the self an idiosyncratic and specific direction that in its lifelong unfolding can be called a *lifeplan* for the self."

According to this formulation fulfillment comes from being in "harmony" with the self's lifeplan, while failing to uncover or actualize this inner blueprint leaves one forever feeling unfulfilled.

Compare this to Joko Beck: "True self is nothing at all. It is the absence of something else. An absence of what?" (1989, 101). It is an absence of, we might answer, not only a "false self" but any notion at all of a "true self" or "lifeplan" that we seek to discover within our lives. The true self of Zen is *no-self;* simply the non-self-centered response to life as it is. How should we as psychoanalysts understand this Buddhist concept of self-centeredness? I would offer this simple definition: *self-centeredness is the perspective of the isolated mind.* That is, the perspective of someone who believes his or her self to be essentially private, interior, autonomous, and separate.

No Transcendence

In the absence of a self-centered or "isolated mind" perspective, it is our moment-to-moment functioning that manifests our essential embeddedness in life. This "true" self is neither inside nor outside; it is neither an inner plan nor a union with a greater or transcendent Being. There is nothing "beyond" being just this moment. This realization illustrates the "anti-transcendent" aspect of Zen that I alluded to before. Putting an end to dualism and essentialism does not catapult us into a "higher" realm, though that may be the initial impression conveyed by a kensho experience like the one described by Austin. Ultimately, Zen endeavors to put an end to any conception of a higher realm. *Enlightenment is precisely the thorough abandonment of any notion of enlightenment.* To convey the radical force of this definition to American ears, I have sometimes said that the common goal of Zen and psychoanalytic practice is *putting an end to the pursuit of happiness.* As psychoanalysts, we can recognize many variations on the fantasy of enlightenment—fantasies of immunity or detachment, immortality or uniqueness, perfect equanimity or freedom from emotionality. All represent ways the isolated mind imagines perfecting itself in its isolation. But as Stolorow and Atwood remind us, the isolated mind is a myth, and the mind's true nature, whether we are aware of it or not, is intersubjective or interconnected. And what it is connected to and part of is a real and messy world. Awakening from a dream of isolation, we return in laughter and in tears to the one real world we have been part of all along. Happiness is no longer something to pursue, to be attained by acquiring something outside of ourselves, but is the natural byproduct of *being ourselves.*

One of my favorite *New Yorker* cartoons shows a guru out playing golf with two young disciples. As he takes a mighty swing at the ball, one young monk whispers to the other, "If he's so enlightened, why can't he lick that slice?" This is a wonderful koan, one that echoes the dilemma posed by a traditional case from the *Mumonkan,* in which an old teacher is punished by being reborn as a fox for five hundred lifetimes after he had made the error of claiming that an enlightened man is forever freed from all past karma. But even though we may no longer dualistically label it a problem, our golf ball may still veer uncontrollably to the right. Long years of conditioning remain to be worked through, and life, even if not viewed dualistically, will still contain difficulties. Being a guru, like being an analyst, must require a fair measure of self-awareness and self-control in the face of frustration or narcissistic injury, and the young disciples in the cartoon have a right to expect their guru not to angrily fling his clubs into the lake after a missed shot, not to scream that their whispering made him flub his drive, and not to be in a snit for the rest of the day over his bad score. The tendency to be frustrated or narcissistically injured will be dramatically reduced by a practice that reveals there is no essential self to defend. But if we imagine that our practice will lead us to a transcendent state where we are totally impervious to the vicissitudes of our lives, we fall into a trap set by the momentary sense of perfection we derived from our experience of oneness. We will always remain embodied, mortal, living in a world of right and wrong, good and bad, life and death. That's where we live and where we need to function: seeing patients who believe they are ill, working with students striving to relieve their suffering. Dropping a dualistic and essentialist perspective doesn't take us out of this world; it allows us to move and function more freely in it—more freely because less defensive and less deluded about its nature.

Loss and Gain

Just as the true self of Zen is the absence rather than the presence of something, enlightenment is not something we can be said to *gain* from practice. Kodo Sawaki Roshi said, "Gain is delusion; loss is enlightenment." Although in psychoanalytic circles we are more likely to speak of *gaining* insight, the Zen way of speaking of loss is perhaps analogous to our saying that defenses or resistances drop off in the course of therapy. When a patient lives her days feeling misunderstood, frustrated, and resentful that nobody ever gets where she's coming from and then, one day, encounters an analyst whose empathy at last allows her to feel that another human being truly understands her, a lifetime of mistrust and despair and anger may drop off in a moment of intense relief. In Buddhist terms, we might say that part of her "self" dropped off, the part that was organized around a particular representation of her "self" and others, and of the impossibility of being understood. What remains is nothing extraordinary, simply a self no longer at odds with itself or the world—"body and mind dropping off," in Dogen's (1983) phrase, denotes the dropping off *all separate* experience of body and mind. This state of no separation is what is called "no self." This no-self is not without structure or boundaries in the usual psychoanalytic sense. Rather, it is fluid, spontaneously, and meaningfully engaged with life. In traditional Kohutian self psychological terms, we might say *that for the no-self all experiences are mature selfobject experiences*. That is, there is an engagement with any and all moment-to-moment experience that provides an ongoing opportunity for the exercise of the self's values and ideals—or in traditional Buddhist terms, its wisdom and compassion. It is this *functioning* that is the hallmark of no-self experience—not some mystical, oceanic dissolving of boundaries.

Constancy

I've stressed the importance of functioning because it is central to another dilemma and misconception concerning the emptiness of self and the meaning of no-self. Buddhism teaches that the self, along with everything else, is empty, changing, and impermanent. How then do we account for constancy? These days I manage to visit Joko in San Diego only once or twice a year, but when I visit, even though I know everything changes, there's something about her that I expect to be the same. For instance, I don't expect her to one day say that she's given up Zen to devote all her energy to playing the stock market! If there's no permanent "self" that is Joko, what am I counting on?

Stephen Mitchell (1991) has noted that analytic theories tend to organize themselves around two fundamentally different perspectives on "self" experience: either self as "relational, multiple and discontinuous" (126) or self as integral, separate, and continuous. Is the Buddhist notion of the impermanence of the self congruent with Mitchell's picture of the self as multiple and discontinuous, in that each posits a succession of transient "selves"? From one perspective yes, but Mitchell's multiple selves are essentially a succession of isolated minds, each in a different "relational configuration" (128). Lacking any realization of intrinsic oneness or interconnectedness, each, despite being "impermanent," can remain self-centered in its perception, motivation, and functioning. And that lack of fundamental embeddedness or interconnectedness poses the problem, within Mitchell's framework as well as that of Buddhism, of whether there can be any consistent ethical values that cohere and remain consistent through a range of constantly changing relational configurations.

How then does Zen reconcile the impermanence of self with the experience of constancy, and particularly with the constancy of core ethical values? To answer that question we need to look more closely at different levels of "self" experience.

Zen postulates what we would call an ongoing "unconscious" level of perception, understanding, and responsiveness that is separate from the self-centered concerns of the personal ego. It is part of what we are by virtue of being human. The Zen master Bankei (1622–93) referred to this innate quality as the Unborn. The Unborn isn't something that has to be created or uncovered; it's what we spontaneously and naturally already are. Only our self-centeredness makes us unaware of its continuous natural functioning. It operates on what we are used to thinking of as a number of different levels, both perceptual and conceptual. Unlike the psychoanalytic version of the Unconscious, however, the unborn isn't "inside" us; if anything we could be said to be an aspect of it. For instance, Bankei told his audience that the workings of the Unborn could be seen in the fact that

> while all of you here are turned toward me, intent only on hearing my sermon and wondering, "What's Bankei going to say?" you aren't trying or not trying either to hear or not hear the cawing of the crows and the chirping of the sparrows out in back. But even so, once they start to chirp and caw, you recognize and distinguish the crow's kaa-kaa and the sparrow's chuu-chuu. And it's not only for crows and sparrows; everything here, when you perceive it with the Unborn, will be simultaneously distinguished and you won't overlook even one thing in one hundred or one thousand. …You're distinguishing everything you see and hear like this, without producing a single thought, is the marvelously illuminating dynamic function, the Buddha Mind that is unborn. (Haskel 1984, 75)

But the Unborn doesn't operate just on the level of perception. Wisdom and compassion are innate human attributes that can function as spontaneously as sight and hearing—but these are especially liable to be interfered with or obscured by overlays of self-centered thought and delusion. According to Bankei,

> All delusions, without exception, are created as a result of self-centeredness. When you are free of self-centeredness, delusions won't be produced. For example, suppose your neighbors are having a quarrel, if you're not personally involved, you just hear what's going on and don't get angry. Not only do you not get angry, but you can plainly tell the rights and wrongs of the case—it's clear to you as you listen who's right and who's wrong. But let it be something that concerns you personally, and you find yourself getting involved with what the other party says or does, attaching to it and obscuring the marvelously illuminating function of the Buddha Mind. Before, you could clearly tell wrong from right, but now led by self-centeredness, you insist your own idea of what's right is right. (Haskel 1984, 24)

What should we as psychoanalysts make of Bankei's claim to be able to spontaneously tell right from wrong? First of all, I would say that Bankei's sermon is illustrating the difference between the workings of the "prereflective unconscious" and the "dynamic unconscious" (Stolorow and Atwood 1992, 33). It is the dynamic unconscious, the repository of "expectations and fears" (34) that most corresponds to intrusive self-centeredness in Bankei's example. It is the prereflective unconscious that is the "spontaneous" organizer of experience. No doubt, Bankei probably needed to be more cautious about what he took to be "spontaneous" or "natural," and it has been a dangerous pitfall for practitioners and masters alike to assume that their own post-kensho response to every new situation has been once and for all purged of self-centeredness and is now entirely spontaneous, natural, and compassionate. As Gregory Bateson (1987) warned, the surest way to be trapped by an epistemological system is to assume that you don't have one and perceive reality "directly." As analysts, we might add the same caveat with regard to unconscious dynamic organizing principles.

But Bankei, I think, is also offering a demonstration of what I've been saying about the necessity of there being *some* underlying layer of values,

ideals, and other organizing principles in order for there to be any functioning of the non-self-centered self. These organizing principles, which will form
the basis of his automatic judgments of right and wrong, simply aren't part
of his notion of "self." And because they operate as spontaneously as seeing
and hearing, there is no separation between Bankei and their functioning. In
Bankei's own terms, it is not as if there is a permanent core of *personal* values
underlying a layer of self-centered concerns; rather, he envisages a *universal
capacity* for a natural, fluid responsiveness that is revealed when self-centeredness
drops away. And whatever is left over when self-centeredness drops away has,
if nothing else, the subjective *feel* of direct, unmediated experience—whatever
an epistemologically sophisticated observer may say to the contrary. Austin,
who as a neurologist specializes in how the brain organizes and processes
information, finds himself convinced that "the feeling that ultimate reality is
being perceived constitutes *the raw data*" [Austin's italics] of kensho experience. Not so unlike Bankei, he concludes it "reveals innate neurophysiolog-
ical capacities" (Austin 1998, 600). Perhaps it is only the isolated mind,
preoccupied with its sense of separateness from the world, that worries about
what epistemic filters it must be using in its struggles to reconnect with a
split-off reality. In the zendo, students are called to the morning's first sitting
by the rhythmic sound of a wooden gong, the *han*, on which is inscribed a
verse that exhorts them to be "like a fish, like a fool." Simply enter into the
swim of things, never once thinking the word "water."

Bankei, like the fish, is completely at home in his world. One might say
there is a perfect "fit" between self and world in Bankei's Zen—if "fit" means
a natural embeddedness in life and doesn't imply a preexistent separation
between self and world that needs to be overcome. Contrast this view with
Eigen's account of Bion's notion of intrinsic deficit: "[Bion] calls on us to face
the fact that our ability to process experience is not up to the experience we
must process…. The deficiency in our equipment begins whenever processing of experiencing begins, a primary process deficiency. We can not keep up
with experiential impacts…. Our equipment produces states it cannot handle…. It is doubtful we can ever catch up with ourselves, or do ourselves justice, whatever level of processing we tap" (Eigen 1998, 99–100). But as the
contemporary poet and Zen teacher Philip Whalen has quipped, "Plenty of
people will tell you that it is the Fate of Man to be eternally a day late and a
dollar short. Don't you believe it" (1972, 19).

An old koan asks, "Why can't the person of great strength lift up a leg?" (Aitken 1991, 132). Here the riddle of no-self is posed in terms of the duality of mind and body. But for one thing to act on another, they must be two separate things in the first place. The person of great strength—and the koan means a person of great spiritual strength and realization—knows no separation, and he doesn't do anything *to* or *with* his body or his strength—he simply moves and functions. Strength, understood in its broadest sense, stands for the sum of one's unselfconscious and un-self-centered capacities. Today, we would be tempted to parse these into separate categories of innate talents, acquired skills, preconscious values and ideals, and unconscious organizing principles. Much of what appears as spontaneous or natural action in such traditional Japanese disciplines such as calligraphy, pottery, or the martial arts is the result of an intensive discipline and training that makes the activity not just second nature but, for all intents and purposes, nature. Reduced to a riddle, this koan is easy to understand; as a challenge to live an unselfconscious, unalienated life, it is one we work on forever.

The answer to the problem of Joko's constancy thus lies both in the consistent absence of something and in the consistent presence of something. What is consistently absent is intrusive self-centeredness. What is consistently present is a "spontaneous" responsiveness and functioning, so much a part of her "self," she does not "possess" it or even experience it *as* part of herself. Aitken Roshi sums it up in the simplest possible terms: "The self is still present—but it is not self-preoccupied. It washes the dishes and puts them away" (1996, 49).

Structural Change

Zen practice aims at radical transformation of both the prereflective and dynamic unconscious as defined by Stolorow and Atwood (1992). In terms of Heinz Kohut's (1977) self psychology, compensatory structure is established based on new non-self-centered values and ideals, and forms the basis for "spontaneous" compassionate responsiveness. In ego psychology terms, W. W. Meissner has referred to the process of fundamentally restructuring the ego ideal as "transvaluation" (1992, 398). However we conceptualize it, a radical transformation of self-organization occurs. Meissner was, I believe, correct to emphasize the "constructive and synthetic" (395) aspect of this process, rather than to focus solely on the collapse or dissolving of old structures. Meissner's description of the transformation of Ignatius of Loyola emphasized the newly empowered, enlivened, engaged sense of self that rose from the ashes of his earlier identity.

Zen, unlike psychoanalysis, which tends to view old patterns of organization as something to be gradually outgrown or moved beyond developmentally, sees its role as directly confronting and challenging old patterns of self-experience. The difficulties inherent in Zen practice, the emotional and physical difficulties that emerge in the course of long hours of sitting, and the conceptual difficulties that arise by having our usual frame of reference radically challenged by the seeming incomprehensibility of a nondualistic, non-essentialist perspective as encapsulated in koans, all combine to undermine preexisting modes of organizing and mastering experience. In this sense, the experience of *not* being able to answer a koan may be as important as finally "passing" it. One's self-image and self-importance, along with all one's usual modes of "knowing," may be threatened or undermined in the face of the seeming unsolvability of the koan. A story (perhaps apocryphal) that made the rounds in one Zen center some years ago told of a student so enraged by the Roshi's repeated refusal to accept his answer to his koan that he threw himself on the teacher and tried to strangle him! Who was the student? A famous psychoanalyst!

Traditionally, Zen has described this destabilizing, disorienting phase of practice as "Great Doubt," and it is particularly associated with what are often the long years prior to the resolution of the first koan, "Mu." Great Doubt is resolved only by Great Death, the collapse of the old self system, a collapse that allows the emergence of a new non-self-centered mode of perception. Western self psychology has a thoroughly developmental orientation, and the changes that emerge in the course of psychoanalysis are usually couched in metaphors of growth and development, certainly not in ones of dying. Dream imagery, however, may give us a metaphoric handle on the Buddhist way of speaking.

Walking along a familiar street, I suddenly came upon my own dead body in the gutter. Astonished, I bent down to examine the corpse closely, to prove to myself that it really was my own dead body. As I did so, a black-robed figure appeared and asked me my name. "Barry Magid," I answered. Pointing to the corpse, the figure again asked my name, and again I answered, "Barry Magid." A third time, the figure pointed to the dead body and again asked my name. This time, I could only reply, "I don't know." The figure now said, "You can have anything you want." I was dumbstruck, and didn't know what to ask for, when I noticed he was now holding a can of soda. I pointed to that and asked for a sip, which he gave me. I then walked away, dazzled by the sunlight on the street as I walked.

A colleague, upon reading a version of this dream, immediately recalled a similar one of his own: "I had a dream at a moment of great personal transformation …of driving around in a car with my own dead body, looking for a convenient place to leave it—it had to do with finally letting go of a life consisting almost exclusively of taking care of others and of realizing, at long last at the ripe old age of twenty-six, that I too existed and counted" (anonymous personal communication).

Even taken out of context, I think we can see how each of these dreams could illustrate the sudden dissolution of an old set of organizing principles, the "death" of an old identity and the emergence of a new, more open sense of self and of possibility. In Aitken's words, the Great Death of realization is "death to a life of abstraction and birth to intimacy with things as they are" (1990, 134).

Deliberately placing difficulty in the path of the student has always been a central part of Zen training, in a way seemingly antithetical to the recent turn in psychoanalysis away from "optimal frustration" (Kohut 1971) and toward "optimal responsiveness" (Bacal 1985). Perhaps the example of Zen can remind analysts that the optimal response may sometimes take the form of a difficulty that challenges or disrupts old patterns of organization.

A BIGGER CONTAINER

For the dismantling of old structures of subjectivity to result in a breakthrough rather than a breakdown, the student must have basic skills of affect regulation at his disposal. Zen has traditionally tended to take these for granted as the byproduct of individual discipline and effort, part of the basic level of maturity expected of a monk. Looked at from a psychoanalytic perspective, we can begin to say more about the intersubjective context in which affect regulation develops through meditation.

Most of the changes that result from meditation practice come not from dramatic so-called enlightenment experiences but from the slow, structure-building aspects of sitting itself. Like analysis, meditation practice creates a long-term relationship with a figure who becomes the object of transference longings and expectations. Like analysis, meditation practice creates a setting for the eliciting and working through of intense fantasies and affects. Like an analysis, meditation trains us to stay with, tolerate, and explore thoughts and feelings normally felt to be too painful or frightening to endure. This is what I mean by the "structure-building" aspect of practice. By "structure" I simply mean the capacity to tolerate and meaningfully organize our affective experience. The absence of this capacity is reflected in the subjective sense of being overwhelmed by experience, of intolerable anxiety in the face of certain affects, leading either to the unconscious repression of the dreaded thought or affect or to conscious avoidant behaviors. Another manifestation of this insufficiency is the subjective experience of inner emotional emptiness or deadness, which can lead either to immobilizing depression or compulsive, addictive attempts at self-stimulation. Meditation teaches us to literally sit with and through all of these states in a way that progressively builds our capacity to tolerate, regulate, and organize our affective experiences. There's nothing mystical about this aspect of practice. The first rule of a sitting practice is to sit still. That means sitting still through restlessness, not scratching itches, not wiping a dripping nose, and not moving a foot that has fallen asleep or is in pain. Beginners will often feel close to panic at the thought of following this simple rule. They may have fear of being trapped or going stir crazy when they think of being unable to respond to such basic aversive cues.

Long periods of meditation can be physically painful. Meditation can be boring. During long hours of sitting our mind wanders, and wanders in ways that we gradually recognize as repeating itself in characteristic ways and patterns. Whatever happens, whatever we feel, we learn to stay with it, observe it, experience it. Joko Beck has called this structure-building aspect of practice building "a bigger container" (1989, 50). As a teacher, Joko demands nothing more or less than emotional honesty from a student. Over and over she emphasizes that practice is not about becoming somebody else, or attaining any particular state, but rather settling deep into the physical and emotional reality of this moment. She asks us to be attentive to the emotional or affective coloration of each moment. "Where," she might ask, "is that feeling in your body? Is there a tension or tightness in your throat, your neck, your belly, as you allow yourself to fully feel this moment? Feel the resistance to fully being present that is manifesting as that bodily tension." Practice with her means learning to sit with resistance, to identify resistance in the form of bodily tensions, to plumb the emotional history of those tensions, moment after moment.

When we sit, we do not try to become calm or peaceful or to quiet the mind; rather, we practice staying with and in the midst of whatever feelings arise. However, simply sitting still for regular periods of time every day, does end up having a steadying and centering effect. Following the breath and labeling thoughts initially leads to building up a stable internal "observer" who is not buffeted by conflicting emotions or swept up by the flow of association or rumination. A meditator becomes increasingly able to interrupt repetitive or obsessive trains of thought and sit in a "wordless" silence with the anxiety or bodily tension that ordinarily accompanies such thinking. At this point, the observer dissolves into the experience of just sitting. It is this progressively increasing capacity to tolerate previously intolerable, warded-off affect states that provides the core structure-building dimension of Zen practice. Like psychoanalysis, Zen practice is *a structured, relational context for eliciting, tolerating, and working through one's patterns of organizing affective experience*, including affects that have been previously repressed or dissociated. The long hours of physically difficult sitting, the relationship to an idealized teacher, and the student's own expectation of transformation are powerful elicitors of both repetitive and selfobject transferential patterns. Furthermore, the group context of practice can elicit strong twinship transference experiences that help the individual to feel what he is going through is a shared, understood, and bearable form of difficulty, even when at its most extreme. All this contributes to an increased capacity to contain and stay with hitherto unbearable states of physical and emotional pain, uncertainty, and disorientation as old dualistic patterns of organizing one's sense of self and the world are made manifest and challenged by practice.

Unlike psychoanalysis, in Zen it is not *primarily* the sense of feeling understood by another person that provides the container for affect. Rather, the individual's own capacity for affect tolerance and regulation is strengthened both by the experience of sitting itself and by sitting within the enabling, selfobject context of the group and the student-teacher relationship. These provide the "affect-integrating, containing and modulating intersubjective context" (Stolorow and Atwood 1992, 54) that allows previously dissociated traumatic affects to be safely re-experienced and worked through. Dualism, far from being a merely abstract philosophical perspective, is the hallmark of dissociated affective experience. No spiritual practice can truly undo a dualistic perspective without engaging and working through previously dissociated experience. Otherwise, momentary experiences of "oneness" will only serve to further split off and sequester dissociated traumatic affects with a false promise of attaining a transcendent state beyond the reach of the old trauma.

Psychoanalysis cures, from the perspectives of self psychology and intersubjectivity, by (1) "providing missing developmental experiences—what Kohut originally meant by selfobject transferences," and (2) providing "responses from the analyst that counteract invariant organizing principles that are manifestations of ...the repetitive dimension of the transference" (Atwood and Stolorow 1997, 521–22). As I have tried to indicate, Zen training tacitly provides powerful selfobject experiences, without, or rarely, ever explicitly acknowledging their role. In the past, such provisions would simply be part of the expectable background of monastic life. In a modern, psychoanalytically informed Zen practice, the selfobject dimension of the student-teacher relationship—along with its disruptions and repair—can be more directly addressed.

The invariant organizing principles that are manifestations of the repetitive transference are a large part of what Buddhism refers to as "self" or "ego," terms that have been used interchangeably over the years in translation of Buddhist texts. That the Buddhist concept of ego is not congruent with the Freudian use of the word should by now be evident. The Buddhist's goal of dissolving the ego doesn't mean aspiring to a loss of toilet training. However, the Buddhist version of "self" does contain elements that pertain to a subjective sense of personal mastery, as well as patterns organized around a sense of defectiveness or deficiency. Even though self-centeredness in the long run is the root of our suffering, nonetheless it retains a powerful short-term appeal! To directly challenge the hold of our self-centeredness is to face the anxiety and doubt it keeps in check.

As the case of our original face shows, who we think we most essentially are is a problem with both deep philosophical and psychological roots. It is one thing to have a momentary realization of the emptiness of the self, and quite another to work through a lifetime of unconscious organizing principles and self-representations. Students commonly have momentary flashes of insight only to unreflectively return to a characterological stance based on an ingrained sense of specialness, entitlement, dependency, or victimhood. A psychoanalytically informed meditation practice will not allow a student to focus on a momentary attainment but will instead emphasize how a moment of realization goes against the grain of the unconscious organization of day-to-day experience, repeatedly picking out the ways in which the old patterns subtly seek to reestablish themselves.

THE STUDENT-TEACHER RELATIONSHIP

What about the relationship of a student to a Zen teacher? How analogous is it really to that of a patient and a psychoanalyst? Is the Zen student-teacher relationship intrinsically shaped by issues of hierarchy and authority, while only the analytic relationship offers genuine mutuality and relatedness?

Many who have had the terrible experience of having someone else's version of reality imposed on them will fear re-traumatization in submitting to any authority. The potential for re-injury is just as real in analysis as in any religious practice, though an intersubjective stance will be perhaps more readily attuned to the danger, and more mindful of the impact of the analyst in inadvertently recreating old patterns of pathological accommodation. And yet only a new experience of authority and expertise, exercised in an untraumatic and validating manner, can redeem authority, discipline, and hierarchical, and didactic relationships for someone previously traumatized by their misuse. Any attempt at an artificially contrived mutuality, one that in effect denies the latent differences in authority and power inherent in professional or student-teacher relationships, tacitly reinforces the patient's or student's view of authority or hierarchy as intrinsically untrustworthy aspects of the relationship that the analyst/teacher is uncomfortable in acknowledging and wielding. Ideally, the Zen teacher exercises a non-self-centered authority, an authority of skillful means, responsive to the particular needs and defenses of the individual student. What does that look like? There is no one answer to the question, because just as analysts and schools of analysis differ widely, no single style characterizes all Zen teachers or how they operate. One popular characterization of the Zen master—initially emphasized, or overemphasized, by D. T.

Suzuki (1960)—casts the teacher as a master of paradox who uses koans to drive the student to a conceptual impasse leading to a wholly new, nonconceptual, nondualistic way of being. That approach might be said to be characteristic of certain Rinzai teachers, for whom extreme austerity and strictness were the guarantors of authentic insight. Perhaps we can draw analogy with the classical Freudian insistence on a pure analytic neutrality and abstinence as the guarantors of the transference neurosis. The strictest teachers were the ones who were called "grandmotherly," since they compassionately offered their students the most direct experience of the Way, like a lychee fruit already peeled and ready to swallow (Aitken 1990). One such grandmotherly teacher, Luzu, is said to have responded to all his students' questions by turning his back to them and silently facing the wall (Cleary 1990). The contemporary American Zen abbot John Daido Loori has said that in all his years with his Japanese teacher he never received a word of approval. "The most I got out of him was a grunt or 'go deeper' or 'not good enough'" (1994, 23).

But contrast this way of teaching with the following description of Shunryu Suzuki's style. A new student who had been intending to go to Japan to study Zen came to the zendo saying that

> he'd read some books about Zen and enlightenment and now he wanted to meet the real thing.... Suzuki told him...it might be good to have some experience with Zen practice in America first. He got a cushion from the altar, placed it in the aisle, and showed [him] how to sit. He corrected his posture, pushing the small of his back in, pulling his shoulders back and his chin in. He pushed his knees down gently, showing him how to put his hands together with the left palm on the right palm and the thumbs touching just enough to hold a piece of paper between them. He told him to keep his eyes half open, and to place his attention on the in and out of his breath. He advised him in the future to wear looser pants, so his legs would cross more easily....This was not at all what [the new student] expected. The books on Zen were full of dramatic interchanges between monks. But there was

something about this priest that made him want to
return. Beneath the charm [he] sensed authority and
humility. (Chadwick 1999, 171–72)

This is a teaching that challenges not by paradox or confrontation but by
its very simplicity. Or, if we experience a paradox, it is that we cannot believe
that the answer to all our questions is so simple. Expecting the extraordinary,
we are surprised by the ordinary. Just sitting. Sitting itself is the answer. We
are so sure that Zen is something extraordinary, we are surprised when it
turns out to be so ordinary. Just sit. And yet, who can manage to obey that
simple injunction?

Here's what my teacher, Charlotte Joko Beck, wrote about the authority
of the teacher: "The last words of the Buddha were, 'Be a lamp unto yourself.' He didn't say, 'Go running to this teacher or that teacher, to this center or that center'—he said, 'look—be a lamp unto yourself…. There is only
one teacher. What is that teacher? Life itself…. Now life happens to be both
a severe and endlessly kind teacher. It is the only authority that you need to
trust. And this teacher, this authority, is everywhere'" (1989, 15–16).

How can we come to terms with the paradox inherent in a Zen teacher
telling us, "Be a lamp unto yourself"? Isn't such an admonition as useless as,
"Be spontaneous"? The tension that must be resolved here is actually
between the tendency to believe that *either* there is someone with all the
answers whom I will defer to as my teacher *or* I must be my own authority:
I don't need anybody to tell *me* what to do! Paradoxically, we need the structure of practice and the ongoing presence of a teacher precisely to break
through this false dichotomy. And when it collapses, life becomes our
teacher. Buddha's exhortation "Be a lamp unto yourself" does not mean you
should become preoccupied with the light of your own self-experience (especially your enlightenment experience). He means we should use our realization to illuminate the life all around us. Seeing and responding to our life is
what real practice is all about. Once when I was ending a visit to Joko, I suddenly found myself aware of her advancing years, and it occurred to me that
any time with her might be my last. Becoming tearful, I said, "I may never
see you again." She responded, "I don't care if I ever see you again. That you
know how to practice is what's important." This brought me up short, but
it has proved truer and truer to me over the years. When my wife Deborah

was killed in a plane crash, I called Joko and thanked her for giving me the resources to go through the pain of that terrible loss. More and more, when someone would ask me what Joko would say about something, I simply started talking about it myself—there seemed no boundary between my sense of practice and hers. That is true intimacy, and life itself is the true teacher that never leaves.

Empathy

I have spoken mainly about how aspects of Zen can be understood from a psychoanalytic perspective. Perhaps I should conclude with a few words about the impact of Zen training on my analytic practice. What does it mean to be a Zen psychoanalyst? Has my analytic stance been altered in any fundamental ways by my Zen training?

In fact, working as I do from a self psychology background, I believe the basic analytic stance of empathic inquiry needs little direct input from Zen. Empathy by definition is a non-self-centered stance. As Yamada Koun Roshi has said, "Zen practice is a matter of forgetting the self in the act of uniting with something" (quoted in Aitken 1996, 81). Substitute "uniting with *someone*" and you have Zen and the art of empathy. One necessarily suspends one's own worldview (as best as one can) and endeavors to see life through the eyes of the patient, immersing oneself in the subjectivity of the other. The patient's subjective experience of *feeling understood* is the one necessary and sufficient criterion for how empathic we are. Incidents of misunderstanding are clear enough signs of my self-centeredness intruding. I do believe I have a greater capacity to sit and stay with another person's affective experience as a result of my Zen practice. But there is little in my basic analytic stance that I've consciously altered because of Zen. For me, empathy remains a far more reliable and less self-centered approach than one that keeps its focus on the analyst's state of mind, even one that emphasizes the analyst's commitment to "not knowing." Bion's analytic mystic (Eigen 1998), with his gaze firmly fixed on the Unknowable Void of O, runs the risk of placing his own purity of mind ahead of the patient's simple desire to feel understood. Echoing the old Chinese master Nan ch'uan (Aitken 1990, 126), I'd say to him, "Forget about Unknowable Reality, your ordinary mind is the way." What is this ordinary mind? Simply a mind unentangled in the isolated mind's dualistic fantasies of delusion and enlightenment, a mind that has forgotten about its own condition.

Form and Formlessness

Zen is, on the one hand, simply the act of sitting and paying attention. Yet, on the other, it is also a branch of a foreign tradition with more than two thousand years of history behind it, an enigmatic and esoteric literature with elaborate rituals accumulated over centuries of practice in a religious and monastic context. American Zen can take the form of either a transplanted Japanese monastery or a suburban house indistinguishable from its Southern Californian neighbors. My own Ordinary Mind Zendo started out in an empty office in a New York City high-rise apartment building. In one office, I meet with patients; the adjacent office was turned into a zendo. Increasingly, a number of patients who come for therapy once, twice, or three time a week have added one or more meditation sessions (often along with a daily sitting practice at home) to their weekly routine. By and large, the transitions from couch to cushion and back again have gone smoothly, reflecting, I believe, a perception by all concerned that what happens in the two settings is, in fact, one practice. Whether through the vehicle of empathic inquiry or through just sitting, the goal of experiencing life as it is—including all the split-off affects accumulated by a lifetime of trying to *avoid* life as it is— remains constant.

Although the form of traditional Zen practice—no less than the use of the couch in a traditional psychoanalysis—may strike some as arbitrary, authoritarian, or artificial, it is only through the skillful use of forms, discipline, and relationship that liberating change can occur. This is just as true for psychoanalysis as it is for Zen. We need the form of the zendo or of the analytic hour to get our attention and to hold it. The free, non-self-centered use of form is the true formlessness, or *no-form*. In Zen, we often hear the phrases *just doing, no doing,* and *not doing* used interchangeably to indicate functioning free from separation or self-centeredness. Just sit. Speak without using your lips. "Not knowing" needn't imply dumbstruck wonder—it can also be the non-self-centered, spontaneous, and *expert* response to whatever arises, whether it takes the form of a swordsman parrying a blow or a doctor stanching the flow of blood.

Like Wittgenstein's (1953) philosophy of language, in the end, Zen leaves everything just as it found it. But how hard both analyst and client must work to do so! Without the hard work, we seem unable to leave our life alone and *just live*. Faced with the dilemma of suffering, consciously and unconsciously we seek an antidote or an escape. And by seeking to escape our suffering we turn our life inside out, contorting our "ordinary mind" into an "isolated mind" that seeks to distance, control, and dissociate an inner "me" from outer pain. We chase after enlightenment or other special states of consciousness that will relieve all suffering and guarantee perfect happiness, or so we've heard. Whether our project is the flight from pain or the pursuit of happiness, the outcome is the same, a life in flight from itself and from this moment. And this moment turns out to be the only answer there is, the only self that there is, the only teacher, and the only reality. All hidden in plain sight.

Zen practice, especially when united with the dynamic insights of psychoanalysis, offers us this paradox: a discipline that promises freedom, a hierarchical relationship that fosters true independence, a form that gives formlessness, a transformation that allows everything to be just as it is.

Commentary

PSYCHOANALYSIS AND BUDDHISM: TWO EXTRAORDINARY PATHS TO AN ORDINARY MIND

PHILIP A. RINGSTROM

If it is at all possible to demystify Zen Buddhism—a daunting task—few authors have accomplished it better than Dr. Barry Magid has. His chapter makes clear that Zen Buddhism can be thought of as a psychology in its own right, one organized by a system of principles, concepts, and values. A system, however, that often feels like a fistful of sand that perpetually disappears from one's grasp.

This is because Zen is a system of paradoxes. So when Zen is compared to psychoanalysis, it illuminates those details lost in the dark shadows of psychoanalytic thought. By bringing into juxtaposition the elusive natures of both systems of thought, Magid's chapter shows how each one reckons with our human need to use ideas to shore up our often fictional, yet experientially all-too-real, self-centered narratives. While Magid points out numerous ways in which Zen and psychoanalysis dovetail, he also captures why we need both complementary systems of thought, since each one can be antidotal to the potential excesses of the other. My discussion of Magid's chapter will be less a critique than a series of comments and questions.

A central way in which Zen dovetails with psychoanalysis involves both systems' investigation of the often arbitrary distinctions or boundaries we make between ourselves and all of that to which we are connected and related. It is in these distinctions that we can identify how our experience of isolation, alienation, and anomic is often primarily a suffering of our own making. But Zen Buddhism and psychoanalysis approach this discovery differently. In Zen the student is taught to "just sit" and notice every moment in which his thoughts or feelings are tinged with fear or anger, indicating a resistance to what is happening, to judgments about himself and others, to how he is being treated, or to what he is not getting.

The psychoanalytic method accomplishes something quite similar, but more through the encounter of the subjectivities of the analyst and analysand. It involves the process of "free" association and often encourages the examination of transference. In this manner, the patient comes to discover his fears and anger and other prejudices, just as the Zen practitioner does. In both systems, prejudices are evidence of the organizing principles that shape one's worldview. While such principles are illusionary in one sense, they do in fact serve the essential function of organizing our daily experience.

A critical distinction that to my knowledge appears missing in psychoanalytic literature is between two broad classes of organizing principles, that is, between what I am calling *variant, developmental, adaptive organizing principles* and what has heretofore been referred to as *prereflective, invariant organizing principles* (Stolorow, Brandchaft and Atwood 1987). The *adaptive organizing principles* constitute the structure upon which fluid experiencing depends, because they supply organization to the onslaught of information that would otherwise overwhelm any human being. Despite their ongoing function, however, they remain open to adaptation and change—that is, open to the process of accommodation to restructuring, which even allows for rapid shifts in context that are the unpredictable "elements" of spontaneity. By contrast, *invariant organizing principles* are the rigidified structures that impede fluid engagement with one's surround. They resist the common goal of Zen and psychoanalysis, which is to embrace and accept things as they truly are. This lends itself to one possible interpretation (certainly only one of many) of what Freud meant in his provocative proclamation that the nature of cure in psychoanalysis involves "transforming your neurotic misery into the common unhappiness." I think that Freud was capturing what Ronna Kataznick (1999) refers to as the distinction between "inevitable suffering" and "optional suffering." "Inevitable suffering" involves unavoidable losses in life, such as death and certain vicissitudes of growing old. "Optional suffering" involves misery caused by our unwillingness to accept these inevitabilities, as well as all of the neurotic machinations we put ourselves through to avoid them.

Enlightenment, according to Magid's "bottom-up" view of Zen, is not about transcendence but about no longer interspersing self-absorbed thoughts or feelings that separate us from experiencing the circumstances of our life. Our most habitual and pernicious ways of doing this are often the least visible to us. They are embodied in the *prereflective invariant organizing principles* that automatically prejudice us in every moment, disallowing us to be our more spontaneous, free, and creative selves.[1] These principles contrast with how *variant, developmental organizing principles* allow us to be in spontaneous engagement with reality, that is, in a state of mutual and reciprocal influence with our surroundings. Illustrations of such mutually shaping moments include a spontaneous engagement between two new lovers, a parent's first encounter with his or her newborn infant, or a chance meeting with a wild animal wherein the mutual curiosity of both human and animal overrides each one's fear.

Such moments of spontaneity may come closest to contacting the true self, not so much in the sense of the fulfillment of an innate self-plan seeking its pathway to development than in a developmentally co-constructed version of self that is less encumbered by the strictures of unconscious invariant organization. Moments of being one's true self are really mostly about the loss of self-consciousness—the watchdog of self-centeredness. This involves what Magid described as "a mutual embeddedness in life [that] doesn't imply a preexistent separation between self and world that needs to be overcome."

Clearly one shared curative intent of Zen and psychoanalysis is to dramatically reduce one's attachment or fixation upon one's *prereflective invariant organizing principles* which have served primarily as mechanisms that attempt to halt time, institute fictional states of permanence where there are none, forbid the acknowledgment of loss, and in some cases institute ritualized substitutions such as addictive/compulsive behavior to fill in a sense of emptiness. In this vein, Magid's inclusion of the Zen teacher's admonition "Gain is delusion; loss is enlightenment" seems especially apt. In this realm of understanding, however, contemporary psychoanalysis—with its growing understanding of the traumatic developmental conditions that are prone to foster such omnipotently controlling thought—may have a distinct advantage. Zen's lack of a comparable system of thought may well prove to be to its liability.

Contemporary psychoanalysis reckons that the development of a fluidly constituted sense of self—sufficiently organized to lose "itself" (that is, lose one's self-consciousness) and enter into spontaneous involvement in the moment—is a byproduct of a developmental attachment system of recognition and attunement by a child's caretaker(s). It involves parents who are capable of recognizing and responding to the subjectively burgeoning organization and reorganization of their child's development without fear of losing their own parental subjectivity.

It is Zen's lack of knowledge about and respect for the psychological vicissitudes of such developmental systems theory that naively invites the "one-size-fits-all" discipline of certain Zen teachers. Magid cautions that such teachers unwittingly underestimate the pernicious "role of compliance" of devotees who have "formed a morbid dependency on the teacher or otherwise succumbed to some form of pathological accommodation, masochistically enduring a painful training solely as a way to maintain a tie to an idealized selfobject." Similarly, Magid finds within contemporary psychoanalysis an antidote to this, suggesting, I think, that empathy can be an enormously underestimated tonic in Zen. He writes:

> When a patient lives her days feeling misunderstood, frustrated, and resentful that nobody ever gets where she's coming from and then, one day, encounters an analyst whose empathy at last allows her to feel that another human being truly understands her, a lifetime of mistrust and despair and anger may drop off in a moment of intense relief. In Buddhist terms, we might say that part of her "self" dropped off, the part that was organized

around a particular representation of her "self" and others,
and of the impossibility of being understood.

And, in psychoanalytic terms, we might say that she has dropped off some
of the tenacious grip of an invariant organizing principle that she can never
be understood.

As important as empathy is, I still think that it is important to underscore
that gaining insight into one's unconscious organizing principles (the fundamental canon of psychoanalysis) is a crucial part of differentiating those principles that are fluidly changing "structures" from those that are invariant.
Indeed, one way of thinking contextually about psychopathology is that the
function of invariant organizing principles is to enforce modes of repetitive
and overbearing order upon the normal chaos of human existence. Invariant
organizing principles "anxiously" dam up at every turn the experience now
colloquially referred to as "going with the flow."

A new question within contemporary psychoanalysis is, Does insight alone
effect change to unconscious invariant structures? While psychoanalysis has
traditionally favored insight, contemporary psychoanalysis appears to be
becoming more open to the "perturbation" variety of change suggested by
Magid's view of Zen, wherein its process confronts and challenges old patterns of self-experience. Stolorow (1997) and Gabriel Trop, Melanie Burke,
and Jeffrey Trop (1999) appear to be grappling with this in their inclusion of
nonlinear dynamic systems theory (Thelin and Smith 1994) in their views on
intersubjectivity. In promoting the attitude of cultivating the improvisational
in psychoanalytic treatment, I have argued that in certain instances, *invari-
ant-organizing principles* may only yield to unpremeditated, purely spontaneous action by the therapist (Ringstrom 1999).

Magid sees Zen's "confrontational" style as at times more beneficially disruptive to old patterns, leaving little in place and clearing room for "new
structure" (or at least potential for it). The "new" is not "something" per se
but a state of "emptiness" or nonprejudicial readiness for the spontaneous
moment, the spontaneous gesture (Winnicott 1971). I think that the term
"emptiness" may overstate the case, wherein new, variant, reciprocally responsive organizing principles may be a more accurate phenomenological depic-
tion of our human condition. Magid, I think suggests this in his allusion to
the "Unborn," that quality that pertains not to what "has to be created or

uncovered" but to "what we spontaneously and naturally already are."

Psychoanalytic thinking, generally respectful of the need for and therefore value of the old self-system, can be antidotal to the potential excesses of Zen. By contrast, Zen assiduously seeks that system's collapse into oblivion, in what Magid calls the resolution of the Great Doubt by the Great Death. Contemporary psychoanalysis recognizes that a precipitous collapse of the old self-system often replicates the trauma of an individual's development. It can reintroduce the experience of a crushing belief system embodied by a parent annihilating a child's burgeoning sense of self-experience. The Zen neophyte and analytic patient may find themselves in comparable positions to the child. Under such circumstances, the reactivation of rigid invariant organizing principles formed to protect the child's emerging self-system from either real or imagined threat becomes essential.

Zen and contemporary psychoanalysis complement each other in that both proffer liberation from old, fixed, rigidified ways of being. Ironically, the Zen approach seems more akin to classical analysis than to contemporary psychoanalysis. It appears to emphasize a transient attachment serving only as a means for teaching the Zen student the pathway to affective tolerance, rather than promoting an ideology favoring a lifelong utilization of others for solace and understanding in moments of pain and grief. Zen seems to share the value of separation/individuation and autonomy in classical analysis, arguing that through practice one can "go it alone."

It's worth noting that the latter philosophical value has been challenged considerably by numerous contemporary analysts, including Kohut who cautions us never to outgrow our need for selfobject responsiveness from others. And others (Beebe and Lachmann 1992; Benjamin 1988, 1995; Stern 1985) argue that we share a ubiquitous and lifelong need for inter-affectivity and subject-to-subject relating.

Although Magid clarifies that his psychoanalytic identity is most comfortable with self psychology as well as the intersubjective perspectives of Stolorow and Atwood, in another way he seems wedded more to the value of autonomy and of "going it alone" found in the classical perspective. This corresponds with the teachings of his Zen teacher, Charlotte Joko Beck. One anecdote supporting this is Magid's report of her having upbraided his tearful and frightened lament over her advancing years and the possibility of never seeing her again with the comment "I don't care if I ever see you again—that you know how to practice is what is important." This value of "going it alone" was underscored by Magid's comments at the 23rd Annual Conference on the Psychology of the Self during the discussion of a paper on trauma by Robert Stolorow (Stolorow 1999; Ringstrom 1999). Comparing the death of Stolorow's wife with the death of his own, Magid offered that their respective traumatic losses differed considerably in terms of their differing expectations about others' responsiveness. Stolorow shared that his trauma was exacerbated by the loss of the very person—his wife, Daphne Socarides Stolorow—upon whom he would normally have relied to help him deal with such a devastating event. By contrast Magid said he never expected anyone to understand his experience and that he had to deal with it on his own. It was the resources Joko had taught him that he relied on "to go through the pain of that terrible loss," not Joko herself or any other person.

Is it possible that being less wedded to an attachment model, Magid can more easily forget himself in his role as analyst and adopt a seemingly Zen-like practice of *decentering*? Does he, that is, wed himself to his patient's perspective by adopting something like the mode of clinical action prescribed by some self-psychologists to facilitate empathy? Even if this were so, it would seem important to bear in mind the caveat that Stolorow has forcefully put forward—that one cannot possibly understand an other without in some manner utilizing one's own organizing principles. Psychoanalysis can never escape having to sail between the Scylla of too great an intersubjective *conjunction* and the Charybdis of too great an intersubjective *disjunction* (Stolorow and Atwood 1992) between the analyst's and patient's organizing principles.

Ultimately, Magid's essay captures how Zen and psychoanalysis operate as beautifully complementary systems of thought, each balancing out the other's potential excesses. Whereas psychoanalysis can be seen at times as taking the sense of self too seriously, foundering on its reification of concepts that lend themselves to the illusion of a permanent self, Zen can be seen as too assiduously pursuing the experience of oneness in its quest to dissolve experiences of boundaries, dualism, and essentialism. The latter quest becomes excessive when the integrity of self-experience becomes glibly written off as the workings of the obstructive ego, better to be forgotten than understood. Magid's essay goes very far in bridging these two complementary systems—modes of personal transformation not so much into someone else as into who we really are.

Reply

THE PATH IS ORDINARY TOO

BARRY MAGID

Any attempt to establish a genuine dialogue between Zen and psychoanalysis might best begin, as Philip Ringstrom graciously has done, with an acknowledgment that "Zen Buddhism can be thought of as a psychology in its own right" and that each system involves the "investigation of the often arbitrary distinctions or boundaries we make between ourselves and all of that to which we are connected and related." For a long time, it would have been hard to find many analysts who were willing to agree that they and the Zen masters were, if not exactly in the same business, each in their own way offering comprehensive descriptions and solutions to the same set of human problems. Once we can agree that the concepts and goals of the two systems are not wholly incommensurable, we can begin an exchange of ideas and experience that has the potential to enrich both systems. There may always be areas where we strongly and irreconcilably disagree—just as there are between classically and intersubjectively oriented analysts—but we will have begun to talk the same language.

One linguistic and conceptual sticking point between psychoanalysis and Buddhism has always been over the meaning of "self," and what could be understood in psychoanalytic terms about the latter's assertion that the self is "empty" or that it could "drop off." In trying to come to terms with this conundrum, Phil Ringstrom makes an excellent point in distinguishing two aspects of the self's organization of experience: *variant, developmental, adaptive* organizing principles and *prereflective, invariant* organizing principles. This distinction does, I believe, take us at least part of the way in clearing up the usual psychoanalytic confusion about Zen's claim to put an end to "self." It is indeed just those "rigidified structures," as Ringstrom puts it, "that impede fluid engagement with one's surround" that are one aspect of what Zen calls the "self" that drops away, and which psychoanalysis can agree could "drop off" without the person dissolving into nonentity. Ringstrom's understanding of "no-self" highlights what he calls "spontaneous engagement with reality" and he sees both Zen and psychoanalytic practices as modes of "cultivating the improvisational." The koan "Nansen Kills the Cat" would seem to exemplify the kind of improvisational spontaneity Ringstrom particularly values. In that story, Nansen comes upon two groups of monks arguing about a cat. Grabbing the cat, Nansen challenges them to "say a word" [of Zen]. When none of the monks can reply, he kills the cat. Later, he tells his student Joshu the whole story. Joshu immediately takes off his sandals, puts them on top of his head, and leaves the room. Nansen calls after him, "If you had been there, I could have spared the cat" (Yamada 1979, 76). Just the sort of improv I imagine Ringstrom would admire. But what would he make of the following seemingly simple exchange, which took place years later when Joshu was now the master of his own temple: "A monk asked Joshu in all earnestness, 'I beg you, master, please give me instructions.' Joshu said, 'Have you eaten your rice gruel yet?' The monk answered, 'Yes, I have.' Joshu said, 'Then wash your bowls'" (45).

Ringstrom's own examples of fluid, meaningful encounters include the "spontaneous engagement between two lovers, a parent's initial encounter with his or her newborn infant, or a chance meeting with a wild animal." But even this short list demonstrates his apparent assumption that the only true alternative to rigidity is to be found not in ordinary events but in extraordinary moments of intensity, excitement, and novelty. However, this privileging of spontaneous, improvisational, and dramatic encounters neglects another, perhaps even more important, aspect of the functioning of no-self: the workings of our ordinary mind, which may display nothing particularly novel, dramatic, or idiosyncratic. This is the Zen of daily activity: chopping wood, carrying water, riding the subway. The "Zen" of these activities isn't to be found in our being able to do them in some special, hyperattentive, or creative way. Rather, we just do them. And just doing them means not being addicted to novelty or excitement or the specialness of our own individual way of doing things. To act without "self" is to function fully and nonseparately in the moment at hand *regardless of that moment's content.* Zen asks us to reexamine our relation to all the ordinary, repetitive, simple acts of daily life—things we do over and over every day, without necessarily any new "mastery" or "developmental progress" being made. Can we redeem our experience of the repetitive and the quotidian from the assumption that it must necessarily be compulsive, rigid, or boring?

The aspect of unconscious mental functioning that encompasses the capacity to experience joy in the simple tasks and perceptions of everyday life is not part of the "rigidified" invariant unconscious, but neither does it fit comfortably under Ringstrom's improvisational "variant, developmental, adaptive" principle. It's the self that "washes the dishes and puts them away" (Aitken 1996, 49), the self that is engaged in the moment and that forgets itself in the moment. Nothing special. Nothing especially creative about it. Just there and alive.

Do you think you should be able to spot the Zen master on the subway? Eido Roshi tells a story about his own teacher, Soen Nakagawa, who as a young monk was traveling on a train with his teacher, Gempo Roshi. In the middle of the crowded car, the old teacher squeezed himself inconspicuously into the corner, while Soen sat down on the floor in full lotus and meditated for the entire trip. Afterward, Gempo gave the young monk hell for it. "Zazen isn't a performance! Under such circumstances ...you must think of others and make yourself as small as you can. *That* is zazen" (Nakagawa 1996, 16).

I am somewhat taken aback by Ringstrom's picture of Zen practice as advocating a "go it alone approach." In fact, I was immediately reminded of the movie *A Fish Called Wanda,* in which Jamie Lee Curtis's character confronts her none-too-bright ("Don't call me stupid!") but philosophical pretentious brother, played by Kevin Kline, by pointing out that "the central message of Buddhism is *not* every man for himself!" ("And the London Underground is *not* a political movement!") How could a practice that is defined by erasing the barriers of separation between self and world and self and other—indeed a practice that maintains that the very perception of those barriers constitutes a delusion—advocate "go-it-alone"? But it is a charge I've heard before from relationally minded analysts—that meditation is fundamentally a solitary activity, while analysis (at least in its two-person psychology mode) is defined by relationship and interacting subjectivities. To view Zen or other meditation practices in such a way is, I believe, to perceive them from the perspective of the isolated mind. From that dualistic perspective, we are all ultimately alone, and must struggle to reach out across an existential void in order to establish affective connection with others. But doing away with the perspective of the isolated mind means being able to experience the interconnectedness that exists from the very beginning—there is no need for us, as isolated individuals, to reach out or establish it—it is what is always already there whether we perceive it or not.

But let me look at the two instances Ringstrom cites where I seem to him to be advocating "autonomy."

In the first instance, Ringstrom quotes from my extemporaneous (and perhaps awkwardly formulated) discussion of Robert Stolorow's description of the emotional trauma of his wife's death (subsequently published as Stolorow 1999). At issue was the nature of such a trauma. Stolorow suggested that his trauma was compounded by the loss of the very person whom he would otherwise have relied on to see him through such a terrible event. He, rather unexpectedly, also seemed to me to be suggesting that it was somehow the universal nature of trauma itself that he responded the way he did. I say "unexpectedly" because one would think an intersubjective approach would instead emphasize the highly variant, contextualized nature of one's response to trauma, as to any other life event. My remarks, therefore, were first of all a matter of presenting what felt like a qualitatively different response to a similar traumatic loss. And my immediate reaction, that no one could understand what I was going through and that I had to deal with it one my own, was a description of the *effect* the trauma had on me—not my notion of how, from a Zen perspective, I ought to handle it. Now that I've had a chance to read the published version of Stolorow's talk, my reaction is somewhat different. I was particularly struck by this sentence: "It is not just that the traumatized ones and the normals live in different worlds; it is that these discrepant worlds are felt to be essentially and eradicably incommensurable" (Stolorow 1999). The sense of living in a private world, one that is "essentially incommensurable" with that of others, seems a perfect description of the perspective of the isolated mind, which Stolorow and Atwood described, in part, as the belief that "each individual knows only his own consciousness and is thus forever barred from direct access to experience belonging to other people" (1992, 9). Now I would say that, in both of our cases, the trauma of a loved one's sudden death precipitated a transitory re-experience of ourself as an isolated mind—although the immediate subjective experience of that isolation took on differing qualities that were co-determined by our own individual personal histories and our differing intersubjective milieus. Perhaps the next edition of the DSM-IV should find room for "post-traumatic isolated mind syndrome"!

Likewise, my exchange with Joko, in which I tearfully expressed a fear that I would never see her again, might also be understood as a momentary return to an isolated mind perspective—precipitated here merely by the fantasy of her death. And her response, rather than insisting that I have the courage to go it alone, was a reminder than in practice, *there is no such thing as alone*. In self psychology terms, this exchange could be understood in terms of the disruption and interpretative repair of the selfobject tie. Disrupted by our impending physical separation, a feeling of our essential connectedness was restored by her words. Ringstrom cites Kohut and Beatrice Beebe and Frank Lachmann as contemporary analysts who urge us never to imagine we can achieve a place of perfect, separate autonomy, but rather retain "a lifelong need for inter-affectivity and subject-to-subject relating." Certainly, Zen would concur with the anti-transcendent aspect of that reminder. But there is also the danger that psychoanalysis may construe the nature of affective connection or attachment far too narrowly and in ways that can foster a lifelong dependency on a very costly version of professional "subject-to-subject relating."

Within the framework of self psychology, one mark of developmental maturity is the progression from *specificity* to *nonspecificity* in what is experienced as a selfobject. In other words, we progressively move from a state in which only very specific, near-perfect affectively attuned empathic responsiveness by a particular, often idealized other is capable of restoring the self's cohesion in the face of post-traumatic fragmentation, to a more mature state in which the self's own stably internalized values, ideals, and identifications with idealized mentors become the basis for meaningfully organizing and affectively managing even intensely traumatic situations. In this state, grounded in a matrix of lifelong practice and a sure awareness of the interconnectedness of all being, one never feels one is "going it alone." In our service, we chant, "Each moment, life as it is, the only teacher." When practice reaches the point of truly listening moment by moment to this teacher, one indeed has a teacher that is always by one's side.

Ultimately, it makes no sense in Zen to say we sit "alone." Sitting itself represents and expresses our identity as Buddha—all of us together, throughout space and time, partaking of this all-pervading Buddha-nature—our common heritage of oneness, emptiness, and impermanence. Writing in the thirteenth century, the Japanese master Mumon wrote about the experience of passing the koan "Mu": "Those who have passed the barrier are able not only to see Joshu face to face, but also to walk hand in hand with the whole descending line of Zen masters and be eyebrow to eyebrow with them. You will see with the same eye that they see with, hear with the same ear they hear with" (Yamada 1977, 13).

Perhaps a modern-day psychoanalyst, though thoroughly comfortable in her own professional skin, might say the same regarding Kohut—a revered mentor whose worldview has been so thoroughly assimilated as to be part of the marrow of her own professional being and whose perspective is always present in her day-to-day practice. Even psychoanalysts need not practice alone.

We all need to learn to experience connection and interconnectedness on a spectrum that runs from intimate, one-on-one relating to an abiding, grounding awareness of the fundamental interrelated and co-determined nature of all existence. Psychoanalysts and Buddhists have specialized in understanding the opposite ends of that spectrum. Perhaps the time has come for each side to develop a new appreciation for the pole it has neglected and for the entire spectrum of human relatedness and being.

Note

1.   Of course, variant, developmental organizing principles also operate prereflectively and indeed also constitute some a priori organizational influence that we bring to each moment. They differ dramatically, however, in their openness to being affected in the moment and to being modified by their accommodation to new data. A possible analogy is that variant organizing principles are like the artistic instruction that over time a painter incorporates and makes his own. Later he is free to "throw it away" since he automatically "knows" how laws about composition, value, color, and temperature work in structuring the effects of a painting. Because he now applies such techniques unself-consciously, he more fully engages his creative capacities including "violating the rules" for artistic effect.

References

Aitken, R. 1990. *The Gateless Barrier.* San Francisco: North Point.
———. 1996. *Original Dwelling Place.* Washington, D.C.: Counterpoint.
Atwood, G., and R. Stolorow. 1997. Defects in the Self: Liberating Concept or Imprisoning Metaphor? *Psychoanalytic Dialogues* 7:517–22.

Austin, J. 1998. *Zen and the Brain.* Cambridge: MIT Press.

Bacal, H. 1985. Optimal Responsiveness and the Therapeutic Process. In *Progress in Self Psychology,* vol. 1, ed. A. Goldberg, 202–27. Hillsdale, N.J.: Analytic Press.

Bateson, G., and M. C. Bateson. 1987. *Angels Fear.* New York: Macmillan.

Beck, C. J. 1989. *Everyday Zen.* San Francisco: Harper.

Beebe, B., J. Jaffe, and Lachmann, F. 1992. A Dyadic Systems View of Communication. In *Relational Perspectives in Psychoanalysis,* ed. N. Skolnick and S. Warshaw, 61–81. Hillsdale, N.J.: Analytic Press

Benjamin, J. 1988. *The Bonds of Love.* New York: Pantheon Books.

———. 1995. *Like Subjects, Love Objects: Essays on Recognition and Sexual Difference.* New Haven: Yale University Press.

Chadwick, D. 1999. *Crooked Cucumber: The Life and Teaching of Shunryu Suzuki.* New York: Broadway Books.

Cleary, T. 1990. *The Book of Serenity.* Hudson, N.Y.: Lindisfarne Press.

Dogen. 1983. *Shobogenzo.* Trans. K. Nishiyama and M. Cross. Tokyo: Nakayama Shobo.

Eigen, M. 1981. The Area of Faith in Winnicott, Lacan, and Bion. *International Journal of Psychoanalysis* 62:413–33.

———. 1998. *The Psychoanalytic Mystic.* London: Free Association Books.

Engler, J. 1984. Therapeutic Aims in Psychotherapy and Meditation: Developmental Stages in the Representation of the Self. *Journal of Transpersonal Psychology* 16:25–61.

Freud, S. 1930. *Civilization and Its Discontents.* In Standard Edition, 21:64–145. London: Hogarth Press, 1961.

Fromm, E., D. T. Suzuki, and R. de Martino. 1960. *Zen Buddhism and Psychoanalysis.* London: George Allen and Unwin.

Haskel, P. 1984. *Bankei Zen.* New York: Grove Press.

Kohut, H. 1971. *The Analysis of the Self.* Madison, Conn.: International Universities Press.

———. 1977. *The Restoration of the Self.* Madison, Conn.: International Universities Press.

Loori, J. D. 1994. *Two Arrows Meeting in Mid-Air.* Rutland, Vt.: Charles E. Tuttle.

Magid, B. 1999. Surface, Depth and the Isolated Mind. In *Progress in Self Psychology,* ed. A. Goldberg, 15:107-19. Hillsdale, N.J.: Analytic Press.

Meissner, W. W. 1992. *Ignatius of Loyola.* New Haven: Yale University Press.

Merton, T. 1997. *Dancing in the Water of Life.* New York. HarperCollins.

Mitchell, S. 1991. Contemporary Perspectives on Self: Toward an Integration. *Psychoanalytic Dialogues* 1:121–47.

Nakagawa, Soen. 1996. *Endless Vow.* Introduction by Eido Shimano. Boston: Shambhala.

Ringstrom, P. 1999. Discussion of "The Phenomenology of Trauma and the Absolutisms of Everyday Life: A Personal Journey," by R. Stolorow. Read at 23d Annual Conference on the Psychology of the Self. Toronto, Ontario. November.

———. 2001. Cultivating the Improvisational in Psychoanalytic Treatment. *Psychoanalytic Dialogues.* 11:727-54.

Rubin, J. 1996. *Psychotherapy and Buddhism: Toward an Integration.* New York. Plenum Press.

Shafii, M. 1973. Silence in the Service of the Ego: Psychoanalytic Study of Meditation. *International Journal of Psychoanalysis* 54:431–43.

Silverman, S., F. Lachmann, and R. Milich. 1982. *The Search for Oneness.* New York: International Universities Press.

Stern, D. 1985. *The Interpersonal World of the Infant.* New York: Basic Books.

Stolorow, R. 1997. Dynamic, Dyadic Intersubjective Systems: An Evolving Paradigm for Psychoanalysis. *Psychoanalytic Psychology* 14:337–46.

———. 1999. The Phenomenology of Trauma and the Absolutisms of Everyday Life: A Personal Journey. *Psychoanalytic Psychology* 14:337–46.

Stolorow, R., and G. Atwood. 1992. *Contexts of Being: The Intersubjective Foundation of Psychological Life.* Hillsdale, N.J.: Analytic Press.

———. 1994. *The Intersubjective Perspective.* Northvale, N.J.: Aronson.

Stolorow, R., B. Brandchaft, and G. Atwood. 1987. *Psychoanalytic Treatment: An Intersubjective Approach.* Hillsdale, N.J.: Analytic Press.

Thelin, E., and L. Smith. 1994. *A Dynamic Systems Approach to the Development of Cognition and Action.* Cambridge: MIT Press.

Trop, G., M. Burke, and J. Trop. 1999. Contextualism in the Human Sciences, 4:202-23.

Uchiyama, K. 1983. *Refining Your Life.* Tokyo: Weatherhill.

Van de Wetering, J. 1999. *Afterzen.* New York: St. Martin's Press.

Whalen, P. 1972. *Imaginary Speeches for a Brazen Head.* Los Angeles: Black Sparrow Press.

Winnicott, D. W. 1965. *The Maturational Processes and the Facilitating Environment.* New York: International Universities Press.

———. 1971. *Playing and Reality.* New York: Basic Books.

Wittgenstein, L. 1953. *Philosophical Investigations.* London: Basil Blackwell.

Wolf, E. 1988. *Treating the Self.* New York: Guilford Press.

Yamada, Koun. 1979. *The Gateless Gate.* Los Angeles: Center Publications.

CHAPTER 7

Transference and Transformation in Buddhism and Psychoanalysis

POLLY YOUNG-EISENDRATH

Both Buddhism and psychoanalysis have the goals of alleviating suffering and increasing compassion. By suffering I mean specifically the Buddhist notion of *dukkha,* which is typically translated as "suffering" in English. Dukkha can be understood to refer to a state of being off-center or out of balance, like a bone slightly out of its socket or a wheel riding off its axle. I will use the word "suffering" here to designate a state of being in which we are out of kilter, a subjective disturbance that may be as mild as a momentary frustration or as severe as a depressive or psychotic state.

Buddhist discourses on dukkha are wide ranging and deal with both physical and mental suffering, but for my purposes I am referring to the mental anguish that we create through our perseverations, distortions, fantasies, and internal commentary. Much of this anguish is rooted in our desire to have things go our way and the resultant feelings of humiliation and despair when they do not. This suffering is distinct from the pain or adversity that is inescapable and out of our control. The teachings of Buddhism imply that the realities of limitation, impermanence, finitude, interdependence, and change—fundamental to all existence—are difficult for us to accept. Our longing for omnipotence makes acceptance difficult. If we can find insight into and equanimity with these realities, according to Buddhism, we will reach a condition in which suffering does not exist, although pain and adversity continue.

I believe that insight and compassion, as I describe below, are central to the transformation of suffering in both Buddhism and psychoanalysis. In this essay I will compare and contrast the ways that these two processes work specifically through the relationships between teacher and student (in Buddhism) and between therapist and patient (in psychoanalysis). Because the literature is vast in both disciplines, I will focus especially on my own experience as a student of Zen Buddhism and as a Jungian psychoanalyst who works with individuals in face-to-face psychotherapy sessions (once or twice per week), as well as on-the-couch analysis sessions (two to four times per week). Additionally, I do couples psychotherapy in a dyadic team with my husband; I mention this here because a lot of my understanding of projection and identification, in relationships, has been illuminated through working with couples. When I use the term "psychotherapy" or "therapy," I am referring to all psychodynamic therapies *including* psychoanalysis. When I use the term "psychoanalysis" I mean to refer specifically (not to exclude psychotherapy) to the depth psychologies—those approaches especially designed to examine unconscious images, desires and motives per se.

Suffering and Insight

Human beings create suffering through evaluating, desiring, fantasizing, aggrandizing, and diminishing both objective and subjective events and experiences in their lives. An easy example would be the negative fantasies of revenge and feelings of anger and frustration that can overtake us because of a small inconvenience like a traffic jam. Much more complex and multilayered are the compulsive self-loathing and self-mutilations that may preoccupy an adult who has experienced trauma or abuse in childhood. Whether an experience is painful, pleasurable, or neutral, our own wishes, desires, and confusions can transform it into transient, repetitive, or permanent suffering.

Freud and Jung and other early psychoanalysts spent the better part of their careers investigating states of transient, repetitive, and permanent mental anguish, along with other seemingly irrational or nonsensical aspects of life (e.g., dreams). They discovered that even seemingly meaningless suffering (for example, a compulsion to repeat a destructive experience) could be understood as intentional and purposive from the perspective of hidden or unconscious desires and motives. The strangest and most troubling human actions could be rendered meaningful when certain developmental facts were known. As the contemporary psychoanalyst Carl Strenger says, "the fundamental step which Freud took at the beginning of his career was to radicalize the principle of humanity and to apply it to phenomena which were previously exempt from it. Neurotic and psychosomatic symptoms began to be seen as humanly intelligible rather than as phenomena which were only amenable to physiological explanation" (1991, 62). It is the hallmark of all forms of psychoanalysis to show that a close study of any human action will lead to a knowledge of its causes and purposes, either in the present moment or in the circumstances of an individual's development.

One translation of the famous Dhamapada says: "All that we are arises with our thoughts. With our thoughts we make the world" (Byram 1993, 1). Our thoughts lead to our actions, our actions to our habits, and finally our habits to our character. All forms of Buddhism teach that our intentions are vitally connected to our actions and our character. Similarly, Strenger says that psychoanalysis is committed to the idea that human behavior is "intentional action all the way down"; psychoanalysts believe that by correctly understanding the meanings of thoughts and actions "we help the patient take full responsibility for who he is, and give him the freedom to change if he truly wants to" (1991, 63).

In both psychoanalysis and Buddhism, accurate insight into the causes and consequences of our suffering opens the door to the possibility of freeing ourselves of it. Buddhism offers insight into the *universal* conditions and causes of suffering (ubiquitous human striving for security and stability, and ignorance or denial of impermanence and change), whereas psychoanalysis offers insight into the dynamics of *personal* suffering (inner conflicts, deficits, complexes, projections, and identifications).

Compassion and Transformation

And yet both Buddhism and psychoanalysis rely on more than insight for the transformation of suffering. The development of compassion for oneself and others transcends interpretations and insights in both practices, in that compassion emerges spontaneously in unique and surprising ways. By compassion, I mean a kind and loving response to the distress and suffering of another or oneself. Compassion is more than pity, sympathy, or the urge to help. The Sanskrit word *karuna*—translated as "compassion"—is related to the lamenting or mournful groan of the sort that naturally comes forth when we see another being in pain or difficulty. But true compassion allows us to respond to a difficulty in a way that is truly helpful, rather than simply reacting and giving advice, trivializing, or taking over. We might say that true compassion is an effective form of concern and caring that contains within it the awareness of the actual difficulty at hand.

In Buddhism, many teachings and activities are aimed at increasing compassion and even at perceiving this very world as a fundamentally compassionate place. Anyone familiar with Buddhism will know that the cultivation of compassionate feeling and knowledge is a central aspect of the three components of the spiritual path: ethics *(shila)*, concentration *(samadhi)*, and wisdom *(prajna)*. Certain methods of Buddhist philosophical analysis (e.g., Madhyamika or the philosophy of the Middle Way; for a contemporary English translation see Garfield 1995) have led to the conclusion that nothing in this world—neither selves nor persons, neither things nor organisms—exists objectively and inherently as independent of anything else. No being or thing exists independently of any other being or thing. Existence is, rather, a state of interbeing or webbed interrelationship with everyone and everything. This profound interdependence is a reality that human beings have difficulty seeing and feeling because of their universal adaptation of developing a sense of individual self. Many methods and arguments in Buddhism lead to the direct realization of this profound interdependence and the emergence of an abiding compassion and connection with all of life. When fully cultivated this kind of compassion intrinsically helps oneself as much as others.

In psychoanalysis, there are, in my view, two reliable means by which compassion is cultivated, although they are rarely described fully. The first is the patient's engagement in, and eventual awareness of, an unobjectionable idealizing transference to the therapist or analyst. By "transference" here, I mean the sustained projections of certain states, images, and feelings into another, in a way that prevents the recognition of the other as different from the projections. In this essay I will use "transference" to refer to such a projective state and "countertransference" to refer to the affective reactions to the transference. Although these two states are difficult to hold distinct, because the one quickly elicits the other, I will use the terms simply to differentiate the two states.

My term for this unobjectionable idealizing transference is the "containing-transcendent" transference, modifying the term used by the contemporary analyst Arnold Modell, who names a "dependent-containing transference" underlying the transformative analytic or psychotherapeutic relationship (1991, 46–52). In the way I use it here, this containing-transcendent transference is distinct from the specific transference of conscious or unconscious emotional patterns and images from childhood dynamics and complexes. I prefer "transcendent" to "dependent" because this form of transference is filled with the hope of transforming one's suffering and one's life, as well as transcending other kinds of limitations in a way that is similar to spiritual transcendence. This containing-transcendent transference is experienced first in the patient's hope that *this* therapist or analyst is knowledgeable and caring enough to be helpful in alleviating suffering. Eventually, or even at the beginning of treatment in some cases, the patient may also imagine that the therapist is a highly developed or spiritually powerful person. In short, this is the transference of the patient's own developmental potential for wisdom and compassion for self and other, as well as the patient's inherent capacity (however unconscious or nascent) to transcend suffering.

These kinds of idealized feelings and beliefs about the therapist/analyst are enhanced by, and even dependent upon, the analytic or psychotherapeutic setup: the relative anonymity of the therapist/analyst, the ethical conduct of the therapist, and the predictability of the therapeutic ritual. By "ritual," I mean the regular time-space-fee routines, the relative lack of retaliation (that friends and family may regularly engage in) against the patient on the part of the therapist, certain ways of speaking, and the absence of social chatter.

Later I will elaborate on the transformative effects of this kind of transference, but for the moment I want only to note that the *effective* therapist/analyst *must* eventually be imagined as someone who is compassionate and powerful enough—spiritual enough, if you will—to be helpful. The psychoanalyst Irwin Hoffman (1998) calls this the "mystique" of the analyst contributing to the therapeutic action of the treatment.

> With regard to therapeutic action ...there is something to the simple idea that the analyst is an authority whose regard for the patient matters in a special way ...that ...we do not try to analyze away, nor could we, perhaps, even if

we did try…. Regard for the analyst is fostered partly by
the fact that the patient knows so much less about him or
her than the analyst knows about the patient…. The analyst is in a relatively protected position …that is likely to
promote the most tolerant, understanding, and generous
aspects of his or her personality. I think of "idealization"
partly in interactional terms (as in "making the other more
ideal") because the analytic situation and often the patient
actually do nourish some of the analyst's more "ideal" qualities as a person. (203)

The *absence* of the containing-transcendent transference results, I believe,
in a situation in which there are no enduring therapeutic effects, no matter how accurate are the insights discovered by the therapeutic partners.
Moreover, the containing-transcendent transference may be the patient's
first encounter ever with someone or something that seems to transcend
suffering and promises renewal.

The second means by which psychoanalysis promotes compassion is
through the ongoing mutual inquiry into the patient's suffering. Over time,
both analyst and patient deeply appreciate the discovery process in which they
have engaged, and recognize how they have depended on each other in the
most unlikely moments when things felt especially tense or frightening. This
recognition of *interdependence* leads to the awareness in both that they suffer
not alone, but with each other and others. Ultimately, this can also lead to an
appreciation of the multiple layers of meaning in one's own or another's
suffering. As analyst and patient see and encounter this human dilemma, they
become more compassionate for all human beings.

The Transformative Relationship

Psychotherapy attempts to address the issue of human suffering through a relationship—both patient-therapist and patient-patient (in the case of a couple, family, or group). Without going into the particulars of how the different models may
use different methods, I want to recall that there are well-researched common
curative factors among all therapies. The leading category of these is the "therapeutic relationship" that develops between therapist and patient and allows a

process of change and transformation to emerge (see, for example, Strupp 1989).

One of the great treasures of Buddhism is relationship—especially to the *Sangha* or community. In some forms of Buddhism (Zen and Tibetan, for example), there is an additional important relationship of the teacher to a student or disciple. It is this two-person relationship that I will discuss here. A famous medieval Japanese Zen master, Eihei Dogen Zenji (1200–53), the founder of the Soto School, explains that the phrase "master and student practice together" means that there is the weaving of "vines" *(katto)* through the intertwining of the two personalities. Dogen alleges that the verification of true awakening (deep insight into the nature of reality) includes "attaining the other" while still retaining the individuality of self and other (see Kopf 1999, 281–86). Often this notion is conveyed by the caveat that self and other are not one and not two.

Spoken in a more contemporary language, the Western Tibetan Buddhist teacher Pema Chodron describes the importance of the student-teacher relationship for encountering the changing, impermanent, interdependent nature of reality. "When you're willing and able to trust the teacher, that's your first experience of steadfastness…. See, the idea here is that entering into an unconditional relationship with one person is a training for staying open to the paradoxical nature of reality. How do you get to the point where you can open to this world as it is, with all of its violence and beauty and meanness and moments of courage?" (Gross 1999, 45–46). The experience of an effective student-teacher relationship establishes the dependence of *both* on the relationship. Only within the relationship do they each find the particular self and the particular other that they constitute together. Although this sounds quite similar to psychotherapy, I will argue that the "intertwining" of self and other in Buddhism and psychotherapy are, formally speaking, designed to be different and composed of effects and methods that are quite distinct.

The effective psychotherapeutic relationship depends on a kind of unconscious intertwining through projections and identifications (transferences and countertransferences) of the two people involved. In order for this intertwining to be transformative, and not simply repetitive of earlier emotional patterns in the patient's or therapist's life—patterns that may engender suffering in either or both—the therapeutic relationship must offer opportunities for the patient to engage in such projections (to love, hate, revere, and diminish the therapist in the form of old emotional habits) *while* retaining enough objectivity in order to develop insight. This insight, as I said above, is the patient's empirical knowledge, witnessed in the therapy session, of the ways in which she or he is unconsciously setting up certain patterns of relating, feeling, and cognizing that create suffering. With this knowledge, the patient has the possibility of changing. So the effective therapeutic relationship allows for difficult emotional themes to develop, and then attempts to interpret and understand them in ways that are useful to the patient.

In order for this to happen, as Modell (1991) claimed (and I concur), there must be at least two kinds of transference going on in every session, as well as another level of relating in which these transferences can be analyzed and reflected upon. The containing-transcendent transference that I described above is the basic frame that surrounds the dynamic field of the therapeutic relationship, by which the relationship is fundamentally remembered and named as ameliorative of the patient's suffering. Because of its containing function the containing-transcendent transference includes feelings and conflicts about dependence-independence, trust-betrayal, and engulfment-abandonment. These themes are part of the therapeutic setup and not derived primarily from the patient's past, although they may take forms similar to other containing relationships (e.g., to a life partner or parent). To be transformative, this containing-transcendent transference obviously demands ethical behavior, trustworthiness, and professional acumen of the therapist—as well as a willingness on the therapist's part to be idealized and "spiritualized," as I describe below.

If you visualize the containing-transcendent transference as the outer frame of three nested frameworks in the therapeutic relationship, the next frame within is another kind of transference: the transference of old emotional habit patterns of the patient in perceiving, feeling, and thinking about the therapist. (Of course, this kind of transference can emerge from the therapist to the patient, but for the purposes of this discussion, I refer to the patient's transference.) This transference is dubbed "iconic-projective" by Modell and refers to the typical ways in which people unconsciously project images, feelings, and states into another—inviting that other to identify with and play them out in familiar ways (1991, 46–52). Such "projective identification" can be understood as a preconscious or unconscious communication of emotional themes that cannot be fully experienced or consciously expressed by the initiator of the projection. A lot of everyday communication contains significant unconscious projective identifications. Within the therapeutic relationship, this kind of communication can be made conscious, understood, and studied. This process begins with the therapist having a distinctly strong sense of being invited to play out some kind of emotional pattern that would be exciting, damaging, or humiliating to the patient. If the analyst/therapist is able to put into words what is being communicated, without arousing too much defensive resistance in the patient (who, after all, has always taken this to be part of "reality"), both patient and therapist will somewhat transform their perceptions of each other. In this way, an aspect of the patient's suffering will be opened to insight and the possibility of change.

Analytic forms of psychotherapy achieve the transformation of suffering by leaving certain kinds of things unsaid—for example, most if not all of the therapist's aggressive, hostile feelings toward the patient—while putting other things into words. The therapist's "interpretation" of unconscious meaning *is* put into words, phrases, sentences, and gestures to bring out the emotional meanings that have been implied or hidden from the patient's awareness until that moment. For example, the patient may say, "I think you're judging me, rejecting my experience when you say..." at the very moment that the patient is, in fact, unknowingly rejecting something about the therapist. At such a moment, the therapist (myself here) might raise a question: "Perhaps you have some feelings of judgment about me?" Such an interaction can be expanded by patient and therapist into a fantasied narrative about the therapist's aloof, stern manner that gradually turns into a portrait of the patient's parent or older sibling. Often such a verbal portrait is unknowingly developed through the words and emotional images used by both patient and therapist to shape an interpretation. Therapeutic interpretations reflect especially on a patient's silences, gestures, postures, dreams, and implied meanings to show how the patient creates suffering. The therapist's ability to be helpful in uncovering unconscious meaning in these contexts is, of course, at the heart of the technical and professional training in all forms of psychoanalysis and psychotherapy.

The third level of the therapeutic relationship—at its core, so to speak—is what I like to call a "kinship relationship," drawing on Jung's (1966) term of "kinship libido." It has often been called the "real relationship," but all levels of the therapeutic relationship are real, no more or less real than this level. Of this component of an analysis Jung says, "To the extent that the transference is projection and nothing more, it divides quite as much as it connects.

But experience teaches that there is one connection in the transference which does not break off with the severance of the projection. That is because there is an extremely important instinctive factor behind it: the kinship libido" (1966, 233). This kinship engenders "a satisfying feeling of belonging together," says Jung later in the same passage.

Within this kinship relationship, as I see it, patient and therapist experience themselves as human beings who are struggling together to try to bring about the amelioration of suffering in at least one, and more profoundly in both. The patient has hired the therapist do a job that the therapist has been educated to do. The therapist, like any other trained professional, will be more or less able to perform satisfactorily on a particular occasion, relevant to the therapist's state of mind and many other factors.

Naturally the patient feels limited and confused by her or his suffering, but the effective therapist/analyst must also feel the confusion and uncertainty of the task of therapeutic transformation. This allows interpretations and other interventions (such as empathy) to be made with an openness and questioning, a not knowing as well as a knowing. Within an effective therapeutic relationship, I believe the therapist must feel and eventually convey the sense that she also suffers. Here is how Hoffman describes this attitude: "analytic therapists in general can safely assume that they do not have privileged access to their own motives, nor are they able, despite their advantageous position, to know exactly what is best for their patients" (1998, 216).

The therapist's tolerance of uncertainty, openness to questioning, and respect for the interdependence of the therapeutic inquiry will convey her knowledge and acceptance of blind spots. This realistic acknowledgment of the limitation of "expert authority" counterbalances the powerful forces of the containing-transcendent and iconic-projective transferences, inviting the patient also to be open and unashamed in acknowledging human foibles such as unconscious desires, wishes, and fears. And yet this kind of realism must be handled skillfully so that the therapeutic relationship also allows plenty of opportunity for experiencing the two forms of transference. In everyday life, we are constantly immersed in iconic-projective transferences and kinship relationships with friends, family, and strangers. Only in the therapeutic relationship do we encounter a special situation in which we have framed the human condition, and its projective tendencies (recreating the emotional suffering of our habit patterns), in a containing-transcendent transference that tends to "nourish some of the analyst's more 'ideal' qualities as a person" (Hoffman 1998, 203) and promote hopefulness and a desire for self-understanding in the patient as well.

The containing-transcendent and iconic-projective transferences are also major transformative aspects of the Buddhist student-teacher relationship. Because I am a student of Zen and not a teacher, I can comment only from the perspective of the student; as I said earlier, I will use the Zen case as a prototype because it has been my experience. Whereas psychotherapy is designed to reveal and ameliorate the roots of *personal* suffering, Buddhist practices are designed to reveal and ameliorate the roots of *universal* suffering. Universal suffering encompasses personal suffering, so one could think therefore that Buddhist practices should address both. Perhaps if practitioners devoted themselves to *all* of the practices, as sincerely as possible, they would have a real potential of becoming free of both. Indeed, this was the original intention of the Buddha and his followers when they all lived in monastic communities.

Today, perhaps especially among Western Buddhists where the teachings and practices are new and often layperson-oriented, it seems unlikely that Buddhist practices will be so thoroughly embraced as to eradicate personal emotional habit patterns, as well as address the universal issues of suffering. In fact, even experiences of awakening to the nature of reality ("enlightenment") may leave intact such personal suffering. Bodhin Kjolhede, abbot of Rochester Zen Center, says, "Even when people have had fairly deep experiences of awakening, they still have tendencies or afflictions or habit energies with amazing staying power." However, the attitude toward these habits *will* have been transformed. Bodhin continues, "After enlightenment you can still be depressed, but it's not as disruptive or frightening because you see it as transient and insubstantial, like all phenomena" (Hooper 1999, 109).

The power of the Buddhist student-teacher relationship is deeply transformative, primarily through a form of the containing-transcendent transference which carries a projection of the perfected spiritual nature (Buddha Mind or true nature) that the student cannot initially find within herself. The student experiences or sees this quality in the teacher and wants to attain it. In Zen, a teacher who has been sanctioned to teach by her or his teacher has already equaled or surpassed the teacher's attainment and so there is reality to the idea that the teacher is beyond the student in spiritual achievement. And yet, as I amplify below, true and deep spiritual attainment should not, in any way, set a teacher apart from others; the most spiritually adept teachers are often known for being very ordinary people. Paradoxically, a spiritual master in Zen (a roshi) is both a special person whose spiritual realization has been sanctioned by a senior teacher *and* an ordinary human being.

Such a teacher naturally speaks from an authority that the psychotherapist or psychoanalyst lacks. Whereas the effective psychotherapist/analyst may still be almost as neurotic as the patient (although able to use insight and compassion in relation to the neurotic tendencies in a process of becoming freer of them), the Zen teacher is certainly not as ignorant of the nature of reality as the student. Becoming a psychotherapist requires completion of professional training; becoming a psychoanalyst involves that plus additional training and a successful personal analysis. The long and arduous apprenticeship of the Zen teacher or the accomplished Buddhist teacher is a whole way of life that has taken many years to ripen, in addition perhaps to learning many methods and ceremonies and so on. In short, the Zen teacher and student are understood to be fundamentally unequal, spiritually speaking.

This difference in spiritual status effectively eliminates the kinship relationship, at least in the beginning of the teacher-student encounter, and perhaps throughout, depending on the circumstances of how long and closely they work together. The developed teacher has mastered her or his own mind and not merely the knowledge of Buddhism. Many roshis would say something quite different from what Hoffman says above: that they *do* know their own motives *and* what is best for their students. In order for the two to "intertwine" and attain each other, as Dogen Zenji describes, the student must learn the ways and means of her or his true nature. In this process, the student fully integrates and assimilates the projection of the containing-transcendent reality.

Additionally, in Zen the actions of the teacher may be harsh and seem hostile as well as openly caring and compassionate. These extremes are aspects of the teaching and not considered a personal matter, but they tend to stir extreme iconic-projective transference fantasies in the student: images and fears of parental figures and older siblings. Because of the strong containing-transcendent transference, and because of the dependence and trust that accompany it, there also tends to develop some erotic feelings related to loving the teacher, colored especially by the containing-transcendent transference before it is thoroughly assimilated. The student feels vitally dependent on and deeply concerned about the teacher in a situation that is unpredictable in regard to the extremes of the teacher's responses. In the effective development of the student's spiritual abilities, the iconic-projective themes of the student's old emotional habits are pitted against the containing-transcendent transference. Without the benefit of any interpretations of one's personal suffering, the student must stop behaving and feeling like an omnipotent or victimized child through mastering reliable spiritual practices in the always-present relationship to the dedicated teacher.

The two kinds of transference guarantee a strong affective context in the student-teacher relationship—often an emotional cooker—in which the process of spiritual transformation takes place when all goes well. I believe that the emotional themes of dependence-independence, trust-betrayal, and engulfment-abandonment are intensified in the student-teacher bond by the relative absence of the kinship feeling. The contemporary North American teacher Pema Chodron, whom I quoted earlier, describes the process like this:

> The job of the teacher is to help the student experience that their mind and the mind of the teacher are the same. The teacher realizes that the student doesn't understand that, doesn't believe it, and doesn't trust.... Sometimes someone needs love and sometimes harshness. But whatever the teacher does is always about helping you to see layer after layer of defense mechanisms and self-deceptions that block your innate wisdom. You have tremendous devotion because without your teacher you would never have discovered this confidence in your own wisdom. (Gross 1999, 47)

At the point that the student awakens to the reality of the Buddha Mind, the student and teacher are one, although they remain two individuals. This intertwining is very different from the therapist-patient relationship of working through the intertwinings of unconscious projective identifications by interpreting personal emotional themes in the moment they happen, while becoming conscious of the relational consequences of projection.

Differences in Transformation and Transference in Psychotherapy and Buddhism

Psychotherapy was designed to transform individual pain and suffering, not to respond to spiritual questions. And yet, a transcendent reality arises within the containing-transcendent transference. In the development of compassion for oneself and others, the patient discovers what Jung (1969) calls a "transcendent function": an ability to contain tensions, conflicts, and other opposite pulls without prematurely deciding that they are "good" or "bad" or mean this or that (see also Horne 1998; Young-Eisendrath 1997). This function allows the patient to keep an open mind in the face of unconscious impulses, desires, and needs.

Most people seek therapy not because they want to, but because they have to. Typically they have already tried other remedies and sought advice about their suffering. Thus, psychotherapy is only moderately desired by the people who pay for it, at least when they begin. The core process of transformation through the therapeutic relationship involves encountering difficult and overwhelming emotions and investigating their origins and meanings. Engaging in and then attempting to understand many chaotic and troubling emotional states, psychotherapists also feel ambivalent about their commitment to the process. Consequently, patient and therapist are genuinely surprised when they suddenly feel deeply appreciative of their dependence on each other. This experience of interdependence and compassion eventually sustains an open-mindedness and fosters the transcendent function over the course of a treatment.

The student-teacher relationship in Buddhism, by contrast, does not typically encourage the student to express or enact overwhelming or negative emotional states. On the contrary, methods of Buddhist practice are designed to increase equanimity and reduce anger, greed, and ignorance. For this and many other reasons, there is little opportunity to work through intense emotional transferences within the student-teacher relationship, except occasionally during meditation retreats and formal encounters with the teacher. Such encounters with my own teacher were always engaged—sometimes confrontational and sometimes very caring—but tended to address the universal or common, rather than personal, meaning of my experience. Additionally, I was always instructed to turn my attention back to my practice and to let go of the disturbing states of mind.

Both the therapeutic and student-teacher relationships make use of transference, but they do so in different ways and for different purposes. Psychotherapy cultivates the transcendent function through opening insight into enactments and iconic-projective transference within a containing-transcendent transference. The kinship relationship balances the power of the two transferences and keeps the focus on the contract of psychotherapy: the patient has hired the therapist to ameliorate the patient's suffering and nothing more (i.e., not to be a mentor, lover, adviser, etc.). Moving around in these three relational realities, the therapist and patient inevitably increase their compassion and knowledge. The goal of intensive psychotherapy or analysis, as I see it, is the patient's fairly reliable ability to use the transcendent function, keeping the mind open in the face of emotional pressures, in everyday life. By the end of an intensive therapy, the iconic-projective transference should have been thoroughly analyzed and resolved, but the containing-transcendent transference will not have been resolved, may not have been analyzed, and will probably have intensified.

The aim of the Buddhist student-teacher relationship is to change the student's underlying fabric of consciousness so that the student has a clear and enduring perception of the nature of reality: impermanence, finitude, interdependence, etc. The containing-transcendent transference will have dissolved in the process: the student will come to see that she or he is also "a Buddha," an awakened one. To put this in other terms, the student initially believes in one way or another that he or she is not capable of deep spiritual realization, but that only the teacher is. After having successfully engaged in practices and methods that have brought about some insight and some freedom, the student will begin to "attain" the mind of the teacher. If the student continues, eventually the student will have access to the spiritual states the teacher has reached. Under these circumstances, the student no longer needs to project a transcendent reality, but has direct access to it. On the other hand, the iconic-projective transference will not have been interpreted and may not have been dissolved. If there are pathological elements in this transference, they may escape the transformative effects of the student's spiritual development. If that student were to go on to become a teacher, and not have resolved or understood the themes of the pathological iconic-projective transference, those same themes could be enacted in countertransferences with future students.

Betrayals of the Containing-Transcendent Transference

Both the therapeutic and the student-teacher relationship make important use of the containing-transcendent transference as a protective space in which to develop the transcendent function and many other skills. In 1916, Jung wrote that this kind of transference portends a "renewal of attitude" and that the patient, "seeks this change, which is vital to him, even though he may not be conscious of doing so. For the patient, therefore, the [therapist] has the character of an indispensable figure absolutely necessary for life. However infantile this dependence may appear to be, it expresses an extremely important demand which, if disappointed, often turns to bitter hatred" (1969, 74). Jung recognized that this transference expresses a striving (conscious or not) for renewal in a person seeking psychotherapy, and of course in a student seeking a Buddhist teacher. With the power of this transference, the therapist or teacher is experienced as a very potent figure. If the promise of renewal is betrayed or trivialized, the patient/student may fall into a serious psychological illness or come to hate the therapist/teacher, or in the worst-case scenario could even commit suicide because of this terrible disappointment.

The initial experience of this idealizing transference awakens inchoate spiritual yearnings for compassion and wisdom. These yearnings are known often only through the hope that *this* therapist/teacher can be helpful with things that no one else has ever seemed to help with. This hopeful belief can become a conviction that suffering will someday make sense and that life has a purpose. The effective transformative relationship can be disrupted and even permanently betrayed through the dissolution of the containing-transcendent transference. This can happen through an ethical violation or gross mismanagement. On a more subtle level, effectiveness can be breached through a chronic, sometimes unacknowledged suspicion that this therapist or teacher is yet another inadequate, uninformed, or unempathic authority figure who has broken the promise of renewal.

Effectiveness can also be diminished through the therapist/teacher's unwillingness to admit to mistakes or to see his or her own human failings. If the patients/students constantly feel that they cannot speak truthfully or must protect the therapist/teacher, then the containing-transcendent transference is compromised because the therapist/teacher is imagined as too weak. In Buddhism a teacher's unwillingness or inability to deal honestly with criticisms or shortcomings openly within the sangha or community can have a very negative effect on the containing-transcendent transference in the student-teacher relationship. A collective experience that the teacher's authority is sacrosanct—never to be questioned on even practical issues, much less spiritual ones—will exaggerate and reinforce negative iconic-projective transferences in students. Often the hateful and aggressive feelings about the teacher's imagined weaknesses will be split off and felt toward those who do not practice or have different beliefs, such as a spouse or work associate. An overly zealous attitude in a student should be a warning that negative strivings, connected to the idealization of the teacher, are unconsciously overwhelming and so have to be kept under strict control.

The transformative relationship in psychotherapy or Buddhism never really ends; its effects live on forever. Even years after the death of one's revered therapist/teacher, news about her or him—especially shocking news like an ethical violation—can confuse or diminish the transformative effects of the relationship. This is a great responsibility for those who take on these roles. On the other hand, the power of the containing-transcendent transference is not a *personal* matter and does not have to be arranged; it arises spontaneously from the universal hope for transformation of suffering.

Mistakenly identifying oneself personally with the powers of this transference leads to destructive errors and actions, of which there are innumerable examples among charismatic therapeutic and spiritual leaders. Such leaders may demand adherence to their particular ideas or become capricious in their influence because they believe that they personally have some unique powers or methods. The charismatic leader may also ignore certain ethical or social codes of decency, believing that he or she is beyond criticism.

Concluding Thoughts

The complementary nature and approaches of the therapeutic and student-teacher relationships in psychoanalysis and Buddhism are important for gaining clearer understanding of each. Both involve the transformation of suffering and use of transference, but each aims at particular goals and uses some very different methods. And yet, they overlap in regard to the importance of the containing-transcendent transference.

The psychotherapeutic process focuses its attention on the transformation of personal suffering through revealing the emotional patterns that are expressed in the iconic-projective transference, framed by the vitality and security of the containing-transcendent transference. The spiritual process of the student-teacher relationship focuses its attention on the resolution and integration of the containing transference, whereas the iconic transference is tolerated but generally not understood specifically in terms of its personal meanings to the student.

In theory, the Buddhist aim to eradicate the roots of suffering should encompass the kinds of personal suffering that have evolved from the conditions of childhood and personality development, as well as other problematic emotional habits of an individual. In fact, this may not happen because of limitations in the student-teacher relationship or in the level of a student's involvement in and commitment to practice. Consequently, effective psychotherapy may serve an important purpose in the transformation of personal suffering, existing alongside effective practice of Buddhism.

Commentary

SEEKING AND SUBJECTIVITY IN BUDDHISM AND PSYCHOANALYSIS

OWEN RENIK

I find Young-Eisendrath's perspective enormously congenial, and the links she makes between Buddhism and psychoanalysis are quite convincing to me. Reading her essay, I was immediately struck by the fact that Young-Eisendrath came to Buddhism as a seeker. She was looking for something and she found it in the Buddhist way. Perhaps this is somehow true for all

Buddhists, but I suspect that if one becomes a Buddhist through growing up in a Buddhist culture, the nature of the quest and of the discovery are, in certain respects, different than if Buddhism is in some sense exotic, something one comes to unexpectedly. In the latter circumstance, it seems to me, certain possible correspondences between Buddhism and psychoanalysis are more apparent.

This impression is strengthened for me by her initial statement that a goal of Buddhism is to alleviate suffering, particularly when she defines suffering as a *subjective disturbance*. This conception of Buddhism permits me to understand Buddhism as a therapy rather than as a religion. It seems to me that both religions and therapies deal with the work of coming to terms with life conditions. In my view, the hallmark of a religion (whether psychoanalysis-as-a-religion or Buddhism-as-a-religion) is that the goal of the work is defined by the practitioner (priest/teacher or therapist/psychoanalyst) and must be accepted, taken on faith, by the seeker. Thus in religion a measure of unquestionable authority for the practitioner is posited a priori. In therapy, on the other hand, the goal is to alleviate the seeker's *subjective* distress, which means that the goal is defined by the seeker; therefore the relationship between practitioner and seeker is of necessity collaborative rather than authoritarian. The authority of the practitioner, when it occurs in therapy, is earned. This is true in the best case, I would say, across therapeutic theories—for analytical psychologists and psychoanalysts alike.

I was very taken, too, with Young-Eisendrath's discussion of the Buddhist emphasis on how much of human anguish arises out of omnipotent desire. I think every clinician will recognize the truth of this connection. It has become fashionable to observe the narcissism of contemporary Western culture and the unhappiness it produces; but the problem of "wanting things to go our way," as she puts it, is a very long-standing one. Freud certainly was aware of its ubiquity when he quipped that the aim of psychoanalysis is to convert neurotic suffering into everyday human misery. However, the relation between suffering and omnipotent desire was recognized millennia ago, and not only in the East. It was a central concern, for example, of the Stoic philosophers, who said a great deal that can be usefully applied in therapy.

Of course, Young-Eisendrath also states that compassion is a Buddhist goal. She sees compassion as a goal of therapy as well, for psychoanalysts and analytical psychologists. Here, I'm not so sure I completely agree, though our differences may be more apparent than substantive. For me, increased compassion—compassion for others and for oneself, with the two operating reciprocally—is surely an outcome of most, if not all, therapies. But I do not conceive of compassion as a designated therapeutic goal. Rather, I find that a patient's achievement of increased compassion arises as a means to the end of relieving the patient's subjective distress. My patients do not aim to become, and I do not aim to help them to become, more compassionate per se. However, I observe that my patients tend to become more compassionate because they discover that it is a less distressing way to live; and in this endeavor I try to be of help.

Of help how? Young-Eisendrath has some important things to say about therapeutic action in Buddhism and in psychoanalysis. I couldn't be more in accord with her about the centrality of the therapeutic relationship and about what I think is her conception of the therapeutic relationship as *a vehicle for learning*. She discusses the healing effect of learning that apparently meaningless suffering has meaning, and the healing effect of learning that the compulsion to repeat destructive experience can be intentional, if misguidedly so. Both factors are decisively important in successful therapy of any kind. My own sense is that Jung specialized more in the former, his specialization originating in the tremendous relief he felt when he was able to assign timeless, cross-cultural meanings to his deeply disturbing youthful visions. Jung's therapeutic success in his own case led eventually, I believe, to the development of useful analytical psychological techniques like amplification. Freud specialized more in the latter, his specialization originating in a personal need to distance himself from his subject of interest, and to observe its characteristics at a remove—whether he was looking at embryos or hysterical women. That stance led, eventually, to his methodology of gathering the patient's free associations and deducing from them the patient's unconscious motivations.

Now, I believe that what Buddhism may help therapists retrieve and maintain is what is too often lost in both psychoanalysis and analytical psychology: namely, appreciation of responsibility and freedom. Young-Eisendrath tells us that in the *Dhammapada* it is said, "With our thoughts we make the world." This is a hard-won but invaluable insight for each of us. Understanding it and putting it to use is, in my experience, always the central issue in clinical psychoanalysis.

Ironically, and unhappily, the theories that we therapists employ have sometimes pointed us in the very opposite direction from taking on responsibility and helping patients take on responsibility, from identifying and from using our own freedom and helping patients to do the same. The concept of *the repetition-compulsion* in psychoanalysis, for example, encourages us to understand our problematic attitudes and actions as lying beyond choice. It is the very opposite of Strenger's conception, which Young-Eisendrath quotes, of "intentional action all the way down." Certain versions of the concept of *the collective unconscious* in analytical psychology have similar implications, encouraging the opposite of awareness of freedom and responsibility. Besides our theories, our professional organizations and educational institutions, needless to say, tend to pull powerfully away from the recognition that it is with our thoughts that we make the world, and toward the acceptance of received wisdom.

Young-Eisendrath considers at length the role played by what she calls "unobjectionable idealizing transference" and "containing-transcendent transference" in therapy. In her view, several levels of transference are always in operation during an analytic session. She follows Modell's conception of a special psychoanalytic reality. For me, on the other hand, the psychoanalytic relationship is a very ordinary one—although an extraordinarily candid one. I'm quite skeptical about the value of understanding the analytic encounter as taking place within a very special reality, of conceptions that require us to postulate multiple levels of *anything* in operation—let alone multiple levels of transference. I regard transference as a problematic term to begin with; the notion of subspecies of transference acting on different levels makes me think of Ptolemaic astronomy. When we begin to multiply theoretical entities, we are in danger of establishing a cumbersome account of the phenomena at hand that is unlikely to be helpful to us in achieving our practical objectives.

When it comes to the question Young-Eisendrath raises concerning how "idealizing transference" functions in therapy, whether objectionable and unobjectionable forms of it can be distinguished, and whether some idealizations of the therapist should be cultivated through the use of ritual, I think we confront a subject that is much too complicated for me to take up in these remarks without giving short shrift to it in a misleading way. I'll confine myself to underlining only one point. The psychoanalytic relationship is set up to facilitate an analyst actually being a better person in many ways to patients than to friends and loved ones. The result is an authority for the analyst within the therapeutic relationship that is *earned*, and very different from the *unearned* authority that is referred to when one speaks of a patient's positive *transference* to an analyst. We can easily agree that earned authority is useful, unobjectionable, and should be encouraged in any way possible. Whether the same is true of some kinds of unearned authority is an entirely different matter. I couldn't tell what roles Young-Eisendrath thinks unearned and earned authority play in the relation between Buddhist teacher and pupil. I would be interested to know.

I think some of the differences between Buddhist practice and therapy that Young-Eisendrath proposes bear further scrutiny. My impression is that the distinction she draws between the universal causes of human suffering, Buddhism's jurisdiction, and the individual causes of human suffering, therapy's jurisdiction, may not hold up if we look into it deeply. Similarly, when Young-Eisendrath describes her experience of Buddhist teaching as different from therapy because she was not encouraged to express negative feelings toward the master, and because the encounter aimed toward serenity rather than the reliving of the turbulent past, she may be contrasting Buddhist practice with a somewhat obsolete conception of therapeutic practice. Contemporary psychoanalysts, for example, have questioned (rightly, in my opinion) the assumption of aggression as a primary motivation, and have come to see many traditionally expected resentments on the part of patients as iatrogenic, understandably counterproductive responses to a misguided, traumatizing analytic stance. In too many instances, the patient's unfortunate past gets recreated when it should be remediated.

I'll end on this note. Young-Eisendrath quotes the Buddhist teacher Pema Chodron as follows: "The job of the teacher is to help the student experience that their mind and the mind of the teacher are the same. The teacher realizes that the student doesn't understand that, doesn't believe it, and doesn't trust.... Sometimes someone needs love and sometimes harshness. But whatever the teacher does is always about helping you to see layer after layer of defense mechanisms and self-deceptions that block your innate wisdom." I can't think of a more cogent statement of the contemporary view, from an intersubjective perspective, of psychoanalytic process and collaborative technique.

Reply

Increasing Our Subjective Freedom

Polly Young-Eisendrath

It was a pleasure to read the kind and intelligent remarks that Owen Renik wrote in response to my essay. I am grateful for this opportunity for a dialogue in print. He and I share in common many views about the central importance of responsibility, intentionality, and accountability in the aims of clinical psychoanalysis. Regarding the term "psychoanalysis," I refer to my clinical practice under the general rubric of psychoanalysis ("analytical psychology" is my particular orientation) because psychoanalysis is the label used in the public domain for depth psychology in general. Besides, after some years of saying, "I practice Jungian analysis," and then hearing, "Oh, I didn't know that *unions* had analysts!" I am happy now to say "I practice psychoanalysis."

I believe that what is practiced by "psychoanalysts" of all persuasions is different in one important way from many other therapies: we make specific use of the subjective distress created *within* the therapeutic encounter (enactments, projective identifications, transference, countertransference) as a significant (but not sole) means of psychological transformation. The psychoanalytic setup should guarantee that the subjective distress that naturally arises will be able to be studied *in the moment*. Ideally, psychoanalysis allows us to catch ourselves in the act of creating our troubling habit patterns, and it teaches us—or has the potential to teach—that we can change our lives by changing our minds. Renik and I seem to be in strong agreement on this point.

In all, I count eight topics in Renik's very engaging comments that invite some more thinking and clarification on my part. The first concerns my being a seeker. He remarks that seeking Buddhism may result in a different perspective than having been born into it. No doubt he is right about that, but I want to clarify my own chronology. I actually happened onto Buddhist practice (with no prior knowledge of it) in an introductory workshop in Zen to which a friend had invited me. It's true that I *was* seeking a religion grounded in experience rather than dogma, but I knew next to nothing about Buddhism at the time. That workshop took place six years before I decided to become a psychologist and four years before I had my first psychotherapy. I eventually became a Zen student in a formal ceremony seven years before I began my Jungian training in 1979. By 1979, I was most definitely seeking *psychological* solutions to psychological problems that had not been solved through Zen practice.

The second topic is suffering and the goal of alleviating it. Renik may or may not know the Four Noble Truths of the Buddha's teachings (fundamental to the entire practice). The Sanskrit term *dukkha* (defined in my essay) is the core of what is called the First Noble Truth: human life is filled with dukkha. Although dukkha is often translated as "suffering," it is probably better translated as discontent or mental anguish. The emphasis on subjective distress is inherent in the earliest teachings of the Buddha: he calls attention to the distinction between our attitude about our experience and the experience itself. Additionally, he makes clear that certain adversities (such as physical decline and death) fall outside our control, but our response to them does not. The Buddha, in fact, was often called a doctor—a therapist of sorts.

Regarding Renik's comments about faith and authority, I would say that Buddhism begins not with faith but with the knowledge of one's own suffering. Here is how His Holiness the Dalai Lama says it: "Unless you know that you are suffering, your desire to be free from suffering will not arise in the first place" (1997, 38). Where faith, as such, enters into Buddhist practices is in the belief that an ordinary human being, Siddartha Gautama, completely freed himself of such suffering and then outlined methods for others to do the same. One must have faith that it is possible to reach such freedom: that others have done it and that one can do it oneself. This is different from faith in authority; Buddhist faith is based on learning and trying a method for oneself.

This is the basic kind of faith that allows a practitioner to engage in the methods that themselves are very effective in generating experience that is transformative, even from the beginning of practice. The Buddha and many teachers after him are well known for admonishing their followers to discover the truth for themselves and not to seek it from authority. Authority has its place in Buddhism, but that place is never higher than the truth of one's experience. Understanding one's experience is yet another matter, though. This is where the relationship with a community (sangha) or a teacher is vital.

It seems to me, however, that there is quite a lot of permission, within the traditions of Buddhism (not manifest equally in each and every teacher or practitioner), for an individual to move along on the path of spiritual development without the specific advice or authority of a teacher, using the methods themselves. Most of the methods require some basic instructions and some monitoring, but at least some of this can be done by peers who have already practiced. It is largely in understanding the actual experiences encountered through the various practices that a teacher or authority figure is especially useful and helpful.

Teachers of Buddhism must be sanctioned to teach, just as psychoanalysts must be sanctioned to practice, but there are Buddhist traditions for challenging and questioning teachers. Many approaches to Buddhism encourage questions and doubts as long as faith in practice is not undermined. Naturally, as I said in my essay, idealization or fear of the teacher can prevent a sincere dialogue from developing. Open inquiry is less encouraged in psychoanalytic traditions and training programs, in my view, where dogmatic adherence to doctrines can replace sincere questioning. Renik's writing (e.g., Renik 2000) has been a welcome relief in this regard among Freudian psychoanalysts. Of course, Buddhism is almost 2,500 years older than psychoanalysis. From Renik's definition of religion, I wonder if he would say that psychoanalysis—too frequently taken on faith from authority—might be more of a "religion" than Buddhism is. Of course, this is a manner of speaking. Buddhism is certainly a religion, in terms of what it encompasses, whereas psychoanalysis is a psychology.

I agree very much with Renik's point that for either Buddhism or psychoanalysis, the proof is in the pudding for the person who is suffering: Does this method help? Naturally, one has to engage deeply enough in either practice in order to answer this question fairly. It would be radical if psychoanalysts were taught to take "nothing on faith" and to "drop the method when it is no longer relevant," as students of Buddhism often are.

In regard to Renik's response to my statements about compassion, I believe that he and I might in fact agree if we sat down to discuss the issues. I regard compassion as a refined and specific form of empathy. To be deeply empathic with one's own suffering, especially neurotic or defensive suffering, as well as with the suffering of others, one must have cultivated compassion. Compassion is the ability to "suffer with" or to stand in the shoes of another or take an empathic view of oneself in regard to our universal human foibles. I believe that psychoanalytic methods, which make use of our subjective distress in the moment as a means of reaching greater freedom, provide unique opportunities for developing our compassion. In such a moment, we can see how suffering is created and how universal it is; the psychoanalytic setup provides an ideal environment in which to cultivate that wise objectivity that allows us to be compassionate.

This leads me, then, to the core of Renik's response regarding the therapeutic action of psychoanalysis and Buddhism. I fully agree with him about Jung and Freud: Jung specialized in showing that apparently meaningless intentions are meaningful, and Freud in showing us how strong is the compulsion to repeat destructive habit patterns because of our unknown intentions. As a Jungian it's true that I help patients see the universal aspects of their complexes and troubling mental habits in ways that reveal symbolic meaning. For example, an individual's negative Father complex may share in the symbolism of demons and ghouls in a way that can be amplified by reference to myth or story. Most people find relief in seeing that their patterns are widely understood. But Jung was, after all, also a Freudian, and so am I. Trained to use free-floating awareness as a kind of "objective stance," which could also be called "equanimity" in the Buddhist tradition, I observe and study subjective states. Both methods mentioned by Renik—amplification and analytic deduction— are used regularly and frequently in my consulting room.

Regarding responsibility and freedom, I note again that I came to psychological and psychoanalytic theory and practice *after* I became a student of Zen. I have always believed, fully and fundamentally, that psychoanalysis (whatever type) is a way to reduce one's suffering and cultivate an attitude of compassion that allows one to become ever more accountable and wise about the complexity of human motivations and actions. I agree wholly with Renik that some Freudian theories of the repetition compulsion and some Jungian theories of the collective unconscious (notably the theory of Self) have ironically and unhappily led to problematic attitudes about our actions being beyond accountability. Perhaps because of my early training in Zen, as well as my continuing study of Buddhism and practice of vipassana meditation now as well as Zen, I regard psychoanalysis specifically as a method for increasing subjective freedom by discovering and clarifying the domain of personal responsibility in relation to suffering.

Finally, I come to Renik's comments about my ideas concerning the "containing-transcendent transference," about which I have now written at length in other places as well (e.g., Young-Eisendrath 2000a, 2000b, 2001). I feel strongly that we as analysts must be responsible for, and knowledgeable about, the interpersonal and intersubjective effects of the analytic ritual or setup. This setup carries strong contextual meanings that resemble religious and spiritual rituals and settings. We often seem to give only lip service to the powerful influences of our ritual on the therapeutic relationship. The regularity of time-fee-space, the limited personal knowledge of the analyst, the analyst's commitment to ethical conduct and little or no retaliation, and the absence of social chatter are unique and specific interpersonal conditions. The absence of social chatter alone, for example, is rare except in rituals. The responsibility of the analyst for following the effects of the analytic ritual on the patient's transformation is key. Knowledge and monitoring of the containing-transcendent transference (as it interacts with the iconic-projective and the kinship relationship) are, in my view, central components of the therapeutic action. If there is a threat to this transference, or a betrayal of it, the hope for transformation dies. (By the way, in thinking of these "layers" of relationship as a nested model, I am drawing on systems theory, not Ptolemaic astronomy.)

This type of idealizing transference feels deeply unreasonable and even unfair to an analyst or a Zen teacher. Why should I—flawed person that I am—carry any special hope? Because the rituals of psychoanalysis and Zen cultivate an idealization of the analyst or teacher. We analysts and teachers are responsible, then, for conserving the hope for renewal until the other can carry it. If we practice our methods well, the analytic patient and the Zen student will take on the methods and move through a process of transformation. In psychoanalysis, as I have said, this does not resolve the containing-transcending transference, but in the Buddhist relationship, it does or it should.

When Renik says that the "psychoanalytic relationship is a very ordinary one," I believe that he is speaking as an analyst and not as a patient. Even a very experienced anthropologist, who engaged in analytic therapy as part of her study of psychiatric training, found that the "emotional intensity generated by the therapy relationship itself" was more than she could have imagined. In her study, T. M. Luhrmann, a professor of anthropology, comments,

> It is common for an analysand to say that the analyst is the most important person in his life. When I was in therapy, I thought of this attachment as the "Wizard of Oz" phenomenon. For me, my therapist became a floating head that accompanied me everywhere, with whom I had conversations that extended way past my sessions, late at night and early in the morning. Psychoanalysts often explain these intense feelings as the reenactment of childhood experiences, but they probably owe their intensity to the weird asymmetry of the therapeutic relationship. (2000, 104)

Yes, indeed, I would say they do, as do the intense feelings that relate to one's Zen teacher or lama.

I regard my authority as an analyst to rest solely on my effectiveness in alleviating suffering and increasing compassion in my patients and others whom I influence through teaching and writing. How well do I do what I am paid to do? This can be evaluated only through the effects I have. My effectiveness is influenced also by how I speak and write about what I do because these expressions affect people's general understanding of what it means to suffer and to transcend their suffering.

In relation to Renik's final point about the differences between Buddhist practice and psychoanalytic practice, I want to make a couple of comments. First, in all of my experiences with Buddhist teachers in many traditions, I have not encountered even one who wanted to speak with me about the details of my own emotional or interpersonal background, unless these were interfering with my practice. Rather, the focus of our encounters was my developing the methods of responding to all kinds of experience with attention and equanimity. These methods were carefully cultivated through instruction, encouragement, and critical feedback. Perhaps an analogy would be learning to ride a bicycle or to drive a car. We learn how to do these things in a safe environment (for example, a parking lot), trying to do what people in general have done to learn them. Our idiosyncrasies and limitations may enter in, but the focus is on the general method used to master the vehicle. This is analogous to Buddhist practice. Psychoanalysis, on the other hand, might be compared to solving one's personal mysteries or puzzles in the context of becoming freer of their troubling effects. We cannot do the work of psychoanalysis without combing through the details of our personal idiosyncrasies and emotional life.

When Renik reminds us that "many traditionally expected resentments on the part of patients" are "understandable counterproductive responses to a misguided, traumatizing analytic stance," I couldn't agree more. For this reason, I would like analysts to become more accountable for the effects of the analytic ritual on the therapeutic action and relationship.

Doing so, we can tell our patients in advance of our ground rules and our reasons for them, of the kinds of effects that the ritual may carry and the reasons for those, and so on, and get a patient's agreement to the context *before* it begins. I certainly do this before I begin any kind of therapeutic treatment. I am also willing to answer any questions about my methods at any time. None of this has ever interfered with transference of any sort. As a Jungian, I recognize that transferences are always taking place. Only in the analytic setting do we specifically study them and their effects.

I would guess that my approach to analysis should be classified under the contemporary "intersubjective perspective" from what I know about it. I would think that analysts like Renik and myself and others who speak openly about the importance of the therapeutic relationship have more in common among ourselves than our original Freudian or Jungian or Sullivanian or object relational training might indicate. I would like to expand this intersubjective perspective to include responsibility for the powerful effects of the containing-transcendent transference on the therapeutic enterprise.

References

Byram, T., trans. 1993. *Dhammapada: The Sayings of the Buddha.* Boston: Shambhala.

Dalai Lama, H. H. 1997. *The Four Noble Truths: Fundamentals of the Buddhist Teachings.* London: Thorsons.

Garfield, J., ed. and trans. 1995. *The Fundamental Wisdom of the Middle Way.* Oxford: Oxford University Press.

Gross, A. 1999. Unconditionally Steadfast: Amy Gross Interviews Pema

Chodron. *Tricycle: The Buddhist Review*, fall, 43–49.

Hoffman, I. 1998. *Ritual and Spontaneity in the Psychoanalytic Process: A Dialectical-Constructivist View*. Hillsdale, N.J.: Analytic Press.

Hooper, J. 1999. Prozac and Enlightened Mind. *Tricycle: The Buddhist Review*, summer, 38–41, 102–10.

Horne, M. 1998. How Does the Transcendent Function? *San Francisco Jung Institute Library Journal* 17:21–41.

Jung, C. G. 1966. The Psychology of the Transference. Trans. R. F. C. Hull. In *The Collected Works of C. G. Jung*, 16:163–323. Princeton: Princeton University Press. First published in 1946.

———. 1969. The Transcendent Function. Trans. R. F. C. Hull. In *The Collected Works of C. G. Jung*, 8:67–91. Princeton: Princeton University Press. First published in 1916.

Kopf, G. 1998. In the Face of the Other: Psychic Interwovenness in Dogen and Jung. In *The Couch and the Tree: Dialogues in Psychoanalysis and Buddhism*, ed. A. Molino, 276–89. New York: North Point Press.

Luhrman, T. M. 2000. *Of Two Minds: The Growing Disorder in American Psychiatry*. New York: Knopf.

Modell, A. 1991. *Other Times, Other Realities: Toward a Theory of Psychoanalytic Treatment*. Cambridge: Harvard University Press.

Renik, O. 2000. Subjectivity and Unconsciousness. *Journal of Analytical Psychology* 45:2–20.

Strenger, C. 1991. *Between Hermeneutics and Science: An Essay on the Epistemology of Psychoanalysis*. Psychological Issues Monograph 59. Madison, Conn.: International Universities Press.

Strupp. H. 1989. Can the Practitioner Learn from the Researcher? *Psychotherapy* 44:717–24.

Young-Eisendrath, P. 1997. Jungian Constructivism and the Value of Uncertainty. *Journal of Analytical Psychology* 42:637–52.

———. 2000a. Psychotherapy as Ordinary Transcendence: The Unspeakable and the Unspoken. In *The Psychology of Mature Spirituality: Integrity, Wisdom, Transcendence*, ed. P. Young-Eisendrath and M. Miller. London: Routledge.

———. 2000b. Self and Transcendence: A Post-Modern Approach to Analytical Psychology in Practice. *Psychoanalytic Dialogues* 10:427–41.

———. 2001. When the Fruit Ripens: Alleviating Suffering and Increasing Compassion as Goals of Clinical Psychoanalysis. *Psychoanalytic Quarterly*. 70:265–85.

CHAPTER 8

The Finger Pointing at the Moon: Zen Practice and the Practice of Lacanian Psychoanalysis

RAUL MONCAYO

Clearing the Conceptual Ground

Freud conceived of psychoanalytic practice as different from that of priests and counselors (1926). The analyst, in order to function as such, has to renounce the position of an ideal leader, moral educator, or pastoral counselor who will teach or guide the subject.

Freud's intention to distinguish psychoanalysis from pastoral counseling has to be understood within the context of his general psychological critique of religion. It is well known that Freud (1907) labeled religion the obsessional neurosis of humanity and that he was inclined to interpret spirituality as a defense against sexual and aggressive drives. Freud's materialistic stance follows from an eighteenth-century scientific paradigm that had predicted the demise of religion and spirituality. Freud (1927) dismissed the consolations provided by religion as either infantile symbiosis with the mother or infantile dependence on a providential father.

However, as I observed elsewhere (Moncayo 1998d), it is likewise important to remember that trends toward the transformation of religion have coexisted for two centuries in the West alongside the rejection of religion advocated by the scientific paradigm. The enlightenment of humanity promised by the natural and social sciences sought not only the elimination of religion but also a higher form of spirituality or religiosity. Current trends of spiritual renewal within Judaism, Christianity, and Buddhism are the heirs apparent of spiritual tendencies within the Enlightenment.

Since the social sciences sought to replace religion with discourses on human nature, psychology, the problem of suffering, and social emancipation, religion was inclined to transform itself in a dialectical attempt to utilize the Enlightenment to its own advantage. Many have considered psychology and Freudian psychoanalysis in particular as instruments required for a radical cleansing of religion, which would free it from dogma, intolerance, prejudice, and bigotry.

A long list of distinguished psychologists as well as proponents of the pastoral counseling field have developed concepts and theories in search of a purified religion compatible with psychoanalytic thought. They all accept the modern, liberal climate of opinion contained within Freud's psychological analysis and critique of the negative side of religion, yet at the same time most of these authors consider the Freudian view as inadequate to describe the higher, nondefensive, nonpathological aspects of spiritual experience.

The trend toward integrating psychoanalysis and pastoral counseling runs through the works of Jung (1958) and Tillich (1952) and is currently best represented by Hans Kung (1979), the existentialist therapies of Victor Frankl (1962) and Rollo May (1958) and the psychoanalytic revisions of W.W. Meissner (1984), James Jones (1991), and Moshe Spero (1992).

However, although agreeing with the project of expanding the conceptual and experiential horizons of psychoanalysis, I do not endorse an integrative framework for exploring the similarities between spiritual practice and the practice of analysis, for such a framework blurs the difference between the latter and pastoral counseling. The many contradictions between spiritual practice and modern psychotherapy should not be reconciled, in my view, by appealing to a need to introduce explicit spiritual values, a moral order, or a search for meaning in life into the practice of psychoanalysis and psychotherapy. In this essay I will outline a perspective on the relationship between the practice of analysis and spiritual practice that avoids the pitfall of viewing analysis as a form of explicit moral treatment in the narrow sense of the term. If anywhere, the spiritual realm will be found by revisioning the ethical structure of the analytic situation itself.

Finally, spiritual practices such as petitionary prayer, contemplative prayer, and meditation also need to be differentiated. Zen meditation will be used as an example of meditation and authentic spiritual experience; it seems to be the spiritual practice most similar to the analytic attitude. Petitionary prayer is the spiritual practice that lies at the point of maximum conflict with the analytic and scientific attitude. The worshiper petitions a deity just like a child petitions a parent. Contemplative prayer falls somewhere in between petitionary prayer and meditation. The function of contemplative prayer is evocative rather than supplicative, and whereas petitioning always presupposes a theistic spirituality (whether monotheistic or polytheistic), meditation and contemplation can be nontheistic.

According to Kung (1979) psychoanalytic treatment should not only be oriented to the past but should also help the subject with the future meaning of life. Analysis should give people meaning by offering them a value-orientation that guides them away from hedonism, addictions, narcissism, and conformism. In this view, psychotherapy is equivalent to pastoral counseling or to a reorientation of one's conscience. According to Kung, who restates a point made by Jung long before, the healing, redemptive, and renewing forces of religion may be more powerful than pure psychological analysis. This may be so, but, in my opinion these forces are not best exemplified by moral counseling or telling people what to believe and how to behave.

Within the pastoral counseling or the religious existentialist perspective, meaning is usually dualistically posited against lack of meaning, theism against atheism, and being against nonbeing, nothingness, or emptiness. Dualism does not allow a dialectical synthesis wherein opposite terms contain each other. Lacan's work contains the seeds of a positive and intrinsically psychoanalytic conception of emptiness and "senselessness" or meaninglessness. In a non-dual sense, senselessness includes both meaning and no-meaning. No-meaning points to a meaning beyond ego-ideals and moral purposes. For the most part, the existentialist school does not appropriate a positive view of emptiness as the Real beyond meaningful representation. As I will explain more extensively later on, Lacan defines human experience as organized by three dimensions: the Real, the Symbolic, and the Imaginary. The Real refers to that aspect of experience which lies beyond language, image, and logic and yet constitutes their very foundation.

The positive approach to emptiness appears not only in the Zen Buddhist and Taoist tradition but also in the sophisticated Christianity of Meister Eckhart and classical Jewish Kabbalah. Existentialist religious thinkers, as in the case of Tillich, are guided by a moral aim to overcome the threat of nonexistence and nonbeing. Nonbeing is not a threat to existence because existence is always arising out of nonexistence and disappearing into a state that cannot be defined by what we call existence or nonexistence. According to Zen Buddhism, the dual categories of being and nonbeing, meaning and meaninglessness, and existence and nonexistence are not applicable descriptions of the spirit of nonduality or the non-dual spirit.

Similarly, while there are important metavalues transmitted through the psychoanalytic situation, these values do not emanate from the place of the moral will. The latter is always caught in dualistic views of good and evil. From a dialectical perspective, that which is believed evil always contains some good and vice versa: that which is believed good contains some evil. If some idea of evil is too despised, then the mind will not be at peace with itself and thus still under the influence of evil. In psychoanalytic terms, moral will is to be located at the level of the superego. The superego derives from primitive sources, and its judgments operate with the energy of aggression and destruction. It divides rather than unifies the subject. The Spanish Jewish Kabbalist Moses Cordovero (1981) noted that the demonic forces contained within the function of judgment are always associated with the tree of good and evil, rather than with the non-dual values of the tree of life. Following the biblical metaphor from the Book of Genesis, it can be asserted that the values emanating from the level of the tree of life correspond to those associated with the practice of analysis: values connected with a sublimated death drive or with a death drive that in the end crosses over to the other side, the side of love or Eros.

Elsewhere (Moncayo 1997) I have postulated that both life and death drives have two dimensions: binding and unbinding. The first type of attachment and detachment is linked to the primary process and the pleasure principle, the second type to the secondary process and the constancy or nirvana principles (which I will define later). The life drive or Eros, which produces lasting connections and unifying ties between people, needs to be distinguished from the binding or attachment of desire and the life drive under the pleasure principle. The latter produces temporary unions, which turn into divorces and separations once the tie turns from one of love to one of hate or aversion. This is a life drive at the service of death or a case where, as Freud put it, the aim of life is death. Following Freud, and in contrast to Lacan, in this particular point of theory construction, the pleasure principle needs to be placed on the side of the unbinding and disruptive force of sexual pleasure and not on the side of homeostasis or the constancy of quiescent energy (as Lacan does). Lacan's concept of *jouissance*, (an untranslatable term that encompasses and surpasses the duality of pleasure and pain) represents a particular combination or configuration of life and death, pleasure and pain, under the pleasure principle. This concept has enormous clinical significance given that jouissance is what is at stake in the production of symptomatology and psychical pleasure/pain such as fear, anxiety, and depression.

Therefore, the Eros or life drive that would exist before and beyond the pleasure principle (Lacan's jouissance), is the Eros linked to the binding function of quiescent energy. If the pleasure principle is defined as a principle of homeostasis, then jouissance would lie beyond the pleasure principle (this is Lacan's argument). However, there are less grounds in Freud to link the pleasure principle with the binding function of quiescent energy, which for Breuer (from whom Freud borrowed these concepts) was intrinsically linked to the homeostatic function. Freud always linked the pleasure principle with the free energy of the primary process (Lacan's jouissance). In addition, how could the pleasure principle as homeostasis put a stop to jouissance (as Lacan believes) if jouissance is beyond the pleasure principle?

The constancy or nirvana principle is more fundamental than the pleasure principle although both can be considered as going beyond one another. Nirvana, in contrast to the pleasure principle, becomes indistinguishable from an Eros that produces more lasting bonds and attachments by unbinding or detaching the libido from archaic love and hate objects and thus transforming free energy into a bound or quiescent kind(ness). If the formula for the relationship between the two drives under the pleasure principle is "the aim of life is death," the reverse is true under the nirvana principle. The relationship between life and death under the nirvana principle is a case where the aim of death is life. Pleasure, in this instance, as the pleasure of the good, rather than the good of pleasure, is defined more by a principle of constancy, of lasting connections, of seeing things through to the end, of balance, harmony, and stability.

Zen Buddhism, just like psychoanalysis, is primarily concerned with "the great matter of life and death." Jack Engler (earlier in this volume) argues that within Buddhism life and death cannot be considered inherited drives because there are no *inherent* dispositions. All impulses and dispositions arise according to causes and conditions. This would be true and well except for the fact that inherited and inherent have two different meanings. For example, consider the Buddhist notion of karma that goes beyond a single lifeline of development as well as the notion of collective karma. First of all, karma, or the law of cause and effect, implies that desires and impulses are regulated according to certain laws whether natural or symbolic/cultural. Certain actions generate new desires, and desires themselves lead to new actions. But in either case, karmic law regulates the portal of motor activity. In addition, we share our collective karma with our species and with all species for that matter. Here even the distinction between animal instinct and human drive is blurred. Karmic, symbolic laws organize even animal instincts. This view is consistent both with Buddhism and the theory of evolution. There is continuity between the animal and human realms. According to Buddhist psychology, the eighth consciousness, or storehouse consciousness (which is really unconscious for all practical purposes), contains the karmic seeds, the causes and conditions that form our basic psychic makeup and that are inherited across timelines and lifetimes. Now inheritance can be interpreted in several ways: (1) as a type of rebirth and as influences from previous lifetimes; (2) how dispositions are transmitted from one generation to the next, whether genetically or symbolically; (3) how life in the past (rather than the past life) influences life in the present and in the future. Finally, the fact that we inherit impulses from "prior lives" does not mean that impulses are inherent dispositions. According to Lacan, drives have Imaginary, Symbolic, and Real dimensions. In my opinion, the Real of the drive, represents the inherent emptiness of desire, or the presence of an unborn and unconditioned dimension operative within birth and death, as the death within life and the life within death. Nirvana or death within life represents the mistake of seeking the unconditioned within conditioned or karmic existence. The self-destructive lifestyle of the leader of the rock group Nirvana, who was addicted to heroin and eventually committed suicide, represents an example of this type of mistake. In seeking Nirvana through pleasure he only met his own biological death. The life within death or true Nirvana represents the joy and serenity of the good law of emptiness. If we don't live in ignorance of the law of karma, then pleasure is a function of constancy, of lasting connections, and of seeing things through to the end.

Such metaethics of the tree of life (which constitute both an ethic and a theory) also need to be distinguished not only from a moral or pastoral orientation but also from a purely rationalist or secularist perspective such as that of ego psychology. Ego psychologists, following Freud, distinguish between a repressive morality of the superego and traditional religion and the more flexible and rational restraints emanating from the ego as Freud defined it. In this view, psychoanalysis is guided by the therapeutic imperative of replacing the pathologically repressive constraints of the superego with the flexible, conscious, rational, and voluntary restraints of the ego.

Ego psychologists find secular health values in the rational treatment collaboration between analyst and analysand as described in the concept of a therapeutic alliance. Higher ethics require the rational ego-functions of objective criticism and reflection. However, with the ego psychology model we arrive at a modern, secular, and rational ethic but not yet at a spiritual dimension of experience. Thus, although the mystic and the scientist share a non-moralistic approach to reality, the abstention of moral judgment, as an analytic practice of superego deconstruction and reconstruction, in and of itself does not constitute a spiritual perspective.

Both psychoanalysis and meditation practice can be conceived as vehicles for accessing a larger non-dual mind. In the case of Zen Buddhism, the phenomena/noumena of a larger mind coincide with a spiritual register of experience. In both models and practices the evocation of "Bid Mind" does not occur primarily through the observance of moral or rational guidelines for behavior. Meditation entails an observation of the mind within the mind while abstaining from discriminating between good and bad or subjective and objective mental contents, whereas free association in psychoanalysis suggests a different form of ideation not under the control of the ego. The ego, as the agency of defense and of rationalizing explanations, tends to become a hindrance to the analytic process. Thus, in contrast to how many critics would have it, within this line of analysis it becomes possible to consider psychoanalysis as being more than just a purely intellectual process. In other words, psychoanalysis also conceives of ego-rationality as a defensive operation in need of therapeutic modification or deconstruction.

Thus, it is possible to argue that the defensive egos and superegos of both analysand and analyst have to be set aside in order to evoke a larger dimension of experience. The process of self-transformation in psychoanalysis and meditation experience can be understood, following Zen and Lacan (1960b), not as an ego function, but rather as a process of discarding imaginary ego-representations and revealing benevolent depersonalizations and creative subjective destitutions.

I agree with Meissner when he stresses that so-called mystical experience "does not undermine or destroy identity but in fact has a powerful capacity to stabilize, sustain, and enrich identity" (1984, 151). The meaning of this statement is contained within the etymological sense of the word "mystical." Mystical is associated with mist, with something insubstantial. Mystical experience destroys identity in the sense that it destroys the illusory or imaginary ego-identifications. It is a necessary symbolic death that dialectically affirms a larger and more ultimate form of psychical identity beyond ego identifications. Thus, following Lacan, it becomes possible to argue that mystical experience and psychoanalysis share a practice of subjective destitution and benevolent depersonalization. What is destroyed or deconstructed in such a process are not the ego-functions per se but the imaginary construct of a substantial ego entity. In this regard, Hans Loewald (1978) has also called for understanding the so-called higher psychical functions, not with ego-psychology constructs but rather with positively defined metapsychological concepts. He regarded the primary process and unconscious desire as sources of creativity, renewal, and timeless forms of intuitive knowing.

In contrast to this, the schools of object relations (Fairbairn, Winnicott, Mahler), ego psychology, and self psychology all privilege the importance of developing a coherent or integrated ego or self identity. This fact has been identified by prior authors (transpersonalists such as Jack Engler [1981] and, within the psychoanalytic tradition, John Suler [1993], Jeffrey Rubin [1996], and Mark Epstein [1995]) as the most salient point of difference or contradiction between contemporary psychoanalysis and the Buddhist doctrine of no-self. For a more expanded and thorough analysis of the question please refer to my paper on the subject (Moncayo 1998c).

The above authors have articulated several possible solutions to the self/no-self dilemma. Engler formulated the now widely circulated idea that you have to be somebody before you can be nobody (see Engler's article in this volume for greater clarification). In other words, Engler proposed that the ego has to exist before a no-ego phase can begin. However, this linear developmental argument runs the danger of ego reification illustrated by the following Jewish joke. Once a rabbi came into the synagogue and found the caretaker saying, "Oh God! I am nothing, nothing…" to which the rabbi responded "and who are you to say you are nothing!" In this model being nobody is still under the influence of a false ego construct presupposed as a prerequisite. Not having an ego becomes a positive ego identification. On the other hand, no-self does not mean low self-esteem, low status, or lack of self-confidence because from a Buddhist perspective such a negative ego is still an imaginary ego, nonetheless. No-self from a Buddhist or Lacanian perspective includes human faculties and functions not attributable to an ego. A problem in exercising human functions or with self-confidence does not exactly represent an ego lack. To the contrary, it could be argued that it is precisely the attachment to an imaginary ego that needs to be worked through and let go.

But although Buddhism shares with psychoanalysis a critique of ego illusions and the Imaginary, Buddhism does not explore and track the Oedipal phantasy material that leads to the construction of a false sense of self. The imaginary ego represents what Engler calls "somebody." In psychoanalysis this imaginary ego is analyzed and worked though, not simply dismissed or repressed. However, in working through the imaginary ego, either in Zen or psychoanalysis, the so-called ego functions are not destroyed. For this reason, Buddhism considers these functions to be functions of the true self whereas for Lacan they are symbolic functions of subject. To transcend the ego functions means to have the realization that memory, judgment, and insight or knowing are a function of the interdependence of the larger, unconscious, symbolic structure. I use the term unconscious in a descriptive sense to indicate "Big Mind" and not the repressed unconscious. In truth, neither conscious nor unconscious applies to describe what Buddhism calls consciousness beyond consciousness and Lacan called a "knowing that does not know that it knows."

Much like Buddhism, Lacan believed the ego to be an imaginary, although inevitable, and necessary construction. For Lacan, the emphasis given by the ego, to autonomy, mastery, and individualism, reinforces an imaginary register of human subjectivity. Lacan defines the imaginary register of experience as intrinsically tied to an inevitable function of illusion or misrecognition, thus the term imaginary rather than the more positive term "imagination." (In Lacanian theory the category of the positive imagination is defined by a particular type of relationship between the Imaginary and the Symbolic [Moncayo 2000].) As a dimension of experience, the Lacanian concept of the Imaginary is based on the premise of an imaginary ego as a false construct or fabrication. In addition, as explained below, the fabrication of a substantial ego is also linked to fantasy life and particularly an unconscious phantasy [1] life. Finally, the concept has an ambiguity built into it given that Lacan also links the Imaginary with visual perception and a general theory of optics. For Lacan, truth and reality have a fictional, illusory, or fantastic structure. Here, he differs from Freud who, in classical Western fashion, clearly distinguished between fantasy and reality. In this respect, Lacan also inadvertently comes close to classical Buddhist thought. Suffice it to say for our current purposes that for Buddhism "external, objective reality" may be a more elaborate product of the mind than a mere subjective phantasy, but is still considered a mental construction, nevertheless.

According to Lacan's theory of the mirror phase, when the child captures his/her reflected image in the mirror, he/she acquires an insubstantial bodily ego representation. Lacan links the ego to the imaginary because in his view the ego is tied to the self-image, to how the self sees itself reflected in the mirrorlike surface of the other. Lacan postulates that the evanescent immaterial reflection of a bodily ego in the mirror represents a concretization of the mother's object of desire. "Oh! so it is this who my mother desires or does not desire." Thus, the specular image, the image in the mirror, occupies the same structural position as the phantasized object which constitutes the cause of the mother's desire. According to Lacan, the individual derives his/her own self-image and body-image, his/her narcissism, from an early identification with the mother and her desire. The first total ego-image is framed according to the desire of the other. The ego is a case where the subject constitutes a phantasy object for the mother. It is the identification with this imaginary object that lies behind the identification of a body-ego representation.

From then on the specular image remains as a double of the subject that equivocally can represent either the self or the other. This is the place of projection and imaginary intersubjectivity where the other is narcissistically misrecognized in terms of the ego and where the ego is narcissistically misrecognized as not derived from an identification with the other. From the perspective of the Imaginary, instead of actually seeing the other as a subject, what the self sees in the other is its own reflection. The ego-illusion and misrecognition derives from the fact that the thought of a special and independent individuality arises precisely at the place where the ego is most determined by and dependent on the other. Lacan associated the ego with sibling rivalry and competition, where the other recognized as a brother and a like-minded member of the same species is perceived as capable of displacing and occupying the very place that the ego holds vis-à-vis the mother.

On the other hand, although Buddhism and Lacanian psychoanalysis regard the ego as an imaginary construction, Buddhism, unlike psychoanalysis, is not interested in deconstructing and tracing back the sources of ego identifications or of desires to the familiar and symbolic history of a subject. Here I agree with Rubin when he observes an absence of a psycho-historical dimension within Buddhism. But from a Lacanian perspective, the presence of a psycho-historical dimension does not necessarily provide evidence and support for the actual existence of a substantial self or ego. Beyond the Imaginary, and within the Symbolic, the subject is a metaphor and a name for a series of functions and processes that occur within language and discourse.

For Lacan it is the symbolic order (a set of laws, values, myths, the order of language, etc.) that establishes the structures and functions of the subject that in the ego-psychology school are attributed to nondefensive and "realistic" ego-functioning. For Lacan reality is a social construct given by the culture-bound and law-bound order of language. The rules of language and the rules of kinship are conceived as two fundamental and integral elements of culture. Language and the symbolic unconscious constitute an Other to the subject because they mediate the relationship between the subject and the object, self and other. *Other* is capitalized because the unconscious and language are the larger structures that condition the experience of reality of the subject. In addition, the Other also refers to parental figures and figures of authority from whom the subject receives both social rules and the rules and content of language. Just as the ideal ego and narcissism are derivative objects of the desire of the mother, it is the relationship with the symbolic father that frees the subject from narcissism and from being an imaginary object of the mother's desire. The identification with the symbolic father, in the sense of an identification with symbolic rules and social laws that the father represents, establishes the subject as a pivot of the Symbolic and the Symbolic as a pivot of subjectivity. The Symbolic is what organizes human subjectivity, and insofar as symbolic rules and social laws are embodied in concrete singular "citizens," the subject functions as an agent/pivot of the Symbolic. Herewith, an individual can hardly be distinguished from the grammatical subject of the statement and the attribution and location given by the circulation of a proper name within language and culture. The subject is identical to a name that represents so-and-so within a particular society.

Following Lacan, the permutations of the Cartesian *cogito ergo sum* will be used to illustrate the three dimensions of the subject. "I think (I speak), therefore I am" represents the imaginary ego and the self-image as aforementioned. When utilizing social language, the *moi*, the ego, says, "I think," "I speak." As Bruce Fink has pointed out, when the ego says I speak "What it means thus refers to a level of intentionality that he views as his own; it refers to an intentionality that fits in with his self-image" (1997, 24). This is why Lacan made a conceptual distinction between the enunciating ego and the subject of the enunciation, and between meaning and signification. Meaning is imaginary because "it is tied up with our self-image, with the image we have of who and what we are." Instead, the subject of the unconscious, of the Symbolic, of signification, of the enunciation is conceived by Lacan as an effect of the operation of the signifier. The classical Freudian slips, the parapraxis, the double meanings, the polyvocal significations, in short, all of the formations of the unconscious, are effects of the language-like symbolic structure of the unconscious. All of these psychic formations have the effect of breaking the imaginary homogeneity of what the conscious ego intended or meant to say. The unconscious and the signifier speak through the subject. The thing speaks for itself or "It" speaks in me. In this respect, Lacan (1977b) modified and permutated the Cartesian *cogito ergo sum* by stating, "I think where I am not" instead of the classical "I think, therefore I am." "I think where I am not" represents what Epstein (1995), following Wilfred Bion, calls thoughts without a thinker where, from a Lacanian perspective, thoughts are signifiers that speak for themselves and articulate the symbolic existence of a subject. The autonomy of the signifier or of symbolic thought is experienced as a negation of the ego: I am not. My thoughts work autonomously and not always in alignment with my intentions and desires. But the "I think" aspect of "I think where I am not" refers to the fact that the Symbolic also represents an aspect of me or my subjectivity although not of the ego. It is a larger me doing the thinking activity, although in a way that appears ego-dystonic.

Lacan's aphorism that the unconscious is the discourse of the Other highlights such involuntary and unconscious functioning of language and identity: how the laws of language—the rules of syntax, metaphor, and metonymy—determine how something can and cannot be said, and how the self-imputed sayings of the ego unconsciously represent quotes of and identifications with the discourse of significant others. In this latter sense, the ego consists of identifications with signifiers coming from the Other (both from the symbolic order and significant/signifying others). The ego represents an imaginary use of the Symbolic to stitch and cover over the ultimate nonexistence of both the Other and the subject. When signifiers representative of ideals become invested with the narcissism of an ideal ego, then identifications become idealizations of an ideal father or fatherland and the signifier functions as a false identification. This would also apply to the case of an individual who has over-identified with Buddhism as an ideology.

This brings us to the third permutation of the Cartesian cogito leading to a third dimension of experience and of the subject: the register of the Real. "I think where I am not" needs to be permutated into "I am where I do not think," which signifies the realm of being or nonbeing beyond thought, signification, and representation. Lacan differentiated between social reality and the psychical Real or what in Zen would be called the ultimate reality.

As I mentioned earlier, in Lacanian theory social reality falls under the category of the Symbolic. The Real refers to the Freudian unconscious in the wider sense of the unknown and not just the repressed. Lacan gave varying definitions of the Real among which the following should be noted. The Real and the subject within the Real is a breach or an empty locus or space that allows for a nexus of relations to exist, for the movement of the signifier within a signifying chain. As Fink has pointed out, "In his seminar on the purloined letter, Lacan states that a signifier marks the cancellation of what it signifies. ... Once the subject has said his or her piece, what she has said usurps his or her place; the signifier replaces him/her; he or she vanishes.... The signifier takes the subject's place, standing in for the subject who has now vanished.... This subject has no other being than as a breach in discourse" (1995, 41).

Thus, on the one hand, the subject is represented by a signifier for another signifier; the subject is a metaphor located within the symbolic register. On the other hand, the subject within the Real is a breach or a hole within discourse. Moreover this breach, gap, or hole has been described by Lacan as the point of non-knowledge. As Juan-David Nasio (1992) has stated, "As subject, I realize myself where I do not know." In addition, on the one hand, this point of non-knowing refers to the *lacuna lacunae* in the act of forgetting as an effect of the repression of signifiers *within the Symbolic.* On the other hand, the point of non-knowing also refers to the unknown in the sense of what lies *within the Real* and beyond language and the existing battery of signifiers. In this latter sense the subject within the Real and the point of non-knowledge also functions as a source of new significations. The engendering of a new signification implies that, up until the moment at which this was engendered, a hole existed in the field of the signified or of signification. Since signification is given by the relationship of one signifier to another, when signification is not known (which means there is no signifier for it) one can say that there is a hole in the field of the signified. And it is indeed in this same hole (and not in the act of knowledge or symbolic representation) that the subject is located according to Lacan. The Real is also the Other *jouissance,* which women and mystics are said to experience but know nothing about (the experience that knowledge or language cannot describe). The Real is that which the signifying chain encircles and yet remains inaccessible to language and signification. Therefore, Lacan speaks of a lack or impotence of language to pinpoint the Real. It is this impossibility to symbolize and understand by means of reason and language that lends the Real its essentially traumatic and anxiety-producing quality. Finally, for Lacan the Real is a plenum without fissures, divisions, oppositions, or differentiations, and this Real is to be distinguished from the illusory wholeness ascribed to the Imaginary. When the ego thinks of itself as being whole, in a New Age or humanistic fashion, this is a self-image or an ego-ideal hypercathected with narcissistic energy.

For Buddhism true self is no-self because phenomena in their own being are empty and only exist as a function of the relationship with everything else. What we call our self is a convention, a fabrication or confection. What is actually there are the five streams of existence, namely, forms, feelings, perceptions, mental formations, and consciousness. But there is no permanent or inherent self within these five streams. These five streams are empty in the sense that nothing stands by itself separate from everything else. As Lacan would put it, the self is the other or the other is the self. Thus, emptiness in Buddhism means interdependence. For example, the body is within the stream of form, and each part of the body is interdependent with every other part. The nose is only a nose in relationship to the face, the nose is inherently empty because without the face the nose does not exist. Thus, to express the emptiness of form (nose), a Zen teacher may say something senseless like the nose is hanging from the wall. This statement is meant to highlight that without the face, the nose is meaningless. Another aspect of emptiness is that things are empty because they are constantly changing, the five streams are in a state of constant flux and transformation. Sometimes Buddhism uses the sky or space as a metaphor for emptiness. Space is like that in which everything can move and the groundless ground of existence. The clear blue sky is a metaphor for essence of mind, and the thoughts of an enlightened person are like birds flying in the sky without leaving any traces. Thoughts without a thinker don't give rise to a false sense of self beyond the true-self experience of birds flying in the sky.

It is thus possible to find areas of intersection between the Buddhist notion and experience of emptiness or ultimate Reality and the Lacanian register of the Real. Although Lacan stresses the importance of language as an organizer of experience (of thoughts, feelings, and consciousness) in a way that Buddhism does not, he not only describes language in the language of interdependence but also includes a register of experience beyond language. The finger is the signifier pointing at the moon, but the finger/symbol is not the moon itself within the experiential register of the Real. The Real is that which the signifying chain encircles and yet remains free of a fixed signification within language. The signification of a word or letter depends on its relationship to all the other words and letters within language. Each word or letter in itself is empty of its own meaning, and it is this emptiness that causes the constant dynamic movement of meaning within a signifying chain.

Emptiness as the clear space that allows for the movement and translucency of meaning is the larger "me" that can be reached on the level corresponding to an authentic spiritual function. "I think where I am not" needs to be permutated into "I am where I do not think," which signifies the realm of being or nonbeing beyond signification and representation aforementioned:

our Real self, the nameless Big me that is beyond thought and that is capable of saying: "I am Who I am." (Exod. 3:14)

Moreover, as noted above, the hole in the field of the signified or, put differently, the hole that appears within the Symbolic when the signified is within the Real, the empty a-territoriality or groundlessness of the Real, begets a nonconventional and evolutionary leap beyond the established uses of language and ideology. Thus, no one can really or in truth say "I am" or "I know who I am" because what the "I" is at the level of the Real is unknown. Not-knowing the meaning of identity within the Real, and the fact that no-self or no-ego is more me or myself than the ego, are precisely the source of both new meaning and what articulates the elements of subjective structure. This view is compatible with Suler, who, following Bion and Michael Eigen, describes how nonbeing and "catastrophe are the zero point that infuses and grounds the self" (Suler 1993, 71). Rather than the ego it is nonbeing or no-self that functions as a primordial binding source that holds the self together.

Thus, I have argued in favor of a marriage of the Lacanian concept of the Real with the Buddhist notion of the Real in terms of emptiness. Lacan often described the Real in terms of an absence or a lack within the Symbolic to pinpoint the Real. Such lack alludes to a limitation of language to represent a Real beyond symbolization. Lacan defines the emptiness of the Real as a lack in the Other. This relates to the dread many Zen students report when first attempting to give talks and use words to speak about their meditational experience and realization. Zen teaching describes this predicament as a mosquito attempting to bite into an iron bull. Symbolic castration or psychical impotence would not be too far off in describing this experience.

For Lacan the missing signifiers to represent the Real, the lack in the Other, or the signifier of a lack, constitute the subject as barred, as divided, and as desiring something of the Real that the Symbolic or the Imaginary will never fully grasp. Neither language nor the ego or drives will render the Real to the subject. As experienced in the practice of Zen meditation retreats, the encounter with the Real is impossible and yet also possible at the same time. Such paradox is also conveyed in the Lacanian aphorism "Be realistic: ask for the impossible." Conventionally, to be realistic signifies to only ask or engage in things that are possible. To ask for the impossible is to be unrealistic. In Zen fashion, Lacan turns the conventional understanding on its head. To access the unconventional Real, one must dare to engage in what appears to be impossible at least initially. For example, who as a Westerner would think of spending sixteen hours a day in meditation? Certainly only someone who must be a little bit crazy.

In addition, the lack in the Other can also be linked up with two other properties of the symbolic order as well as likened to the well-known Zen line from the Heart Sutra, "Form is emptiness and emptiness is form." First, given that every signifier is defined only by its differences from other signifiers, this emptiness of meaning of each singular signifier by itself is what sustains the interdependency of meaning within the structure. As noted earlier, nothing stands by itself separate from everything else. Second, the symbolic order is characterized by the fundamental dialectic of presence and absence. In the symbolic order everything exists upon a background of absence. Lacan notes that the signifier is used in the absence of the thing and that signifiers exist only in relationship to other absent signifiers. Thus, in the first case the emptiness of the signifier, or the fact that the self-existence of each singular signifier by itself is devoid of its own meaning (form is emptiness), enriches and supports the meaning of the signifying structure (emptiness is form), while in the second, the emptiness or absence of the thing and of the structure (form is emptiness) supports the symbolic form of the signifier (emptiness is form). In either case, emptiness and dialectical absence (which is also a presence) represent positive terms that do not annihilate either form or structure. Symbolic absence generates the production of new meaning, the shading and cascading of meaning within the function of metaphor and metonymy in language. Thus, within the Lacanian paradigm the lack in the Other represents not only the finitude of discourse and the impossibility of ever having the last word but also a source of creativity and inventiveness. Lacan's barred subject under the Symbolic not only undergirds the positive function of social laws but also the possibility of desire. Symbolic castration under the law of language is the price paid for accessing both desire and the emptiness of the subject.

Thus, when Lacan refers to the subject as a metaphor or a signifier that cancels/produces the subject as a breach or hole within discourse (the self is made of not-self elements), such negative terms (breach/hole) also need to be considered and understood in terms of the positive creativeness of the Buddhist not/naught or of the true self/subject as emptiness. Creative emptiness is more than just the absence of something. No-self is often confused with feelings of emptiness, as the absence of something, or as defensive detachment. It is only within the Symbolic that emptiness appears as a negative lack or hole. Within the Real itself emptiness is a plenum, as Lacan himself has pointed out. It is the Real as an empty plenum *(vacuum plenum)* that turns the hermeneutic wheel of enlightenment and begets the sparks of new poetic significations. Finally, in my view, the no-self or nonbeing under the Symbolic and the Real also has an affective and energic dimension. Nonbeing represents a creative symbolic death that in conjunction with Eros and life provides the quiescent energy that illuminates and holds the self together writ large. The self writ large points to a principle of self-cohesiveness (Engler, this volume) that is given not by a personal self but by the nature of bound energy and the larger interdependent symbolic structure.

Lacan also poses the concept of an anterior lack prior to the lack within the Symbolic (Verhaeghe 1998). The lack within language refers to the fact that once being appears within language it also disappears under language, given that there is a dimension of the Real and of being that cannot be said by language. Being appears as a lack within language to represent the Real (i.e., meditation experience). If you try to speak about the Real you feel lacking. But more fundamentally, there is an element of the Real that is lost in the process of birth itself. Being appears with birth but also disappears under birth. This process is repeated once again in language. What is lost with birth—life and underneath language—is the Real, the unborn, the thing or no-thing without a name. In relationship to this Real, Lacan says that the subject is the unborn and the unrealized. The question for our purposes is whether, following Buddhism, this subject is realizable.

With his notion of alienation of the ego under language and the signifier, Lacan purports to argue (not unlike Buddhism) that the subject has no substance and that therefore there is no self-realization. However, in Buddhism self-realization precisely signifies the realization of no-self or that the ego has no substance. To understand this point within the context of the Lacanian framework we need only apply Lacan's concept of "unknown knowing" *(l'insu qui sait)* or of the "knowing that does not know that it knows" to the question of the subject. Unconscious knowing or not-knowing refers both to repressed knowing in the analysand and unrepressed unconscious knowing in the analyst as manifested in the act of interpretation. Unconscious knowing refers to a knowing subject that does not exist or know as an ego but only as a subject. Unconscious or unknown knowing refers to an ego that is not and to an unborn subject that is or is the part of being lost in the process of becoming and gestation. But what is it? What is this subject? What is this unborn Real that is a no-thing without a name? Here both Lacan and Zen Buddhism tell us that the answer comes from the Real and not from language or the Symbolic. Developmentally for Lacan the subject has to separate not only from the mother and the Imaginary via the father and the Symbolic but also from the symbolic Other and the ideal father by realizing the nonexistence of the Other and of the ego. This paves the way to the real being of the subject, *son être du sujet*. Within Zen Buddhism, the answer to what is the subject or who is at the seat of unconscious knowing comes in the form of a sudden perceptual realization beyond language and logic into the empty essence of reality. In either case the act of autopoeisis, or *se parere*, as Lacan called it, of self-creation or self-realization—the emergence of a new subject or the being of the subject within the Real as well as the emergence of new signifiers and poetic significations—originates beyond mother and father, the Imaginary and the Symbolic, out of the vacuity of the Real and of the subject.

To conclude this section, the Buddhist notion of no-self does not conflict with the Lacanian paradigm given that this is precisely a point where both traditions coincide to a significant degree. Both could be said to converge on the Zen formula that "true self is no-self" or the Lacanian-informed formula that "true subject is no ego." Both formulas illustrate the realization that the true subject requires the symbolic death or deconstruction of imaginary ego-identifications and representations. It is the experience of no-self, of the subject as metaphor, emptiness, and quiescent energy, that grounds and constitutes what has been called the analytic attitude, the therapeutic stance, or what Lacan calls the subjective position of the analyst. As such, the subjective position of the analyst, as representing no-self, the power of metaphor, and bound energy, points in the direction of the evocation of a different state of mind than that associated with ordinary ego-experience. Thus, the practice of what Lacan calls benevolent depersonalization applied to both analyst and analysand constitutes the psychical equivalent of the experience of meditation in Zen and Buddhism in general.

The Direction of the Treatment, and the Subject and Power of the Unconscious

Lacan outlined some of his clinical notions in "The Direction of the Treatment and the Principles of Its Power" (1977c). In Lacanian psychoanalysis, the two elements of direction and power are correlated: for there to be a direction to the treatment the analyst has to renounce the ego-power granted to him/her by the analysand's transference and the therapeutic alliance between them. Rather than the analyst, it is the unconscious of the analysand that "knows" the truth manifesting through the symptom, but due to repression and concomitant disguises, the subject appears to ignore it. From this place of ignorance the analysand searches for an ideal "master" in the analyst.

Freud (1922) described the wish of people to look for leaders and leading ideas to hold authority over them. The analysand comes into analysis wanting the analyst to wield a curative power over him/her. Because of this, Lacan always insisted upon differentiating psychoanalysis from pastoral counseling or any other variety of counseling.

Lacan finds antecedents for the position of the analyst in the Stoics and the Socratic *mayeutics*. Socrates went around town engaging people in conversation about different subjects, appearing to know nothing and being willing to learn from everyone who professed to know. Socrates made profession of no knowledge except that of his own not-knowing. He believed that people know both less and more than what they think they know. To those who appeared to know he showed them that they actually did not know; to those who appeared not to know, he showed them that in fact they did know.

In the example of psychotherapy or the practice of analysis, patients come either positively or negatively predisposed to a therapeutic encounter/interaction. Entering the psychotherapeutic field already requires a certain ego-deflation or symbolic castration on the part of patients. They have to be willing to acknowledge a certain degree of suffering and inability to help themselves on their own. From this place of suffering, stagnation, and helplessness, patients reach out to the therapist/analyst. This is the place of not-knowing, of the subject of the unconscious, and of expecting and sometimes demanding that the analyst know something and wield a curative power.

When negatively predisposed, the ego of the analysand will display resistance and a devaluation of the knowledge of the analyst: "I know who I am, and nobody knows more about myself than me, and I do not think you can help me, and actually I am not doing so bad after all." Using Lacanian theory one can distinguish between the ego and the subject. The *ego* is the small mind of Zen Buddhism that already knows it all and has nothing to learn from anybody. The "I" is at the center of all statements. The ego says, "I know," "I have attained." The *subject* corresponds to the empty Big Mind of the beginner; it is innocent, does not claim to know, and is open and ready for surprises and new possibilities. But the key point is that access to the subject requires an ego-death. Although the ego claims to know, in reality it does not know, because it is the subject that in truth knows. Conversely, although the ego claims not to know, in reality it does know because the subject knows.

At this juncture it becomes all important that the analyst not respond to the patient from the place of his own ego. If the analysand, in the transference asks for a master of knowledge, the analyst should act from the place of not knowing, the equivalent of Socrates showing people that in fact they did know. But it is the unconscious subject of the patient who knows, not the ego. In the analytic situation, this truth cannot be brought forth other than by a renunciation on the part of the analyst. If the analysand claims to know and that the analyst does not, the analyst still responds—without self-consciousness—from the place of a knowing that does not know that it knows. The analyst needs to acknowledge that the individual knows but point in the direction of unconscious knowing by the subject and not the ego.

Therefore, according to Lacan, in order to renounce the power that the analysand gives the analyst at the outset of analysis, the analyst must make three payments or symbolic renunciations: with his/her person, with words, and with the core of his/her being. Such payments describe the spiritual depersonalization of the analyst and will be considered one at a time.

PAYMENT WITH ONE'S PERSON

To let go of the social ego requires a form of subjective destitution, at least a partial retreat from social behaviors and conditions, and a letting go of what Jung called the social mask or persona, our favorite ego-images and verbal platitudes. The analytic or therapeutic relationship is not a social relationship: it differs from professional work relations with peers, superiors, and subordinates, and it differs from relationships with lovers, teachers, family, and friends. It also differs from relationships with priests in that the analyst is not a moral guide or a guru. The analyst, like the Buddha, is no more than an arrow pointing inward to the patient's own intrinsic mind as the locus of truth and liberation.

In work relations, a certain measure of success, of striving toward goals and objectives, is expected from the ego. The ego is expected to know something under the performance requirements governing work relations. Nothing of this sort is expected in analytical practice. Analysis is the place where the ego can fail miserably, and all ego-ideals be suspect and subject to deconstruction. Even the most ungrammatical form of language will be accepted in analysis. Moreover, psychoanalysis thrives on mistakes, for they are access points or gateways to the unconscious. A Zen saying describes the life history of a Zen teacher as that of one continuous mistake or of one mistake after another. In addition, for the analysand the renunciation of a social relationship suspends the mental defenses operative through social discourse and results in an openness to inner experience.

In social, sexual, and familiar relations the ego desires, expects, and even demands things from others. The analyst pays with his person when renouncing those dispositions in relation to the analysand. The analyst must ultimately renounce even the desire to cure or provide a successful treatment to the patient. The reverse only intensifies the ego-resistance of the patient to the treatment. But then what are the gratifications "permitted" to the analyst? Money and livelihood for one thing. But this should not lead one to think that greediness toward money on the part of the analyst could not become a hindrance to the treatment and the therapeutic relationship. Ultimately the practice of analysis is a spiritual satisfaction.

Paying with one's person also requires renouncing personal values. Does this mean that there are no values implied in the therapy situation? I want to argue that the abstention of judgment implies values of a different order, or metavalues. Renunciation implies that values are there. Rather than ignore them or be value-blind, we need to go beyond them. We renounce values in order to achieve values on a different level. This point about metavalues will be elaborated and expounded further on.

For example, whenever a therapist encounters homophobia or dislike of homosexuality, or heterophobia or dislike of heterosexuality, sexism or dislike of men or women, addiction to prostitution or racism and anti-Semitism, it is not fruitful to try to reform the analysand into adopting the correct values. This will only engender argument and ego battles and wreck the therapeutic relationship. Rather, abstaining from preaching one's values will facilitate an exploration of the themes and conflicts that lie at the root of such ethical failures. In the long run, such abstention stands a much better chance of preventing problematic social attitudes and values.

I am not advocating a value-free or "objective" scientific approach. As I have established elsewhere (Moncayo 1998a), subjectivity is always implicit in any relationship between a knower and a known. It is not possible to avoid a subjective position. The question becomes one of how to work with our subjectivity in order to realize a subjectivity without a subject and effect a subjective or spiritual destitution. Truth is rectified error within the context of a permutation of subjective experience. Psychoanalysis, as I already observed, thrives on mistakes, and the life of a Zen teacher is that of one mistake after another. Ego-ideas and ego-ideals, in the sense of ideological false views (i.e., I am good at this, or my country, theory, teacher is the best), must be let go moment to moment, one piece at a time. To acknowledge being wrong and give up ego attachments to erroneous beliefs and assumptions requires a certain humility and sobriety of mind that is common to both the spiritual and scientific attitudes. It is this attitude that clears and prepares the mind for new insights to arise.

PAYMENT WITH WORDS, THE LANGUAGE OF THE UNCONSCIOUS AND OF NONDUALITY

The second renunciation is to pay with words. Another aspect wherein the therapeutic relationship differs from a social relationship is the type of dialogue that characterizes the use of language in analysis. This aspect of analysis coincides with what Dogen calls one of the eight awarenesses of an enlightened subject: avoiding idle speech. In contrast to a symmetrical dialogue where one person talks and another person responds, an interpretation, in the analytic sense of the term, means that one person speaks more and another speaks less. In addition, the analyst not only has to speak less but has to speak in a different manner. Within the psychoanalytic situation, dreams and unconventional linguistic formations, such as slips, puns, jokes, and so forth, are matched by the use of interpretative speech on the part of the analyst. As Roberto Harari (1985) has pointed out, interpretation requires fine tuning and a skillful use of words meant to evoke something different from conventional or ordinary speech.

Moreover, from a Lacanian perspective interpretative speech is not the speech of ordinary life in two significant respects: first, in analysis the analyst needs to allow what is equivocal, paradoxical, and ambiguous instead of expecting and utilizing forms of linear directive speech; and second, an interpretation should not be a move whose goal is to obtain something. In other words, interpretative speech, like poetical language, needs to be distinguished from any form of instrumental or communicative discourse. Interpretation does not aim at communication as a means for something else or at asking someone to do something, but rather aims at simply evoking and invoking a particular signification.

In passing, it should be noted that Jung (1953) had already realized the significance of paradox as a form of spiritual expression. He pointed out that all religious statements contain logical contradictions that are impossible in principle. Only paradox comes near to expressing the non-dual basis of life. Nonambiguity and noncontradiction are one-sided and therefore unsuited to express nonduality.

According to Lacan, *lalangue*, as the text or language of the unconscious, escapes the grammatical or formal logical organization of discourse. The signifying chain is composed of key signifiers that are polyvocal and equivocal in nature. Moreover, what is evoked by a paralogical use of language is the experience of the unconscious, which for our purposes has certain similarities with a spiritual definition of experience. Within Zen Buddhism the realm of a non-dual reality—equivalent to a spiritual register of experience—is expressed by a nondualistic or unconventional use of conventional language. Metaphorical intuitive utterance transgresses and elevates the ordinary meaning of words. Our thesis here is that because the reality of the Zen Buddhist "Bid Mind" includes a core experience beyond language and symbolization, its expression within language requires a different use of language from that of formal social/logical language and the language of science.[2]

For example, a student asks the Zen ancestor Joshu, "What is spirituality?" Joshu responds, "A puddle of urine in the Buddha land [or holy land]." The student then asks, "Could you show it to me?" and Joshu responds, "Do not tempt me." In another case, the student asks, "What is Buddha?" and the teacher responds, "Ten pounds of flax" (or cloth symbolizing the four layers of robes worn by a Zen priest). Far from simply constituting heretical statements, such senseless or nonsensical enunciations are aimed at dislodging the student from ego-ideals, from imaginary, dualistic conceptions of Buddha and spirituality. Spirituality is not something sacred and pompous opposed to something mundane or ordinary. In another example, the Zen teacher asks, "What do you hit in order to get the cart to move, the horse or the cart?" The ordinary dualistic response would be "The horse, naturally!" But in the classical Zen story, the teacher responds that you hit the cart instead!

A deviant, innovative, and surprising utterance plays with the binary structure of formal language to make it say something that escapes the determining duality of social language. But from a purely social conventional point of view, such speech constitutes a payment with one's person because it risks being perceived as unusual, peculiar, foolish, and even downright deviant.

Lacan also made a distinction between empty and full speech. The analysand often wastes time by focusing on trivialities or rationalizations that remain far removed from the causal core of the subject's suffering. Thus analysis, as the discourse of the unconscious, is concerned with unfolding not so much the well-known story line but rather the unknown dreams and unconscious core themes and phantasies.

In listening, the analyst needs to localize in the flux of speech the capital elements or signifiers, the signifying diamonds and nuggets amid the coal and dross of ordinary speech. Thus, to pay with words is to elevate the use of words as done by the dreamwork. It implies a conversion of being to a more truthful and essential state. But just as the dreamwork is constructed or woven by a larger unconscious subjectivity than the ego, so in interpretative speech the speaking ego or enunciator should be canceled as much as possible in favor of the enunciation from the place of no-self. In order to raise the analytical function, the analyst needs to speak from the place of no-self (the unknown knowing subject), where the ego as the enunciator is canceled as much as possible in favor of allowing the power of the signifier to transform and illuminate the subject. The *aphanisis* (disappearance) of the ego results in the epiphany (appearance) of the subject: true subject is no-ego (Moncayo

1998c). Thus, the cognitive ego is not the agent of insight but rather is the subject that bears witness to the lightning of wit and knowing contained within the treasure chest of the signifier.

In addition, the interpretative saying should be concise, with little emphasis on rational syntaxis and conjunction. Sayings should be surprising and fresh. Thus, defined in this way, the use of language in psychoanalytic practice acquires a remarkable similarity with the proverbial use of language in spiritual discourse. Both imply an enunciation from the place of no-self and the corresponding *aphanisis* or disappearance of the ego.

Thus, the fact that a spiritual register of experience and the Lacanian dimension of the Real exist outside language does not mean that we are left in a position of not being able to say anything about the core of our experience. Silence does not necessarily possess more truth value to express the Real—although sometimes it may. By now it is well known that Lacan's aphorism "The unconscious is structured like a language" should not be interpreted as meaning that the structure of the unconscious is identical to the structure of social language. Rather, the unconscious has the structure of a different kind of language—the language of the unconscious. This is precisely the meaning we give to our statement that the evocation and expression of the Real requires a different use of language. As we've seen, Lacan even gave a different name to the symbolic language of the unconscious: *lalangue*. *Lalangue* thrives on the homophonic or metaphorical rather than grammatical or syntactic elements of language.

Herewith are presented two case vignettes as examples of *lalangue*. The first will primarily exemplify the homophonic element, the second the metaphoric. An analysand had been struggling over not wanting to have "two sessions a week." He was also in conflict with seeing his struggle as having anything to do with the analyst. At the beginning of the next session he made a comment regarding the waiting room: "Your waiting room is too weak." I have said that *lalangue* appears as a deviant or peculiar predication. Somebody could say that this must be a grammatical mistake; no English speaker would say that a waiting room is "too weak"! And yet the fact remains that this was an educated native English speaker. The analyst responded by saying, "Two a week is too weak." Again, a deviant predication is matched by a peculiar interpretation. This analysand, who, for purposes of confidentiality will be represented here by the letter J. (the signifier is what represents the subject for another signifier—the analyst) and who was marked and effected/affected by being named after an Aunt whom his father envied (the subject appears first in the Other), was caught in an imaginary ego-struggle with the analyst. To the resistance of his imaginary ego, two sessions a week represented an imaginary form of castration. I say imaginary, because he was not ready for a symbolic renunciation (castration) of his ego-resistance. Thus, he wanted to tell me in some way that it was not he but I who was weak. He chose the small size and poor taste of the waiting room to say this. On the other hand, the unconscious text chose a word or signifier ("weak") that was homophonically linked to the two signifiers that represented castration in his mind ("two a week"). The analysand was making an imaginary or ego-defensive use of the symbolic link, whereas the analyst appeals to the *aphanisis* or disappearance of the imaginary ego and the appearance or epiphany of the metaphoric subject as an effect of the signifier. Once the text of *lalangue* becomes linked via the act of interpretation, it is no longer a question of an imaginary ego-to-ego relationship. The subject is represented by the signifier and the laws of the Symbolic.

In the second example, an analysand is telling me how he has been able to be effortless and timely in his current university studies. He jokes that he is dictating and that I should write down what he is saying. He associates this to being effortless in playing the trumpet as a young boy until he had to put in effort to match the high notes of another student. Both of these comments served as introductions to his problem of not being able to put any effort into writing and finally finishing his dissertation. Then his associations go to his obsessive thoughts that his parents will die. He grew up in fear that his mother would die, and he says that his father wants to live forever but that he wants him to die. I interpreted that his efforts are geared toward remaining a child of his mother and not growing up. If his parents die then he has to be a man instead of his mother's boy. Being a man for him means paying a price, such as losing his hair and not having feminine objects of desire. (In prior sessions, the analysand had spoken about his fears as well as his desires to be a grown-up responsible man. He feared losing his hair like his father. He also had a dream where he was pregnant with a boy.) His response to my intervention was to quote a revered figure of his to the effect that being a man means having the baton of the phallus. "That's having something," I said, "whereas for you being a man has represented not having hair like your father. Baldness is the baton."

"Baldness is the baton" represents the symbolic phallus as a resisted absence that nevertheless generates a symbolic consistency and efficacy for the subject. It is also interesting that Zen priests symbolically shave their heads as a signifier of renunciation. Obviously, Zen priests would interpret head shaving not in this way, but as a symbol of non-attachment. Nevertheless, psychoanalysis focuses on self-representation as a function of identification with objects of desire. This is what Engler (this volume) calls being somebody. "Somebody" refers to the ideas we have about ourselves with or without hair. Even becoming a priest could acquire the meaning of something or someone to be desired. In addition, the symbolic *act* of interpreting an unconscious idea/meaning may have a similar effect to the symbolic act of shaving the head. Both are aimed at releasing the subject from fixed ideas or self-representations. However, Zen focuses on how subjective experience is reflected in the external meaning of an act, whereas psychoanalysis focuses primarily on a dialectic between concealed and revealed meanings.

Internally, the self-idea, the being somebody, is a hallucinated or phantasized object, whereas externally the phallic object/signifier is revealed as empty or as a purely symbolic form. A Zen act has the advantage of directly taking the subject beyond the dualities of language, but an analytical act of interpretation, conceived as a non-dual use of language, leaves the subject open, bare, and without the option of defensively hiding behind formal appearances of detachment or authority.

Payment with the Core of One's Being, the Desire of the Analyst, and the Question of Metavalues.

The third payment required of the analyst is payment with the core of his or her being. Lacan invents the concept of the desire of the analyst and declares it the hub around which all analysis turns. Why? Because Lacan believed that Freud not only created a new discursive situation but also invented a new subjective position: that of the analyst.

Lacan states that the desire of the analyst is something different from the desire of the other. He also remarks that it is neither the vocational desire to be an analyst nor the personal desire of each analyst: it is an impersonal desire for death—not for dying, but for death. Death here represents what is known in Zen as the great death of Nirvana. This kind of symbolic death is beyond birth and death as we usually know them. The desire for death or of death is not a death wish in the usual sense of the aim of the death drive in terms of hetero- or auto-aggression. A desire of death involves not doing what is customary with desire, which is to attempt to be desired. The analyst must first seek to be desired but then ensure that the analysand directs this desire toward others. This is the most difficult renunciation to accept because it requires that the analyst relinquish the ideal (egoic) position in which the analysand has placed him or her. This is what is stoic about the analyst—the analyst has to auto-induce or self-introduce a narcissistic wound. At this juncture the importance of termination can be clearly discerned. There is something deadly both in the desire of the analyst and the termination of analysis in the sense of the cutting off and non-attachment associated with the death drive. Although analyst and analysand have had a very intimate and profound relationship, perhaps the most intimate and private relationship the analysand has ever had with anyone, the relationship has to inevitably end. This appears to be contrary to Eros, that always leans toward union and synthesis. If it were simply a matter of love, the analysis would never end. Why would the analysand leave another who has understood the alphabet and letters of their experience and has possibly helped them more than their own parents. The relationship with parents, for example, never ends. On the side of the analyst, why would the analyst leave another who loves and cherishes them? Therefore, Lacan has argued that for the analysis to end, the analyst has to become a discardable waste product (from letter to the litter). As one Zen ancestor once said, "Buddha is a shit-stick." (In olden times, sticks were used as the equivalent of toilet paper.) From this vantage point, one can understand why the analyst's desire is a special subjective position requiring a payment with the core of one's being. The analyst must work on something having to do with his or her own desire. This makes it the most decisive and fundamental of the three payments. It is only on the basis of such payment that one can tolerate paying with words and with one's person. Only if the analyst declines to put himself/herself in the position of being desired for life can he/she attack his/her own ego-identity by leaving aside values, choices, and other narcissistic gratifications.

With the notion of payment with the core of one's being we return to the question of revisioning the ethical structure and the intrinsic spirituality of the analytic situation. I mentioned earlier that the values emanating from the level of the tree of life of nonduality (of good and evil) correspond to those associated with the practice of analysis. Analytical values are related to a sublimated death drive or to a death drive that in the end crosses over to the other side, the side of Eros. Regarding so-called health values, the Buddha, like Freud, is known to have used the well-known parable of the surgeon. The doctor has to extract the arrow from the body, cutting and temporarily causing more pain, in order for the wound and the body to heal and live. The practice of cutting, separating, *desetring* or nonbeing, discarding, letting go, and nonattachment are all the manifestations of a non-dual good connected with the symbolic register of the death drive. It is in this sense that Lacan linked the symbolic order to the function of the death drive. However, I am also linking a sublime reach of death or nirvana with Eros, which is something that Lacan did not explicitly do. Thus, in unison with the gospel and genesis I submit that there is a life that leads to death and a death that leads to life, or, put dialectically and nondualistically, there is life within death (under the nirvana principle) and death within life (under the pleasure principle). I argue that the Eros, which I associate with what Lacan called the second death under the symbolic order (i.e., the "no" of the father "kills" the ego as an imaginary object of the mother's desire), precisely refers to a distinction between the jouissance of the Other, and an Other jouissance that others (e.g., Miller 1997) have found implicit in Lacan's work.

The deadly aspect of mystical experience destroys identity in the sense that it destroys the illusory or imaginary notion of ego. Zen practice, for example, is commonly referred to as leading to an ego-death. It is a necessary symbolic death that dialectically affirms a larger and more ultimate form of psychical identity. Thus, I have stated that mystical experience and Lacanian psychoanalysis share a practice of what Lacan calls subjective or mental/psychical destitution and benevolent depersonalization.

The same can be said with respect to paying with one's person as a form of renunciation or negation of personal values. I have argued that the abstention of judgment implies values of a different order or metavalues. In a way I am using Abraham Maslow's (1968) concept of metavalues but conceive of them in the context of a Zen Buddhist concept of nonduality, the Freudian/Lacanian/Buddhist understanding of a symbolic death, and the Freudian/Nietszchean notion of a transvaluation of psychical values.

It is well known that moral values, or what I am calling superego values, operate within a classical dual relationship to desire. In addition, superego values are often fervently desired and compel one to forbidden desire.

The dividing, aggressive component of superego judgments, although having a social utility, nevertheless need to be neutralized under the influence of a non-dual Eros that is not the opposite of hate and that is cultivated and evoked by the renunciations contained within the desire of the analyst. The life of desire, of dual love, quickly turns into hate and deadly aggression, and hate, once socialized, quickly turns into dual morality and resentment. Thus, both dual desire and morality end up on the shore of a death that is the end of life. I have also mentioned that the desire of the analyst, which is a desire for emptiness or for no particular object, can be seen as a desire for death, for nirvana, for the serenity of a symbolic death that gives rather than ends life. It gives life because a desire for emptiness, or an emptiness at the root of desire, regenerates rather than negates or ends desire. A desire not to desire would still be just another desire. Emptiness as the end/aim of desire is not the end or extinction of desire. Thus, the desire of the analyst is also Buddha's desire. And Buddha's desire or the desire of the analyst, although beginning from the condition of death and suffering produced by a dual life of desire and morality, generates a transvaluation of psychical values that illuminates the meaning of a second symbolic death at the service of life and "rebirth." On this latter shore, life and death, Eros and nirvana, do not constitute polar elements but constitute two sides of the same ground.

Freud spoke of the transvaluation of psychical values in reference to the workings of repression: what was pleasant becomes unpleasant and vice versa. The moral good replaces the good of pleasure by turning the latter into something bad, and the bad of frustration into something good. The practice of analysis reverses this process: the moral good or superego becomes suspect, and the bad of desire becomes once again something good and acceptable to the analyst. But since psychoanalysis is not a hedonism, this cannot be the end of the story. Becoming intimate with one's desire is not equivalent to the fulfillment of human desire, which is something impossible.

The dialectical reversal and transvaluation whereby the good becomes bad, the bad becomes good, life becomes death, and death becomes life, the crossing over to the other side, are classical examples not only of the workings of the psyche, of analysis as a therapeutic practice, but also of spiritual practices that seek the non-dual unity of reality by turning one term into its opposite.

In addition, this dialectical reversal also operates in intersubjective relations. For example, at first the analysand comes representing the side of suffering, division, death, the "I am dying, I cannot live like this," and the analyst represents the possibility of life, unity, love, and reconciliation. At the end of analysis a transvaluation of these values needs to take place. The analyst needs to move to the place of the second death, of a spiritual death that renews life by renouncing the desire to be desired and ultimately ending the relationship with the analysand. The analysand needs to move from the place of death and suffering to the place of recovering the possibility of love and of loving someone else, not the analyst.

The place of the second death is that of the freeing of the libido from archaic objects in the transference and therefore also eventually from the analyst/therapist. It is an experience equivalent to grief and grieving the lost objects as images that define the ego or with which the ego is identified; and therefore the second death also represents a loss at the level of the ego, a subjective permutation and psychical destitution. Finally, the peace of nirvana, of the second death, is associated with nonpathological grief because it represents freedom from attachment and an eventual return to the natural quiescence of the mind.

The relationship between a symbolic death and the desire of the analyst can also be observed in what can be called the sacrificial aspect of the position of the analyst as support for the transference. To exercise the analytic position, the analyst needs to withstand the love and hate of the analysand as a function of transference and not as response to past or present behavior of the analyst toward the analysand. The analyst takes on the problems of the analysand as if they were his own, insofar as the analyst will be perceived by the analysand as having done this or that to him or her, either literally or figuratively. Moreover, if we follow the Kleinian school with the concept of projective identification, the metaphor is complete: the analyst gets to feel and experience mental states that are not his own in order to metabolize them and return them to the analysand in a more benevolent and favorable form. Moreover, if the analyst is hated and verbally attacked in the transference, the analyst is not to respond in kind but rather merely provide interpretations. Here the similarity between the position of the analyst and that of the archetypal Christ is relatively obvious. According to Catholic dogma Jesus took on the sins of the world in order to enact the function of a huge recycling container for the thoughts, feelings, and actions of the human world. From this perspective, one can get another glimpse regarding the intrinsic spirituality of the analytical situation, which does not require even a single mention of an ethical or religious counsel or teaching.

Finally, it can also be argued that the desire of the analyst produces what Maslow (1968) named a B-cognition, or a knowing of being that is impersonal, without human desire, unmotivated, unattached, and not centered or based on the ego. Maslow likened the B-cognition to what Krishnamurti called choiceless or desireless awareness. Such an awareness bestows the ability to perceive the ineffable, that which cannot be put into words. A choiceless or desireless awareness is another way of talking about paying with one's person in terms of renouncing personal choices and preferences and paying with the core of one's being as a desire not to be desired.

From this vantage point, it becomes possible to arrive at a different understanding of the meaning of the alleged consolations provided by both religion and psychoanalysis. The consolation provided by psychoanalysis needs to be included in the equation because, as a therapeutics, psychoanalysis encompasses a solution to the problem of suffering, even if only partially. Psychoanalysis prides itself on being able to tolerate absences or lacks: of perfection, religion, an ideal sexual relation, an ideal marriage or society, and so on. Psychoanalysis denounces the imaginary crutches and consolations provided by religion as either infantile and dysfunctional symbiosis with the mother or infantile dependence on a providential father. Both of these forms are seen as being intrinsic to the symbolic lies and imaginary deceptions of love. However, the psychoanalytic tolerance of absence is the cultural analogue to the religious function of renunciation, nonattachment, and the ability to be alone in the face of the Real. *Analytic absence* cannot be dualistically regarded as sheer absence. Such absence produces not a positive fetish, an imaginary phallic or religious object, but an ethical presence, a psychical and energic position/state within the analyst. For the analyst it functions as a source of consolation in the sense of a core of being associated with self-control, equanimity, and a therapeutic stance.

Commentary

WHERE IS THE "SPIRIT" IN A SPIRITUAL CONCEPTION OF PSYCHOANALYSIS?

M. GUY THOMPSON

The juxtaposition of Zen Buddhism with the notoriously abstract conceptualizations of Jacques Lacan may come as a surprise to those who view Lacan's output as anything but a spiritually informed psychoanalysis. Yet Raul Moncayo makes a compelling argument that there are at least some aspects of Lacan's theory and clinical philosophy that parallel the teachings of Zen. Although Moncayo's essay is limited to a relatively narrow reading of this thesis, it nevertheless offers insight into the nature of Lacan's maddeningly impenetrable oeuvre as well as Zen practice itself.

Moncayo begins with a cautionary statement to the effect that a proper integration of Buddhism and psychoanalysis should not be confused with attempts to enjoin religious and therapeutic principles in the form of pastoral counseling and the like. Indeed, Moncayo includes the work of Jung, Tillich, Frankl, May, Meissner, and Jones as that of only some of the many analysts whom he believes have confused pastoral counseling with psychoanalysis. Rather, he seeks to exploit those aspects of religious practice—in this case, Zen—that affect the mind of the psychoanalytic patient in a positive manner. Specifically, he sees pastoral counseling as an inherently "suggestive" therapy that transforms the role of the practitioner from one whose principal task is to *listen* into a mandate to "guide" one's charge toward becoming a morally enlightened individual. It is Moncayo's intention to outline a perspective on the relationship between the practice of analysis and spiritual practice that avoids the pitfall of viewing analysis as a form of explicit moral treatment in the narrow sense of the term. Instead, he characterizes Zen as an example of a spiritual experience that shares similarities with the so-called analytic attitude.

That said, I found it confusing at the start as to what Moncayo intends by "spiritual practice." Is the word "spiritual" employed in a specifically religious context or should it be understood as a more secular (e.g., ontological) concept in the sense that Heidegger (1962), for example, employs it? This is a distinction of no small import. Virtually all religions, including Buddhism, use the term "spiritual" in an explicitly religious context. Judaism, Christianity, and Islam, for example, speak of the spirit or "soul" as that aspect of the individual that survives death and encounters heaven or hell sometime after; moreover, while alive one's spirit is capable of some form of communion with God, though the specific nature of such communion varies from one religion (or sect) to the next. Hence the spiritual person is "in touch" with God, and will meet God in the hereafter. Whereas most schools of Buddhism do not speak of God specifically, they nevertheless recognize a subtle process of continuity that survives death and is subsequently reborn as a human or other life form in the next life; the Buddhist endeavors to live in such a way as to avoid this ceaseless cycle of death and rebirth.

Because Moncayo says nothing about his understanding of the term "spiritual," we are left wondering what is specifically spiritual about a Zen-informed practice of Lacanian analysis. If it simply implies an increase in one's capacity for compassion for others, why call this spiritual? Many analysts would argue that an increase in one's capacity for love is a common benefit of analytic treatment, but they wouldn't necessarily term this capacity spiritual in nature. Yet Moncayo, in his effort to distinguish a proper psychoanalytic use of Zen from the pastoral variety, seems to part company with those analysts who embody an explicitly "spiritual" agenda.

On the other end of the spectrum Moncayo is critical of analysts who view psychoanalysis as a purely rational or intellectual exercise that is devoid of a spiritual foundation, such as the ego psychology model that lacks a "spiritual dimension of experience." As anyone who is familiar with Lacan's writings knows, he views ego psychology as emblematic of everything that has gone wrong with the evolution of psychoanalysis since Freud's death. I suspect many American analysts will find this argument somewhat tired and, perhaps, overstated. After all, Moncayo cites Loewald, one of the most prominent ego psychologists in America, as an example of someone he perceives as *not* guilty of this shortcoming! Perhaps what Moncayo means by the phrase "spiritual dimension of experience" is too subtle a notion by which to measure entire schools of analytic practice. More to the point, he takes issue with those analysts who endeavor to form a therapeutic alliance (a cardinal principle of ego psychology) because, in his view, such alliances are rationalistic in nature. But Moncayo's point is well taken when he suggests that many analysts (ego psychological or otherwise, I would argue) reduce free association to little more than a means of obtaining data about the patient's unconscious instead of a specifically non-rationalistic mode of thinking that has the potential for facilitating an experience with one's Being. However tantalizing this observation may be, I believe his argument would be more compelling were he to explore what he means by the spiritual dimension to the free associative experience in more detail.

Readers who are not already familiar with Lacanian analysis will find Moncayo's treatment of its theoretical foundations challenging, to say the least. The principal concepts that bring Zen and Lacan together on the theoretical front are their respective views about the nature of the ego or self, and a comparison between the Zen notion of the "void" or "emptiness" and Lacan's conception of the "Real" or unconscious. For example, Zen Buddhists see the self as an illusion, thus the purpose of Zen practice is to gain insight into the self's true nature. Lacan argues that the ego of the structural model is also an illusion and that the true subject is "other" than the ego, so that the latter is little more than the seat of resistance to the analytic process. This cuts against the grain of just about all the other psychoanalytic schools (with the possible exception of Melanie Klein) and lends Lacanian analysis its radical bent. In Moncayo's view the purpose of free association is to short-circuit the dominance of the ego's rationalistic nature by allowing for the "subject" to slip through the ego's defenses in the form of parapraxes and the like. This can also be compared to the Zen koan whereby the Zen master speaks in riddles and paradoxes in order to shock the disciple into yielding to a form of consciousness that is not dependent on intellectual gymnastics. This point is well taken and is an interesting departure from conventional psychoanalytic practice.

The respective characterizations of Zen's "no-self" and Lacan's "unconscious subject" dovetail with their respective theories about the Void and the Real. Because there is no self in the conventional sense, human experience can be characterized as one of emptiness, a thesis reflected in Heidegger's conception of Being and Sartre's (1956) notion of "nothingness" (which was inspired by his reading of Heidegger and Nietzsche). One of the principal goals of Zen is to recognize that our existence has this "empty" quality, including the identifications that comprise one's ego, eliciting a frame of mind in which one is compelled to question assumptions, a principle shared by most schools of psychoanalysis. Lacan puts his own special twist on this by claiming that the ego is incapable of recognizing its true nature. Hence the Real can never be "known" directly but can only be experienced in a noncognitive, paradoxical fashion. This sounds more like Nietzsche than

Freud, and no doubt both Nietzsche's and Heidegger's influence comes through in some of Lacan's most novel concepts. As Moncayo emphasizes, even words ultimately fail us because one's truth cannot be captured "in" words but can only be approximated or experienced *through* words, a conclusion that will come as a surprise to those who hold that Lacan reduces the analytic experience to language. It seems that this is also a point where Moncayo, following Zen, goes further than Lacan in emphasizing the limited function of language in the analytic process. Moncayo sounds even more like Heidegger than Lacan does when he characterizes the principal goal of analysis as "an encounter with Being."

Conceptually, one can see that both the Zen and Lacanian emphases on the empty nature of the self should serve as a foil to those patients (or adepts) who favor intellectualization as their defense. This takes us to the section of Moncayo's essay where he explores how Lacan puts these theories into practice, in the context of the treatment situation. Here one would expect Moncayo to seize on the most controversial (but arguably, the most "Zen") of Lacan's technical interventions, the "short session," but Moncayo neglects to discuss this pivotal issue. Instead, he frames Lacan's clinical philosophy in the guise of "three forms of payment" that the analyst must observe in his or her analytic stance with patients. One of Lacan's principal concerns was with the manner in which patients typically fashion their transference with the analyst. Lacan believed that patients, engaging in a form of what Kohut termed "idealizing" transference, unfailingly view their analyst as a fount of wisdom who has all the answers to what is the matter with them and how they should set out to fix it. Accordingly, he saw the analyst's principal task as one of thwarting the patient's efforts to lure the analyst into assuming this role. According to Moncayo, "in order to renounce the power that the analysand gives the analyst at the outset of analysis, the analyst must make three payments or symbolic renunciations: with his/her person, with words, and with the core of his/her being." These three forms of "payment" go something like this:

1. Payment "with one's person" more or less follows Freud's rules of neutrality and abstinence, in that the analyst views the nature of his relationship with patients as inherently different from other kinds of relationship with which analytic patients are typically familiar,

including relationships with peers, superiors, subordinates, lovers, teachers, friends, and so on. This is because the analyst should resist the role of guide or mentor who sets out to "treat" the patient's illness in the manner that a psychiatrist, for example, would be expected to, or to cater to one's needs in the manner that a friend or lover might. Like one image of the Zen master, the analyst should be inscrutable and not be fooled into helping patients "succeed" at their endeavor but, on the contrary, helping them fail. Only then will they be capable of truly questioning what they are doing by recognizing that the project of making their ego "feel good" has made them a slave to social convention. According to Moncayo, "the analyst must ultimately renounce even the desire to cure or provide a successful treatment to the patient," thereby relinquishing whatever need the analyst may have to please his patients by gratifying their demands for satisfaction.

Here Moncayo raises the issue of spirituality once more when he says that "the practice of analysis is a spiritual satisfaction," not a material one. This again begs the question as to what Moncayo means by the term "spiritual," but it would appear to mirror, at least in this context, Freud when he said that patients who crave the analyst's love must learn "to give up a satisfaction which lies to hand …in favor of a more distant one, which is perhaps altogether uncertain, but which is psychologically …unimpeachable" (1915, 170). (Does this signal a "spiritual" dimension to Freud's technical principles as well?)

2.   In the analyst's "payment with words" the rule of abstinence is even more pronounced in that the analyst takes care to measure his words in order to increase their effect. This pertains to the use of interpretation, and in Lacan's hands interpretations should not endeavor to "explain" the patient's experience but should rather take the patient by surprise, by startling and unsettling the patient's cozy relationship with his ego. The Zen-like aspect of this technical principle can be discerned in the view that interpretations should be paradoxical in nature, prompting patients to access a "higher" form of insight. Similarly, the Zen master avoids idle chatter and speaks only when he has something to say.

3. Finally, "payment with the analyst's being" dovetails with Freud's admonition against "therapeutic ambition," by monitoring one's countertransference in order to avoid the innate tendency to be "helpful" when help is asked for; in effect, this elicits from the analyst a form of sacrifice in his abandoning the wish to effect miracles and any hopes of terminating the treatment with the patients' gratitude for all he has done for them. Moncayo sees this as the most fundamental of the three "forms of payment" expected of the analyst, the reason being that unless analysts can overcome their need to be loved by their patients they will be incapable of tolerating the two other "payment" schemes.

Moncayo observes there is something stoic about this principle, depriving the analyst of a warm or comfortable relationship with his patients, a sacrifice that many contemporary analysts will dispute but that "classical" analysts have been advocating for some time. Indeed, there is something ironic about Lacan's criticism of that very school of analysis—ego psychology—that has elevated the standard for the use of abstinence considerably further than even Freud intended, in a manner that reflects Lacan's predilections.[3]

The remainder of Moncayo's essay returns to the question of the ego (or self) in both Zen and Lacanian analysis and the manifestation of "ego death" as a therapeutic aim. The notion of some form of death, psychological or otherwise, is a hallmark of Lacan's work, and Moncayo gives the notion due importance in his essay. But what precisely is meant by such a term? One of the criticisms of Lacan's thesis is that it appears to reduce analysis to the destruction of narcissism, embodied in the patient's love of himself. It should be noted that, despite Lacan's claims to "return to Freud" in his theoretical formulations, this is contrary to Freud's thesis that the typical neurotic is not *sufficiently* narcissistic. This is especially cogent with the obsessional neurotic, a class of patient Lacan devoted his analytic technique to treating. In Freud's view the obsessional is already so guilt-ridden and dissociated that he is incapable of living his desire, opting instead to serve "moral" values that rationalize sacrificing his desires for the purported "benefit" of others.

This raises the issue of Lacan's "short session" that Moncayo fails to mention in his essay, a technique, arguably more than any other, that reflects the paradoxical nature of Zen. Briefly, Lacan felt that guaranteeing patients fifty-minute sessions no matter how they use them only encourages them to waste the allotted time by saying nothing of consequence until the session is about to end. In order to subvert such strategies Lacan opted to end his sessions without warning, sometimes five minutes into the session, without apology or explanation. The patient was obliged to wonder why the session ended in such a fashion and returned the next day fearful of a repetition of the same. According to Stuart Schneiderman (1983), Lacan was also prone to charging his patients whatever fee he decided from one session to the next (but *not* based upon the length of the session), taking an occasional swig of whiskey, counting his money while his patient was free associating, and any number of other strange behaviors, all for the purpose of unsettling the patient's expectation as to how the analyst should behave.

By such behavior, Lacan elevated the rule of abstinence to unprecedented levels, all for the purpose of shattering the patient's (egoic) expectations, and ostensibly shocking the patient into a more rarefied state of consciousness. Whether such ploys proved successful we do not know, because the very concept of "success" has also been abandoned along with any other expectation! Yet according to Freud, this form of punishment is not likely to work on obsessional neurotics because such tactics will likely excite them even further by fueling their insatiable guilt. In practice, Freud (1919) advocated a diminished use of abstinence with this patient population in order to avoid falling into a trap. (It was only with those hysterics who thrive on attention that he advised a pronounced dosage of withholding.)

It is therefore surprising that Moncayo would end his essay with the proposition that the aim of analysis is for the patient to "love someone else, but *not* the analyst." With the employment of such measures one wonders, *how?* It is difficult to see how simply thwarting the patient's quest for the analyst's love would *in itself* enhance the patient's capacity to love anyone. Moreover, Moncayo proposes that analyst and patient alike are joined in common cause by a *mutual suffering through deprivation*, even comparing the position of the analyst with that of Christ who "suffered for the sins of mankind." It seems to me this sentiment smacks more of Catholicism than Zen. Indeed, Lacan's outlook has been characterized as one of "catholicizing" psychoanalysis for precisely this reason, due to the prominence he places on the experience of thwarted expectations. My understanding of Zen is that it advocates a more benign sensibility. If anything, Zen is an inherently joyful exercise that aspires to elicit the adept's capacity to love *in and through the Zen master's example.*

It goes without saying that love is rarely discussed in the psychoanalytic literature, and according to many it should be avoided. On the other hand, when one talks about the spiritual dimension to psychoanalytic practice, the need for love and its presence should not be ignored. I would venture that the spiritual aspect of Zen (or any other religion) always, in some measure or other, pertains to love, even when one exercises a restraint that is guaranteed to disappoint. However compassionately such restraint is exercised and however noble one's motives for employing it, the expression of love is deservedly anticipated, even if its manifestation is given in the form of a handshake, a smile, or the tone of one's voice. I would hope that Lacan's method of analysis, however Zen-like, can find a place for the expression of love, even at its most measured level.

Reply

PSYCHOANALYSIS AS A SECULAR AND NONTHEISTIC SPIRITUALITY

RAUL MONCAYO

I would like to thank Michael Thompson for his thoughtful comments on my essay and will attempt to address his major questions more or less in the order raised. The review of an author as thoughtful as Thompson provides any writer an invaluable opportunity to clarify and reformulate the basic cogency of the arguments.

Noting Thompson's comment about the difficulty of Lacanian ideas for readers who are not familiar with his thought, I would like to acknowledge that the impenetrability of the style is something that is common to both Zen and Lacan. Both use language and concepts in a non-dual way in order to invoke an enigmatic dimension of experience and of the mind that cannot be described by the binary (dual) and lineal characteristic of language and formal logic. Zen koans and Lacanian aphorisms, like poetry, use the evocative (and perhaps even provocative) more than the explicative function of language. To speak/read what is impossible to speak/read can be quite a frustrating (although ultimately rewarding) experience, not unlike the experience of analysis. In this regard, in both meditation and analysis, the actual practice illuminates and facilitates a way through explanation and knowing. Without the experience, the concepts discussed may be more difficult to understand. Moreover, new ideas and perspectives may be preceded by what Lacan called "not understanding"—or not knowing, as Zen would have it. This not understanding leads to practice, which then may lead to understanding. Having said this, wherever possible, I will make every effort to clarify and unpack the concepts but without compromising the content of what needs to be said.

The first major question raised by Thompson addresses the difference between a spiritual and a secular conception of the mind/spirit. As I observed, the Enlightenment sought not only the elimination of religion but also a more authentic form of spirituality. Four ways of conceiving the relationship between psychoanalysis and spirituality arose under the influence of the Enlightenment. First, there is the secular version of spirituality that objectifies and demystifies religious illusions under the guidance and purview of reason and the scientific process. In this category only the secular perspective remains. However, what is lost in the process is the evocation of a dimension of human experience that was realized within the experiential field of traditional practices and remains unaccounted for by the secularization process. For example, many scientists believe that spiritual experience is an illusion better accounted for by scientific categories. It could be argued that because psychoanalysis, and perhaps science in general, historically gave only a partial and biased account of spiritual phenomena and experience, they remain vulnerable to the same dogmatic fundamentalism that they criticized in religion. In fact, many have criticized orthodox psychoanalysis as being tantamount to a secular form of religion in the bad sense of the term. Religiosity in this regard, whether in science or spirituality, represents a rigid adherence to concepts or methods that function as basic articles of faith.

A second trend of Enlightenment spirituality, within the Western spiritual traditions themselves, kept the baby of what is specific and true to the spiritual field, but threw out the bath water of religion by absorbing the secular critique of its field. The pastoral counseling field would be a good example of this trend. By incorporating the techniques of psychotherapy within a religious context, religions are able to neutralize the more radical and atheistic expressions of secular knowledge regarding the soul (psyche). In this instance, the secular disappears under the spiritual principle.

Thirdly, it is within the context of the struggle between the secular and the sacred that Buddhism was introduced into the West. Buddhism arrived free of a historical antagonism between science and religion. In addition, Buddhism could be seen either as a religion or as a practical philosophy of life and in general spoke of a middle way or a non-dual relation between the secular and the sacred. Here nonduality represents a both/and rather than an either/or relationship between the two principles. Thus, the transformation of religion under the enlightenment can also be considered as leading toward a nontheistic spirituality such as that found within the Zen Buddhist tradition. Nontheistic spirituality stands as a third alternative to traditional and contemporary theism and secular scientific atheism. In Buddhism, the secular remains active within a spiritual perspective (the secular within the sacred) as reflected in Buddha's famous advice not to believe in anything unless it is proven true within experience. Finally, within this framework, a fourth category becomes plausible wherein the spiritual remains implicitly active within the secular paradigm (the sacred within the secular). In other words, the secular mind may also contain unrecognized and unthematized intrinsic spiritual elements or seeds undestroyed by the secularization process. It is in these last two categories (the secular within the sacred and vice versa) that psychoanalysis and Zen Buddhism may have a supplementary rather than a complementary relationship.

In addition, as argued elsewhere (Moncayo 1998d), spirituality can also be distinguished from religion, since the first refers to an immediate, intrinsic, and direct experience as well as to an actual form of practice (e.g., meditation), whereas the second alludes to extrinsic, institutional, and conventional religiosity as a mechanism of social affiliation and control. As a construct, spirituality can also be used to designate a spiritual liberalism or a liberation spirituality characterized by an attitude of openness, free of the constraints of religious orthodoxy, traditional authority, or convention. Spirituality in the case of Zen Buddhism, for example, is also distinguished from the "New Age" phenomenon because it is linked to an ancestral symbolic lineage where, as the Zen tradition would say, the spirit/mind of Buddha has been directly and intrinsically transmitted and confirmed from teacher to disciple for generations. Within what is known as the New Age movement, there are many self-proclaimed unauthentic "masters" who, nonetheless, derive substantial profit from the spiritual supermarket. Within Buddhism, this tendency is known as spiritual materialism.

Spirituality as defined in this essay also needs to be distinguished from the mere interpretation of texts, from a simple sociohistorical constructivism, and from analyses of language and discourse (rhetorics). For the school of hermeneutics, there is no self-understanding that is not mediated by signs, symbols, and texts, whereas in Zen there is a transmission of a psychical Real (to use both a Buddhist and Lacanian concept) outside all scripture or beyond the bounds of words and the symbolic order. Zen teaching recommends a direct plunge into the Real itself through the experience and practice of "thinking nonthinking" while following the breath in the lotus posture. Self-understanding in Zen consists of a perceptual realization of the self-nature as emptiness and no-self. Here signs, symbols, and texts do not mediate self-realization. Lacan's work also differs from the school of hermeneutics in that it includes a register of experience that is beyond words and the symbolic order (the Real). But Lacanian psychoanalysis also differs from Buddhism because its relationship to the Real takes place through a special use of language and working through of unconscious phantasies (what Lacan calls the phantasm).

Nevertheless, given that self-realization in analysis does takes place on the basis of the Real, I propose that the psychoanalytic profession, like Zen, is also a kind of lineage requiring a mind-to-mind transmission beyond the study of texts, intellectual knowledge, and the clinical uses of the analytic process. Such mind-to-mind transmission, which is transmitted through the being of the analyst via the personal analysis, lies right at the edge of what can be articulated within language. Nevertheless, it forms the basis of what Lacan calls the desire of the analyst (the desire not to be desired), which supports the subjective state that the analyst must experience for there to be a direction to an analysis. The analyst is animated by a search for a state of being or a psychic function that will enable him or her to carry out the analytical task. Thus, analysis is not technical know-how; it involves not simply factual information but also the activation of a state of being within the analyst that Lacan calls the analyst's subjective position. However, most Lacanian analysts believe that analysis instills a state that is never spontaneously present in the psyche but is an original creation of psychoanalysis, a new subjective position. Nevertheless, psychoanalytic theory may be at a loss to account for the meaning and nature of such a psychic function/state.

It is not a purely rational or intellectual ego state associated with professional ideas or identifications; it goes further than that. Perhaps like the mind of Zen meditation, the analyst's mode of being is the function of a consciousness beyond consciousness that is neither totally unconscious nor conscious in the sense of an ego state.

Similarly, we've seen that Lacan (1977) spoke of the psychic function of "unknown knowing" or a "knowing that does not know that it knows." In Zen, the mind that is beyond knowledge and ignorance is called Buddha's "don't know mind." In contrast to faith in beliefs or concepts, faith in experience tends to include rather than exclude doubt. Given that beliefs create a dichotomy between faith and doubt, between what you believe and what you don't believe, faith in experience and in emptiness devoid of fixed ideas generates a space and a hole in which new ideas and signifiers may emerge. This is an experience and a state of open-mindedness and nondefensiveness necessary for both the analytic or scientific attitudes and an authentic spiritual perspective.

But for Buddhism the function of Buddha consciousness (a consciousness beyond consciousness) is a natural expression of Buddha-nature (according to Buddhism, the universe, as it is, already exists in a state of enlightenment, although without practice this state cannot be realized). Lacan's theory, like Buddhism, presupposes a dimension of experience that brings psychoanalysis closer to a spiritual realm than ever before. However, the two conceptions of the Real are not identical, and their difference parallels the distance between the realm of Buddha-nature and the realm of purely secular or profane experience. This is notwithstanding the fact that in Zen, emptiness or spirituality is something totally ordinary, as reflected in the story of Joshu described in my essay. In the relations between, on the one hand, the profane versus the sacred and, on the other, psychoanalysis versus Buddhism, psychoanalysis considers "the profane within the sacred," whereas Zen upholds "the sacred within the profane" or ordinary. In the Freudian sense, religion, for example, is an anal fixation with purity and cleanliness: purity or holiness is purely of the nature of shit. Freud's theory, which comes under the principle of "the profane within the sacred," is geared toward debunking pompous, dualistic religiosity (the profane and the sacred as only separate, unrelated terms). However, once this task has been accomplished, the Buddhist principle of "the sacred within the ordinary" still applies. In the Zen case, shit or urine itself expresses Buddha-nature. Nonetheless, both perspectives have a bias toward missing each other's insights. This is another example of a potentially supplementary relation between Buddhism and psychoanalysis.

The further point of contact between the secular and the sacred, which Thompson alludes to, concerns the question of being. I mentioned that, to the best of my knowledge, the existentialist school does not appropriate a positive view of emptiness as the Real beyond meaningful representation. The Real refers to that aspect of experience that lies beyond language, image, and logic and yet constitutes their very foundation. In addition, the Real, as a foundation or a groundless ground, remains empty of any fixed meaning. But emptiness as a spiritual experience in Buddhism differs from the concept of emptiness as a philosophical concept of existentialism. Sartre (1956), for example, has a nihilistic conception of nothingness as an absence without presence. Consider, for example, his anxiety-producing nothingness, which also appears in the clinical manifestation of depression and character disorders. Emptiness in Buddhism is both absence and presence at the same time.

For Lacan human beings are speaking beings. They are constituted as such by the Other or the laws of language, and in this process and within language human beings become lacking beings or a lack of being. Let me clarify what this means. First of all, it should be kept in mind that with his concept of the Symbolic, Lacan also links the laws of language with the incest prohibition and the "no" that the father represents. Language is deployed to both symbolize and reinforce a socially and developmentally prescribed separation: from nature and from being the object of the mother's desire. It is this loss that structures being as a lack of being. To speak means to have sustained a certain loss under language. Thus, to be a speaking being means to have a lack of being that in turn leads to desire as a desire for being or a "want-to-be." The core of being and of the subject is this lack of being as well as a desire to recoup the loss under language via unconscious phantasy. Phantasy takes the subject beyond the lack or nothingness of being and supplies a sense of being. For example, consider the case of an analysand who presented the symptom of becoming paralyzed and speechless when faced with a desired woman. The Symbolic governs verbal intercourse between men and women and requires that subjects own and symbolize the loss involved in language. In the case of this analysand, such a loss was compensated for by two phantasies at work in his predicament. One is that he was excited by a recurrent phantasy of a woman with a penis or a "phallic woman," although he did not realize that when faced with an actual desired woman this phantasy also evoked the loss it was meant to compensate for. A woman with a penis embodies her omnipotence, her lack of lack, and therefore of desire for a man. This lack of desire of the phallic woman (for him or any other man) is what he experiences as his own lack of manhood, although his complicity in this remains unconscious. On the other hand, he was also paralyzed on account of another phantasy: that he is a special agent type of character who is fearless, defies all odds, and has all women. This type of man that he would like to be is the kind of man he was not vis-à-vis "the woman." So instead of working through the loss of being under the Symbolic and language, the analysand disclaimed the lack and instead sought refuge in the phantasies that paralyzed him.

However, the concept of being has an ambiguous and contradictory status within Lacanian theory. On the one hand, Lacan argues that being appears only within the symbolic register of experience: human beings are speaking beings. On the other hand, the Symbolic produces being as a lack or absence of being and therefore the ego seeks being within phantasies and the Imaginary. Within the Symbolic the ego is always under the threat of disappearing and of feeling as a nothingness with respect to the totally different experience of being that imaginary phantasies seem to offer. Thus, human beings access being through language and at the same time language precipitates the disappearance of being within the subject. Lacanian theory advances two contradictory propositions: being appears only within language and being disappears with language. In my opinion, this dialectical contradiction can be resolved by thinking of the lack of being as a non-being in a dialectical relationship with being. Between the Symbolic and the Real, being and nonbeing are different and yet contain one another, whereas between the Symbolic and the Imaginary, nonbeing is completely devoid of being and vice versa. Rather than think of the lack of being as an absence of being or a nothingness, which is the opposite of being, if the lack of being is conceived of as the nonbeing or emptiness at the core of being, then emptiness or nonbeing is being itself.

In spirituality, desire is turned inward and away from finding being within the realm of unconscious phantasy and the Imaginary register. Strictly speaking, whether in Zen or psychoanalysis, there is no liberation from desire itself because such would imply another desire. What becomes possible is to leave the object of desire unfixed and mutable and thereby access the opening of being into emptiness. Since no one object can fill the gap of being, working through the loss at the core of being, instead of appealing to phantasy to prevent the loss, transforms the "nonbeing of being" into the "being of non-being" or dual nothingness into non-dual emptiness. Here being folds upon itself and into the opening of the hole or lack within being or the "nonbeing of being." So if in language "being is a lack of being or a nonbeing," in spirituality the approach to the Real is through the opening of nonbeing within being. In other words, nonbeing is realized as being without the mediation of phantasy. In addition, within the "nonbeing of being" in language, the sacred or the holy manifests thanks to the "holeness" or lack of closure, that is, lack of a lid that could give a fixed meaning to a text. A sacred text can be interpreted in many different ways in interaction with what the text alludes to (the Real) but cannot capture. In this way, the meaning of a text always remains open because language lacks a last or final word that could close textual meaning and the meaning of the Real. In this sense, the Real functions as an inexhaustible source of new meaning that manifests along the double axis of what is said and what is not said (about the Real). What words fail to say expresses the nonbeing within the being of the text or of discourse.

I turn now to the question of the variable-length session, which, as Thompson correctly points out, I neglected to discuss in my essay. There are several reasons for the neglect. First, I have already addressed this practice in a psychoanalytic paper (Moncayo 1997), although not in relation to Zen Buddhism. Second, my thesis concerned a more general notion of benevolent depersonalization of the analyst as a form of practice similar to Zen. Third, the variable-length session can be misunderstood because of established prejudice in the psychoanalytic field regarding its use. After all, Lacan was expelled from the International Psychoanalytic Association for this practice. Thompson himself seems to partake of those prejudices when he describes this kind of practice as a kind of punishment. It is often said that the relationship between the analyst and analysand under the variable-length session is primarily a negative sadomasochistic relationship. On the other hand, I do agree with Thompson that the variable-length session is a practice where Lacan and Zen do in fact coincide. In Zen, compassion is often expressed via the wisdom of the symbolic sword, as a symbolic act that cuts through the attachments to false views and rationalizations. I like to call this a form of symbolic empathy for the subject (in my essay I indicated how the Lacanian notion of the subject differs from an ego concept) associated with the function of the symbolic father and mother (the mother who, like the father, is also at the service of the Symbolic). Let me give you another clinical example to illustrate the notion of the symbolic mother. An acculturated Latina patient asked a supervisee of mine if this clinician could sell the patient's tamales in the clinic where she was seen. The clinician said "no" and the patient proceeded to fire her as her psychotherapist. The patient then told her next psychotherapist that my supervisee had refused to sell her tamales because the clinician thought that both the patient and this kind of work were beneath her social class. The patient proceeded to complain how this act constituted mistreatment and a humiliation without any awareness of how inappropriate her demand could be or the way in which she was asking the clinician to become a sort of employee of hers. The symbolic mother (the mother associated with the function of prohibition) is represented by the "no" of the clinician, whereas the imaginary mother (the phantasized way the client interprets the meaning of the prohibition) is represented by the clinician that she thought mistreated her.

Lacan was critical of an imaginary maternal empathy championed by object relations theory (currently the dominant form of psychoanalysis within the International Psychoanalytic Association), for while it wittingly or unwittingly undermines the symbolic function of the father, it reinforces the defenses of the imaginary ego. (The Latina patient's problem from her perspective was not that she wanted the clinician to be the daughter and she the mother, but that the clinician mistreated her.) Imaginary empathy is prone to interpret the complaints of the analysand, which Lacan would associate with the imaginary mother, as actual parenting faults and deficits, and to attempt to give to the analysand the love they did not receive from the parents, although ultimately doing a disservice to the subject along the way. Rather than helping the analysand come to terms with the symbolic function of the mother and the father, imaginary empathy may help shore up imaginary ego-constructs and keep alive the expectation that the "object" of love and the ego-ideal could in fact be attained and realized.

Finally, Thompson also raises the question of whether a radical destruction of narcissism runs contrary to Freud's work, particularly in reference to the obsessive patient. In addition, Thompson seems to identify a critique of narcissism with the death of desire. I will have to be brief, because to do justice to this question would require an examination of the concept of narcissism that goes beyond the scope of this essay. It all depends on the definition of narcissism. My thesis is that what Thompson calls a radical destruction of narcissism actually constitutes a further development and differentiation within narcissism. I postulate four degrees of differentiation within narcissism. Lacanian theory agrees with the prevailing intersubjective theory of narcissism, and Lacan may in fact have been one of its precursors. Lacan has been credited with coining the term *intersubjective*. Primary narcissism is an intersubjective condition whereby subject and object, mother and child, have not been differentiated. As Winnicott has noted, mother and child share the breast. The beginning of a differentiation starts with the mirror phase whereby the ego or ideal ego is defined by the specular image (image in the mirror), which involves an identification with the mother's desire (for further explanation see above). This would be secondary narcissism according to Freud's second theory of narcissism, given that he used the terms "ideal-ego" and "ego-ideal" interchangeably and did not differentiate them. The ego-ideal constitutes a further or tertiary differentiation within narcissism in relationship to the symbolic recognition of the father. But here Lacan subjects the ego-ideal to a critical analysis not found in Freud, at least in a systematic fashion.

According to Lacan, (the name of) the father is placed in lieu of the absence of the maternal gift. Because the mother has the power of the gift (to love or not love, etc.), the boy and the girl experience a sense of insufficiency and dispossession vis-à-vis the mother. The father appears to the child as the possessor of that which the mother wants and lacks (imaginary phallus) and, therefore, he is perceived as a potential safe haven against the perceived omnipotence of the mother. This state of affairs results in a first imaginary love/identification for/with the father. This is the beginning of the ego-ideal and of the desire to be recognized by the father. However, in Lacanian theory, the father only appears to have the imaginary phallus or whatever the child imagines the phallus to be. In actuality the symbolic phallus (as a function that facilitates separation and protects the child from the dread of maternal omnipotence) is never there; it remains always beyond and absent. In addition, the idealization, the love/hate for the father as the presumed holder of the imaginary phallus, produces imaginary castration because it perpetuates the experience of being deprived of an object that in actuality does not exist or is only an imaginary construction. For Lacan the symbolic phallus or the symbolic father is not an object of the senses; it has no image or word; it is rather a nothing, a nonbeing, and a zero that, nonetheless, constitutes a pivot and support for the life of the subject. Lacan finds support for the concept of the symbolic father in the Holy Writ. The symbolic father of the Bible either does not respond with a name, is nameless, or responds with letters the meaning of which is unclear. Such refusal to give a name reveals the emptiness of the Other. The Other knows he/she is nothing.

In this way, the ego-ideal and the imaginary father are subjected to a further fourth degree of differentiation. This is the rock of symbolic castration and the most difficult of narcissistic wounds: the symbolic father and phallus are also found to be lacking, a zero or a nothing. Once the illusions regarding the ideal father and the disillusions regarding the lack and limitations of the father have been cleared in the transference, the father remains as an empty symbolic function, without a name or image but still a function nonetheless. The task of the analyst is to serve as a support for this function by ultimately being empty of content that could define the identity of the analysand. This paves the way for the real being of the subject or the emergence of a new subject. Thus the recognition of the emptiness of the Other leads to a fourth degree of differentiation within narcissism, which coincides with what Kohut called a cosmic narcissism marked not by grandiosity and elation but by solemnity and a serene inner confidence. Such end-state narcissism is differentiated from first-degree primary narcissism (or the oceanic feeling, as Freud called it) because it includes all the mediations/separations introduced by the paternal function. The postulate of there being four degrees within narcissism should put to rest the concern that Zen meditation experience is identical to a primal form of narcissism.

Finally, with regard to the obsessional structure, Lacan argued that the key problem concerns the death of desire and the existential question "Am I dead or alive?" Obsessive persons question whether they are alive, because of their absence of desire and their general pessimistic view of life. In addition, obsessions with death and the dead father are central features of the obsessional structure. In this regard, Thompson, Freud, and Lacan would agree that desire in the obsessive needs to be brought back to life, rather than deadened any further. However, from a Lacanian perspective, the obsessive is struggling against the lack within desire more than against a forbidden desire.

In Lacan, the struggle between desire and the law does not occur between two dual terms external to one another, but is internal to a dialectic within desire itself. In other words, it is not that the obsessive does not desire because the law of the father forbids him to do so, as the usual psychoanalytic understanding would have it. The obsessive attempts to eliminate desire because desire represents a lack of being and a lack in the Other. The obsessive defends against desiring the other or vice versa because desire appears to the obsessive as a signifier of imaginary castration. For example, an obsessive usually deprecates a woman when she desires him. He only wants her when he fears (and wants) the rejection that proves her to be a fatal, indifferent, phallic woman. When a woman's desire for the obsessive is present, then such desire reveals her as a lacking being, which is what the obsessive needs to defend against. This is shown by the example of an analysand who, the night when a desired woman finally began showing signs of desire for him, dreamt the following dream. He was naked with her in foreplay with a strong erection, when suddenly the situation turned sour and a feeling of dread and anxiety began to prevail. He had seen her breasts and the sense that her breasts were small instilled in him the thought that what she really wanted was to cut off his penis. The imaginary castration threat only appeared once the woman began to desire him and this desire signified the presence of a lack (symbolized by the small breast).

Thus, ultimately, rather than simply attributing the fear of castration to actual behaviors of the father (and the analyst acting in a more benign and loving manner than the historical father), the obsessive needs to be reoriented to come to terms with a threat within desire itself. This, of course, is not to deny that many obsessives may have had authoritarian fathers, but simply to emphasize that the recognition of this fact, together with the provision of a corrective emotional experience, are not enough to reconcile the obsessive to his desire. Rather than defend against the lack produced by the presence of the imaginary father, as if there could be desire without lack, the obsessive needs to accept and go through the lack that goes with desire. Only then will the obsessive have access to desire. This is the illusion: that the lack and the law are external to desire, and that one could have desire simply by eliminating the law and the lack thereof. Thus, by being solely and simply empathic and soft with the obsessive, one runs the risk of perpetuating the illusion of a world of desire without symbolic lack. By resisting the lack, what is being resisted is desire itself. Conversely,

I have argued that working through the lack and emptiness of the Other leads precisely to Eros and a recovery and discovery of the capacity for love and desire. Finally, it is important to also note that, more often than not, the obsessive may have been pampered, indulged, or loved too much by his or her mother, precisely as a defense against the lack symbolized by the desire of the father. To use a gratifying approach with an obsessive would only reinforce the death of desire and the death of the lack of being that sustains it.

Notes

1. Within some schools of psychoanalysis, unconscious "fantasy" is spelled "phantasy."

2. A few words are needed to account for the obvious differences between the Lacanian Real of unconscious experience regarding sex, and the psychical Real in Zen meditation experience. This question addresses the differences that Freud and Jung had in reference to the nature and content of the unconscious. A more developed account of the subject is developed elsewhere (Moncayo, 1998b). Clearly, in Zen the non-dual Real that is expressed through a permutation of conventional dual language differs from the play of the signifier and free association in relationship to the Real of sexuality and aggression in the Freudian/Lacanian Unconscious. One refers to unknown-knowing regarding no-self, the other to unknown-knowing regarding the Real of unconscious desire and sexuality. I argue that they both refer to an "It" but that the "Id" symbolized in both conceptions is different although related. Sublimation is what elevates an object (id) to the dignity of the emptiness (It) at the core of the object (the It of id or what Lacan calls *das Ding*—German for "the thing"—and the id of It). An example of this is given in my chapter wherein Joshu defines spirituality as a puddle of urine in the Buddha land.

3. See Thompson (1994) for a discussion on how Freud's analytic technique does not conform to "classical" standards.

References

Bion, W. 1995. *Attention and Interpretation*. Hillsdale, N.J.: Jason Aronson.

Cordovero, Moses. 1981. The Palm of Deborah. In *Anthology of Jewish Mysticism*. New York: Judaica Press.

Dogen. 1975. *Shobogenzo*. Tokyo: Japan Publications.

Engler, J. H. 1981. Vicissitudes of the Self According to Psychoanalysis and Buddhism: A Spectrum Model of Object Relations Development. *Psychoanalysis and Contemporary Thought* 6:29–72.

Epstein, M. 1995. *Thoughts without a Thinker*. New York: Basic Books.

Etchegoyen, H. 1991. *The Fundamentals of Psychoanalytic Technique*. New York: Karnac.

Fink, B.1995. *The Lacanian Subject*. Princeton: Princeton University Press.

———. 1997. *A Clinical Introduction to Lacanian Psychoanalysis*. Cambridge: Harvard University Press.

Frankl, V. 1962. *Man's Search for Meaning*. Boston: Beacon Press.

Freud, S. 1907. *Obsessive Actions and Religious Practices*. In Standard Edition, 9:117-27. London: Hogarth Press, 1959.

———. 1915. *Observations on Transference-Love (Further Recommendations on the Technique of Psycho-Analysis III)*. In Standard Edition, 12:157–71. London: Hogarth Press, 1958.

———. 1919. *Lines of Advance in Psycho-Analytic Therapy*. In Standard Edition, 17:157–68. London: Hogarth Press, 1955.

——— 1922. *Group Psychology and the Analysis of the Ego*. New York: Norton, 1959.

——— 1926. *The Question of Lay Analysis*. In Standard Edition, 20:183–250. London: Hogarth Press, 1959.

——— 1927. *The Future of an Illusion*. New York: Double Day/Anchor Books.

Fromm, E. 1950. *Psychoanalysis and Religion*. New York: Bantam Books.

——— 1960. *Psychoanalysis and Zen Buddhism*. San Francisco: Harper Colophon.

Greenson, R. R. 1978. The Working Alliance and the Transference Neurosis. In *Explorations in Psychoanalysis*, 199–224. New York: International Universities Press.

Harari, R. 1985. *Discurrir el psicoanalisis*. Buenos Aires: Nueva Vision.

Heidegger, M. 1962. *Being and Time.* Trans. J. Macquarrie and E. Robinson. New York: Harper and Row.

Jones, J. W. 1991. *Contemporary Psychoanalysis and Religion.* New Haven: Yale University Press.

Jung, C. G. 1953. *Psychology and Alchemy.* In Collected Works, vol. 12. Bollingen Series, no. 20. New Jersey: Princeton University Press.

———. 1958. *Psychology and Western Religion.* In Collected Works, vol. 11. Bollingen Series, no. 20. New Jersey: Princeton University Press.

Kung, H. 1979. *Freud and the Problem of God.* New Haven: Yale.

Lacan, J. 1960a. *Livre VIII, Le Transfert.* Paris: Editions du Seuil.

———. 1960b. *Seminar no. 7: The Ethics of Psychoanalysis.* New York: Norton, 1988.

———. 1975. El reverso del psicoanalisis. Buenos Aires: Paidos.

———. 1977a. Le Seminaire XXIV, L'insu que sait. Unpublished.

———. 1977b. The Direction of the Treatment and the Principles of Its Power. In *Écrits.* New York: Norton.

———. 1977c. The Agency of the Letter in the Unconscious or Reason since Freud. In *Écrits,* New York: Norton.

Loewald, H. 1978. *Psychoanalysis and the History of the Individual.* New Haven: Yale University Press.

Maslow, A. 1968. *Toward a Psychology of Being.* New York: Van Nostrand Reinhold.

May, R. 1957. *Man's Search for Himself.* New York: W. W. Norton.

Meissner, W. W. 1984. *Psychoanalysis and Religious Experience.* New Haven: Yale University Press.

Miller, J. A. 1997. The Drive Is Speech. *Umbr(a),* 1.15–33.

Moncayo, R. 1997. Freud's Concepts of Drive, Desire and Nirvana. *Umbr(a),* no. 1.

———. 1998a. Cultural Diversity and the Cultural and Epistemological Structure of Psychoanalysis. *Psychoanalytic Psychology,* 15:262–86.2

———. 1998b. The Real and the Symbolic in Lacan, Zen and Kaballah. *International Journal for the Psychology of Religion* 8:179–96.

———. 1998c. True Subject Is No-Subject: The Real, Symbolic and Imaginary in Psychoanalysis and Zen Buddhism. *Psychoanalysis and Contemporary Thought,* fall, 383–422.

————. 1998d. Psychoanalysis and Postmodern Spirituality. *Journal for the Psychoanalysis of Culture and Society* 3:123–29.

————. 2000. The Metaphoric Function and Fundamental Emptiness of the Subject and the Name of the Father in Lacanian Psychoanalysis. Unpublished.

Moncayo, R., and R. Harari. 1997. Principles of Lacanian Clinical Practice. *Anamorphosis, Journal of the Lacanian School of Psychoanalysis* 1:13–28.

Nasio, J.-D. 1992. The Concept of the Subject of the Unconscious. *Cinq Leçons sur la Theorie de Jacques Lacan.* Paris: Rivages.

Ricoeur, P. 1970. *Freud and Philosophy: An Essay on Interpretation.* New Haven: Yale University Press.

Rubin, J. B. 1996. *Psychotherapy and Buddhism: Toward an Integration.* New York: Plenum Press.

Sartre, J.-P. 1956. *Being and Nothingness.* Trans. Hazel Barnes. London: Methuen.

Schneiderman, S. 1983. *Jacques Lacan: The Death of an Intellectual Hero.* Cambridge: Harvard University Press.

Smith, J., ed. 1991. *Psychoanalysis and Religion.* Johns Hopkins University.

Spero, M. H. 1992. *Religious Objects As Psychological Structures.* Chicago: Chicago University Press.

Suler, J. R. 1993. *Contemporary Psychoanalysis and Eastern Thought.* Albany: State University of New York Press.

Thompson, M. G. 1994. *The Truth about Freud's Technique: The Encounter with the Real.* New York: New York University Press.

Tillich, P. 1952. *The Courage to Be.* New Haven: Yale University Press.

Verhaeghe, P. 1998. On the Lacanian Subject. In *Key Concepts of Lacanian Psychoanalysis,* ed. D. Nobus, 164–89. London: Rebus Press.

CHAPTER 9

A Well-Lived Life:
Psychoanalytic and
Buddhist Contributions

JEFFREY B. RUBIN

To live! To live! So natural and so hard.

—James Schuyler, "Hymn to Life"

Buddhism has entered the consulting room and psychoanalysis has entered the Buddhist monastery in dramatic ways in recent years. We live and practice in a psychoanalytic universe in which Buddhist teachers are in therapy, psychoanalysts meditate, and spiritual seekers simultaneously pursue contemplative paths and analysis. More and more of my patients indicate during the first session that they seek a therapist who is open and attuned to the spiritual dimension of life. And probably a third of them (some of them therapists) meditate. And some of the Buddhists among them have had dreams about their experiences at Buddhist retreats that they want to explore in therapy. The burgeoning dialogue among therapists, researchers, and spiritual seekers about the possible relationship between the Western psychoanalytic and Eastern meditative traditions has yielded crucial insights about human development, conceptions of selfhood, psychopathology, and cure (Engler 1984; Rubin 1996).

Psychoanalysis and Buddhism each have something rare and vital to contribute to the challenges and difficulties of living in our world. The capacity of these two wisdom traditions to help us live with greater self-awareness, self-acceptance, care, compassion, morality, and freedom is essential in a world permeated by self-blindness, self-hatred, powerlessness, and alienation. In this chapter I will explore what light psychoanalysis and Buddhism can shed on a life well lived.

My strategy will be as follows: First I shall explore why illuminating the nature of the good or well-lived life is important to psychoanalysis. Then I shall examine why psychoanalysis is in a unique position to elucidate the well-lived life. Then I shall explore diverse and divergent psychoanalytic perspectives—including classical psychoanalytic, Jungian, Kleinian, object relational, interpersonal, self psychological, and intersubjective—on the good life. I suggest some implications for such issues as the nature of self, morality, and freedom. Buddhist teachings drawn from the Theravadan, Zen, and Tibetan traditions, which I intersperse throughout, offer a counterpart to psychoanalytic ones, thereby illuminating hidden presuppositions of psychoanalysis as well as helping us raise new questions and gain new insights about the good life.

There is considerable talk these days of a "dialogue" between the Western psychotherapeutic and Eastern meditative traditions. From my perspective such a dialogue has actually rarely occurred. Most often, there is what Freud in a different context termed a "monologue without interruption," by which I mean, each tradition operates as if it is the royal road to truth and healthy living and rarely learns from the other. Freud and many of his colleagues pathologized and marginalized religion and spiritual experiences,[1] tending to view religion and spirituality through the Eurocentric and intellectually imperialistic lens of a Western psychology that reduced religious beliefs and practices and the spiritual quest to infantile meanings and functions. The Eurocentrism of psychoanalysis is illustrated by Freud's reaction to Romain Rolland, a poet and student of the Indian mystic Ramakrishna. Responding to Freud's critique of religion in *The Future of an Illusion*, Rolland indicated that Freud's perspective had much merit but that it neglected the most important source of the attraction of religion, namely, the "oceanic feeling," a "sensation of 'eternity,'" a feeling as of something limitless, unbounded." In *Civilization and Its Discontents* Freud admitted that he could not discover this "oceanic" feeling in himself and voiced discomfort in coping with these "obscure modifications in mental life" (1930, 73). He pathologized religious and spiritual experience, viewing them as a regressed state connected to infantile helplessness and as engendering "limitless narcissism." Subsequent psychoanalysts, with rare exceptions (e.g., Loewald 1978; Kovel 1991), have followed Freud's lead and also neglected and pathologized this facet of self-experience.

Psychoanalysis in its myriad contemporary postclassical relational forms—object relations theory, self psychology, interpersonal psychoanalysis, social constructivist analysis, and intersubjectivity theory—has deeply enriched classical psychoanalysis. In many ways relational analysis has moved beyond some of the cultural ethnocentrism and closed-mindedness of the early years of psychoanalysis. That Eurocentrism is, however, alive and well in psychoanalysis was brought home to me recently when I heard an eminent and otherwise highly open-minded psychoanalyst within the relational fold make disparaging and unreflective remarks about religion at a psychoanalytic conference. While part of the history of religion is certainly a story of persecution and idolatry—one has only to think of the Crusades or contemporary religious fundamentalists of various persuasions—it is also a story of compassion and wisdom. There is a great danger of conscious and unconscious idealization of religion and the spiritual quest. Psychoanalysts have deeply illuminated uncritical deification of religion. But it is unanalytic, by which I mean counter to the psychoanalytic spirit to take anything on faith—including psychoanalytic atheism—which in my clinical experience can itself be defensive and impoverishing, denying the divineness and fullness of life and being.

While Eurocentrism may be on the wane, contemporary writers in the West often adopt a polar opposite approach, what I have termed "Orientocentrism" (Rubin 1996), idealizing Eastern contemplative disciplines and treating them as the center of the psychological and spiritual universe. Orientocentrism is alive and well when authors are attached to Buddhism as the source of indubitable truth, don't question its universal validity, and are resistant to how non-Eastern disciplines such as psychoanalysis might enlighten it. Buddhism usefully highlights the dangers of *attachment*, which refers not to the work of John Bowlby and his co-workers on the centrality of psychological connectedness or attachment to a person in human development and psychological transformation, but rather to a fundamental human predilection that causes inevitable and ubiquitous suffering, namely the irrational clinging to any facet of experience, ranging from the belief in the

existence of a permanent, unchanging, autonomous self to the ultimate validity and universality of one's preferred psychotherapeutic or Buddhist theory.
Most of the recent literature on psychoanalysis and Buddhism is not Buddhist
enough in a certain sense: authors are *attached* to Buddhism. When one uncrit-
ically deifies Asian thought and practice, its blind spots *and* the potential value
of psychoanalysis are inevitably neglected. Treating Buddhism *or* psychoanalysis as a received truth, rather than a human and thus fallible creation that
has pockets of unconsciousness, renders us insufficiently reflective and critical
of it. It causes us to ignore its blind spots and its limitations. In the case of
Buddhism, it causes us to avoid the embarrassing but essential questions that
are crucial to the transplantation of Eastern contemplative theories and practices into the West, such as: Why have there been so many scandals in American Buddhism involving teachers—those supposedly self-realized
beings—who have sexually exploited students, engaged in financial impropri-
eties, and struggled with addictions?

The literature on the potential interface between psychoanalysis and Eastern contemplative thought has moved, thankfully, beyond the intellectual colo-
nialism of the Eurocentric perspective of Freud and many subsequent Western
psychologists and clinicians. Now the dialogue between psychoanalysis and
Buddhism needs to move beyond Orientocentrism. We need a *close encounter
of a new kind* between the Western psychoanalytic and Eastern meditative and
contemplative traditions. In such a *dialogue of reciprocity* there would be mutual
respect, the awareness of differences, and a receptivity to learn from each other
(Rubin 1996, 1999). To have such a dialogue there cannot be an attachment to
either Buddhism or psychoanalysis as a privileged and infallible source of wisdom. Cross-fertilization can occur only when there is a willingness within each
tradition to learn from and be transformed by the other.

For you to understand my perspective on the interface of psychoanalysis
and Buddhism, I must say a few words about the context from which I think
and write. It is a perspective that does not fit into familiar, singular, or existing
categories or schools of thought or practice, whether psychoanalytic or Buddhist. Because it may lack some of the comforting landmarks that we are deeply
conditioned to expect, we may be left slightly disoriented. My perspective is a
sensibility or a *space of thinking*—a transitional one in D.W. Winnicott's sense—
not a *school* of thought. Traditions of thought and practice give one insight
and direction, as well as a community to identify with. They provide solace and

further knowledge. But they can be enslaving as well as enabling. Identifying with a particular school of thought—being attached to it in the Buddhist sense—whether Buddhist or psychoanalytic, pushes away other parts of reality. The sensibility I am pointing toward is a liminal space, a middle way in the Buddhist sense, that sees life as more complex than any theories—including my own. "Truth" is not the province of a particular school of thought. Sometimes it thrives in the interstices between different disciplines and modes of thinking, where fertile and novel perceptions and questions may arise.

There is, as Taoism teaches us, a Way that is not bound by any particular way, which is no set way. One can embrace and appreciate many systems without being bound by them. In order to do this we need to forgo the comfort and security of identifying with either the psychoanalytic or the Buddhist tradition as the sole source of truth. Then we can dance in the spaces between them—tacking back and forth—freer to use what is best from each.[2]

At least three questions are central to the project of an integrative cross-cultural psychology: What does each tradition uniquely illuminate and what does each omit? How can psychoanalysis help spiritual seekers? How might contemplative disciplines such as Buddhism enrich psychoanalysis? Both psychoanalysis and Buddhism would be transformed by such a project. Then we might have a more fully integrative approach to the art of living.

Given psychoanalysts' avowed commitment to moral neutrality, it may sound strange at first to speak of psychoanalysis and the good life. The good life or the full life is not something that psychoanalysis usually is or should be prescriptive about. One of the many virtues of psychoanalysis is that unlike ancient spiritual traditions or contemporary psycho-spiritual writings, it does not legislate or provide formulaic answers to the Socratic question of how one should live. There are many virtues to such an attitude, including the minimization of coercive external impositions, the protection of the patient's autonomy, and the openness to many different ways of living.

Given the neglect of health in psychoanalysis and its reluctance to engage values, psychoanalysis seems like an unpromising candidate for illuminating the well-lived life. In fact, psychoanalysis may not seem to offer anything to this topic unless we approach it *psychoanalytically*, by which I mean, reading psychoanalysis against its grain, questioning standard interpretations of analysis (even by psychoanalysts), searching for latent as opposed to manifest meanings and implications in psychoanalytic formulations, and treating what psychoanalysts leave unsaid as sometimes just as meaningful as what they say. To take up a "Freudian" attitude toward psychoanalysis itself is to be interested in *unconscious* facets of psychoanalytic theory and practice (Rubin 1998). The psychoanalytic legacy about the good life includes no explicit instructions about how we should live and may only be germinally present in analytic writings. Psychoanalysts are not always consciously aware of what their writings imply about the well-lived life. There are implications about a life well-lived in psychoanalytic writings and uses to which psychoanalytic perspectives can be put that analytic thinkers may not always have consciously intended and of which they may not always be consciously aware. Often they have not integrated what they write into their way of living.

It is often assumed outside psychoanalysis—occasionally even within it (e.g., Molino and Ware 2001)—that psychoanalysis is *normalizing*, by which I mean, a form of social control and conformity. But psychoanalysis is transgressive and denormalizing as well as constraining. Psychoanalysis exemplifies its conservativeness when it knows too much beforehand about how successful human development or psychoanalytic treatment proceeds. When this happens the patient is placed on a Procrustean bed, and potentials for treatment and growth are narrowed. Psychoanalysis illustrates its potential for offering liberation when it challenges its own authority and transforms, overcomes, or extends its normative standards. Fertile and suggestive perspectives on the good life emerge when psychoanalysis destabilizes its own authority.

While psychoanalysis has usefully eschewed a prescriptive perspective on values, it offers a variety of suggestive perspectives on a life well lived. Here I will attempt to explore some psychoanalytic versions of, to borrow a phrase from W. H. Auden, "the dreams of Eden," or visions of the good life. Reflecting on them not only opens up tacit knowledge encoded within psychoanalysis but also contributes to living a fuller life.

The quest to live a good life has a venerable history. The central concern for individuals whom Erich Fromm calls "masters of living" (1995, 17)—Lao Tzu, Buddha, Socrates, Aristotle, Epicurus, Jesus, the Prophets, Montaigne, Thoreau, Nietzsche, Marx, and Albert Schweitzer, among others—was how humans should live. Two ways of thinking about this broad and important topic dominate contemporary thinking: a secular, materialistic ideal and a spiritual one.

François Rabelais ends his satirical masterpiece *Gargantua* with the construction of the Abbey of Thélème. In Thélème wealth, happiness, and pleasure are the goals of life. In our world the good life is often linked to similar hedonistic images: the unlimited freedom to "have it all," to purchase and accumulate; the ability to obtain ceaseless pleasure, luxury, and ease; the capacity and power to shape one's life and to segregate oneself from noxious external impingements including any unwanted obligations and constraints. The popular media—movies, televisions, books, magazines, and newspapers—exalt this kind of life. A large percentage of people in our society find this goal enormously compelling. Even those who decry the vacuity of this ideal often judge themselves according to whether they actually embody it. Believing, along with AT&T, that "It's all within your reach," the vast majority of people unconsciously (or consciously) believe that if they achieve these goals then they will be happy.

Yet even very wealthy people experience a great deal of alienation, emptiness, stress-related disorders, and the feeling that "there has to be something more."[3] That there is no direct correlation between financial wealth and emotional health is probably not news to any analyst who has listened to the disillusionment and sometimes despair of their wealthier patients. "Having it all" or attempting to achieve it does not constitute a life well lived and in fact is sometimes an obstacle to it. This is not surprising. The most remarkable feature of the Abbey of Thélème, after all, was its thick walls, not its sensuous delights. Inside the abbey one has privacy and is secluded from the outside world. But one also cannot see the "other side." Good fences, claims Robert Frost, make good neighbors. They also make good prisons. The wall at Thélème incarcerates its inhabitants and also keeps outsiders out.

There is a countervailing perspective on the good life that is increasingly popular nowadays—the "spiritual" point of view. Spiritual perspectives on the good life cannot be placed in a monolithic formula. But they share several features that offer a powerful challenge to our ceaseless pursuit of wealth and leisure: the attempt to discover and embody an essential, authentic self; the idealization of selflessness; and the belief in an uncontaminated realm "beyond ego" that it is humanly possible to experience. A growing number of people find such spiritual ideals compelling. But the rash of scandals in spiritual communities in recent years, involving rampant egocentricity and a complete lack of moral accountability, cast grave doubt on spiritual images of the good life and the ideal of selflessness. As does the incidence of addiction among growing numbers of Buddhist teachers.

Psychoanalysis reveals the limitations of secular and spiritual pictures of the well-lived life. While many contemplative traditions acknowledge that humans confront resistances to growth and have great difficulty changing, they tend to lack the comprehensive understanding of and systematic approach to unconsciousness that psychoanalysis offers.

The unconscious—what Jung thought of as the unknown as it lives in and through us—confirms the fallibility of the analyst and the guru. Our inability to know ourselves completely means that there will always be areas of both ourselves and the interpersonal and external world that remain opaque and undiscovered. The spiritual ideal of achieving perfect and complete knowledge of ourselves is, as Jung recognized, a romantic wish that has seduced spiritual seekers.

Psychoanalysis critiques the "apsychological," or non-psychologically sophisticated moralities of contemplative traditions because of the way they oversimplify psychological life and ethics and their neglect of human development and personal history. Psychoanalysis demonstrates how accounts of the good life coming from the contemplative traditions neglect the ubiquity of self-deception, overlook the shaping role of the past (the way our individual and family histories close down certain possibilities and delimit how we relate to ourselves, to others, and to the world), and underestimate the stubbornness of character, transference, and unconsciousness (Rubin 1996). Contemplative traditions neglect the way intentions and actions may have multiple unconscious meanings and functions. Altruism in a spiritual practitioner may hide vanity and sanctimony. Self-denigration may masquerade as spiritual asceticism. And humility can be fueled by a sense of non-entitlement or fear of competition no less than a recognition of the suffering and limitation generated by an excessively possessive relation to a theory, material object, or psychological or spiritual practice.

The problems with both contemplative and secular conceptions of a life well lived leave us adrift lacking a guiding vision or a framework for action. The dialogue between psychoanalysis and Buddhism can make a significant contribution to this topic. Psychoanalysis seems, at first glance, ill equipped for elucidating the good life because of its "tragic" world view (its focus on illness not health), its concern with the isolated unencumbered individual,[4] and its commitment to moral neutrality. The "tragic" worldview refers to a recognition of the inescapable mysteries, dilemmas, and afflictions pervading human existence (Schafer 1976). Tragic does not necessarily imply, contrary to popular usage, "unhappy or disastrous outcomes" (47), but rather a steadfast recognition that time is irreversible and unredeemable; humans are beings moving toward death, not rebirth; choices entail conflict and compromise; and suffering is inevitable. Religious consolations are unrealistic in the tragic vision.[5] Deriving from and intimately connected to its tragic worldview; psychoanalysis is a psychology of illness that neglects health, creativity, intimacy, and spirituality.[6] Psychoanalysis, as Winnicott aptly noted, has "yet to tackle the question of what *life itself is about*" apart from illness (1971, 98). The Standard Edition of the works of Freud, for example, contains over four hundred entries for neurosis and pathology and not one for health. Because psychoanalysis has focused on pathology, it tends to conceive of health as an absence of illness rather than the presence of well-being, as Freud's "pathography" of Leonardo da Vinci illustrates. To read psychoanalytic accounts of the "ends of analysis"—personal integration, heightened reality testing, a capacity to "love and work," greater ego strength, enlarged ability for self-reflection and self-analysis—is to understand why artists and spiritual seekers all too often believe that there is more on earth (I don't know about heaven) than psychoanalytic accounts of the good life suggest. Contemplative perspectives on the human condition imply that psychoanalysis contributes to suffering by its tragic and secular worldview and by systematically underestimating human possibilities for healing and health. It is thus not surprising that the concept of the good life rarely appears in the psychoanalytic literature.

Illuminating the nature of the good life is important for psychoanalysis for at least two reasons: the first is clinical, the second is cultural. Psychoanalysis is not value-neutral. The analyst has a vision of the good life, even if he or she does not consciously formulate it and moreover insists that analysts should have no vision apart from the analytic method, neutrally applied. To know when to terminate a treatment, the analyst must have an image of cure; to know what a cure *is*, one must have a vision of the good life. These visions shape our daily work in hidden ways that are no less important because they are unconscious. In fact, they are more formative because they are hidden.

The second reason the topic of the good life is important has to do with the problematic place of psychoanalysis in the contemporary world. We live in a demoralized world in two senses: many people feel discouraged and beaten down; and we live in an age where morality is the exception, where hedonism reigns in most domains of human conduct. Elected officials, religious figures, executives, media personalities, entertainers, and professional athletes all do what enhances the self and are without scruples or concern for their impact on others. In a world that resembles a moral free-for-all, where anything goes, where everything from reason to revelation can be deconstructed and debunked, people are left with no foundations or guiding direction for action. Many people then feel cast drift. Egocentricity, hedonism, trendy psycho-spiritual quick fixes, and self-anesthetizing behavior move in to fill the breach. Is it surprising that we feel moral malaise?

Psychoanalysis is in a good position to illuminate the good life for at least three reasons: First, psychoanalysis is a sanctuary from the cognitive oversaturation, emotional disconnection, and pressure to live one-dimensional lives that permeates our culture (Rubin 1998). As such, it provides a heuristic, emotionally intimate, and relatively non-impinging context for exploring such questions of ultimate concern as how one should live. Second, psychoanalysis is in a position to illuminate the good life because it has access to depths of human subjectivity that are not explored anywhere else in daily life. Psychoanalysis appreciates unconsciousness, which religious and spiritual disciplines all too often neglect. It is also a "hermeneutics of suspicion"— challenging and attempting to demystify taken-for-granted motives and meanings (Ricoeur 1970). Third, psychoanalysis, unlike postmodernist discourse, is critical yet reconstructive, demystifying yet affirmative. Psychoanalysts question the authority humans often irrationally invest in others, yet they do not deny expertise. Psychoanalysts recognize that there is no objectivity, but they do not usher in a disabling nihilism. Psychoanalysts throw out the baby of self-mastery, yet they do not drain the bath water of self-complexity (Rubin 1998).

And yet, despite the potential of psychoanalysis to illuminate the good life, one could search in vain for psychoanalytic citations on this topic. Erich Fromm (1947, 1998) and Leslie Farber (1976) are in a distinct minority in addressing this important and neglected topic. There are at least five reasons this topic has been neglected in psychoanalysis. (1) Hitching its star to science was one important way that psychoanalysis tried to legitimize itself in an inhospitable world. Neutrality was central to the self-image of science. The legacy of neutrality made analysts queasy about contaminating the treatment. It is thus normal analytic practice for the analyst to refrain from expressing any ideas about the good life to the patient. (2) Psychoanalysts have resisted writing about resistance to the terminal phase and termination of treatment. Since it is in this phase of treatment that reflections on cure and the good life may explicitly play the most central role, neglecting this facet of the treatment has meant that the issue of health has been incompletely addressed by psychoanalysis. (3) The fully analyzed patient (or analyst!) is more readily viewed as a fiction in contemporary psychoanalysis. Recognizing the illusory nature of perfectionistic ideals of a "complete analysis," we analysts may neglect the topic of health, broadly construed. (4) Psychoanalysis, with its tragic worldview, is a psychology of illness, focusing on what goes wrong in development. The best humans could achieve, according to Freud, was to transform "neurotic misery into common unhappiness" (Breuer and Freud 1895, 304). Suffering is inevitable, Freud felt, because of the inherent tension between our biological nature, especially our instinctual nature, and the dictates of civilization. We are driven creatures who create our own suffering through the clash between our asocial, somatically based sexual and aggressive fantasies and drives and the constricting and repressive demands of civilization. A life simply without tension is as good as it gets. Human suffering, according to Freud and most subsequent psychoanalysts, can be lessened although not eliminated. In a world in which suffering cannot be eradicated, the good life involves the capacity to live with clear-eyed rationality, to peel away distorting illusions including erroneous religious hopes for salvation, to bear life's burdens with greater clarity and stoical equanimity, and to love and work with a measure of success and fulfillment. (5) With its "hermeneutics of suspicion," psychoanalysis tends to debunk what is positive in the search for the hidden and seamy underside of apparently constructive ideals and behavior. Is it any wonder then that analysts, to borrow from Shakespeare, "know what we are but not what we may be."

Psychoanalysis and the Good Life

The examined life is, for Freud, essential to the good life. Freud continued and radically extended the centuries-old Augustinian tradition of deep self-investigation with his writings on the unconscious, transference, resistance, and dreamwork. Human reflection, action, and morality have been greatly complicated ever since Freud plumbed the unconscious. The unconscious is another word for the ubiquity of self-deception, the impossibility of complete self-awareness, and the possibility of exquisite creativeness. We are not transparent to ourselves. Actions and intentions have multiple conscious and unconscious meanings and functions. There are several morals to this story: in such a world we have an endless capacity to deceive ourselves and to do evil; we can never completely know ourselves; we have an exquisite capacity for unconsciously communicating with ourselves and healing ourselves; and the examined life is never-ending (Rubin 2003).

"Turn your eyes inward," writes Freud, "look into your own depths, learn first to know yourself." A central assumption of Buddhism is that without a formal training—such as meditation—most people sleepwalk through life unaware of the actual texture of their experience. Without specialized training we get emotionally highjacked by thoughts, feelings, and fantasies. We plan, obsess, daydream, and worry. We tend to endlessly rehash the past and anticipate the future. Meanwhile we miss the present.

Participating in therapy and ongoing self-analysis obviously cultivates greater self-awareness. Buddhism also recommends meditation: a careful, nonjudgmental attentiveness to whatever is occurring in the present moment. I think of it as the mind turning to investigate its own workings in an experience-near manner. The purpose of meditative practice, contrary to popular misconception, is not to make anything special happen—such as silencing or emptying the chattering mind—but to relate to whatever is happening in our experience (no matter how confusing or disturbing) with a spirit of self-friendship, that is, with tolerance and a sense of inner spaciousness and acceptance.

The Vietnamese Zen teacher Thich Nhat Hanh gives an example of mindfulness in daily life: "While washing the dishes you might be thinking about the tea afterward, and so try to get them [the dishes] out of the way as quickly as possible in order to drink the tea. But that means that you are incapable of living during the time you are washing the dishes. When you are washing the dishes, washing the dishes must be the most important thing in your life. Just as when you are drinking tea, drinking tea must be the most important thing in your life" (Nhat Hanh 1987, 24).

Meditation or mindfulness is an incomparable means of developing self-awareness, fostering our capacity to cultivate moment-to-moment awareness or attentiveness. A Zen story illustrates the way the mindfulness that Buddhism points toward is more extensive than what we ordinarily mean when we think or talk about awareness. "Nan-in [a teacher of Zen] was visited by Tenno [a student and aspiring teacher of Zen], who, having passed his apprenticeship, had become a teacher. The day happened to be rainy, so Tenno wore wooden clogs and carried an umbrella. After greeting him Nan-in remarked: 'I suppose you left your wooden clogs in the vestibule. I want to know if your umbrella is on the right or left side of the clogs?' Tenno, confused, had no instant answer. He realized that he was unable to carry his Zen every minute. He became Nan-in's pupil, and he studied six more years to accomplish his every-minute Zen" (Reps 1919, 34).

Meditation cultivates the capacity to hear when we listen, see when we look, and taste when we eat. Formerly inaccessible thoughts, feelings, and fantasies emerge. We develop the capacity to sit with and through a wider range of feelings. Our tolerance for the different facets of our experience expands. We become more self-accepting. We also become more present. We can more easily deeply commune with ourselves, other people, animals, and nature. Empathy and compassion are deeply cultivated (Rubin 1996).

Our culture is permeated with the implicit as well as explicit search to transcend the dizzying complexity of inner life and embodied existence. The notion of the unconscious casts severe doubt on the dream of self-mastery and self-transcendence. When complete self-awareness is viewed as an illusion, as it is within psychoanalysis, then the examined life is seen as never ending. Mental health and the good life then become a process not a destination. Melanie Klein (1960) pointed to the irreducibly fluid nature of mental life—the way, that is, that we experience alternating states of being, each with its own particular style of relatedness and defensiveness. Mental health, from this Kleinian perspective, involves skillfully navigating the ever changing and sometimes turbulent waters of our lives without drowning, rather than transcending difficulties forever and reaching a static, conflict-free state of being.

In Japanese aesthetics there is a great emphasis on *wabi sabi*, (Koren 1994, 7) sometimes described as the beauty of things imperfect, impermanent, and incomplete. Eschewing the illusory ideals of perfection that permeate our culture, psychoanalysis joins Japanese aesthetics and Zen in a *this-* (rather than other-) worldly conception of living, which provides a realistic ideal and also mitigates the quick-fix mentality that reigns in our culture. The implication is that the good life entails engaging and embracing life moment-to-moment in its messiness and complexity rather than seeking to achieve a permanent and irreversible state of health that is beyond and devoid of suffering and conflict.

People demand it and forfeit it, seek it and lose it—what is this desideratum we call freedom? Freedom, as John Maynard Keyes somewhere said, demands eternal vigilance. It requires interminable self-examination. Freedom is often talked about in contemporary popular and academic discourse in polarized terms: we are free *or* we are determined; we are puppets of language and history (according to postmodernists) *or* we are capable of "just saying no," of "just doing it" (as self-help gurus and television ads claim). The work of Freud in particular and psychoanalysis in general suggests that the terms of these debates are problematic because they polarize what are mutually interconnected and reinforcing experiences of being, namely, having conditioning and having the capacity for reflection and self-transformation. Freedom for Freud was always contextual and relative, never absolute: what I—as a practitioner of yoga who continually experiences the reality of constraints—think of as a *freedom-within-structure*. While we are all authors of our own lives, our authorship is not without limitations. We are also determined. One can never transcend what Shakespeare termed "the ten thousand shocks that flesh is heir to," but one can gain a measure of freedom. This is what Peter Gay, in a felicitous phrase, terms Freud's "deterministic psychology of freedom" (1990, 89).

For Sandor Ferenczi the possibilities for freedom were more radical than for Freud. For Ferenczi it was possible not only to experience mental health but to lead a more unfettered life. In his reflections on dissolving transference and super-ego formations and living elastically in "The Elasticity of Psychoanalytic Technique" (1928), there are intimations of the freedom that he believed and hoped psychoanalysis at its best could foster:

> It is the business of the real character analysis to do away
> with, at any rate temporarily, any kind of super-ego,
> including that of the analyst. The patient should end by

ridding himself of any emotional attachment that is independent of his own reason and his own libidinal tendencies. Only a complete dissolution of the super-ego can
bring about a radical cure. Successes that consist in the
substitution of one super-ego for another must be
regarded as transference successes; they fail to attain the
final aim of therapy, the dissolution of the transference…. The ideal result of a completed analysis is precisely that elasticity which analytic technique demands
of the mental therapist. (99)

The good life, for Ferenczi, was the uncoerced and liberated life. We don't
free-associate in order to be cured, claims Ferenczi, we are cured when we can
free associate (1927, p. 79), by which I think he meant: when we can live with
greater playfulness, freedom, authenticity, and spontaneity rather than social
conformity, automatic compliance, or self-neglectful responsibility for others.

With freedom comes responsibility. Contemporary popular and academic discussions of suffering, evil, and ethics tend to establish false contrasts:
splitting moral accountability and empathy. Right-wing political commentators demand moral accountability but are unempathic toward the poverty-
stricken or oppressed. Liberal apologists for the downtrodden express
empathy for their plight but sometimes neglect moral accountability. At its
best, psychoanalysis encourages empathic understanding of the experience of
the oppressed or of the evil-doer, while also acknowledging moral responsibility. "Moral responsibility," for Hans Loewald (1978, 8), involves "appropriating" one's history, by which he means reworking, reorganizing, and
transforming the legacy of our past so as to create a unique life in the present. This involves integrating and drawing on our histories rather than being
excessively detached from or driven by them. If we are either too detached
from our past or too entangled in it. our lives are either depleted or enslaved.
We are then not morally responsible in the present.

For Loewald, human life is devitalized if we neglect our past. The past
is the potential wellspring of our life in the present, the root of our sense
of ourselves and our world, our meanings and our passions. Our past experiences—even negative ones—are like manure that fertilizes the garden of
our lives, adding depth and texture to the way we live in the present.

The past is defensively evaded when psycho-spiritual traditions treat only the present as real and the past as illusory and counsel spiritual seekers to "let go" of it. Many spiritual seekers strive to become detached from painful experiences in their past rather than engaging and integrating them into their lives in the present. The past is also neglected when popular self-help writings recommend that we just "get over" our past.

If we voluntarily sever links with our past we create a discontinuous sense of our own history, which leaves us adrift and devitalized in the present. And we are then condemned, as Santayana warned, to repeat our history and thereby impoverish our life in the present. I suspect that this is one reason some meditators struggle with the same conflicts over self-care and intimacy even after years of meditating.

The person who avoids his or her emotional life by, let us say, minimizing or repressing losses or trauma through cultivating detachment may well be at the mercy of the feelings he or she has disowned. I am thinking of a Buddhist who suffered traumatic losses as an adolescent and trained himself to detach from painful feelings. After college he began meditating and refined his capacity to disavow disturbing emotions. He denied his pain, never mourned his losses, adopted a super-independent stance toward life, and phobically avoided painful arenas of life including dependence on others for emotional sustenance. The disavowed losses still haunted and impoverished his life years later. As an adult he had little intimacy and minimized emotional pain, which he was immunized from. He avoided whole facets of life that threatened to trigger unpleasant feelings and deep emotional anguish. His capacity for intimacy and for empathizing with the emotional pain of others, for example, was deeply compromised.

If we are too immersed in the past—haunted by old memories and experiences—then we betray the present. We greatly diminish the aliveness of the present when we accommodate it to old scenarios and expectations. We are prone to unreflectiveness and hyperreactivity. We have no panoramic perspective on our experience or our life. Our life resembles an emotional roller coaster. Submersion in our own subjectivity also compromises our relationships with other people. We view them egocentrically—only in terms of how they affect us—rather than as separate beings with their own unique values, wishes, and needs. Our relationships are then fraught with conflict and disappointment.

Appropriating our history, in Loewald's view, entails drawing on our experience as a crucial resource for life. The past is not so much outgrown but woven into our current life. An important aspect of appropriating our histories is what I have termed "self-creation," building a personally authentic and meaningful life in the present by creatively reworking and transforming our experience (Rubin 1998). When we draw upon the experience and meanings embodied in our history but are not subsumed by them, our lives in the present have greater meaning and richness. Such a life is neither a sterile imitation of another's existence, nor a reactive rebellion against ways of living that we may in fact value, but is a life that has texture, vitality, and depth and is authentically one's own.

Ordinarily such moral accountability, like freedom, is elusive. We are usually quite attached to our sense of ourselves and our view of the world, which makes us rigid. We want the world and our lives to unfold according to our vision of it. When life does not conform to our expectations, we become frustrated and angry. *Attachment*, not money, is the real root of all evil, Buddhists might argue. For such attachment leads to an egocentric perspective. We place ourselves at the center of the universe. We become more selfish and greedy, less kindhearted and less open to the uniqueness of others. Attachment leads to emotional and intellectual intolerance.

Attachment in psychoanalytic circles takes various forms. We may hold that the theory we believe in or the school of thought we identify with is the only valid one, and we denigrate the theories and allegiances of other therapists. When challenged we get defensive instead of curious about what another viewpoint might teach us. What Buddhism terms *nonattachment*, or a nonclinging and nonpossessive relationship to ourselves, to others, and to the world, is central to freedom, compassion, and wisdom.

A story from the Zen tradition illustrates what Buddhism means by attachment and nonattachment.

> Two Zen monks, Tanzan and Ekido, were once traveling together down a muddy road. A heavy rain was falling. Coming around a bend, they met a lovely girl in a silk kimono and sash, unable to cross the intersection. "Come on, girl," said Tanzan at once. Lifting her in his arms, he

carried her over the mud. Ekido did not speak again until
that night when they reached a lodging temple. Then he
no longer could restrain himself. "We monks don't go
near females," he told Tanzan, "especially not young and
lovely ones. It is dangerous. Why did you do that?" "I
left the girl there," said Tanzan. "Are you still carrying
her?"(Reps 1919, 18)

Engaging the world, not renouncing it, is essential in psychoanalysis and
Buddhism. There are periodic warnings in Buddhism about the dangers of
detachment. Paul Reps retells the story of an old woman in China who had
supported a monk for over twenty years. She had built a little hut for him and
fed him while he was meditating. Finally she wondered just what progress he
had made in all this time.

To find out, she obtained the help of a girl rich in desire. "Go and embrace
him," she told her, "and then suddenly ask: 'What now?'" The girl called
upon the monk and without much ado caressed him, asking him what he was
going to do about it. "An old tree grows on a cold rock in winter," replied the
monk somewhat poetically. "Nowhere is there any warmth." The girl
returned and related what he had said [to the old woman].

"To think I fed that fellow for twenty years!" exclaimed the old woman in
anger. "He showed no consideration for your need, no disposition to explain
your condition. He need not have responded to passion, but at least he should
have evidenced some compassion." She at once went to the hut of the monk
and burned it down (Reps 1919, 10).

An ethos of asceticism, renunciation, and melancholia haunts psychoanalysis as well as Buddhism. Assuming that mental health involves a stoical
life of clear-eyed rationality without illusions, many psychoanalysts since the
time of Freud tacitly or explicitly counsel renouncing, foregoing, or abstaining from unrealistic or illusory desires and wishes. That this "appetite lost"
(Phillips 1998) may breed a somber and melancholic soul seems insufficiently
discussed in psychoanalysis.

If "appetite lost" is a central facet of the classical vision of the good life,
then "appetite regained" (Phillips 1998) is crucial to what I would provisionally term the "aestheticist" wing of postclassical psychoanalysis. Not
the somber, stoical rationalist but the heroic, individuated artist, with her

creativity, authenticity, spontaneity, and aliveness striving for authentic self-expression and self-transcendence, embodied for Winnicott—as it did years before for Otto Rank—the good life from this vantage point. There is more to life than confronting our fate with clarity and dignity, according to Rank. We could also create something enduring—through contributing to one's community, raising a happy child, or fashioning a work of art—that might outlast us and thus grant us the opportunity to go beyond ourselves and perhaps transcend our tragic fate. This, for Rank, is essential to a well-lived life. The good life, for contemporary analysts along this aestheticist axis such as Adam Phillips and Michael Eigen, involves curiosity, exuberance, and ecstasy.

Freud's work on the unconscious and dreamwork offers an unsuspected doorway into the enriching universe of "appetite regained." There is a deep human predilection to reduce or narrow down the mysterious and wondrous abundance that we call life. "Newton's vision and single sleep," Blake terms it. We search for our essence, speculate about our destiny. Doing so is reassuring. It creates an apparent order—a world that can be mapped. Emily Dickinson said it thus: "The Soul selects her own society / Then shuts the door / On her divine majority / Obtrude no more ...I've known her from an ample nation / Choose one / Then close the valves of her attention" (1957, 8). The nature of dreamwork—particularly its dense complexity and its idiosyncratic meaning and nature—suggests that we are all (even the most prosaic among us) artists capable of creating fertile, unique, and often surreal dreamscapes that capture with brilliant lucidity and specificity our hopes and fears, our demons and saviors.

The dreaming experience is not something that happens only when we are asleep. "Oh, these humans of old knew how to dream and did not need to fall asleep first," wrote Nietzsche (quoted in Duerr 1985, 114). The dreaming mode of thinking—the creation of condensed and displaced symbols and images related to unfinished emotional feelings, fantasies, and conflicts from our past that are triggered by experiences imbued with unsuspected meanings—happens when we are awake as a backdrop to our conscious thinking and feeling.

The dreaming experience—and the uniquely creative way that Freud, Jung, and Winnicott, among others, taught us to play with dreams—is applicable to daily life. If we take the dream as a model for the unconscious operation of thought, and if we take free association and evenly suspended attention as potentially creative ways of speaking and listening that encourage the emergence of unconscious facets of our experience, then we would experience our emotional life and the world in a more fertile and creative way. One of my supervisors in psychoanalytic training illustrated this when he encouraged me to listen to intellectual discourse and everyday speech, no less than patients, with that meditative state of mind that Freud (1912) termed "evenly hovering attention" (Zvi Lothane, personal communication). Then the world—the sights and sounds of daily life, the images and ideas in novels or movies, the artwork in our homes and offices, the people we converse with, the plays and music that move us, the sensuous pleasures we relish—are potentially pregnant with unsuspected meanings. Overdetermined, emotionally charged, condensed, and displaced images that symbolically encode unresolved emotional conflicts and unrealized potentials from the past are evoked by these and other experiences in the present in what Bollas, in a felicitous phrase, terms the "dreamwork of one's life" (1992, 53). As we develop the capacity to play with and associate to these images in an uncensored and unfettered way, a variety of further meanings emerge and point in unpredictable directions. New insights, questions, pathways, and dreams are generated by our secondary process reflection upon and interpretation of these evocative trains of thought and emotion. Our internal creativity may lie fallow for a while until an experience in the present triggers new condensed and displaced images resplendent with evocative possibilities, which we then decode. And so on and so on.

The external environment, as well as our emotional life, can be reanimated when we are attuned to the dreamwork of our lives. How we experience the world is shaped, in no small measure, by how we look. Winnicott taught us that a child's torn blanket was, for an imaginative toddler, not a worthless and disposable item but a precious possession. A teenager asks his mother to drive to the back of a small shopping center near where they live. She does. When they arrive he is overjoyed while she is perplexed. Because she only sees debris—garbage cans from the restaurants and stores, worn stairs, and chipped rails—she cannot fathom why he wanted to go there and why he is so happy. "You are not looking at this place as a skater would," he tells her. He has noticed that she has failed to recognize that the fire hydrant, staircase, and ledge were a heavenly course for an in-line skating and skateboarding enthusiast such as himself.

A unique perspective on the nature of the self, as well as moral responsibility, emerges when we are receptive to the dreamwork of our lives. Postmodern discourse recognizes the complexity of the self but then makes an unwarranted and erroneous epistemological leap and claims that our existence is illusory; a Lacanian mirage. Psycho-spiritual writings, on the other hand, herald the finding of an authentic, idealized, essential, selfless self. Contemporary popular culture offers a less "spiritual" but equally essentialistic vision of the self. "You be you," Nike commercials beseech us. But are we singular? And do we have a particular destiny?

Seeing the self as like a dream, by which I mean, as a dense, complex, and multi-faceted phenomenon—a work of art in progress—presents an illuminating perspective on self-experience. It also offers a critique of the nihilism of postmodern views and the essentialism of popular and spiritual conceptions of self.

Western secular culture fosters self-inflation. In Western culture the self is often treated as the highest good. The desires of the isolated individual are worshiped. This often breeds narcissism, which is implicated in a great range of evil and is the source of great suffering in our world. In Eastern meditative traditions self-centeredness is viewed as a villain, the cause of greed and immorality. Spiritual traditions celebrate the virtues of selflessness. While the spiritual sense of self opens up new possibilities for living, there are also pathologies of spirit, for example, the "spiritual materialism" of contemplative seekers who use spiritual experiences as a mark of distinction in competition with others, or experiences of fusion that lead to self-effacement, not self-transcendence.

But "regard for the self is not evil," Abraham Heschel reminds us. "It is when arrogating to the self what is not its due, enhancing one's interest at the expense of others or setting up the self as an ultimate goal that evil comes into being" (1955, 400). I have repeatedly witnessed among meditators whom I know, and have treated, the way in which Eastern contemplative viewpoints can breed self-neglect. This occurs when one uses meditation to detach from rather than engage one's troubling past and when one treats others as more important than, instead of equal to, oneself.

In the work of Fromm, Winnicott, and Kohut, among others, psychoanalysis suggests a third, more constructive option to the alienating hedonism of secular individualism and the self-nullifying potential of renunciative spiritual doctrines. Altruism and self-care are both essential aspects of a balanced life, according to these and other psychoanalysts.

By highlighting our complexity and fluidity, contemporary relationally oriented analysts such as Stephen Mitchell, Irwin Hoffman, Michael Eigen, Robert Stolorow, George Atwood, and Philip Bromberg suggest that it is possible to recognize our multidimensionality without falling into the postmodernist fallacy of jettisoning our individuality/singularity. They also make us more skeptical about the singular, essentialistic, and authentic self of contemplative and pop psycho-spiritual writings. A richer sense of human subjectivity is possible when we reflect upon the, fluid, multidimensional self depicted in psychoanalytic writings. Intersubjectivists describe the possibility of a life that is imbued with greater insight, self-stability, flexibility, affect tolerance, and more complex experiences of self (see, for example, Stolorow, Brandchaft, and Atwood 1987). The self is then like a symphony orchestra with many instruments—rationality and passion, will and surrender, insight and action—that need to play together in harmony (Rubin 1996).

Jung radicalizes and enlarges psychoanalytic views of the self. For Jung the field of what constitutes the well-lived life expands from the individual's self-realization and self-actualization to what we might think of as a spiritual self or sense of the universe. There are, for Jung, at least three facets to the life well lived: individuation, wholeness (integrating opposites—including so-called male and female values—and becoming multidimensioned people), and living with a "religious attitude." Individuation involves the development of our uniqueness and our full humanity. The Jungian emphasis on the integration of opposites is important because of what the Greeks and the Stoics termed *antakolouthia* or the "mutual entailment of the virtues" (Murphy 1992). We ordinarily think of virtues as self-sufficient, complete, and, as it were, capable of standing on their own. But no virtue or quality—even apparently valuable ones such as honesty or awareness—is virtuous by itself. A well-lived life requires the balancing and integration of seeming opposites. Honesty without compassion, for example, is cruelty. Awareness devoid of action remains merely intellectual knowledge. The third crucial facet in a life well lived for Jung, a religious attitude, is a feeling of being embedded in a larger life, a world imbued with depth, sacredness, and meaning and approaching that world with reverence and scrupulous attentiveness.

Buddhism implicitly says that there is more to being human than having an integrated and cohesive self. The integrated self, which is the acme of mental health in psychoanalysis, is viewed by Buddhists as an *arrested, suboptimal state of development*. For contemplatives, to be fully human is to move beyond the psychoanalytic and commonsense belief that one's life is the ultimate value. Buddhism implicitly points to a vital and neglected facet of self-experience, what I have termed the *nonselfcentered* or *spiritual self*, by which I mean a non-self-preoccupied state of being in which one is open to the moment without a sense of time, unselfconscious but acutely aware, self-"forgetful" yet not self-neglectful, highly focused and engaged although relaxed and fearless (Rubin 1996; 1998).[7] Many of us have had such experiences—perhaps communing with nature or a loved one, meditating or praying, playing sports, or creating art.

Compassion is a crucial ingredient of a life well lived according to Buddhism. Psychoanalysts such as Fromm and Kohut have emphasized the importance of empathy, concern, and compassion as well as authenticity, self-realization, and creativity. Buddhism also emphasizes compassion but widens its sphere, which suggests that psychoanalysis has underestimated human possibilities in this area. The compassion Buddhism points to is more than empathy—that is, more than the ability to enter into and share another's suffering. In dissolving the barriers between self and other, the nonselfcentered self ushers in a different kind of consciousness of self in relation to others. When self-experience is less self-referential and self-preoccupied, and more self-expansive and interconnected, we feel more in touch with people and nature. Then instead of asking, What is the other doing (or not doing) for the self?—the question we usually focus on in psychoanalysis and daily life—we ask, What might the self do for the other?

Cultivating the experience of nonseparation and intimacy toward all people, including those who may wish to harm us, leads to what Tibetan Buddhists term "great compassion" (Gyatso 1999, 124). This widens the circle of compassion to include all living beings, not simply those closest to us. Morality can be viewed in more universalistic and less exclusive ways because of the concern for the other as well as the self. This fosters a radical sense of responsibility toward others that includes ethical conduct toward strangers as well as family and friends.

Gandhi's relationship to a potential assassin illustrates the great compassion that the Dalai Lama is pointing toward. A man was sent to assassinate Gandhi.

The assassin sat in the audience at one of Gandhi's public lectures. The assassin was so moved by the power of Gandhi's spiritual teachings that he scrapped his plan. He prostrated himself in front of Gandhi after the talk and tearfully apologized for his plan. Take a moment and imagine yourself in the identical situation. What would you say to a person who told you that they had just moments ago planned to kill you? …Gandhi's response was: "What will you tell your boss—the man who sent you—about your failure to carry out your plan?"

In the foregoing, I have highlighted several key dimensions of a life well lived within psychoanalytic and Buddhist writings. What are the morals of the tales that psychoanalysis and Buddhism tell? The good life is protean: there is no single best way of living. Each person must discover and create the best way to live. Since inner experience is fluid rather than static, this changes from moment to moment. But the good life always asks us to engage life with care and attentiveness in all its complexity rather than attempting to transcend struggle; it asks us to operate on all cylinders rather than perfecting partial domains of experience, and to integrate and balance complementary qualities (awareness and moral action, rationality and ecstasy) rather than cultivating particular isolated virtues. We need to strive to be free even as we continually confront how we are determined. The good life entails attunement to the other as well as cultivation of the self. Living with compassion and empathy as well as authenticity and vitality are crucial.

Rudyard Kipling believed, perhaps like many of us, that "East is East and West is West and never the twain shall meet." But dancing in the spaces between psychoanalysis and Buddhism and fostering a cross-pollinating dialogue between these two wisdom traditions might greatly enrich the quality of our lives and aid us in experiencing a well-lived life.[8]

Commentary

MANAGING TRAFFIC ON THE BRIDGE BETWEEN PSYCHOANALYSIS AND BUDDHISM

CHARLES SPEZZANO

As interest has intensified in the task of building bridges between psychoanalysis and spiritual traditions, the difficulty of holding the tension between the two sides has become evident. Can a bridge-building essay hold this tension, keep the bridge up, and convey the sense that the whole task is worth continuing to pursue—because psychoanalysis and the spiritual tradition, in this case Buddhism, will enrich each other? Jeffery Rubin's essay accomplishes these difficult tasks. His arguments that psychoanalysis can find a useful account of compassion in Buddhism, and that Buddhism can find in psychoanalysis a useful guide to more healthy integration of one's personal history into a more alive awareness of self and world in this moment, are especially compelling and worth special attention.

Equally compelling and useful is Rubin's use of D.W. Winnicott's transitional space concept to ground the notion of not being attached even to Buddhism itself. I have to confess that I have always been what the New Yorkers of my youth used to call a "sucker" for this idea of transitional space. It seems to be the main point of analysis as I have come to practice it. That is, my aim is to help patients open up mental space in which they can play with affects, images, or ideas (question them, transform them, or link them to other affects, images, or ideas). So, I read Rubin as trying to balance the notion that there is no leverage, whether psychological or spiritual, for lifting oneself into the good life with the notion that the unconscious might be a kind of leverage for the next best thing: questioning any account of psychological life and ethics that tries to lift us up by making things seem uncomplicated.

Having set the stage for his careful balancing act, Rubin moves on to argue that psychoanalysis is unique in its "comprehensive understanding of and systematic approach to unconsciousness." Psychoanalysis brings us face to face with complexity and conflict at every turn, but, Rubin argues, it suffers from the absence of a theory of well-being, since it is mostly (except, perhaps, for Winnicott and a few others) "a psychology of illness that neglects health, creativity, intimacy, and spirituality." Here, I thought, as I reread this part of Rubin's essay, he had slipped something in: at first the issue was only that psychoanalysis neglected spirituality, but now the assessment (indictment) had been enlarged (to sustain the balancing act on which the essay depends for its momentum) to include a neglect of all aspects of well-being.

Once this move is made it becomes crucial for Rubin's further efforts in the essay, but I can only partially accept the notion that psychoanalysis has implicitly defined health and well-being as only the absence of illness and that it has neglected not just spirituality but also health, creativity, and intimacy. Freud clearly thought that a pleasurable sublimation of libido was possible in many areas of life. There have been analysts (Winnicott, Marion Milner, and Rollo May, to name just a few) who have written about creativity as something other than what happens if you are not psychologically ill. Intimacy was clearly part of W. R. D. Fairbairn's vision of analysis, a vision in which it is strongly suggested that if you analyze repressed bad objects you will make contact again with your capacity to be excited about good objects. I could go on and try to mitigate each of the charges that psychoanalysis neglects health, creativity, and intimacy, but Rubin is right that there are few ideas in wide circulation in psychoanalysis that refer to well-being, beyond Freud's having commented that the good life involves being able to love and work with pleasure and passion and that analysis aims to free oneself from neuroses to live that good life. As Phillip Rieff put it in *The Triumph of the Therapeutic*, psychoanalysis is not a salvation psychology. In fact, Rubin's indictment is a notion I have been disturbed by for many years since reading *Beyond Ego*, where two chapters in the section "Psychological Well-Being: East and West" discuss meditation as a useful or necessary road to well-being and the good life besides Western forms of therapy. More specifically, the editors introduced that section with this observation: "Traditionally, psychologists and philosophers have tended to avoid defining the highest good for humanity, resorting to negative terms in defining health as the absence of disease and good as the absence of evil. Health by definition is only 'not sick'" (Walsh and Vaughan 1980, 119).

Sometimes I think that psychoanalysis has presented a picture of the mind in which the pleasure of being alive is felt when one connects to a good object with a sense of mutual love or when one is working passionately (with some combination of excitement and autonomy). At other times I spin this differently and say that psychoanalysis has left the impression that joy, for example, might be felt at any given moment, barring internal barriers to having one's normal share of it, without one having to do anything specific to bring it about (other than not engaging in any anxiety-catalyzed unconscious defensive activity). As Rubin says near the end of his essay, in his vision of life, "awareness devoid of action remains merely intellectual knowledge."

So, I got over my initial hesitation about Rubin's indictment and went on reading the essay accepting the notion that psychoanalysis certainly has not made a big deal about how to live the good life, especially since Rubin addresses what had really bothered me about his indictment, namely, that, despite having been unable to formulate a convincing account of the good life, analysts in daily practice all have some notion about it (and its associated value system). Perhaps that notion has remained hidden because we have been trained not to dispense advice or communicate our personal visions of the good life to patients. That leads me to want psychoanalysts to develop better theories about well-being and the good life, because when we have the sense that our interpretations are informed and shaped by consensually accepted theories, we are less squeamish about implicitly nudging a patient to think or imagine, if not to act, in a certain way.

In any case, Rubin goes in another direction: people cannot depend exclusively on psychoanalysis (not even when we include lifelong post-analytic self-analysis) in their striving for well-being, health, creativity, and intimacy. I agree with this, but wonder if it needs to be said more as a corrective to the literature than because patients or analysts have actually believed that analysis is the whole path to the good life. If, as Rubin suggests, patients have gotten the message from their analysts (or we have gotten the message from the literature we have created) that "a life simply without tension is as good as it gets," none of the people I have analyzed have bought that message, and analysts themselves have all sorts of other ways in which they are committed to enhancing their own well-being—even beyond spending August in the Hamptons catching up on *New York Times* fiction bestsellers. Nonetheless, we haven't integrated any theory of joy into our theories about therapeutic action. So, I appreciate Rubin's nudging us toward a general acceptance of the idea that we all will (and should) do more than immerse ourselves in analytic self-reflection in our pursuit of the good life. I also appreciate his eloquence and persuasiveness in offering Buddhist meditation as one way to enhance our sense of what we may be.

Oddly, when developing this idea, Rubin starts out with the Buddhist assumption that specialized meditation training cures us of our universal illness (my phrasing) of sleepwalking through life. What makes this seem different from psychoanalysis wanting to cure us of neurotic self-deception, I have to assume, is that for Rubin meditative practice actively trains one to have a healthier relationship to "whatever is happening in our experience …with a spirit of self-friendship." Even so, I found myself confused because Rubin seems to say that there is a sort of psychoanalytic equivalent to Buddhist meditative contact with the present experience, namely, free association (which, in turn, one might say is what psychoanalysis trains us to do better). Rubin ends this part of his essay with an implication that Ferenczi was deviating from the kind of psychoanalysis generally associated with Freud and Klein, in which the good life is acceptance of the limits of the Oedipal compromise or the depressive position. Ferenczi was veering off more toward the kind of psychoanalysis that would eventually become associated with Winnicott, where the patient ends up not just more tolerant of being a conflicted and limited unconscious subject but more playful, free, and authentic. At this point, I was reading Rubin as saying that Buddhist meditation is either a natural enhancer of such a Ferenczian-Winnicottian analytic agenda or a necessary addition to it.

But then Rubin suddenly led me around a corner into another neighborhood: morality. He had hinted that this was coming earlier in the essay by talking about values, but it still took me by surprise when I realized we had moved from freedom to be in the present (an agenda of both meditation and, seemingly, some theories of analysis) to the issues of how freedom demands responsibility and empathy and how "contemporary popular and academic discussions of suffering, evil, and ethics" tend to falsely split the concerns about responsibility from those of empathy. Psychoanalysis "at its best" (i.e., in Loewald's writings), Rubin began to argue, does combine attention to both "empathic understanding of the experience of the oppressed or evildoer, while also acknowledging moral responsibility," whereas Buddhism might push one toward detachment from the emotional reality of one's history and thereby limit one's sense of empathy and moral responsibility. On the other hand, Rubin argues that Buddhism can balance a psychoanalytic emphasis on dwelling on the past (or, better, integrating it) with detachment from the past: "What Buddhism terms *nonattachment*, or a nonclinging and nonpossessive relationship to ourselves, to others, and to the world, is central to freedom, compassion, and wisdom."

I thought here that Rubin might be intending to elaborate the notion that Buddhism potentially teaches analysts not to get overly attached to their theories, but, having made that point, he returned to the idea that analysis is traditionally characterized by "an ethos of asceticism, renunciation, and melancholia." He also returns to the comparison of traditional "appetite lost" classical analysis versus the "appetite regained" attitude of what Rubin calls the "aestheticist" brand of "postclassical" analysis, emphasizing "curiosity, exuberance, and ecstasy." This time around, however, Rubin suggests that we should not be too quick to include Freud in the appetite-lost, renunciation and resignation school of analysis because, in his writings on dreams, Freud opened a doorway to recognizing the inherently playful and imaginative tendency of the mind. "The external environment, as well as our emotional life, can be reanimated when we are attuned to the dreamwork of our lives."

Following what to me was another sudden twist, Rubin then returned to the issue of moral responsibility. He offered the argument that dreamwork, if we are receptive to it, becomes a psychoanalytic perspective not only on the nature of the self but also on moral responsibility. To Rubin the dream reveals a self that is an evolving work, or art in progress, and not a postmodern series of discontinuous selves. In other words, the psychoanalysis of dreams has always been a third alternative to either "the nihilism of postmodern views" or "the essentialism of popular and spiritual conceptions of self" because psychoanalysis, from Freud to Winnicott, has been on a trajectory of recognizing the dreaming mind as a constantly changing and yet continuous organ. As a result psychoanalysis avoids the self neglect to which meditative traditions are vulnerable and, especially in the work of such authors as Fromm, Winnicott, and Kohut, steers a course through the Scylla of "alienating hedonism of secular individualism" and the Charybdis of "self-nullifying potential of renunciate spiritual doctrines."

I was a bit confused here since, in most of the essay, the spiritual had been associated with the life-enhancing, but I understood that there are different spiritual traditions and Rubin was focusing here on the self-denying side of spiritual traditions and contrasting that with what he sees as the best of psychoanalysis, which—in the writings of Mitchell, Hoffman, Eigen, Stolorow, Atwood, and Bromberg—balances altruism and self-care, as well as balancing self-multidimensionality with individuality/singularity. Jung adds another ingredient to a blend of what is common to good spirituality and good psychoanalysis. He expands the field of what constitutes the good life "from the individual's self-realization and self-actualization to the universe," the psychoanalytic equivalent of a spiritual sense of being one with the universe.

Rubin concludes that what psychoanalysts have not been telling patients, are not now telling them, and probably will not tell them anytime soon is that they should be "open to the moment without a sense of time" or "engage life with care and attentiveness in all its complexity rather than attempting to transcend struggle." While we have written as if we hope, in psychoanalysis, that patients will come to live with "authenticity and vitality," we have not written much about telling them to start "living with compassion and empathy."

I cannot tell if Rubin believes that we should start telling patients to live more compassionately and empathetically, or just that we should value other traditions and practices in which such advice is given (since it isn't likely to be given in analysis, or shouldn't be). I don't think this issue is a small matter. It touches on the whole question of whether we try to keep ourselves limited, as much as humanly possible (which, many of us now believe, is not as possible as words such as *detached, objective, abstinent,* or *neutral* suggest—regardless of what we had been taught they mean), to pointing out what analysands are doing and not in any way tell them to do something that they are not doing. This goes further than the focus of Rubin's essay takes him.

Rubin chose to not use any clinical vignettes, but I want to give one (I don't think we can address any topic fully without clinical examples). A patient came to me because a previous therapist had abruptly moved to the East Coast. The patient seemed to have learned much about himself and his inhibitions about loving and now was living with a woman he seemed happily engaged with and was planning to marry. Yet a fairly crippling medical symptom was plaguing him, which had been investigated by all sorts of specialists and deemed psychosomatic. That this symptom had plagued him virtually unabatedly throughout the previous analysis had never seemed to bother his previous therapist (who, as far as I know, was not bound by some "classical" rules, but appeared to have been an avid student of Winnicottian-relational-intersubjective perspectives). After a year, the patient and I reached an understanding: his symptom was not the result of anxiety but a way to regulate anxiety; that is, it led him to do something specific that, when he did it, relieved not only the physical symptom but his anxiety as well. So I suggested he learn a method of breathing, which gives people something to do when they became anxious. My decision was based solely on the fact that we had achieved an understanding, that he had been suffering for almost six years, and that, as far as I could tell, he was going to keep the symptom because it was his best anxiety-regulating strategy.

The practice of deep and meditative breathing substantially reduced the presence of the symptom, but eventually he had to face his own reluctance to make the practice part of his everyday life and to use it "religiously" (as he put it) whenever he felt his anxiety rising and the symptom coming on. He had another fantasy (which we were able to analyze as, partly, an angry and resentful identification with his father) that life had broken him and life should fix him (without his having to do anything). He was then faced with a decision about whether he would do the one thing he had learned to do to regulate his anxiety.

On an even broader scale, many years ago I was teaching one of my first seminars at the Colorado Center for Psychoanalytic Studies and the senior analyst with whom I was teaching, Gary Martin, pointed out that just because a patient (in this case a man in his twenties or thirties) realizes in analysis that his conflicts, anxieties, and defenses have inhibited him from participating in the social encounters through which we learn to relate to people as lovers and intimates, that does not mean that now, after his realization, he suddenly knows how to do what he might have learned years earlier had he not been so inhibited. Later, I developed a way of pointing out to patients that, while listening to them describe their unsuccessful experiences in certain human situations over and over, it occurred to me that they never reported considering doing or saying anything such as (fill in the blank here). This, I realize, treads close to what, for some analysts, is a dangerous practice of making behavioral suggestions, but I assess it to be a good form of Winnicott's attitude of making psychoanalytic something that might easily not be psychoanalytic. Winnicott is often reported as having held the attitude that I describe thus: "I do as much analysis with each patient as we can do together, but if they need something that is not, strictly speaking, analysis, then I try to do that as well...and so what?" I believe that sometimes this is overused (as the transitional space notion can be) to justify doing anything that pops into one's mind when faced with human suffering, but it is better understood as being a way to make analytic use of something not normally thought of as part of the practice of an analyst. So, I don't just say, "Hey, why don't you try this," when I can see a way to say, "I notice that you tell a story in which the character played by you might easily at a certain moment be expected to at least consider doing this or that, but never once have you mentioned considering doing it."

So, I want to leave Jeffrey Rubin, to whom I am grateful for his continuing to write in a way that makes me think about these issues, with this idea: that we struggle in analysis not only with valuing other practices but also with the whole question of what we, as analysts, might do when we notice not what patients *are* doing (intrapsychically or interpersonally) but what they are *not* doing (and when we find this not-doing striking, given that we all listen through our values and personal visions as well as through that collective wisdom we call psychoanalysis). This is a big question to which he draws our attention in a specific, thought-provoking, and elegantly written way.

Reply

BEYOND EUROCENTRISM AND ORIENTOCENTRISM

JEFFREY B. RUBIN

East and West
Can no longer be kept apart.

—Goethe

I, too, have ropes around my neck, I have them to this day,
pulling me this way and that, East and West, the nooses
tightening, commanding, choose, choose.... Ropes, I do
not choose between you.... I choose neither of you and
both. Do you hear? I refuse to choose.

—Salman Rushdie, *East, West*

There has been a burgeoning interest in recent years in the relationship between the Western psychoanalytic and Buddhist meditative traditions. This nascent dialogue, of which this book is a part, several generations removed from earlier interest among psychoanalysts such as Carl Jung, Erich Fromm, Karen Horney, and Harold Kelman, offers the promise of expanding the resources and depth available to analysands and meditators in pursuing their chosen paths of self-investigation and transformation. This conversation has already illuminated perspectives on psychopathology, visions of selfhood, cure, and change.

I am grateful for the opportunity of being a part of this historic dialogue between these two wisdom traditions. I am also appreciative of the chance to respond to Dr. Charles Spezzano's thoughtful and detailed discussion of my essay. Cross-cultural dialogue—as the dialogue between psychoanalysis and Buddhism must truly be called—is a difficult enterprise, fraught with the potential for misunderstanding. I respect Spezzano for engaging in this perilous project and earnestly grappling with my thinking. I appreciate his attentiveness to my argument, the way he tried to get inside my thinking, and his depth and creativity.

I will respond to several questions and comments stimulated by his commentary. His commentary may be missing a central focus of my essay when he reads me as trying "to balance the notion that there is no leverage, whether psychological or spiritual, for lifting oneself into the good life with the notion that the unconscious might be a kind of leverage for the next best thing: questioning any account of psychological life and ethics that tries to lift us up by making things seem uncomplicated." He seems to read me as saying that given the fact that true liberation is not possible, psychoanalysis's hermeneutic of suspicion is the next best thing. The heart of what I am trying to do is articulate the essence of what psychoanalysis and Buddhism offer to accounts of a life well-lived. In my essay, I try to convey the variety of ways that psychoanalysis and Buddhism can aid us in living a well-lived life. I assert that there is a pathway to freedom—one that each tradition cultivates in different but synergistic ways, both in the mode of never-ending self-examination. While psychoanalytic perspectives on unconsciousness make a crucial contribution to this endeavor, from my perspective they are not "the next best thing" but an indispensable facet of the quest to live a more sane and enlightened life.

In his response to my essay, Spezzano focuses more on what Buddhism offers psychoanalytic visions of the well-lived life than the other way around. Perhaps this is inevitable, given that he is much more familiar with psychoanalysis. But this approach eclipses my central concerns, at least as I think of them. The most radical facet of my perspective, at least as I see it, is not, as Spezzano claims, the way spiritual traditions such as Buddhism and their associated practices might complement analysis but the reverse issue: what psychoanalysis offers spiritual traditions. If Freud and the vast majority of his colleagues were guilty of Eurocentrism, by which I mean, the conscious and unconscious deification of European and North American standards and values, then most recent writings on psychoanalysis and Buddhism have been guilty of the opposite danger, what I have elsewhere termed "Oriento-centrism" the conscious and unconscious idealization of Asian beliefs and practices and the consequent neglect of the potential value of psychoanalytic wisdom (Rubin 1996; 1998). Orientocentrism is different from what the cultural and literary critic Edward Said (1978) terms "Orientalism," by which he means the pervasive tendency in Western scholarship on non-Western cultures—particularly the Middle East (but applicable with the appropriate changes to Asian cultures)—to be intellectually imperialistic, creating a distorted other ("the East") as a foil to aggrandize "the West." Orientocentrism is the opposite of Orientalism: the deification, rather than the denigration, of Asian thought.

Eurocentrism is illustrated in psychoanalysis by the automatic and unquestioning pathologizing and marginalizing of religion and spiritual and mystical experience. Orientocentrism emerges when authors focus on what "the East" offers "the West," but neglect (if not ignore) what the "the West" might offer "the East." To neglect what psychoanalysis offers Buddhism is to unconsciously adopt an Orientocentric perspective.

My work begins from a deeply felt sense of the bankruptcy of an either/or logic. I am interested, as I have written elsewhere, in a perspective "beyond Eurocentrism and Orientocentrism," by which I mean a dialogue between psychoanalysis and Buddhism in which there is mutual respect, a recognition of differences, and a willingness to learn from each other (Rubin 1996; 1998; 1999). From the liminal space of a both/and perspective, the capacity of psychoanalysis and Buddhism to enlighten each other emerges more readily. It is this mutual enlightenment that I feel is the most radical and the most illuminating facet of the dialogue between psychoanalysis and Buddhism.

I would find it interesting to hear more about Spezzano's reaction to my perspective on psychoanalytic and Buddhist accounts of a life well-lived. For example, does he think that the Dalai Lama is correct in claiming that there are greater possibilities for compassion than are dreamt of in psychoanalytic psychologies? What does Spezzano think of what I claimed psychoanalysis has taught Buddhists about a life well-lived?

And yet, he raises an interesting and important question when he asks whether I am saying that Buddhist meditation is a natural enhancer of or necessary addition to psychoanalysis. I believe it is both. As I have written elsewhere (Rubin 1996), meditation provides an operationalizable technique to cultivate and refine evenly hovering attention, the state of mind Freud recommended for optimal psychoanalytic listening. Teaching meditation in psychoanalytic training would, from this perspective, deepen and polish psychoanalytic listening.

It can be said that Buddhism neglects meaning, insofar as, though it offers reflections on the meaning of the universe, it does not reflect on the meaning of individual behavior, symptoms, dreams, and so forth. Psychoanalytic attention to meaning could enrich meditative practice, offering an invaluable tool in making sense of the unconscious thoughts, feelings, fantasies, and somatic symptoms and sensations that arise in meditation practice.

Spezzano indicates that he is confused when I refer to the potentially harmful effects of meditative practice, especially given the fact that much of my essay focuses on the life-enhancing aspects of Buddhism. He resolves this apparent contradiction by concluding that there are different spiritual traditions, some life enhancing and others self-denying. The point I was making in my essay, however, was not that some spiritual traditions are life enhancing, whereas others are self-denying, but rather that Buddhism itself is a complex tradition containing both strands.

He raises another vitally important question when he asks whether I am saying that we should tell patients to live more compassionately and empathically, or whether we should just value other traditions and practices in which such advice is given. This is, as Spezzano identifies, outside the scope of my essay, which attempts to delineate what each tradition offers to accounts of the well-lived life. I hoped with my essay to plow the land and open up a space so that this important question and other related ones about technique could ultimately be explored.

I think the next step in the dialogue is to address this question as well as the question with which Spezzano concludes his essay, namely how we analysts respond to what patients are not doing in treatment and their lives. I hope that these and other new questions, insights, or vistas will emerge as the reader engages my essay and Spezzano's thoughtful commentary.

Rudyard Kipling believed, perhaps like many of us, that "East is East and West is West and never the twain shall meet." In *East, West,* a recent collection of his stories, Salman Rushdie (1994) offered an opposite perspective, quoted at the head of this reply: "I too have ropes around my neck, I have them to this day pulling me this way and that, East and West, the nooses tightening, commanding choose, choose … Ropes I do not choose between you … I choose neither of you and both. Do you hear? I refuse to choose." East may be East and West may be West, but in my experience, if we are open to what psychoanalysis and meditative traditions might teach us and allow the twain to meet, then our lives and the lives of those we work with, might well be transformed and greatly enriched.

Notes

1. Analysts such as Jung, Silberer, Pfister, Horney, Kelman, Fromm, Milner, Rizzuto, Meissner, Ulanov, Roland, Coltart, Grotstein, Suler, Magid, Cooper, Rudnick, Morvay, Eigen, Spezzano, and Gargiulo, among others, have appreciated religion and approached it non-reductively. I discuss this elsewhere at greater length (e.g., Rubin 1996, 1998).

2. This notion arose as a result of my own playing with Bromberg's (1998) "standing in the spaces."

3. The Dalai Lama points out that poorer nations have sanitation-related illnesses, while more highly urbanized, industrialized nations such as the United States have a greater preponderance of stress-related ones (Gyatso 1999, 9).

4. This is more true of classical analysis, although shades of what Stolorow and Atwood term the myth of the isolated mind persist even in contemporary analysis (Rubin 1998).

5. Analysts such as Ferenczi, Jung, Horney, Fromm, and Winnicott, among others, embraced a more affirmative and less tragic conception of the world.

6. Rank, Fromm, Milner, and Eigen, among others, are, of course, exceptions.

7. Since Buddhism speaks of the illusoriness of the autonomous, self-identical, independent self, it would object to this way of thinking about self-experience. Buddhism's critique of our taken-for-granted sense of self usefully highlights the transitory nature of consciousness and self-experience. But in highlighting the fluid nature of mind it neglects its substantial, historical nature and the recurrent patterns of thought and action that shape our character and our experience of self and relationships. The non-self-centered self is my own attempt to preserve the germ of truth in Buddhist formulations without subscribing to its problematic facets.

8. This chapter was enriched by dialogues with George Atwood, Jerry Gold, Jerry Gargiulo, Jo Ann Magdoff, Louise Reiner, and Mary Traina.

References

Bollas, C. 1952. *Being a Character: Psychoanalysis and Self Experience.* New York: Hill and Wang.

Breuer, J., and S. Freud. 1895. *Studies on Hysteria.* In Standard Edition, 2:1-309. London: Hogarth Press, 1962.

Bromberg, P. 1998. *Standing in the Spaces: Essays on Clinical Process, Trauma, and Dissociation.* Hillsdale, N.J.: Analytic Press.

Corbett, L. 1996. *The Religious Function of the Psyche.* New York: Routledge.

cummings, e. e. 1972. *Complete Poems.* New York: Harcourt Brace Jovanovich.

Dickinson, E. 1957. *Poems.* Boston: Little, Brown & Company.

Duerr, H. P. 1985. *Dreamtime. Concerning the Wilderness and Civilization.* Cambridge, Mass.: Basil Blackwell.

Engler, J. 1984. Therapeutic Aims in Psychotherapy and Meditation. *In* Transformations of Consciousness, eds. K. Wilber, J. Engler and D. Brown, 17–51. Boston: Shambala.

Farber, L. 1976. *Lying, Despair, Jealousy, Envy, Sex, Suicide, Drugs, and the Good Life.* New York: Basic Books.

Ferenczi, S. 1927. The Problem of the Termination of the Analysis. In *Final Contributions to the Problems and Methods of Psycho-Analysis,* 77–86. New York: Brunner/Mazel, 1980.

————. 1928. The Elasticity of Psychoanalytic Technique. In *Final Contributions to the Problems and Methods of Psycho-Analysis*, 87–101. New York: Brunner/Mazel, 1980.

Freud, S. 1912. *Recommendations to Physicians Practicing Psycho-analysis*. In Standard Edition, 12:109–20. London: Hogarth Press, 1958.

————. 1915–16. *Introductory Lectures on Psycho-Analysis*. In Standard Edition, 15:243–63. London: Hogarth Press, 1963.

————. 1922. *Two Encyclopedic Articles: Psychoanalysis*. In Standard Edition, 18:235–54. London: Hogarth Press, 1955.

————. 1927. *The Future of an Illusion*. In Standard Edition, 21:5–56. London: Hogarth Press, 1961.

————. 1930. *Civilization and Its Discontents*. In Standard Edition, 21:64–145. London: Hogarth Press, 1961.

Fromm, E. 1947. *Man for Himself.* New York: Henry Holt.

————. 1995. *The Essential Erich Fromm*. New York: Continuum.

————. 1998. *The Art of Being*. New York: Continuum.

Gay, P. 1990. Freud and Freedom. In *Reading Freud: Explorations and Entertainments*, 74–94. New Haven: Yale University Press.

Gyatso, Tenzin [Dalai Lama]. 1999. *Ethics for the New Millennium*. New York: Riverhead Books.

Heschel, A. 1955. *God in Search of Man: A Philosophy of Judaism*. New York: Farrar Straus and Giroux.

Klein, M. 1960. On Mental Health. In *Envy and Gratitude and Other Works (1946–1963)*. New York: Dell, 1975.

Koren, L. 1994. *Wabi-Sabi for Artists, Designers, Poets and Philosophers*. Berkeley: Stone Bridge Press.

Kovel, J. 1991. *History and Spirit: An Inquiry into the Philosophy of Liberation*. Boston: Beacon Press.

Loewald, H. 1978. *Psychoanalysis and the History of the Individual.* New Haven: Yale University Press.

Molino, T., and Ware, C., eds., 2001. *Where Id Was: Challenging Normalization in Psychoanalysis*. London and New York: Continuum.

Murphy, M. 1992. *The Future of the Body*. Los Angeles: Tarcher.

Nhat Hanh, T. 1987. *The Miracle of Mindfulness*. Boston: Beacon Press.

Phillips, A. 1998. *The Beast in the Nursery*. New York: Pantheon Books.

Reps, P., ed. 1919. *Zen Flesh, Zen Bones: A Collection of Zen and Pre-Zen Writings*. New York: Anchor Books.

Ricoeur, P. 1970. *Freud and Philosophy: An Essay on Interpretation*. New Haven: Yale University Press.

Rosenbaum, R. 1999. *Zen and the Heart of Psychotherapy*. Philadelphia: Brunner/Mazel.

Rubin, J. B. 1996. *Psychotherapy and Buddhism: Toward an Integration*. New York: Plenum Press.

———. 1998. *A Psychoanalysis for Our Time: Exploring the Blindness of the Seeing I*. New York: New York University Press.

———. 1999. Religion, Freud, and Women. *Gender and Psychoanalysis* 4:333–65.

———. 2003. *Close Encoutners of a New Kind: Passion, Ethics and the Good Life in Psychoanalysis and Buddhism*. Forthcoming.

Rushdie, S. 1994. *East, West*. New York: Pantheon.

Said, E. 1978. *Orientalism*. New York: Vintage Books.

Schafer, R. 1976. *A New Language for Psychoanalysis*. New Haven: Yale University Press.

Schuyler, J. 1993. Hymn to Life. In *Collected Poems*. New York: Farrar Straus and Giroux.

Stolorow, R., B. Brandchaft, and G. Atwood. 1987. *Psychoanalytic Treatment: An Intersubjective Approach*. Hillsdale, N.J.: Analytic Press.

Wallwork, E. 1988. A Constructive Alternative to Psychotherapeutic Egoism. In *Community in America: The Challenges of Habits of the Heart*, ed. Charles Reynolds and Ralph Norman, 202–14. Berkeley: University of California Press.

Walsh, R., and Vaughn, F., eds., 1980. *Beyond Ego*. Los Angeles: J. P. Tarcher.

Winnicott, D. W. 1971. *Playing and Reality*. London: Tavistock.

List of Contributors

Neil Altman, Ph.D., is a supervisor and faculty member for the New York University postdoctoral program in psychotherapy and psychoanalysis. He is co-editor of the journal *Psychoanalytic Dialogues*, author of *The Analyst in the Inner City*, and co-author of *Relational Child Psychotherapy*.

Joseph Bobrow, Ph.D., is a Zen teacher in the Aitken-Harada tradition. He teaches at Deep Streams Institute in San Francisco, which offers Zen practice, continuing education for psychotherapists on the interplay of Buddhism and psychotherapy, and community service (applying Buddhist and psychoanalytic principles and practices in school-based programs for teenagers in the probation system). He is also a personal and supervising analyst and faculty member at the Psychoanalytic Institute of Northern California. He is the editor for *Groundwater: The Journal of Buddhism and Psychotherapy*. He has a private practice with adults and children in San Francisco.

Jack Engler, Ph.D., teaches and supervises psychotherapy in the department of psychiatry at Cambridge Hospital and Harvard Medical School. He is a founding member of the Insight Meditation Society in Barre, Massachusetts, and is a faculty and board member of the Barre Center for Buddhist Studies. He has co-edited and co-authored several books including *Transformations of Consciousness: Clinical and Contemplative Perspectives on Development* (with Ken Wilber and Daniel Brown); *The Consumer's Guide to Psychotherapy* (with Daniel Goleman); and *Worlds in Harmony: Dialogues on Compassionate Action* (with the Dalai Lama and others). He is in full-time private practice in Cambridge, Massachusetts.

Mark Finn, Ph.D., is a consulting psychologist at North Central Bronx Hospital, co-editor of *Object Relations Theory and Religion: Clinical Applications*, and author of "Tibetan Buddhism in Comparative Psychoanalysis." He has been a student of Buddhism since 1975, mostly within the Karma Kagyu tradition of Tibetan Buddhism, but with beneficial interactions with the Zen and vipassana communities.

James A. Grotstein, M.D., is a clinical professor of psychiatry at the UCLA School of Medicine and supervising and training analyst for the Los Angeles Psychoanalytic Society/Institute. He has authored several books including *Splitting and Projective Identification* and *Who Is the Dreamer and Who Dreams the Dream?*

Robert Langan, Ph.D., is a faculty member and supervising analyst at the William Alanson White Institute, a faculty member at the Institute of Contemporary Psychotherapy, and an editorial board member for *Contemporary Psychoanalysis*. His first encounter with Tibetan Buddhism while with the Peace Corps in Nepal sparked a lifelong interest in Buddhism that included explorations of meditation and the vipassana tradition. He has written a number of articles including "On Free Floating Attention" and "I Thou Other: Fluid Being in Triadic Context."

Barry Magid, M.D., received Dharma transmission from Charlotte Joko Beck and is a Zen teacher at the Ordinary Mind Zendo in New York City. He is a supervisor and faculty member at the Postgraduate Center for Mental Health and the Institute for Contemporary Psychotherapy and is the author of *Ordinary Mind: Exploring the Common Ground of Zen and Psychotherapy* and the editor of *Freud's Case Studies: Self Psychological Perspectives* and *Father Louie: Photographs of Thomas Merton by Ralph Eugene Meatyard*.

Stephen A. Mitchell, Ph.D., was a training and supervising analyst at the William Alanson White Institute and a supervisor and faculty member at the New York University postdoctoral program in psychotherapy and psychoanalysis. He was the founding editor of the journal, *Psychoanalytic Dialogues* and is the author of several books including *Relational Concepts in Psychoanalysis; Hope and Dread in Psychoanalysis; Influence and Autonomy in Psychoanalysis;* and *Can Love Last: The Role of Romance Over Time*.

Raul Moncayo, Ph.D., is a Lacanian analyst, a Zen priest at the Berkeley Zen Center, and a faculty member at both the California School of Professional

Psychology and the Lacanian School of Psychoanalysis, Berkeley. He has practiced at the Berkeley Zen Center since 1978 and is a senior student of Roshi Mel Weitzman. He has published a number of articles including "True Subject Is No-Subject: The Real, Imaginary and Symbolic in Psychoanalysis and Zen Buddhism" and "The Real and Symbolic in Lacan, Zen and Kabbalah."

Stuart A. Pizer, Ph.D., is faculty member, supervising analyst and past president at the Massachusetts Institute for Psychoanalysis; visiting faculty and advisory board member, Toronto Institute for Contemporary Psychoanalysis; contributing editor for *Psychoanalytic Dialogues;* and author of *Building Bridges: The Negotiation of Paradox in Psychoanalysis.*

Owen Renik, M.D., is a training and supervising analyst at the San Francisco Psychoanalytic Institute and former editor-in-chief for *Psychoanalytic Quarterly.* He is the editor of the book *Knowledge and Authority in the Psychoanalytic Relationship* and co-editor of *The Place of Reality in Psychoanalytic Theory and Technique.*

Philip A. Ringstrom, Ph.D., Psy.D., is a senior training analyst and supervising analyst, faculty member, and member of the board of directors at the Institute of Contemporary Psychoanalysis in Los Angeles, California, and has a full-time private practice in Encino, California. He has been published in a number of journals including *Psychoanalytic Dialogues, The Bulletin of the Menninger Clinic, Psychoanalytic Inquiry,* and *The International Journal of Psychoanalysis;* he is a publication reviewer for *Psychoanalytic Dialogues* and the *Journal of the American Psychoanalytic Association;* and he is one of fifteen international panelists on the psychoanalytic internet site *PsyBc.com.* He has sustained an interest in Buddhism that began over twenty-five years ago.

Jeffrey B. Rubin, Ph.D., practices psychoanalysis and psychoanalytically-oriented psychotherapy in New York City and Bedford Hills, New York. He has taught at various psychoanalytic institutes and universities including The Postgraduate Center for mental health, The Object Relations Institute of New York, The C. G. Jung Foundation of New York, Yeshiva University, and Union Theological Seminary. He is a faculty member at the Harlem Family Institute and is the author of *Psychotherapy and Buddhism; A Psycho-*

analysis for Our Time: Exploring the Blindness of the Seeing I; and the forth-coming *Psychoanalysis and the Good Life: Reflections on Love, Ethics, Creativity and Spirituality; The Mystic in Sneakers;* and *Close Encounters of a New Kind: Passion, Ethics and the Good life in Psychoanalysis and Buddhism.* He has been a student of Buddhist meditation and yoga since the late 1970s, and his primary teachers have been Joseph Goldstein, Jack Kornfield, Christopher Titmuss, Joel Kramer, Dolphi Wertenbaker, and T. K. V. Desikachar.

Charles Spezzano, Ph.D., is a training and supervising analyst at the Psycho-analytic Institute of Northern California and a member of both the Los Angeles Institute and Society for Psychoanalytic Studies and the International Psychoanalytic Association. He is a contributing editor for *Psychoanalytic Dialogues* and a member of the editorial board of the *Journal of the American Psychoanalytic Association,* as well as the author of *Affect in Psychoanalysis: A Clinical Synthesis* and co-editor of *Soul on the Couch: Morality, Religion, and Spirituality in Contemporary Psychoanalysis* and *Psychoanalysis at Its Limits: Navigating the Postmodern Turn.*

Neville Symington, D.C.P., is a psychoanalyst with a private practice in Sydney, Australia. He has been president of the Australian Psycho-Analytical Society, chairman of the Sydney Institute for Psychoanalysis, senior staff member of the Tavistock Clinic in London, and chairman of the Psychology Discipline for the Adult and Adolescent Departments at the Tavistock Clinic. He has authored several books including *The Analytic Experience; Narcissism: A New Theory; Emotion and Spirit; The Spirit of Sanity; The Clinical Thinking of Wilfred Bion* (co-authored with Joan Symington); and *A Pattern of Madness.*

M. Guy Thompson, Ph.D., is founder and director of Free Association, Inc., in San Francisco; personal and supervising analyst at the Psychoanalytic Institute of Northern California; past president of the International Federation for Psychoanalytic Education; and president of the Northern California Society for Psychoanalytic Psychology. He is author of *The Death of Desire: A Study in Psychopathology; The Truth about Freud's Technique: The Encounter with the Real;* and *The Ethic of Honesty: The Fundamental Rule of Psychoanalysis.*

Sara L. Weber, Ph.D., is a faculty member at the William Alanson White Institute; assistant professor of psychology and education in the department of clinical psychology at Teachers College, Columbia University; and assistant professor at the Derner Institute, Adelphi University. Her spiritual interests began early, inspired by a Lubavitch grandfather and her Kabbalistic meditation experiences at summer camp. Currently she is attracted primarily to the vippassana meditation tradition and Tibetan Buddhism.

Polly Young-Eisendrath, Ph.D., is a psychologist and practicing Jungian psychoanalyst in central Vermont and a clinical associate professor of psychiatry at the University of Vermont Medical College. She began studying Zen Buddhism in 1971 as a student of Roshi Philip Kapleau, and in 1999 she went on to become a student of vipassana teacher Shinzen Young. She has published twelve books (translated into twenty languages) and many book chapters and articles. She lectures internationally on the topics of resilience, women's development, couple relationship, and the interface of contemporary psychoanalysis and spirituality. Her most recent books are *Women and Desire: Beyond Wanting to Be Wanted; The Psychology of Mature Spirituality: Integrity, Wisdom, Transcendence* (co-edited with Melvin Miller); and *Awakening and Insight: Zen Buddhism and Psychotheraphy* (co-edited with Shoji Muramoto).

ABOUT THE EDITOR

Jeremy D. Safran, Ph.D., is a professor of psychology in the Graduate Faculty of Political and Social Science at New School University, where he was previously director of clinical psychology. He is also a senior research scientist at Beth Israel Medical Center. Dr. Safran completed psychoanalytic training at the New York University Postdoctoral Program and is on the board of directors of the International Association for Relational Psychoanalysis and Psychotheraphy. He has been a long-time student of both Zen and Tibetan Buddhism and has studied with Karma Thinley Rinpoche since 1984. Dr. Safran has authored several books including: *Negotiating the Therapeutic Alliance: A Relational Treatment Guide* (with J. Christopher Muran); *Emotion in Psychotherapy* (with Leslie Greenberg); and *Interpersonal Process in Cognitive Therapy* (with Zindel Segal). He has a private practice in New York City.

INDEX

WISDOM PUBLICATIONS

WISDOM PUBLICATIONS, nonprofit publisher, is dedicated to making available authentic Buddhist works for the benefit of all. We publish translations of the sutras and tantras, commentaries and teachings of past and contemporary Buddhist masters, and original works by the world's leading Buddhist scholars. We publish our titles with the appreciation of Buddhism as a living philosophy and with the special commitment to preserve and transmit important works from all the major Buddhist traditions.

To learn more about Wisdom, or to browse books online, visit our website at wisdompubs.org. You may request a copy of our mail-order catalog online or by writing to this address:

WISDOM PUBLICATIONS
199 Elm Street
Somerville, Massachusetts 02144 USA
Telephone: (617) 776-7416
Fax: (617) 776-7841
Email: info@wisdompubs.org
www.wisdompubs.org

The Wisdom Trust

As a nonprofit publisher, Wisdom is dedicated to the publication of fine Dharma books for the benefit of all sentient beings and dependent upon the kindness and generosity of sponsors in order to do so. If you would like to make a donation to Wisdom, please do so through our Somerville office. If you would like to sponsor the publication of a book, please write or email us at the address above.

Thank you.

Wisdom is a nonprofit, charitable 501(c)(3) organization affiliated with the Foundation for the Preservation of the Mahayana Tradition (FPMT).